# THE THEATRE IN SEARCH OF A FIX

# ROBERT W. CORRIGAN

# THE THEATRE IN SEARCH OF A FIX

*Shambaugh Library*

**DELACORTE PRESS / NEW YORK**

*Design by Julian Hamer*

Library of Congress Cataloging in Publication Data

Corrigan, Robert Willoughby, 1927–
The theatre in search of a fix.

1. Drama—Addresses, essays, lectures.   I. Title.
PN1731.C6        809.2        72–12862

FOR

JANE

# ACKNOWLEDGMENTS

*Several of the essays in this collection have appeared, in whole or in part, in the following publications:*

"Tragedy and the Tragic Spirit": Originally appeared in *Tragedy: A Critical Anthology* edited by Robert W. Corrigan. Used by permission of Houghton Mifflin Company.

"Aeschylus and the Vision of Tragedy": Originally appeared in *Aeschylus* (Laurel Classical Drama Series) edited by Robert W. Corrigan. Copyright © 1965 by Dell Publishing Co., Inc.

"The Tragic Turbulence of Sophoclean Drama": Originally appeared in *Sophocles* (Laurel Classical Drama Series) edited by Robert W. Corrigan. Copyright © 1965 by Dell Publishing Co., Inc.

"The Drama of Euripides": Originally published in *Euripides* (Laurel Classical Drama Series) edited by Robert W. Corrigan. Copyright © 1965 by Dell Publishing Co., Inc.

"Comedy and the Comic Spirit": Originally appeared in *Comedy: Meaning and Form* by Robert W. Corrigan. Copyright © 1965 by Chandler Publishing Company. Used by permission of the publisher.

"Aristophanic Comedy: The Conscience of a Conservative": Originally appeared in *Greek Comedy* (Laurel Classical Drama Series) edited by Robert W. Corrigan. Copyright © 1965 by Dell Publishing Co., Inc.

"Some Thoughts on Roman Drama": Originally appeared in *Roman Drama* (Laurel Classical Drama Series) edited by Robert W. Corrigan. Copyright © 1966 by Dell Publishing Co., Inc.

"The Modern Theatre": Originally appeared in *The Modern Theatre* edited by Robert W. Corrigan. Copyright © 1964 by Robert W. Corrigan. Used by permission of The Macmillan Company.

"Ibsen's *Ghosts* as Tragedy": Originally appeared in *Educational Theatre Journal*, Volume XI, No. 2, 1959. Used by permission.

"Strindberg and the Abyss": Originally appeared in *A Dream Play and The Ghost Sonata* by August Strindberg. Copyright © 1966 by Chandler Publishing Company. Used by permission of the publisher.

"The Plays of Chekhov": Originally appeared in *Chekhov: Six Plays*. Used by permission of Holt, Rinehart and Winston.

"Character as Destiny in Hofmannsthal's *Electra*": Originally appeared in *Modern Drama*. Used by permission.

"The Collapse of the Shavian Cosmos": Portions originally appeared in *Laurel British Drama: The Twentieth Century* edited by Robert W. Corrigan, copyright © 1965 by Dell Publishing Co., Inc.; and in *Laurel British Drama: The Nineteenth Century* edited by Robert W. Corrigan, copyright © 1967 by Dell Publishing Co., Inc.

"The Transformation of the Individual in the Modern Theatre": Originally appeared, in different form, in *The New Theatre of Europe, Volume I*, edited by Robert W. Corrigan. Copyright © 1962 by Dell Publishing Co., Inc.

"The Disavowal of Identity in the Modern Theatre": Originally appeared, in different form, in *The New Theatre of Europe, Volume II*, edited by Robert W. Corrigan. Copyright © 1964 by Dell Publishing Co., Inc.

"Thornton Wilder and the Tragic Sense of Life": Originally appeared in *Educational Theatre Journal*, Volume XIII, No. 3, 1961. Used by permission.

"The Theatre in Search of a Fix": Originally appeared in *Tulane Drama Review*. Used by permission.

"Engagement/Disengagement in the Contemporary Theatre": Originally appeared, in part, in *The New Theatre of Europe, Volume I* edited by Robert W. Corrigan; and in *The New Theatre of Europe, Volume III* edited by Robert W. Corrigan, copyright © 1968 by Robert W. Corrigan.

"Anger and After: A Decade of the British Theatre": Originally appeared, in part, in *Laurel British Drama: The Twentieth Century, The New Theatre of Europe, Volume I* and *The New Theatre of Europe, Volume III*.

"The Achievement of Arthur Miller": Originally appeared in *Arthur Miller: A Collection of Critical Essays* edited by Robert W. Corrigan. Copyright © 1969, Prentice-Hall, Inc., Englewood Cliffs, N. J. Used by permission of the publisher.

# CONTENTS

# III. THE THEATRE IN A COLLECTIVE SOCIETY

# IV. THE PRESENT AND ITS POSSIBILITIES

# PREFACE

THE ORIGIN of this book can be traced back to a meeting in a New York hotel room almost fifteen years ago. I was then the editor of the new and still struggling *Tulane Drama Review* (now *The Drama Review*) and this soon-to-become-important magazine had caught the attention of an editor at George Braziller. He wrote to me in New Orleans and asked that we meet the next time I was in New York. We did, and that meeting changed my life in many profound ways. When the little man entered the hotel room I noticed how young he looked (he still looks twenty years younger than he is), but I was more impressed by his energy and quickness of mind. He knew the theatre well, the range of his reading of literature was almost encyclopedic, and his knowledge of philosophy was so great that he could have been a university professor rather than an editor in a publishing house. We hit it off at once and over the years that followed that spark has matured into a deep friendship, the kind of friendship which earlier times were not embarrassed to acknowledge as having the quality of fraternal love. Since that time my friend Dick Huett has been *my* editor. (To be sure there have been times when I was unfaithful in this relationship, but I always came home again.) The book we first talked about (a collection of pieces from *TDR*) was eventually published by Grove Press which Dick had joined as an editor. Then he moved to Dell where he took on the huge task of editing their Delta and Laurel editions. I went with him, as it were, and we are still there together. At Dell Dick and his close friend and colleague, Ross Claiborne, launched numerous

ambitious and imaginative projects and they gave me more opportunities than one man could ever fulfill. But more important than
the opportunities is the fact that this relationship shaped my growth
as a writer and critic. We had marvelous and heated debates; Dick
would never let me short-change myself and he insisted on pushing
ideas as far as possible. He was a stickler on style, but never in a
way that was inhibiting. But finally it was Huett the philosopher
who turned my mind to those ideas and themes in the theatre which
have since become my central concerns not only as a critic but as
an educator as well.

Although it may be hard to believe, he did not want me to be an
anthologizer. Every so often he would say, "After you've finished
editing this volume you're going to write the book we've talked so
much about." I knew he was right but it's hard to break bad habits.
Finally, he and Ross decided to do it for me. The three of us met for
lunch at the Yale Club in the fall of 1965 and I was told that they
were going to publish a collection of my essays. This would be my
"first" book and from then on I would be expected to write the
kinds of books we had so often discussed. I agreed with them and
set to work, but fate (and my own nature) intervened and here it
is nearly seven years later and the undertaking is just now finished.
First I became totally involved creating the School of the Arts at
New York University, and then I moved to Los Angeles in the summer of 1968 to be the first president of the yet-to-be-created California Institute of the Arts. The task of building Cal Arts from
scratch was enormous and there wasn't time for anything else. I
scarcely thought about the book, although we always dutifully mentioned it whenever we saw each other. Finally, however, the ultimatum came: It had to be finished by the fall of 1972 or the project
would be abandoned. Again fate intervened. For on the very day
that I received Dick's letter informing me of this, I had made what
was in effect an ultimatum to the Board of Trustees of the Institute
that quickly led to those decisions which culminated in my resignation as president in May of 1972. So I could turn again to the book
and thank God for that. I had been working around the clock under
unbelievable pressures in an atmosphere of tension. To be relieved
of all that so suddenly created a real problem of decompression and
only the necessity of finishing the book made it possible for me to
work through this difficult period with some ease. Now it is finished

and I hope to turn my attention to writing those books Dick Huett and I have so often discussed.

The title of the book was the title of an essay I published in *TDR* in 1961. It became the introduction of the Grove anthology which started it all. Its connotations were ahead of its time then, and it still seemed appropriate in the late 1960s when the drug culture was coming, as it were, into bloom. I questioned whether it was still pertinent today, but as I thought about the state of the theatre I was convinced that those issues which by implication that title addresses are still very much the central issues that today's theatre must face up to. So I have retained it. While the book is a collection of essays written over a fifteen-year period, I have rewritten or revised most of them in an attempt to achieve a continuity of idea and theme. Ten of the essays were originally published as introductions to Dell editions; six are new and are published here for the first time; and the remaining ten were published as articles or introductions to other books. (I should like to thank the publishers of these essays for permitting me to include them in the book. They are: The Macmillan Company, "The Modern Theatre"; Houghton Mifflin Company, "Tragedy and the Tragic Spirit"; Chandler Publishing Company, "Comedy and the Comic Spirit" and "Strindberg and the Abyss"; Holt, Rinehart and Winston, "The Plays of Chekhov"; Prentice-Hall, "The Achievement of Arthur Miller"; *The Educational Theatre Journal,* "Ibsen's *Ghosts* as Tragedy" and "Thornton Wilder and the Tragic Sense of Life"; *Modern Drama,* "Character as Destiny in Hofmannsthal's *Electra*"; and *The Drama Review,* "The Theatre in Search of a Fix."

I should also like to acknowledge my gratitude to those other editors and publishers who have been so helpful to me during the past fifteen years, and particularly I want to thank Arthur Wang, Howard Chandler, William Parker, John Poindexter, and the late Jack Case.

Finally, I must acknowledge my admiration for and debt to Herbert Blau. I know he knows what a major part he has played in my life and how his powerful imagination has helped to shape my own "idea of a theatre."

R.W.C.

*Los Angeles*
*June, 1972*

# PART ONE

# THE CLASSICAL SOLUTION

# 1

# TRAGEDY AND
# THE TRAGIC SPIRIT

THE FACTS of tragedy have haunted the spirit of every man in all ages, and for this reason the subject of tragedy has usually interested those who feel the need for a more intelligent awareness of themselves and the world in which they live. This has always been true, but never more so than it is today when we feel that our lives are perched precariously on the brink of continual disaster. The number of books and articles on tragedy and the tragic written in the past quarter of a century is overwhelming, and the very fact of their existence indicates that the conditions of our world have forced our imaginations to dwell once again on the facts of suffering, failure, and death.

Until World War II, "tragedy" was a dirty word in public parlance (we destroyed its power by indiscriminately using it to describe any kind of painful experience), and in academic circles it had become an honorific term reeking with a musty nostalgia for past ages of glory. It was argued that tragedy, the great flower of aristocratic societies, was dead and that all attempts to revive it in a democratic and egalitarian age were doomed to failure. Even the mighty Ibsen seemed small when placed next to Aeschylus, Sophocles, and Euripides, or Marlowe, Shakespeare, Corneille, and Racine. So said the professors. On the surface the students agreed and they read their Sophocles with dutiful respect, but they really liked O'Neill, no matter how tin his ear was supposed to have been. In fact, it is now clear that tragedy hadn't died at all, it had just gone underground for a couple of centuries. Dostoevsky, Nietzsche, and Kierkegaard had told us so, but most people were not convinced. Dunkirk, Belsen, and Hiroshima changed all this, and once again tragedy has taken its place as an accepted part of our lives.

Looking back, it is easy to see how and why the subversion of tragedy occurred. After the Restoration and on into the eighteenth century, England had a new deal in politics and religion; the emerging middle-class economy was burgeoning and creating a new prosperity; a growing confidence in the methods of empirical science tended to dispel personal doubts; and the bright flame of the Enlightenment cast its light on all that had been dark and mysterious. Man may have been "Born but to die, and reasoning but to err," but as Pope went on, there was a plan, for those who would but look:

> All nature is but Art, unknown to thee;
> All Chance, Direction, which thou canst not see;
> All Discord, Harmony not understood;
> All partial evil, universal Good . . .

On the Continent, the romanticism of Rousseau and his followers had a similar effect on popular attitudes about tragedy. The Curse of Adam was a social blight, not an innate quality of man. Individual man was born good and was then corrupted by his society. But society could be changed, and it was the duty of all men of goodwill to work for its improvement. In reducing Evil to evils, catastrophe was institutionalized and therefore made remediable. Thus, by insisting that human suffering and failure are not so much the result of our essentially divided nature as the effects of impersonal and external social forces, Rousseauian romanticism tended to dissolve tragic guilt—although it should be noted that it was also largely responsible for creating the psychology of victimization.

The nineteenth century was more or less officially the century of progress, and tragedy was given little place in either official life or official art. The "Cult of Life" emerged victorious (in theory at least), and the tragic view of life was seen as the great enemy which had to be suppressed at all costs. Victorianism, with its sturdy morality, its conservatism, its willingness to compromise, and its ability to assimilate alien views into its unique brand of optimism, was riding high on the crest of a wave of material expansion and unthought-of prosperity. The voices of doubt and dissent were there, of course, but they were seldom heard. And in America we were too busy getting the land settled to worry much about aesthetic abstractions like tragedy.

At the turn of the present century, rumblings from the underground and occasional eruptions could be heard. The theatre especially had begun to change. We see it first in the later plays of Ibsen, such as *The Master Builder*, and in Strindberg's *Miss Julie* and his post-inferno plays; it rises to a frenzy in the works of the German Expressionists. Even a Fabian optimist like Shaw, who for so long had an answer for everything, began to come up with the most improbable solutions to the question of "What's to be done?" And as the final curtain descends with Saint Joan crying out, "O God that madest this beautiful earth, when will it be ready to receive thy saints? How long, O Lord, how long?" we know that the answer is, "Never!" So we pass through the era of Maxwell Anderson and Clifford Odets and enter the Age of the Bomb. All the debates about the common man being tragic (invariably any discussion of tragedy will sooner than later evoke the question, "Is *Death of a Salesman* a tragedy?") are ample, if not always eloquent, testimony that tragedy is once more a central concern of many thoughtful people.

But as soon as we acknowledge the renewed possibility of tragedy, we invariably exclaim: "Where is it?" People turn feverishly to the giants of the past or to Aristotle's *Poetics* and bemoan the fact that while our world may certainly be tragic, it is not very hospitable to the nobility and grandeur that we tend to associate with tragedy as a dramatic form. In our lament we reveal that for all of our interest in the subject we really do not understand it very well. We reveal the commonplace assumption that there is in Western culture a persisting "idea of tragedy" that can be defined in terms of certain formal or structural characteristics. The history of the Western theatre documents the fact that nothing could be further from the truth.

It seems to me that a much more effective way of dealing with the subject would be to distinguish between *the form of tragedy,* which constantly changes—even in the work of a single dramatist—and *the tragic,* which is a way of looking at experience that has persisted more or less unchanged in the Western world from the time of Homer to the present. Santayana once wrote: "Everything in nature is lyrical in its ideal essence, tragic in its fate, and comic in its existence." The tragic writer in all ages has always been chiefly concerned with man's fate: ultimate defeat and death. Sophocles, Shakespeare, and Ibsen were tragedians because they were, in large measure, concerned with the individual's struggle with fate; and for them, as for all writers of tragedy, this struggle is seen as a conflict with necessity, or what the Greeks referred to as *Ananke*. Necessity is not some kind of social disease that those who would change the world can ignore, soften, or legislate out of existence. Necessity is the embodiment of life's smallness, absurdity, and fragility; it is the acknowledgment of the limitation and mortality of all human experience. Man's struggle with necessity has been expressed in many forms and in varying contexts throughout history, but it is the constant of tragic drama and, insofar as they can be related, it is the bond that links each of those writers whom we refer to as tragedians. But such a view of life does not necessarily have anything to do with artistic form; one need not be an artist at all to hold such a view (certainly the late Adlai Stevenson saw the world in this way); and it is a view that is as compatible with the lyric poem or the novel as it is with drama.

The tragic view of life, then, begins by insisting that we accept the inevitable doom of our fate, and this fact is the mainspring of all tragic drama. However, our experience of tragedy tells us that it is more than this. The great tragedies of history also—and with equally compelling force—celebrate the fact that, while a man may have to learn to face and accept the reality of necessity, he also has an overpowering need to give a meaning to his fate. If man's fate, no matter how frightening, has no meaning, then why struggle? "If," as Kierkegaard wrote in *Fear and Trembling*, ". . . there were no eternal consciousness in a man, if at the foundation of all there lay only a wildly seething power which writhing with obscene passions produced everything that is great and everything that is insignificant, if a bottomless void never satiated lay hidden beneath all—what then would life be but despair?" But, like Prospero, we tend to trust that our ending is not despair, and our experience with tragic drama is sufficient testimony to our capacity to give meaning to our fate.

The spirit of tragedy, then, is not quietistic; it is a grappling spirit. And while the nature and terms of the struggle vary in direct relationship to the individual dramatist's belief in the meaning of the struggle, in every great tragedy we sense the validity of a meaningful struggle and the real possibility of it. Thus, tragic characters may win or lose; or more precisely, they win in the losing and lose in the winning. But it is the struggle itself that is the source of the dramatic significance, and it is out of this struggle with necessity that heroism is born.

When we think of tragic heroes, we usually think first of their great nobility of spirit. Oedipus, Faustus, Lear, or Solness may be right or wrong; they may suffer and be destroyed; but the emotional depth and intellectual capacity each of them brings to his suffering condition stamps him with the mark of greatness. We admire the hero because he resists the forces of Fate.

In this regard, as has so often been the case, Aristotle—or at least the usual interpretations of *The Poetics*—has misled us. That quality of human will which dares to stand up against the universe and struggle with necessity is called *hubris* by Aristotle, a flaw and therefore undesirable. We must never forget that this interpretation of *hubris* is an expression of the fourth-century Greek's admiration (or need) for moderation in all its forms. While the turmoils of the preceding century may have prompted the widespread acceptance of this Aristotelian attitude, to apply it as a judgment or think of it as describing what happens in tragedy is nonsensical. For tragedy reveals that *hubris* is that quality in man which defies the *status quo* of being human: It is the protest against the limitations of being a man. Whether this resistance takes the form of an inordinate and monomaniacal pursuit of a finite goal or is an arrogant and suicidal aspiration toward the infinite, it cannot be considered as only a character defect. Rather, it is an integral part of human nature; it is the necessary counterpart of man's capacity as a feeling and thinking being. This explains why the action of tragedy seems creative and destructive at the same time, why the spirit of tragedy is the spirit of achievement. It is an end (usually death) and it is a fulfillment, a complete realization filled with a heightened sense of life.

It is the paradoxical nature of this confrontation with fate which leads the hero into what Karl Jaspers has called "boundary situations," those areas of experience where man is shown at the limits of his sovereignty. "Here," as Richard B. Sewall puts it in his *The Vision of Tragedy*, "with all the protective coverings stripped off, the hero faces as if no man ever faced it before the existential question—Job's question, 'What is man?' or Lear's 'Is man no more than this?' " At this frontier, the hero, with faith and those generalizations derived from his experience, attempts to map his universe. What happens finally in tragedy is a failure of maps; in the tragic situation, man finds himself in a primitive country that he had believed his forefathers had tamed, civilized, and charted, only to discover they had not. One of the great holds that tragedy has always had on the imagination is that it brings us into direct touch with the naked landscape. The playwright begins by moving the hero into what Conrad referred to as the "destructive element," and then he presses these boundary situations to their fullest yield. In the midst of "the blight man was born for," the tragic dramatist demands of his hero what Hamlet demanded of himself: "How to be!" Thus, in carrying the action to the uttermost limits, the playwright is able to explore the farthest reaches of human possibility.

Man's tragic condition is that he is doomed by fate to defeat. The affirmation of tragedy is that man's spirit triumphs over his fate. This mortal encounter between the tragic and tragedy—between life and form—is the chief source of tension and turbulence in what we call tragic drama. Paradoxically, death in some form usually triumphs, but heroism is born out of that mortal struggle and its spirit lives on long after the corpse has been interred.

Finally, however, the real key to the understanding of tragedy lies in recognizing that all tragedy has its roots in human struggles and springs from the basic dividedness of man's nature. All drama is built upon catastrophe (literally, a shift in direction)—any event which overturns the previously existing order or system of things. As such, catastrophe itself lacks moral meanings; it is equally capable of producing joy and happiness or sadness and grief, depending on the context in which it occurs. The most important characteristic of tragedy—the one distinguishing it from all other dramatic forms, especially melodrama—is that all significant "catastrophic" events are caused by the inner dividedness of the protagonist and not by some external force. *King Lear* and *The Duchess of Malfi* have many things in common, but because Lear is clearly brought low by the dividedness of his own nature while the Duchess, in spite of her inner conflicts, is ultimately destroyed by forces not of her own making and over which she has never had any control, we consider Shakespeare's play a tragedy and Webster's a melodrama. A similar distinction can be found in classical Greek drama; certainly there is as much suffering in *The Trojan Women* as in *Oedipus the King*—probably more. But because the King of Thebes is responsible for his own suffering in a way that the victimized women of Troy are not, we correctly believe that the difference between the two dramas is one of kind and not degree. This is an important distinction, because if the catastrophes of experience are considered to be the result of an external force—whether it be a divinity, a power of nature, or some societal pressure—then the individual is ultimately not responsible for them no matter how much he might suffer because of them. Tragedy cannot exist if the protagonist does not eventually come to recognize that he is morally responsible for his deeds and that his acts are the direct offspring of choices he has made. Professor Robert B. Heilman, in his very important book *Tragedy and Melodrama: Versions of Experience*, argues that the tragic character is one in whom is incorporated "the dividedness of a humanity whose values, because they naturally elude the confines of formal logic, create an apparently insoluble situation." These divisions may and do take many forms, but they always present alternatives and demand that man choose between them. And choice implies consciousness, for alternatives are not really alternatives if they do not in some way live in the hero's consciousness. Thus division is not only the occasion of self-knowledge, it is the very material of self-knowing. And self-knowledge derived from the irreconcilable conflicts within us is the very stuff of tragedy.

Such is the turbulence of the tragic, and if we are to rescue those plays which celebrate these abiding conflicts from those dusty repositories where most masterpieces of culture are usually stored, we must find ways to rediscover that tension of struggle against fate which is inevitable when men try vainly but nobly to impose a meaning on their own lives and on the world around them. If we are to succeed in this we must recognize that the constant in tragedy is the tragic view of life or the tragic spirit: that sense that life is, as Scott Fitzgerald once put it, "essentially a cheat and its conditions are those of defeat." This spirit can and does take many forms —both in drama and life—but it is always there as a backdrop to man's fate. Tragedy has always been both a celebration and a protest of this condition, and it is as possible in our day as it ever was. If only we would stop looking for another Shakespeare or Sophocles we might discover that *Mother Courage* is as much a tragedy as is *Coriolanus* or *Ajax,* or that *The Master Builder* or *A Long Day's Journey into Night* say as much to our time about the tragic nature of our existence as does *Oedipus the King.*

A failure to understand what tragedy is about can have important and undesirable consequences for our grasp of reality; confusion on this subject may result in our losing touch with certain ideas that are an indispensable means of contemplating and understanding and experiencing the human catastrophes that surround us everywhere.

# 2

# AESCHYLUS AND
# THE VISION OF TRAEGDY

AESCHYLUS is usually referred to as that grand titan who was the "father of tragedy." In the sense that for the Greeks of the fifth century B.C. a tragedy was, as Norman J. DeWitt put it, "any play based upon the legends of the historical aristocracy" performed at the festivals of Dionysus, this title is deserved. He was indeed chiefly responsible for taking the protean forms of the early ritualistic choral dances and making them into a play with definite and more or less fixed characteristics. But Aeschylus was not, at least as we use the term today, a writer of tragedies.

I believe that the tragic writer in all ages has always been concerned chiefly with man's fate and a man's fate is that he is ultimately doomed to defeat because he is born to die. For the Greeks of the fifth century this struggle with Fate is seen as a conflict with necessity (*Ananke*). Although this struggle does exist in the plays of Aeschylus, it is not central to them nor can it be for several reasons.

Karl Jaspers, in his important little book *Tragedy Is Not Enough*, points out that "the mythical mind sees the world's basic disharmony reflected in the multiplicity of gods." In such a world, tragedy, as we have come to know it, cannot exist, for tragedy has its roots in human struggles and springs from the basic dividedness of man's nature. If the catastrophes of experience are considered to be the result of divine struggles, then man is not responsible for them no matter how much he might suffer because of them. Only when

11

there is one supreme god is it possible for man to be the source and
subject of tragedy. At the same time, it is impossible for tragedy to
exist if man does not believe he is morally responsible for his deeds.
Such a sense of responsibility is difficult, if not impossible, to
achieve without a belief in something beyond man's finite condition. As Jaspers puts it, "Where there is no sense of the infinite vastness of what is beyond our grasp, all we finally succeed in convey-
ing is misery—not tragedy."

The conditions necessary for the existence of tragedy do not obtain
in the world of Aeschylean drama. Most of his extant plays reveal
the Greek world to be in a state of transition from a more or less
primitive mythic dispensation to the stability of a state-oriented
social order, and Aeschylus seems ultimately to be more concerned
with the emergence of Zeus the Fulfiller than he is with the sufferings of mortal men and women. In a sense, Aeschylus' greatest
achievement was that he made the Greek drama possible for tragedy. By the end of *The Oresteia*, Zeus is firmly established as Lord
of the universe, a position that was not challenged, in the theatre
at least, until some of the later plays of Euripides. The establish-
ment of Zeus provided the playwright—particularly Sophocles—an
ultimate perspective that informs and judges human actions. Sophocles does not pretend to understand the authenticity or vastness of
his power. Or, to use more modern terms, Sophocles' world is one
of being, a world of essences; the Aeschylean universe, by comparison, is in a state of becoming, it is a world of existences.

In fact, it is probably correct to describe Aeschylus as our first
existential playwright (which may, by definition, make it impossible for him to be a tragedian). Many critics have pointed out that
Aeschylus is not really interested in his characters or why they behave as they do. They are monolithic and we are seldom if ever
permitted to see beyond their imposing, granite-like surfaces. They
are brought into situations where they must inevitably come into
conflict; they clash, and we see what happens. But what Aeschylus
is really interested in is "what is done"; for him the essence of human action is found in the act of decision, not in the reasons that
the decision was made. From an early play like *The Suppliant
Maidens* to *The Oresteia* of his maturity we see that Aeschylus'
dramatic strategy is to create an impossible situation that the hero
must resolve through action. We know nothing of King Pelasgus'
inner life and little of Orestes', but this is unimportant because

Aeschylus is more interested in the situation to be resolved than in the characters who participate in the resolution. Like a chemist making an experiment in his laboratory, Aeschylus constructs an action with a view to isolating the quintessence of action. But the question of the significance of that action is another matter. It is generally believed that self-knowledge derived from the irreconcilable conflicts within us is the very stuff of tragedy. But there is very little of this in Aeschylean drama. There are irreconcilable conflicts, to be sure, but we never feel that the human characters have created them because of their own irreconcilable needs, nor do we sense that they are capable of or responsible for resolving them. "Tragedy is real," says Jaspers, "because irreconcilable opposition is real." But Aeschylus, the poet, delivers us from tragedy by resolving the irreconcilable on the higher plane of the gods. The demand for action is imposed by the gods and ultimately the responsibility for the resolution is theirs as well. For this reason, to quote Jaspers again, in the plays of Aeschylus tragedy is "conquered by the awareness of a larger context of fundamental reality."

In a sense, Aeschylus' plays might best be described as "divine comedies" peopled with Homeric heroes. Certainly, with the exception of Orestes—and we shall come to him presently—we find no heroes in Aeschylus' plays who begin to resemble Antigone, Oedipus, Medea, Hamlet, Lear, or even Mrs. Alving and Nina Leeds. It is a commonplace that Aeschylus is the playwright of a nation experiencing profound changes, and that his plays mirror the revolutions in religion, law, government, and social structure that had been taking place in the preceding century. But it is not so readily noted that, as the Greek world view changes, so too do those standards by which men judge the moral qualities of heroism. Thus, although Prometheus, Agamemnon, and Clytemnestra are towering figures who command our moral attention, they lack tragic stature because there is no possibility for moral action in *Prometheus Bound* or the *Agamemnon*. They are heroes in the old epic sense—essentially uncomplicated, with stature based upon social position and/or physical prowess, and whose achievements and transgressions confirm or reflect more the will of whimsical gods in conflict than the results of conscious, self-motivated choice. It is clear, of course, that Aeschylus is rejecting the values, customs, and standards of heroism of the Homeric world, but in his plays—at least the ones we still have—his chief concern is with the new dispensation of the Olympian deities and not with the moral significance of human suffering.

With the coming of Orestes in *The Choëphoroe* the possibility of a new heroism emerges. He is the prototype of the tragic hero in Western literature, but he himself is not such a hero. He does make a moral decision, he is torn in the making of that decision, and he is hunted and haunted after he has acted on that decision. But one all-important condition is missing that denies him the status of a tragic hero: there is no ultimate perspective by which his actions can be judged. The action of *The Eumenides* must move beyond the judgment of Orestes, not only because of Aeschylus' overall design, but because there can be no judgment of Orestes until matters have been straightened out in heaven between the gods of the old and new orders. Orestes is the potential tragic hero, and we can see this clearly only if we turn our attention specifically to the trilogy itself.

Practically everyone seems to agree that the action of *The Oresteia* deals with the transfiguration of the patterns of justice and the metamorphosis of persuasion from a morality of vengeance and vendetta to a morality of social law and the ultimate achievement of true justice. Throughout the three plays Aeschylus presents a constantly shifting yet continually related series of situations that demand an answer to the question, What is justice? But it must be made very clear that he is not writing "The Tragical History of the House of Atreus." The formative principle of the trilogy is to reveal the ideal adjustment between opposing principles and forces in the quest for a vision of justice. This is not so much a dramatic action—which is chosen and made—as a destiny that is fulfilled.

In *The Oresteia* we have the occasion of tragedy without the substance of it. Actually, as several commentators have suggested, there are two worlds in the plays: one immanent and the other transcendent. This is true of most Greek plays, but unlike the world of Sophoclean tragedy, the realm of the gods is not as yet fixed and accepted in the Aeschylean universe, and there are, therefore, no inviolable standards of justice by which to judge the actions of men. This means that everything in *The Oresteia* is double and in a constant state of change; both men and gods are on trial, and a change of attitude on the part of the gods will be reflected in the actions of the human characters, and all of the violence and destruction, division and discord that erupt in the House of Atreus is meant to reveal a similar condition in the realm of the gods as well. (In this regard, it should be remembered that, unlike the Judeo-Christian concept of God, the Olympian deities were not believed to be eternal. They were born and grew.)

We can see this double development by comparing briefly the *Agamemnon* to *The Choëphoroe*. In the former play we are shown a world of moral violence that has created social and political chaos involving both gods and men. Within the play, however, there is no growth and no action; there are no internal divisions within the characters, and they never react to one another. Each of them acts out of pride for what he or she believes to be justice, and they collide like mighty stars in an empty space. But as flawed as they are by their pride and the thirst for revenge, they are victims of a moral chaos that they did not create and which they feel no responsibility to correct. For all their epic stature, like the Homeric heroes, they are the pawns of the gods.

A different spirit pervades *The Choëphoroe*. The revengeful Apollo, who had to have Cassandra as a victim in the *Agamemnon*, is now the god of light leading the untainted Orestes to his horrible but necessary task. The spirit of vengeance has begun to recede and the spirit of social responsibility is taking its place. There is no way to account for this change if we look for the cause in the human characters. What happens makes sense only if we see that the laws of cause and effect have given way to the principles of maturation; for in *The Oresteia*, Aeschylus is finally more concerned with the coming to maturity of the gods than he is with the tragic struggles of the human actors.

The issues raised by the struggles of the House of Atreus in the first two parts of the trilogy cannot be resolved by the mortals involved in them. Both sides are right and both are wrong, and Orestes must therefore be judged—if there is to be judgment at all—by a new and higher law. Thus, in *The Eumenides* the two strands of the play that have been woven together more and more tightly in the *Agamemnon* and *The Choëphoroe* are finally fused. But as the action passes beyond the limits of the human condition, it also goes beyond tragedy. The moment Athena enters the scene, the human struggle with necessity is undercut by the likelihood of divine intervention, and the possibility that Orestes may be acquitted destroys the tragic sense of his being trapped without a chance of escape.

The great debate begins—this scene provides persuasive evidence that the informing image of all Greek tragedy is based not on the forms of religious ritual, but is shaped by the Athenian courts of law—and the cases for a world order based upon the imperatives of the instincts as opposed to the rigid but more reasonable concepts of social law are presented. The jury votes and there is a tie. Athena must decide, and she sides with Apollo and Orestes. But, significantly, the play does not end with Orestes' acquittal. Before there can be a final resolution, Athena must persuade the Erinyes to accept her judgment. Persuasion, which had heretofore been the partner of a justice by vendetta, must be transformed so it can be incorporated as a working principle into the new justice of social law. Athena succeeds, and the Erinyes become the Semnai, the Holy Ones. This accomplished, the new vision of justice has been realized, and the trilogy can end in a ritual celebration.

Aeschylus has conquered tragedy by creating a mythical visualization of a world guided by Zeus, *Dike* (justice), and the gods. Zeus and Fate (*Moira*) are finally united, and in that union the possibility of a perfect justice has been achieved. Such a resolution, however, is religious, not tragic.

Finally, it must be seen that, although the action of the trilogy has been resolved in the realm of the gods, it could not have been accomplished without the willingness of men to struggle and suffer for a new justice. William Arrowsmith, in his important essay "The Criticism of Greek Tragedy," points this out in his discussion of the play.

> In this world, tragedy can only work itself out through time and suffering, and Zeus himself is powerless to act until the heart of man happens on the beginnings of a true justice. For justice without the wisdom to sustain it would have been a meaningless gift, and wisdom, as the Chorus tells us, is learned in suffering.

A hero capable of such wisdom, who is willing to suffer for justice, is indeed of a new breed. The old heroism of the Homeric world has given way to a heroism based on moral responsibility, and this transformation makes the Greek world possible for tragedy. This was Aeschylus' greatest achievement, and it is for this reason that we can rightly call him the "father" of Greek tragedy, even though, to our knowledge, he never wrote one.

# 3

# THE TRAGIC TURBULENCE OF SOPHOCLEAN DRAMA

SOPHOCLES, alas, has been allowed to become a cultural monument. In contrast to Euripides, whose atonalities seem so akin to those of the mid-twentieth century, Sophocles is usually thought of as the poet of serenity, the champion of self-restraint, and the hero of a hard-won spiritual peace. His plays are hailed as great landmarks of balance and harmony, in which form and idea are perfectly conjoined. Like Goethe, Mozart, and Dante, he is a classic; and as such he is taught and revered, but seldom—at least not in the theatre— are his plays enjoyed as living works of art. With a few exceptions, notable in their rarity, most productions of Sophocles' plays with their hollow ranting, posturing gestures, wooden movements, and Old Vic-ish choruses are dreadfully dull. The prevailing attitude seems to be: "By all means, let's teach Sophocles in school, but if we must have Greek drama in our theatres let's do one of the modern versions—preferably French—such as Anouilh's *Antigone*, or Giraudoux's *Electra*; or, if we are going to be really experimental, we'll try Cocteau's *The Infernal Machine*." To think this way is to do both ourselves and Sophocles a disservice, and, more important, it in no way takes into account the generative power of the Greek theatre. Sophocles can stand such a misunderstanding, but we suffer a profound cultural loss that is as unnecessary as it is dangerous. In order to avoid this, I share William Arrowsmith's belief that the first obligation of the scholars and critics of Greek literature is to help us regain that sense of vitality and turbulence—Arrowsmith's "the turbulence of experience, and the turbulence of ideas under dramatic test"—which make Greek drama exciting theatre.

The failure of most interpretations of Sophocles' plays is the total disregard for the turbulence of this tension. In much the same way as the Bible has been devitalized by the petty moralizing of most Sunday school stories, the critic, in his need to clarify, tends to over-simplify and thus destroys that marvelous rage of the blood which courses through the plays. We must discover ways to restore for both readers and audiences the dynamics of Greek drama in pro-duction (Artaud referred to it as "the physics of Greek tragedy"); and more particularly we must find the means that will encompass that turbulence which we know must have characterized the plays of Sophocles when they were first produced in the fifth century B.C.

If we are to be successful in this, I believe that from the very be-ginning we must refrain from our tendency to categorize Greek drama and should acknowledge the futility of searching for an "idea of Greek tragedy." It is a commonplace that Aristotle's famous definition of tragedy is not descriptive of the majority of the thirty-three extant plays. And the more recent theories, such as "with purpose, through passion, to perception" or the ritualistic-origins approach, are equally inadequate. Even a structural definition proves unsatisfactory as soon as one attempts to make it into a gen-eralized principle. What formal consistency does one find when he compares *Antigone* to *Oedipus the King*, or to *Electra*, or *Oedipus at Colonus?* (Not to mention trying to compare the plays of Aeschy-lus and Euripides in terms of structure!) As I have already indi-cated, for the Greeks of the fifth century, a tragedy (a "goat song") was "any play based upon the legends of the historical aristocracy" performed at the festivals of Dionysus. It may very well be true that these festival performances originally had religious and ritual significance, and this may account for certain common conventions shared by each of the playwrights; this fact may even explain why certain plots and themes were continually used; but by the time of Sophocles the Dionysian festivals had lost most of their religious significance and drama had moved from the realm of religion to that of art, hence the ritual origins of the Greek theatre are of little or no help when it comes to understanding the meaning, signifi-cance, or dynamic of any one play. In the end, formal explanations

of Greek drama are as limited and limiting as the more popular thematic approaches.

Most interpretations of *Antigone* usually pit a noble Antigone fighting in behalf of a belief in the traditional gods (divine law) against a hardhearted, tyrannical Creon who stands for social and political order (human decrees). First of all, such an abstract formulation is woefully superficial, but more important, it can never be a dramatic action; it captures none of the strife and internal struggle of the play; it is incapable of expressing the dividedness of belief, and, at best, it can only produce a cheap kind of political melodrama.

Rather than seeing Antigone and Creon in dialectic opposition to each other, as Hegel did, we should stress their similarities, remembering that they are of the same family and share a common fate; remembering also that Sophocles—contrary to the assertions of some commentators—never conceived of action in terms of a Hegelian dialectic. The most frightening and morally significant struggles in human life are usually those in which the opposing forces use different means to achieve similar ends in the name of identical values. One need only read the speeches, attacks, and counterattacks in our newspapers to realize that the current struggle between the United States and Russia is of this nature. The labels may be different, the ideologies may seem to be at odds, but both sides claim to be fighting in the cause of freedom; each is striving to free the world from domination by the other. We find a similar condition in the regular flare-ups between big business and the labor unions (which are also big business): both sides in these disputes are seeking greater prosperity, and each claims to be working for the general good of society. People become dramatic when they insist on acting on their beliefs. Dramatic action is the collision of people acting in this way, but dramatic action does not become morally significant until this conflict is fought under identical banners of value.

What distinguishes Antigone and Creon is not principle, for they both claim to act in behalf of love. They are in conflict only insofar as they are both caught up in the family's common fate. What is significant is what happens to them as they fulfill their destinies, as they struggle to give a meaning to their fate. Antigone, in her steely assertion of the principle of love, nearly destroys her own humanity (and thus her capacity to love) and denies the presence of love in others. Her greatness resides in her capacity—in the nadir of loneli-

ness—to push the principle beyond the point of denial to the place of rediscovery—rediscovery of love and her own humanity.

Creon never reaches this stage of self-discovery. He suffers just as much as Antigone, actually more; but because he is morally blind he lacks the capacity and the drive to force his fate to its fullest yield. To the very end of the play he sees himself as a man who has struggled hard for the cause of justice in the name of love, only to suffer the misfortunes of a fickle fate. Creon is a man of intelligence, shrewdness, and strong resolve, but he lacks the humanity necessary to understand his fate. Because of this incapacity he is a victim and therefore can know only the horror of his fate. Antigone's capacity for a greater humanity is the source of her heroism, and while this heroism in no way softens her fate, it does give it a glory that all men aspire to, but few ever achieve.

In this regard, I believe Arrowsmith is absolutely correct when he writes about the play as follows:

> What she (Antigone) first accepts as a fate, the principle of love that dooms her to death, is hardened by her desperate plight and her desperate courage and loneliness; and this in turn hardens her— "Great suffering makes a stone of the heart," as Yeats put it—making her refuse Ismene the same dignity of fate she claims. As she hardens, so does Creon on behalf of the same principle, denying Haemon in order to hurt Antigone, just as Antigone dishonors Ismene in order to honor Polyneices. Still hardened, but increasingly tormented by a loss she does not understand and yet the fate she chose, Antigone is condemned to her symbolic death, walled alive in a tomb, and thus cut off alike from both the living and the dead, the human being still alive, like Niobe, beneath the cold rock of her heroism. And suddenly, as the chorus compares her to a goddess, she knows what has happened, and cries, "I am mocked, I am mocked!" and the rock falls away, leaving that final warm confusion that makes her so human and so lovely.*

The play's turbulence resides in this: each of the characters in the play acts on behalf of the principle of love, but the common fate of Antigone and Creon is that to hold steadfast in the cause of love they must deny others the right to love. Each, insisting that he be allowed the dignity of shaping his own fate, must deny this right to others. Antigone's heroism is born when she, in the moment of

---

* William Arrowsmith, "The Criticism of Greek Tragedy," *The Tulane Drama Review*, vol. III, no. 3 (March, 1959), p. 43.

agony, discovers her failure as a woman and is thus able once again to reassert that humanity which gives meaning and vitality to the principle itself.

There is a similar turbulence to be discovered in Electra's waiting as she endures the ravishing delays of a god not ready to act, or in the persuasions of Neoptolemus and Odysseus as they try to seduce Philoctetes into rejoining the Greek forces at Troy. However, in the rest of this chapter I should like to focus my attention on *Oedipus the King*, probably the greatest, most difficult, and most mysterious of all the existing Greek tragedies. This is not the place for a detailed analysis of the play, but I hope my remarks will at least be preliminary soundings that can begin to express that quality of turbulence which drives this great play.

*Oedipus the King* is usually thought of as one of the world's great detective stories. Oedipus, the great sleuth, the one who has solved the inscrutable Sphinx's difficult riddle, is called upon at the beginning of the play to discover who killed Laius. He follows all the clues and discovers that he himself is guilty of slaying the Theban king.* Unfortunately, as attractive as this interpretation is, Sophocles' text makes it very clear that the question "Who killed Laius?" is not really the issue at all; it is a red herring, for in actuality we never know for sure who *did* kill Laius. There is the generally accepted account of Laius' death, which has a band of robbers—"almost an army"—kill Laius and his small company, with only one man escaping, who then returns to Thebes to tell the story. Then there is a rumored story that Laius was killed by some travelers with no one escaping. Tiresias is brought in and accuses Oedipus, but as Oedipus rightly asks Creon: "If I was guilty, why did not Tiresias accuse me then? He must have known, for he is wise." Creon can only answer: "I do not know," and the matter is dropped. There is Jocasta's version, which substantiates the public version of the story. Finally, there is Oedipus' own description of the man he killed at the place where the three roads meet, which makes it clear that he was all alone. In good courtroom fashion all of these accounts are brought into question in the following dialogue:

---

* This is the basis of Francis Fergusson's carefully reasoned interpretation of the play's action in his admirable *The Idea of a Theater*. I believe it is also the underlying assumption of W. H. Auden's fascinating essay on the detective story, "The Guilty Vicarage," in which he shows that Greek tragedy and the modern detective story share many important common characteristics.

OEDIPUS: You said he told you robbers murdered Laius. If he still says "robbers" and not "a robber," I am innocent. One cannot be taken for many. But if he says a murderer alone, the guilt comes to rest on me.

JOCASTA: But we all heard him say "robbers"; that is certain. He cannot unsay it. I am not alone, for the whole city heard.

The investigation never goes beyond this point. To be sure, the Shepherd who is to unravel it all is called, but by the time he comes, the question "Who killed Laius?" is no longer important and he is never asked. Whether Oedipus killed Laius is never unequivocally determined, and the fact that it is not is not really important to the meaning of the play. With the arrival of the messenger from Corinth the action moves—although it has been going there from the beginning—to the question of Oedipus' identity.

Rather than reading the play as a detective story, I agree with Professor Lattimore, who has shown in his *The Poetry of Greek Tragedy* that the play's action is based upon the general pattern of the lost one found, that *Oedipus the King* is essentially a foundling story. Beginning with Moses, Cyrus, and Romulus, right up to Ernest-Jack Worthing, the foundling story has always been a success story and therefore is usually the plot of a comedy whenever it is employed in the theatre. This is the basis of Mr. Lattimore's interpretation, and he contends that the tension and effectiveness of the play resides in the irony achieved by mounting a tragedy on an essentially comic scheme. With this I disagree! There is no ironic inversion here, for all the way to the end the play *is* a success story. Like the other foundling tales, the action of *Oedipus the King* is a quest either by discovery or deeds for identity. Usually the success of this achievement is the cause for joy and celebration ("Our Perdita is found!"), but in *Oedipus the King* the focus is on the disaster of identity. Oedipus succeeds! He finds and he is found. But whenever a man discovers his identity—who he really is as distinct from what others (his parents, siblings, friends, colleagues, and even his enemies) believe or desire him to be—he becomes conscious for the first time of his own unique and individual struggle with necessity. It is the individual's sense of his own identity that transforms Man's Fate into a man's fate. The tragic view of life insists that the assertion of identity—"I am Jesus, the King of the Jews!", "I am Hamlet, the Dane!"—is inextricably bound to suffering and death, the cross and the grave. There is glory in the discovery of self, but it has a price, and great tragedy has always affirmed this ambiguity.

This central ambiguity of tragic action is expressed in *Oedipus the King* by the interweaving lines of the plot, by the conflicts within and between the characters, and in the image patterns of the poetry, especially the play's central image—Mount Cithaeron. It will be remembered that the foundling is always the child of the wilderness, and in Greece the wilderness is in the mountains, and particularly the wild, barren slopes of Mount Cithaeron. Cithaeron, as Jane Harrison has shown in *Themis,* was the home of all foundlings, especially divinely protected heroes, demigods, and even such gods as Dionysus and Zeus. Most critics, Lattimore's being the notable exception, overlook the importance of Mount Cithaeron in the play and yet it is always there towering above the imaginative world of the play as it does, in fact, range above the city of Thebes. In addition to its continual presence in the imagery of the choral odes, it is also the key image in Oedipus' discovery of his identity. When he returns to the stage after tearing out his eyes, he cries out against his fate, shouting: "Cithaeron, why did you let me live? Why / Did you not kill me as I lay there?" and shortly before he leaves the stage for the last time, humbled and having accepted his fate, he calls up the image of the mountain:

> Let me
> Have no home but the mountains, where the hill
> They call Cithaeron, my Cithaeron, stands.
> There my mother and father, while
> They lived, decreed I should have my grave.
> My death will be a gift from them, for they
> Have destroyed me. . . .

What is the significance of the recurring metaphor of Cithaeron? What is involved in this return to the mountain, the mountain of Oedipus' infancy? Part of an answer can be found in the second choral stasimon.* Coming as it does right after Oedipus' decision to call the Shepherd who is to decide once and for all who killed Laius, it serves as a commentary on the ultimate futility of those investigations of the intellect which would fathom the will of the

---

* This is one of the most remarkable passages in the play and yet it is often cut in production, and Yeats saw fit to reduce its fifty lines to fifteen in his "more poetic" rendering of the text. But both structurally and thematically it is absolutely essential to an understanding of the play's meaning.

gods and solve the riddles of existence. But it is also the overture to that movement of the play which concerns itself with Oedipus' search for his own identity. In linking the quest for Laius' killer with the larger question of existential identity, this choral passage is both a judgment and a foreshadowing. The first thirty-eight lines are particularly significant and worth recalling here:

CHORUS: All actions must beware of the powers beyond us,
    and each word
Must speak our fear of heaven. I pray
That I may live every hour in obedience.
The laws that hold us in subjection
Have always stood beyond our reach, conceived
In the high air of heaven. Olympus
Was their sire, and no woman on earth
Gave them life. They are laws
That will never be lured to sleep in the
    arms of oblivion,
And in their strength heaven is great and
    cannot grow old.
Yet man desires to be more than man, to rule
His world for himself.
This desire, blown to immensity
On the rich empty food of its ambition,
Out of place, out of time,
Clambers to the crown of the rock, and stands there,
Tottering; then comes the steepling plunge
    down to earth,
To the earth where we are caged and mastered.
But this desire may work for good
When it fights to save a country, and I pray
That heaven will not weaken it then.
For then it comes like a god to be our warrior
And we shall never turn it back.
Justice holds the balance of all things,
And we must fear her.
Do not despise the frontiers in which we must live,
Do not cross them, do not talk of them,
But bow before the places where the gods are throned.
Time will come with cruel vengeance on the man
Who disobeys; that is the punishment
For those who are proud and are more than men—
They are humbled.
If a man grows rich in defiance of this law,

If his actions trespass on a world that he should fear,
If he reaches after mysteries that no man should
  know,
No prayer can plead for him when the sword of
  heaven is raised.
If he were to glory in success
All worship would fall dumb.

In effect, the passage says: "Woe to the climbers of mountains! And yet, where would we be without them!" Man's need to overreach himself, to "despise the frontiers in which we must live," to be a hero, is an essential part of human nature; but all attempts to transcend the limits of being human are inevitably doomed to disaster. Most men know they are incapable of reaching "after mysteries that no man should know," but they nonetheless need and admire those heroes who would dare so audaciously to do so. From the time of Hesiod's *Works and Days,* the mountain climb was the symbol in Greek literature of the hero's impossible quest for perfect *arete,* that ultimate achievement of mind and spirit which made man like unto gods. To achieve *arete* requires a tremendous act of will; it is an achievement that only a person with a strong sense of his own identity is capable of attempting and, therefore, it inevitably separates him from the rest of humankind. It is also a demonic quest for it ultimately must transcend the limits of rationality. Oedipus, although unaware of it, has such a demon within him. He finally discovers it, and in his discovery we witness the tragedy of intellectuality.

Our most distinguishing characteristic as human beings is our self-criticizing intelligence. It is the source of our greatness, but it is also the cause of our most profound grief. It creates the occasions for tragedy in one of two ways: either when our reflective thought challenges the authenticity of our impulses, or when our impulses rebel against those threats to their fulfillment which our reason would erect to maintain itself. Nietzsche described this as the conflict between the Dionysian and the Apollonian, but whether we describe this conflict as one between freedom and domination, Eros and Thanatos, autonomy and constraint, gratification and repression, or genuine progress and eternal return, it makes little difference for it is from the conflict of these two natures in each of us that the tragic experience emerges.

The ambiguity of all tragedy, and this is especially true of *Oedipus the King,* consists of the fact that our doomed need to die is the only means of regaining the spontaneity that life loses under the alienating, repressive systems created by the intelligence. This is the curse of Adam! He paid the price of death for an increase in intelligence. His curse dramatizes the connection between death and culture: The same rational process that strengthens man's chances to live also creates the conditions that make death inevitable and even attractive. The great tragedies reenact the necessity and the meaninglessness of this death drama; they show man's ultimate and inevitable alienation, but they also reveal that man's rational faculty is the cause of this condition. This is so because intelligence, in the words of Ralph J. Hallman,

> invites man to overreach himself; it discovers to man his fragmented, corrupt nature; it imposes duality upon experience and thereby sets up conflicts . . . it is the source of all painful paradox. It creates the notion of universality, of eternality, of permanence. Rationality alone can conceive of deathlessness, and it therefore creates in man the urge to become immortal. It forces man to expand his personal, limited, finite experiences to a cosmic scale. Thus, it makes possible the idea of an ultimately meaningless universe. It is an agent of domination; yet it creates the conditions of freedom. It militates against aggression; yet aggression cannot occur in its absence. It softens our motor experiences and makes for indolence. It saps life of individuality by forcing it into institutional molds; yet when the individual discovers it within himself, he becomes the rebel.*

Tragedy, in short, shows why heroes are born, but it also depicts the bankruptcy of intelligence as a measure that one must take in a vain effort to escape the final estrangement.

The foundling story is one of the archetypal expressions of this conflict, and, as Jung and Kerenyi have shown, the Oedipus menace exists in the form of the "eternal child" within every one of us. Imbedded in the psychic structure of each individual, it expresses itself as the most fundamental urge to become ourselves through the process of losing ourselves in a retreat to the Cithaeron of our childhood. It is thus potentiality for self-realization; it is the act of returning to the primordial condition where lies the secret power capable of unbinding the fetters of a coercive world and of releasing the self into full freedom. Intelligence creates the possibility of such

* *Psychology of Literature* (New York, Philosophical Library, 1961) pp. 138–139.

freedom; it dangles before man the chimerical vision of an autonomous existence, and thus taunts him to rebel. But such freedom can never be realized, for no man can fulfill himself apart from an ordered system even though his very nature demands that he try. Perhaps the history of the whole human race can be telescoped into this one tragic contradiction: man demands freedom, but he wills to submit. Only the tragic hero makes a desperately magnanimous effort to achieve spontaneity; only he refuses to compromise. Thus Oedipus is doomed, but not because he had a tragic flaw, but because he refused to accept a ready-made fate. He wanted his own fate—not the gods'! His personal fate may be cut short by his doom, but Oedipus insists upon distinguishing his own responsibility by blinding himself. It is the magnificence of his own declaration of responsibility that makes him so heroic. His fate is *his*, and no one else's. And if he has *hamartia*, it is not a sin or a flaw, but the ungovernable tragic ignorance of all men.

"Oedipus," as we all know, means "swelled foot" when translated from the Greek; but *Oida Pous* also means "on the track of knowledge." Oedipus begins in the play as a hero of knowledge. He would climb Mount Olympus, the home of the gods and the place of wisdom; he has solved the riddle of the Sphinx, which can be answered by an abstraction: MAN. But we must always remember that although the risk of the Sphinx is deadly, its challenge is to the intellect alone. In answering the Sphinx man may be right or wrong, but his answer is rational. But the quest for identity is not a rational undertaking, and here our intelligence fails us. Man's intelligence cannot solve, cover, foresee, or account for all that happens to us. Experience always makes a fool of the mind, for the answer to the question "Who am I?" is an experiential answer and is therefore always unique. Harold Rosenberg, in writing about *Oedipus the King* in his fascinating essay "Notes on Identity," said: "The assumption of tragedy is that in actual existence it is impossible to win, except by way of the destruction itself—and winning through being destroyed is not a rational risk but a transcendental hypothesis." Oedipus attempts to understand everything, including his own identity, in a rational way. But for all of his determination and intelligence there is a dark, nonsensical element in experience that eludes his comprehension and thereby leads him to his destruction. Life begins for Oedipus, as in a way it does for each of us, on Mount Cithaeron. He would climb Olympus, only to discover that man's fate is that he end on Cithaeron. His glory is in the climb and his doom in the fall that is inevitable.

> Yet man desires to be more than man, to rule
> His world for himself. . . .
>
> Out of place, out of time,
> Clambers to the crown of the rock, and stands there
> Tottering; then comes the steepling plunge down to earth,
> To the earth where we are caged and mastered.

Such are the conflicts of turbulence which, as I said earlier, are inevitable when men try vainly but nobly to impose a meaning on their own lives and on the world around them.

# 4

# THE DRAMA
# OF EURIPIDES

A FEW years ago the now deceased French playwright Arthur Adamov wrote: "The destinies of all human beings are of equal futility.
The refusal to live and the joyful acceptance of life both lead, by
the same path, to inevitable failure, total destruction." In this sentence, and in the essay of which it is a part, Adamov is describing
the absurdity that he believes is the essential nature of the human
condition. But he might also have been describing the final meaning of many of the plays written by the world's first "absurdist"
playwright, Euripides. And these plays, much like those of our
twentieth-century Absurdists, have been baffling critics ever since.
In fact, it all began with Aristotle!

In the thirteenth chapter of the *Poetics*, Aristotle refers to Euripides as "the most tragic of the poets." But to say this and nothing
more is to say very little. Like so many of Aristotle's infuriating remarks, it contains a great truth if we can only discover what it is.
To do this we must again refer to that crucial distinction between
tragedy, which is a particular dramatic form, and the tragic, which
is a particular way of viewing human experience. When we talk
about tragedy, we are in the realm of aesthetics; when we discuss
the nature of the tragic, we are in the realms of metaphysics, ethics,
and possibly religion. In short, the difference between the two is
the difference between art and life. This does not mean they are not
related, at times they may seem inseparable; but the distinction is
real.

Even a cursory examination of the existing Greek "tragedies" indicates that Euripides was more conscious that "the destinies of all human beings are of equal futility," that we are all doomed "to inevitable failure, total destruction," than either Aeschylus or Sophocles. But such a view of life does not necessarily have anything to do with artistic form. Thus, to say that Euripides is "the most tragic of poets" is to say nothing about him as a playwright or about the form of his plays. And this, I think, is where all the trouble starts. When we talk about Greek tragedy as a dramatic form, what are we talking about?

Again, Professor DeWitt's observation that "for the Greeks tragedy was any play based upon the legends of the historical aristocracy" is pertinent, and it is related to two other important ideas. The first is that in the fifth century B.C. the Greek audiences (and critics too, if there were any) of Athens were not particularly interested in questions of tragic form. If the plays dealt with the exploits of the legendary heroes of the past, that was all that mattered. Questions of catharsis, reversal and discovery, disastrous or happy endings never seemed to have been raised. Audiences may have preferred Sophocles' plays—the results of the contests would indicate that they did—but it never entered anybody's mind to question whether or not Euripides wrote tragedies. It was not until Aristotle, almost a century later, that matters of dramatic form became important.* So, if we are to understand Greek tragedy, and the tragedies of Euripides in particular, we must cut through the assumptions and methodology of Aristotle's evaluation.

The second implication of Professor DeWitt's statement is that insofar as Greek tragedy had any formal characteristics they were aristocratic. This is not a new idea; critics from Aristotle to Joseph Wood Krutch have maintained this. But it is an important consideration for anyone who wants to understand Euripides, for it implies that the driving force behind all of the conventions of tragedy is a hierarchical order that imparts meaning to all human actions and at the same time transcends them. Man and his society are thought of as microcosmic reflections of a transcending cosmic design, and within this order there are many levels—levels that are analogically related, but that nonetheless manifest differences in degree.

---

* It is interesting to note, and here again I am indebted to Professor DeWitt, that with the exception of Aristotle, and to a lesser degree and for totally different reasons Plato, Greek intellectuals—early or late—were never very much concerned with the subject of tragedy.

This kind of world view is uniquely suited to the form of tragedy, for it automatically produces men who, at least potentially, have heroic stature. Furthermore, it does not deny the tragic sense of life, since these heroes in their involvement with finite issues can easily lose sight of the ultimate cosmic order and thereby be brought low. In their fall, and in the discovery—or more properly, rediscovery—of the cosmic order that they have violated, the order is reaffirmed. This is the affirmation of tragedy to which critics constantly refer. (However, it should be pointed out that such periods, and then only briefly, seldom occur in human history, and that only four or five playwrights—and they not consistently—have ever written that kind of tragedy.) Furthermore, the affirmation of a cosmic order in no way vitiates the tragic fact that man as an individual is always defeated, order or no order. In fact, I would go so far as to say that the affirmation of tragedy is an affirmation of form only, an aesthetic affirmation that may very well be satisfying to the spectator who is outside the action but is of little help to the individual spectator once he leaves the theatre to reenter his own tragic existence.

Be that as it may, the point for us is that Greek tragedy as a form had aristocratic origins. It developed out of an agricultural economy that was ruled by a landed aristocracy and a religion that corresponded to such an economy. The theology of early Greek drama is the theology of Hesiod, and since the festivals were originally ritual celebrations of sacrifice to the gods in order to insure a bountiful harvest, it is no wonder that the emerging form of Greek tragedy is in the pattern of seasonal change—life, death, and rebirth. Thus, both in meaning and form Greek tragedy evolved as a product of the seventh century B.C. To be sure, it went through certain evolutionary refinements, but those changes—although they made for better theatre—did not really alter the fact that the plays were still "goat songs" based upon the rituals of an aristocratic agricultural society.

But, and here is where Euripides comes in, what relevance did this kind of metaphysical and social order have for the Athenian of the fifth century? This was the age of Pericles; Athens was a democracy, and the Hellenistic imperialism that we tend to associate with the fourth century was already in full sway. In short, the world that Euripides was a part of was neither predominantly aristocratic nor agricultural. Fifth-century Athens was an urban, middle-class, artisan society; its economy was based upon production surpluses and trade. Furthermore, Hellenism had its religious reformation too, and profound changes in religious practice and belief were taking place. The traditional gods of Hesiod's *Theogony* were no longer meaningful to the anonymous small businessman living in the city. If anything, he was attracted to the many Oriental cults that the traders had introduced. Even in this increasingly secular age there was still a need for some belief in the supernatural, but this need was becoming more internalized, more personal, private, and mystical. As a result, the individual's relationship to his god was not dependent upon the hierarchical systems of a cosmic order, but was direct and immediate. We have seen similar things happen in Europe and America since the Industrial Revolution, and we have noticed what happens to tragedy when such changes occur, because, as George Steiner said in his book *The Death of Tragedy*, "there is nothing democratic in the vision of tragedy."

And this leads us to the Euripidean dilemma. Both Sophocles and Euripides were tragic writers in that they saw the destiny of man as one of defeat. But they were radically different in that Sophocles —at least until late in his life—accepted the metaphysical system of the Olympian gods and the traditional dramatic form based upon that system. His plays celebrate the values of that system; and his heroes, though they fall, affirm the validity of the cosmic order in their defeat. Euripides, on the other hand, not only doubted the validity of the Olympian deities, but he clearly saw that the inherited forms of tragedy had little or no relevance to the world in which he lived. He was clearly a playwright in a bind.

This is first manifested in Euripides' continual experimentation with dramatic form. Many of his plays are not tragedies except by that broad standard which we established earlier. *Helen* and *Iphigenia in Tauris* are dramatic romances and have much in common with many of our popular contemporary film and television plays of the same genre. *Alcestis* has moments of tragedy, but certainly ends happily. *Medea, Electra,* and *Orestes* are sweeping melodramas that have much more in common with the bloody Elizabethan revenge plays than with those plays which we usually think of as tragic. And so on.

If this is true of Euripides' plots and general themes, it is also true of his use of the traditional conventions of classical drama. For example, the myths upon which Greek tragedies are based are concerned with public experience; thus Euripides was constantly having to "doctor" them so they were somehow capable of expressing individual personal dilemmas. *Hippolytus,* which is a synthesis of several legends, is a good illustration of such "doctoring." Witness the chorus. Traditionally, the chorus represented a public response. It could be, and often was, wrong in its judgments, but it did express communal values and reactions. Clearly, Euripides doubted the existence of such a community of response and yet he was "stuck" with the form. As a result his choral passages become increasingly lyric and function less and less as an integral part of the dramatic action. Instead of interacting and providing a public, a communal, comment and reaction to the events of the plot, the Euripidean chorus is little more than ornamental, and at best it serves as an artificial means of furthering the exposition of events or it helps to create an emotional pressure for the action.

Two good examples of this come to mind. First, one of the weakest moments in *Hippolytus* is when Theseus is cursing and banishing his son while the whole time the chorus is present, knowing the truth. They lament but say nothing. Obviously, they cannot, for if they did the play would end right there; but it is a good example of a playwright saddled with a convention he cannot effectively use. Second, in *Medea,* Medea makes a chorus of Corinthian women swear not to tell of the destruction she is about to bring on the royal household of Corinth; and they take such an oath. Without being sticklers for verisimilitude, we have to admit this stretches our "willing suspension of disbelief" pretty far. In our own terms, it would be similar to Chairman Mao's coming to Washington and announcing to the local chapter of the DAR that he was about to blow up the White House and then persuading those august ladies not to tell anyone about it.

Euripides has a similar problem with his plots. Traditionally, the plot of a Greek tragedy was the working out of an individual conflict that had communal significance. It is this public truth which provides the artist with his means of communication. It enables him to communicate emotion and attitude simply by describing incidents; it gives him a storehouse of symbols with guaranteed responses; it enables him to construct a plot by selecting and patterning events that, because of his community of belief, are significant. The dramatist is bound more by a plot than other artists, because for him plot is essential and the very existence of plot depends on agreement between writer and audience on what is significant in experience. All tragedy, for that matter, is wholly dependent on a conventional view of the significant in experience; we must be sure that the issues really matter before we can consider any outcome to be tragic.

This helps explain why Euripides had such trouble with his recognition scenes. In a Sophoclean play there is a situation that has to be resolved; in the process of resolving it the characters, and particularly the hero, come to a new understanding of themselves and their relationship to the situation, and finally through the situation of their relationship to the cosmic order, the will of the gods. This is the recognition scene, and it is important to see that this scene always leads to a new mode of action. Now, in a Euripidean play there is also a situation to be resolved, but the resolving of it never leads to any new recognition. (In fact, it is interesting to note that usually the hero of a Sophoclean play is in a situation where he must *do* something. Euripides' heroes, for the most part, are trying *not* to do something.) Euripides' characters, if they learn anything, learn nothing about themselves they do not already know from the beginning. Phaedra comes to no recognition, she learns nothing new; neither do Medea and Pentheus, and Agave and Theseus learn only that they made horrible mistakes. Essentially, the characters are static; they do not grow, and the only thing they learn is that "you can't win." All of Euripides' plots are the working out of a situation that has occurred because the characters are the way they are. It is like an experiment in chemistry: take three ingredients, mix them together, and a particular result will occur. The chemicals have no choice in the matter; they cannot even refrain from participating in the experiment.

Finally, we can see the effects of this dilemma in Euripides' language. Of all the Greek playwrights, Euripides was probably the best poet. In Sophocles' works it is hard to find a "great quotation," except in the choral passages, because the meaning is in the action and not in the words alone. Sophocles was a "maker of actions." Euripides was a "maker of words," and his poetry tends to replace action; it compensates for the lack of it. We notice, for instance, particularly in the speeches of the nonroyal characters, the beginning of the *sententiae* tradition, which Seneca later perfected and which is so much a part of the language of the Jacobean dramatists. *Sententiae* are wise, almost platitudinous sayings that give the meaning of statements rather than dramatic meanings. But when statement replaces dramatic process, the theatre, as so many modern plays will attest, is in mortal danger. Euripides, then, was a master at creating poetic meanings, and all of his plays manifest a contextual verbal unity. But this unity tends more and more to be the unity of technique, the necessary compensation of a playwright who finds it difficult, if not impossible, to construct a meaningful action. In short, the structure and form of Greek tragedy—a structure and form determined by the values of a long-dead aristocratic and agricultural society—were not expressive of what Euripides was trying to present thematically.*

It now remains for us to see what the effects of this dilemma had on the plays of Euripides. The first and most obvious effect is to be found in Euripides' handling of the Olympian deities. Many critics have gone on at great length to show that Euripides was satirizing the gods in his plays. Although there seems to be plenty of evidence to support this position, it is really beside the point. There is little doubt that Euripides does not believe in the validity of the gods, but the fact remains that the traditional form requires that he use them. So, and this it seems to me is the important question, since he cannot omit them, what does he do with them? He usually does one of three things:

1. The gods are sometimes just tacked on as useless appendages that have no organic relationship to the drama.

2. They are used in the convention of the *deus ex machina* to provide an artificial metaphysical or aesthetic solution for a situation that has no such satisfactory resolution inherent in it. (Only Euripides consistently needed to resolve his plays in this fashion. Where there is a firm belief in a metaphysical cosmic order, no such device is necessary. Sophocles used it in only two of the extant plays: *Philoctetes*, which, as most critics have pointed out, is Euripidean in theme, tone, and technique; and *Oedipus at Colonus,* which is more of an apocalyptic vision, like *The Tempest,* than a tragedy.)

---

* It must be clearly understood that there is no condemnation of Euripides in this. To those who would accuse him of laziness or lack of inventiveness for not creating a new form that would express what he wanted to say, we can only counter by saying that for plays to be produced in the fifth century B.C. they had to conform to the conventions of the festival theatres. Euripides was not a closet dramatist—which is really a contradiction in terms—and had to do the best he could. In fact, because of his dilemma he may well have been the most inventive of the three great Greek dramatists.

3. The gods are humanized (not for satiric purposes I would insist) in such a way that they become objectifications of the internal,
irrational drives of the human characters.

But if not the gods, what then? The omnipotent ruler of the
Euripidean universe is *Fortuna,* Luck. Time and time again we find
this idea informing the plays:

> . . . I can pass on to my children after me
> Life with an uncontaminated name,
> And myself profit by the present throw
> Of Fortune's dice. . . .

> This is the lot in life I seek,
> And I pray that God may grant it me,
> Luck and prosperity. . . .

> . . . all depends on the luck men have.

> Luck has fallen on your bride, and the
> Gods have blessed her fortune.

> . . . no man among mortals is happy;
> If wealth comes to a man, he may be luckier
> Than the rest; but happy—never.

There is no order in such a world; everything that happens is unpredictable, irrational. But if Luck does rule the universe, what happens to those traditional concepts of tragedy such as Fate, Justice,
and Wisdom? They, too, must take on radically new meanings.

In the plays of Aeschylus and Sophocles, Fate knows what the
metaphysical order is. In such a world man is free to choose what
Fate knows he will choose. Fate may be apart from the cosmic order of the universe, but it works through and has meaning only in
terms of that order. But in a world governed by the metaphysics of
Chance, Fate becomes that particular irrational imbalance which
exists within each individual. Man no longer chooses his fate—or
anything else, for that matter—he is a victim. This is made very
clear in Phaedra's crisis of conscience, a crisis in which Euripides
expresses man's essential nature and his impossible dilemma. In a
world governed by *Fortuna,* in which Fate is internalized, right and
wrong are no longer objective values that the individual may choose;
such values now exist within man and are known only subjectively,
and since the individual can never choose consistently he is always
defeated, and the balance and freedom of a clear conscience can

seldom be attained and never be maintained. Fate, then, is the working out of conflicting irrational forces—forces over which we have no control, leading always to our destruction.

What is true of Fate is also true of Justice. Traditionally, Justice was doing the will of the gods. But in a world where *Fortuna* rules, how can one succeed in doing so? What is the will of the gods? How can you know it? Can one ever be sure? Hippolytus seemed to be doing the will of Artemis—she says he was—and look what happened to him. Pentheus, puritan that he was, believed he was doing the right thing. Theseus served Poseidon and it did not help him any. Which god's will does one serve and how can one serve them all since they contradict each other? Justice disappears in the world of Euripides' plays; if it exists at all, it almost seems to be based on "Don't get caught!"

But if Justice disappears, what happens to Wisdom? In the Olympian universe Wisdom is knowing the will of the gods and then doing it; that is, acting with Justice. If you cannot know the will of the gods, then what do you do? In many of Euripides' plays it is no longer a matter of knowing and doing the will of the gods. Wisdom is a relative thing. If what you do succeeds, you have acted wisely; if it fails, you have not. This is the way the Nurse defends herself after she has failed in presenting Phaedra's case to Hippolytus, and nothing in the play refutes her defense:

> Mistress, you may well blame my ill-success,
> For sorrow's bite is master of your judgment. . . .
>
> Had I succeeded, I had been a wise one.
> Our wisdom varies in proportion to
> Our failure or achievement.

Such relativity of values inevitably leads to a philosophy of moderation. And here again we are mistaken if we believe this Hellenistic virtue was not commonly accepted until the fourth century B.C. To be sure, Aristotle is the first to celebrate the idea of the Golden Mean in philosophic terms, but it was already common currency—if only for the sake of expediency—in the fifth century B.C. In every play Euripides wrote, prudence—the careful taking of the middle way—is shown (and significantly by nonroyal characters) to be the only way a man can survive, if he is lucky. The Ismenes and Chrysothemises of Sophocles' plays who follow this road are the objects of scorn; but the world of Sophocles—however much we may admire it—had very little in common with Athenian life as it really existed. The Sophoclean hero is a nostalgic anachronism; Antigone is a kind of fifth-century Scarlett O'Hara and Creon her Rhett Butler—attractive monuments to the remembrance of things past. And so with Euripides we have the first prudential hero. In a world without meaning and order, in a world governed by Chance, Fate is Carson McCullers' "screaming idiot racing around the world"; Justice is nonexistent, and Knowledge is useless in the fight against our conflicting irrational desires.

We have already indicated something about the nature of the heroes who inhabit this kind of universe, but there is more that must be said about the Euripidean hero. When we think of tragic heroes, the first thing that usually comes to mind is the great nobility of the hero's spirit. An Oedipus, Prometheus, Lear, or Macbeth may be right or wrong; they may suffer and be destroyed; but the emotional depth and intellectual capacity that each of them brings to his suffering condition stamps him with the mark of greatness. We admire the hero because of his spirit of resistance against the forces of Fate. From a cosmic perspective the hero is guilty of a kind of *hubris* in that he would dare to stand up against the universe, that he would be rash enough to affirm some one aspect of experience—whether it be love, power, glory, knowledge—to the neglect of the totality of experience.

The hero is always doomed—as we all are—but it is a glorious doom. And in spite of the critics and aestheticians, we do not think of *hubris* as a flaw of personality. *Hubris* is that power in human nature which causes a man to upset the metaphysical balance of the universe and in so doing trigger a chain of consequences that inexorably precipitates his own doom. As such it is an ambiguous concept. From the point of view of the metaphysical order, it is man's greatest transgression; within the context of human striving, it is man's greatest strength and virtue. *Hubris* is, therefore, both an arrogant defiance of the metaphysical order and a heroic protest against the limitations of that order. But I repeat, *hubris* should not be thought of as a character defect of egotism. It is that part of human nature which makes man's fate inevitably tragic. It is for this reason, as I said earlier, that the actions of our great heroes are both creative and destructive at the same time. For in the hero's downfall both the greatness of the individual and the meaningfulness of the cosmic order he would defy are affirmed. The hero, by pushing into those "boundary situations" of the human spirit, carries man to his furthest verge, but at the same time that cosmic order which the hero would either rebel against or would affirm is standing more firmly than ever at the end of the play.

However, in all of our thinking about the nature of heroes, we have made one crucial assumption: that there is a cosmic or metaphysical order that defines the attributes of the hero's greatness. And it is precisely this order which we have shown is missing in the world of Euripides' plays. In a world governed by an irrational *Fortuna,* action may or may not be heroic; and if the heroic as such is a matter of accident—notice how accident, not design, is the key to a Euripidean action—this is greatly to deflate if not destroy heroic potentiality. Many of Euripides' characters have a greatness of spirit, but this greatness affirms nothing—not even itself—for in the end each of the characters is brought low by irrational forces. But when man has no power in the shaping of his destiny, even if it be a destiny of doom, then he is only a victim. He is a victim in a situation he has not created, that he has no power to change, and for which he can ultimately feel no responsibility. In this kind of world all men are the same; all men are suffering victims. This accounts, I believe, for the emergence and increasing importance of the "little man"—the nurses in *Hippolytus* and *Medea,* Electra's farmer husband, the more fully characterized messengers—in Euripidean drama.

More important, however, is the fact that in a world of victims there seems to be little or no reason for heroism. Increasingly, Euripides is saying that the only chance man has to survive, if he is lucky, is not to get too involved, not to feel too much. In *Hippolytus, Medea,* and *Electra* the servants urge moderation, because in a world governed by Chance one has to play it safe on all sides. Strong, heroic commitment only gets the individual into trouble, and it is a "trouble" that has no affirmation in it. If it is believed that there are no cosmic values, then life itself becomes the greatest value. In such a world "safety first" is the watchword of existence, life insurance is the best policy; and above all, don't antagonize anybody. Such an attitude is obviously inimical to the heroic whether in life or drama. It does not alter the tragic fate of our existence, but when the mainspring of tragedy, the hero, disappears, it does not take long for the form to disappear also.

Related to the disappearance of the hero in Euripidean drama is the attitude toward suffering and death that is manifested in his plays. In the plays of Aeschylus and Sophocles, suffering, though painful, is shown to be a positive and beneficial force in human affairs; for through suffering mankind is able to achieve Wisdom. This view is stated explicitly by Aeschylus in *Agamemnon:*

> Zeus, who guided men to think,
> Has laid it down that wisdom
> Comes alone through suffering.

Indeed, it is a commonplace in Western thought that suffering enhances one's understanding of life; suffering makes one more human and comprehensive; suffering makes one more creative. But there are many (Euripides among them) who look upon these as parlor platitudes. In a world where Wisdom is "safety first" and Justice is Luck, suffering can have no saving attributes. It certainly cannot lead to Wisdom; it is nothing but a meaningless retribution that produces pain and perhaps more suffering. In such a world suffering is significant only because it is suffering. In fact, in most of Euripides' plays there is a kind of perverse reversal of the axiom of "wisdom through suffering." Phaedra, for instance, has Wisdom from the beginning; she knows what the wise and just thing for her to do is. But this knowledge only enhances her suffering and brings with it more suffering. If Euripides' plays affirm anything about the nature of suffering, it is that the human condition is to suffer; life is misery and there is no reason for it, it just is. Those living in Euripides' world very likely *would* have agreed with Arthur Koestler's view of suffering as expressed in *The Age of Longing:*

> What about the famous purifying effect of suffering? Some people suffer and become saints. Others, by the same experience, are turned into brutes thirsting for vengeance. Others just neurotics. To draw spiritual nourishment from suffering, one must be endowed with the right kind of digestive system. Otherwise suffering turns sour on one. It was bad policy on the part of God to inflict suffering indiscriminately. It was like ordering laxatives for every kind of disease.*

Concomitant with Euripides' change of attitude concerning the effects of suffering is the shift in attitude toward death that we find in his plays. If one accepts the view that life is only meaningless suffering, then death becomes the only way out, a blessed release, an

* *The Age of Longing* (New York, The Macmillan Company, 1951) p. 22.

escape from this vale of tears. Death has always been central to tragedy, but usually as an achievement. Death meant the end of the hero's life, but it was also related to the fulfillment of his personality and his aims. This accounts, I think, for our mixed feelings about the traditional hero's death: We are filled with the terror of his end, but we are also moved with admiration by the power of his affirmation. Antigone's death is horrible; it is also great and admirable. The same is true of Oedipus' blinding. But this is not what we feel when Pentheus, Polyxena, Iphigenia or Hippolytus die. Their deaths are so meaningless, so absurd. The best we can say for these deaths is what the characters themselves say—it is an escape. This accounts for the strong death wish that is so much a part of all Euripidean characters. In a world where there can be no reconciliation of feelings and reason, where nothing makes sense, life is meaningless. Death is meaningless too, but it is less painful. Therefore, it is better not to be human, for "Death is the best plan of all."

In all of Euripides' plays, then, the characters are finally acquitted because they cannot know how to act. If he is saying anything, Euripides is saying that men must be tolerant and understanding of each other, because all men suffer and there is no real meaning to suffering in an irrational world. Indeed, Aristotle was right when he called Euripides the most tragic of poets. Euripides was the most tragic because he not only saw that the basic condition of life was defeat, but also because he could not accept the traditional form of tragedy, which, in aesthetic terms at least, was able to conquer the tragic nature of man's existence and thereby provide a temporary victory over, and a temporary affirmation of, that absurd condition in which "the destinies of all human beings are of equal futility."

# 5

# COMEDY AND
# THE COMIC SPIRIT

A FEW years ago in a seminar on comedy I asked the students in the class to give a definition of comedy in one hundred words or less. After what seemed an interminable silence—we all knew that I had asked the impossible, and that the question really reflected my own frustration in attempting to deal with comedy's many baffling problems—a young man reached into his pocket and pulled out a crumpled newspaper clipping and passed it over to me, mumbling something to the effect that "this is it!" Though it was not a definition, it certainly did indicate in a grotesque manner several of the elements related to this complex subject which Dr. Johnson so correctly observed "has been particularly unpropitious to definers." The article read as follows:

### MAN'S CORK LEG CHEATS DEATH
#### KEEPS HIM AFLOAT AFTER LEAP INTO RIVER

A carpenter's cork leg kept him afloat and prevented him from taking his life by jumping into the Mississippi River from a Canal St. ferry, Fourth District police reported Monday.

Taken to Charity Hospital after his rescue was Jacob Lewis, Negro, 52, 2517 Annette. Suffering from possible skull fracture and internal injuries, he was placed in a psychiatric ward for examination.

Police said that after his release from the hospital he would be booked for disturbing the peace by attempting to commit suicide.

The incident occurred about 11:25 P.M. Sunday while the ferry M. P. *Crescent* was tied up on the Algiers side of the river.

Police quoted a ferry passenger as saying he saw the man leap from a rest-room window into the water. When the call was sounded, two employees, James McCaleb, 43, 709 Wilks Lane, and Edward Johnson, 54, 2113 Whitney, Algiers, both Negroes, lowered a boat and rescued Lewis.

He was brought into the boat about 100 yards from the ferry after he refused to grab life preservers the men threw him.

Ferry employees said he told them he had no desire to live. His attempt on his life might have succeeded if his cork leg had not kept him afloat, police said.—(New Orleans *Times-Picayune*)

We cannot help laughing at this report of a thwarted suicide. The situation is ludicrous, if not downright absurd; death and utter despair are cheated in such a preposterous fashion that they are not taken seriously. Even the physical injury is all but ignored, and we are more conscious of the insult—being booked for disturbing the peace—than we are of the pain. And, finally, in its own grim way the story underscores the commonplace that comedy and laughter are serious business.

However, as we enter the realm of comedy we must proceed with caution. There are countless pitfalls to be avoided, the most important of them being the tendency to get so caught up in related but peripheral issues—the psychology or physiology of laughter, the politics of humor, conventions of comic acting, etc.—that we forget the main subject altogether. Nor should we forget the lesson to be learned from the first recorded attempt to take comedy seriously. Recall the prophecy of Plato's *Symposium*: It is early morning and Socrates is still rambling on. He finally begins talking about comedy and proposes his theory that tragedy and comedy spring from the same roots. "To this they were constrained to assent, being drowsy, and not quite following the argument. And first of all Aristophanes dropped off to sleep." "Such was the charm," as Henry Myers has pointed out, "of the first theory of comedy! We leave the *Symposium* with an unforgettable picture of an eminent philosopher putting an eminent comic poet to sleep with a lecture on the comic spirit."

A second warning: In our investigation of the general nature of comedy we must resist falling victim to what I have called the "formalistic fallacy" in the study of dramatic genres. This is the kind of thinking about drama which assumes that comedy of all ages has certain formal and structural characteristics in common. But where in the history of drama will one find such formal consistency? Certainly not in classical Greek or Roman drama; nor in English stage

comedy of the Elizabethan, Restoration, or eighteenth-century periods; nor, for that matter, in the so-called "black" comedy of our
own age. Though it is true that some characteristics of comedy seem
to be "universal"—the presence of lovers, the defeat of an impostor
figure and his subsequent assimilation into the restored social fabric,
an inverted Oedipal pattern in which the son triumphs over the
father, and the presence of violence without its consequences—these
finally have thematic rather than structural significance. The structure of each play is unique, and even within the work of a given
playwright there is an evolution of form which makes it impossible
to consider his work in terms of consistent structural patterns.

The constant in comedy is the comic view of life or the comic
spirit: the sense that no matter how many times man is knocked
down he somehow manages to pull himself up and keep on going.
Tragedy, on the other hand, has always dealt with that rebellious
spirit in man which resists the limitations of being human, including
the limits imposed on him by society. It focuses on man's heroic
capacity to suffer in his rebellion, and celebrates the essential nobility of the rebellious spirit. Thus, while tragedy celebrates the
hero's capacity to suffer, and thereby earn a new and deeper knowledge of himself and his universe, comedy tends to be more concerned with the fact that despite all our individual defeats, life does
nonetheless continue on its merry way. Comedy, then, celebrates
man's capacity to endure; such capacity is ultimately conserving in
spirit and quality. Eric Bentley describes this relationship in his
*The Life of the Drama* as follows: "In tragedy, but by no means
comedy, the self-preservation instinct is overruled. . . . The comic
sense tries to cope with the daily, hourly, inescapable difficulty of
being. For if everyday life has an undercurrent or cross-current of
the tragic, the main current is material for comedy."

However, while identifying the continuing spirit of comedy is essential, it is not enough. Because it does not help us very much
when it comes to explaining why particular plays which we are
accustomed to calling comedies are comic. For, though it is true
that it is almost impossible to say what comedy *is*, we do nonetheless know that it exists and is readily identifiable. We laugh at Volpone even when his situation is desperate, and we are moved to
tears by Charlie Chaplin at the end of *City Lights* in spite of the
ludicrousness of some of the early scenes. Even in those plays where
the laughable and the painful are inextricably combined—for exam-

ple, the Falstaff plays or any of Chekhov's plays—audiences have no difficulty following the right threads in the design. In short, the problems of comedy are seldom artistic; playwrights know how to write plays which their audiences will recognize as comic. The big question is, How do we know?

One important clue in our search for an answer to "How do we know?" is the fact that, invariably, every discussion of comedy begins with (or eventually reaches) at least a passing reference to tragedy. The reverse is seldom true: In most essays on tragedy, comedy is never mentioned. In this regard, an apparent exception to the rule is illuminating. In the beginning of the fifth chapter of *The Poetics,* Aristotle defines comedy as follows:

> Comedy is an artistic imitation of men of an inferior moral bent; faulty, however, not in so far as their shortcomings are ludicrous; for the Ludicrous is a species or part, not all, of the Ugly. It may be described as that kind of shortcoming and deformity which does not strike us as painful, and causes no harm to others; a ready example is afforded by the comic mask, which is ludicrous, being ugly and distorted, without any suggestion of pain.

The two key ideas in this definition are *the ludicrous* and *the absence of pain;* and although it is clear from what follows that Aristotle is more concerned with their tragic contrasts—*the serious* and *the painful*—he does establish two fundamental boundaries of the comic. Let us examine them briefly.

In making this distinction between the ludicrous and the serious Aristotle was not denying the potential seriousness of comedy; rather, much like Plato, he was postulating the idea that comedy, as well as tragedy, derives from positive attitudes toward value. For something to be serious we must assign it serious value, and this can occur only when there exists a larger system of values which we accept as valid and of which the specific value is a part. Thus, while Aristotle describes the ludicrous as a species of the ugly which has no painful effects, it is impossible to set the limits of the ludicrous until the serious has first been defined and accepted. A thing cannot be ugly or immoral until we have first agreed on what is beautiful and moral. This explains why it is we can discuss tragedy (which deals directly with the serious) without reference to comedy, but when talking about comedy must always refer to the standards of seriousness which give it its essential definition.

Thus, for all of its positive characteristics, comedy is negative in its definition. An audience will refuse to react positively (in this case, laugh) to any presentation in a ludicrous manner of what it believes to be the true, the good, or the beautiful. We laugh, for example, at the absentminded professor not because of his learning but because his absentmindedness is not consistent with his erudition. When Trofimov falls down the stairs in the third act of *The Cherry Orchard* it is a comic event. Not because falling down stairs is funny—it obviously is not—but because it undercuts his pompous posturings about love which preceded his fall. Similarly, we can never be induced to laugh at the beautiful *as* beautiful. A beautiful woman is not funny; a beautiful woman who speaks in a high, squeaking voice is very funny because she fails to measure up to the standard which her appearance had previously established. Such a standard may not always be a logically defensible one—more often than not it is not—but it holds in the theatre so long as the audience takes it to be so. Such is also the case with the beautiful but dumb blonde. The dumbness is an analog to the squeaking voice, though there is no logical, necessary relationship between beauty and intelligence.

However, our laughter in these instances cannot be explained in the simple terms of incongruity. For incongruity, no matter how it is conceived—expectation and consequence, tension and elasticity, reality and illusion—does not, as many theorists have maintained, necessarily evoke a comic response, nor is it unique to the comic form. Incongruity has been effectively used in all dramatic forms—serious and comic. It can produce dire emotions as well as side-splitting laughter. The coming of Birnam Wood to Dunsinane in *Macbeth* is unquestionably incongruous, but no one in the play or the audience thinks it is funny. The same is true of Richard III's seduction of Lady Anne. Indeed, as Aristotle pointed out in Chapter XIV of the *Poetics,* to show a terrible act committed by a character from whom we expect love (hence, an incongruous act) is the most effective way of producing a tragic effect. In fact, I believe a good case could be made for the idea that incongruity is the cause of horror in the theatre as well as laughter. What is operative in the ludicrous is not a question of mere incongruity, but a perceptible falling short of an already agreed-upon standard of seriousness which we have set for the object, or which is set by the object for itself.

One boundary of the comic's realm, then, is that line where the ludicrous and the serious meet. We turn now to its other boundary. In *The Life of the Drama*, Bentley characterizes farce as that form in which violence can operate without fear of consequence. He goes on to show how the violence of farce becomes the basic ore of comedy. This observation is significant, but it needs enlarging. One essential difference between comedy and farce is that in the action of the former there are definite consequences (one reason why we say comedy is of greater consequence than farce). But these consequences have had all the elements of pain and permanent defeat removed. Thus it is that the pratfall is the symbol of the comic. This symbol can be carried to its outermost limits by saying that in comedy death is never taken seriously or even considered as a serious threat. Aristotle perceived, correctly, that while the ludicrous (whether it take the form of the grotesque, of exaggeration, or of physical deformity) was the proper subject matter for comedy, manifestations of the ludicrous must be made painless before they can become comic. The writhings of the cartoon character who has just received a blow on the head, the violent events in some of Molière's plays, or the mayhem committed on and by slapstick clowns remains funny only so long as it is quite clear that no real pain is involved. One reason why the violence of slapstick is so effective in films (one thinks of the pies and boppings of the Three Stooges or the Ritz Brothers) is that it is virtually impossible to fear for the characters since the actors have no physical reality. On the stage, if a fight—even one intended to be funny—appears to be an actual fight, the audience may well begin to fear for the actors, that is, take seriously the possibility of pain. Thus it is that whenever a serious deed or event is allowed to enter the field of comedy (as frequently happens) the serious effect must, in some way, be cut off. Such is the case in Jonson's *Volpone,* in which the possibility of the rape is never seriously considered because of the circumstances in which the scene occurs. Similarly, in *The Playboy of the Western World* we never take Christy's threat to murder old Mahon seriously because all of the prior fantasizing about Oedipal murder assures us that the dreadful threat will never be carried out. Conversely, one of the reasons *The Cherry Orchard* is so difficult to interpret is that the line between the characters' self-dramatizing about suffering and actual pain is such a tenuous one. If we miss all the subtle clues Chekhov gives us to indicate that Madame Ranevsky does not really care about the orchard and is actually enjoying being at the center of a teapot drama, then it is impossible for us to think of it as the comedy ("at times even a farce") which Chekhov intended. The same kind of ambiguity exists in *Twelfth Night* with Malvolio. Shakespeare pushes the cruelty almost too far, and if we begin to feel sorry for Malvolio the comic effect of the rest of the play is jeopardized.

From these examples we may draw our second conclusion: comedy operates in that middle zone between the serious and the absurd which Aristotle called the Ludicrous. It is an area which excludes nobility of character, painful consequences, and the consummation of any events which are likely to offend our moral sensibilities.

Another false but widely held assumption about comedy is that there are themes, situations, or character types which are the special province of comedy, or are at least thought to be especially compatible to the comic muse. But if we examine the history of drama, we discover that we must reject the assumption. *Oedipus the King*, for example, is the story of "the lost one found." As such, it is, like *The Importance of Being Earnest*, a "success" story, a story type which traditionally has been particularly well suited to comedy. There is no doubt that *Oedipus the King* is a success story, but no one would ever call it a comedy. The reverse is equally true: *The Playboy of the Western World* is, as I have already noted, a story of Oedipal murder, but no one has ever thought of it as a tragedy.

All of the materials available to the dramatist, whether they be from his own experience, from history, or from the accrued traditions of the drama itself are, in fact, neutral. It is only by the playwright's shaping of them that they take on meaning—a meaning which may be tragic, comic, melodramatic, farcical, or what-have-you. Not to understand this fact is to blur the crucial distinctions which exist between art and life. In life, the meaning we assign to any situation will be the product of personal determinants. But our response to an event which occurs in a play will be the product of the causes built into that play by the playwright. In both cases it is the view and the value assigned to it which will determine whether we consider a situation serious or comic, or remain completely indifferent to it. For example, the "battle of the sexes" is usually mentioned as a typical comic plot. And while it is true that the struggle for power in the home has provided a comic impetus for many plays, beginning with *Lysistrata* right up to *The Last Anal-*

*ysis*, this same struggle is also at the heart of such eminently serious works as *Macbeth* and Strindberg's *The Father*. Or again, a girl surrounded by a host of suitors has been used as the basic predicament of countless comic plots, but surely this is the situation of Homer's Penelope, O'Neill's Nina Leeds, and even (in a perverted way) of Ibsen's Hedda Gabler as well. Nor will it do for us to claim that comedy generates action out of ignorance or wrong reason, since *Oedipus the King, King Lear,* and *Othello* come to mind as readily as *Twelfth Night, Tartuffe,* and *The School for Scandal.* Even plays universally accepted as tragic or comic can be transformed. Tom Stoppard turned *Hamlet* into an absurdist comedy with *Rosencrantz and Guildenstern Are Dead,* and one of the fascinating aspects of Nicol Williamson's interpretation of the Dane was the way he created numerous comic effects simply by making unexpected changes in phrasing. In short, for every comic use made of a given situation, one can find examples of a serious use of the same situation. And the reverse of this is equally true. In each case the deciding factor is the way the artist has used his materials so they will assume a comic or a serious shape. In so doing he will also shape the audience's response to his creation.

One other broad area of misunderstanding needs to be clarified before entering the world of comedy. Living, as we do, in a time when our next tomorrow must always be in question, comedy's tenacious greed for life, its instinct for self-preservation, and its attempts to mediate the pressures of our daily life seem to qualify it as the most appropriate mode for the drama of the second half of the twentieth century. However, one of the most striking characteristics of the modern drama is the way the age-old distinctions between the tragic and the comic (the serious and the ludicrous, the painful and the painless) have been obliterated. This has not been a process of commingling as so many critics have, I believe, erroneously asserted. The combining of the tragic and the comic in a single play is nearly as old as the drama itself—I can trace it back to Sophocles. But what is happening today is something quite different. So much so, that it has become increasingly difficult to use the terms comedy and tragedy with any precision. There are a number of reasons for this.

As indicated earlier, both tragedy and comedy depend upon generally accepted standards of values. Such norms make it possible to establish those hierarchies of seriousness upon which the drama has been traditionally based. It is this public truth which in earlier periods of history provided the artist with his means of communication. It enabled him to communicate emotion and attitude by simply describing incidents; it provided him with a storehouse of symbols with guaranteed responses; it enabled him to construct a plot by selecting and patterning events which, by means of this public criterion, were significant. But once public truth is shattered into innumerable separate and mutually incommunicable private truths, all experience tends to become equally serious or equally ludicrous. Or, as Eugene Ionesco, one of the founding fathers of the Theatre of the Absurd, put it: "It all comes to the same thing anyway; comic and tragic are merely two aspects of the same situation, and I have now reached the stage when I find it hard to distinguish one from the other."

Any examination of the theatre of the past century makes it abundantly clear that the drama's general pattern of development during this time can best be described as a gradual but steady shift away from universal philosophical and social concerns toward the crises and conflicts of man's inner and private life. One of the dominant ideas of the modern *Weltanschauung* is the belief that it is impossible to know what the world is really like. Beginning with Luther's refusal to accept that there was any intelligible relationship between faith and works, the sacramental view of experience gradually disappeared. In rejecting the phenomenal world as an outward and visible manifestation of man's spiritual condition, Luther began a revolution in thought which, because of the achievements of science and technology in the past two hundred years, now makes it impossible for man to attach any objective value to the observations of his senses. This insistence on such a clear-cut division between the physical and the spiritual aspects of reality had a profound effect on the modern dramatist. Inevitably, it made him increasingly distrustful of his sensory responses to the "outside" world, and at the same time it tended to negate whatever belief he might have had in the objective validity of his subjective feelings and sensations. The modern artist no longer holds a mirror up to nature, at least not with any confidence; he can only stare at his own image. He becomes a voyeur to his own existence.

Probably no force in the nineteenth century did more to destroy man's belief in an established norm of human nature, and hence begin this process of internalization in the theatre, than the advent of psychology as a systematized field of study. By convincingly demonstrating that normal people are not as rational as they seem, and that abnormal people do not act in a random and unintelligible way, psychology has made it difficult, if not impossible, for the dramatist to present his characters in a direct way. In earlier times when it was believed that there was a sharp distinction between the sane and the insane, the irrational "aberrations" of human behavior were dramatically significant because they could be defined in terms of a commonly accepted standard of sane conduct. However, once a playwright believes that the meaning of every human action is relative and intelligible only in terms of a unique and subsurface combination of forces, the dramatic events of the plot cease to have meaning in themselves, and they take on significance only as the secret motivations of the characters who participate in them are revealed. (The technique of earlier drama is just the reverse: The motivations of the characters are revealed by the events of the plot.)

Nowhere are the profound effects of these changes of attitude more evident than in those modern plays we call comedies. Historically, comedy has as often as not been exceedingly complex—the typical comic plot is a labyrinth of complexity—but it has seldom been ambiguous. And ours is an age of ambiguity. One of the reasons we tend to dismiss the frothy Broadway comedy as irrelevant or escapist is that it is so clear-cut; it lacks the dimension of ambiguity. Thus, while the playwright may approach experience with a comic sense, i.e., man's need and capacity to endure, he is acutely aware that not only is the serious inseparable from the ludicrous, but also that it is impossible for him to remove the pain of experience from his representation of life if that representation is to have the ring of truth.

We see this clearly in the plays of Chekhov where the ludicrous and the painful are so inextricably linked that they make us laugh with a lump in our throats. O'Neill sensed something similar when in 1939 he remarked:

> It's struck me as time goes on, how something funny, even farcical, can suddenly, without apparent reason, break up into something gloomy and tragic. . . . A sort of unfair *non sequitur*, as though events, through life, were manipulated just to confuse us. I think I'm aware of comedy more than I ever was before—a big kind of comedy that doesn't stay funny very long.[*]

[*] Croswell Bowen, *The Curse of the Misbegotten* (New York, 1959), p. 259.

The most striking thing about Gogo and Didi as they wait for Godot is that they are two irreducible specimens of humanity whose only capacity is to remain comically, tragically, ambiguously alive with the courage of their hallucinations. (Anouilh appropriately described *Waiting for Godot* as Pascal's *Pensées* "acted out by circus clowns.") Finally, Saul Bellow is a great comic artist not because he pokes fun at humanity's shortcomings, but because he sees the comic as the most appropriate weapon in man's struggle for survival in an absurd world. Life as revealed in *The Last Analysis* is a Grand Guignol but with less sense.

With increasing frequency the contemporary theatre reveals (and sometimes celebrates) that to live is to make the comic gesture, or what Pirandello called the comic grimace. Today, the comic view of life is comic in the sense that the lines of the comic mask are indistinguishable from those of the tragic. In them we find that the relationship of means to ends is a paradox. In the theatre of an earlier time we have a sense that a destiny is being fulfilled: As the comic action is completed, all the complexities and disruptions of the plot have been resolved and the social fabric has been restored. We have no sense of such natural or inevitable resolution in the plays of the twentieth century. Whenever the boundaries between the serious and the ludicrous tend to dissolve, clear-cut resolution gives way to ambiguity, fantasy, or philosophic sleight of hand.

And yet this should not be cause for despair, for from its very beginnings comedy, no matter what form it has taken, has always been one of the human spirit's most effective strategies for drawing life into a stalemate in our cold war with existence. Perhaps Aristophanes was right to fall asleep after all. In his infinite wisdom he knew that the lines between comedy and tragedy were at best tenuous, and often artificial. Certainly that latter-day Aristophanes, James Joyce, did. And as we enter comedy's realm we should do so in the litanal spirit which brings *Finnegans Wake* to a close:

> Loud, heap miseries upon us yet entwine our arts with laughters low. In the name of the former and of the latter and of their holocaust, All men.

# ARISTOPHANIC COMEDY:
# THE CONSCIENCE
# OF A CONSERVATIVE

THE GREEK comic poet Aristophanes (*circa* 450–387 B.C.) was certainly one of the giants of the classical theatre; but on rereading his plays today, he seems more like an early-day version of a Barry Goldwater, who had the quick and contentious mind of William Buckley and the raucous sense of humor and comic invention of Al Capp, and whose program was, in effect, to urge the Greeks to repeal the second half of the fifth century. Actually, because of its central concern with society's need and its ability to maintain and preserve itself, comedy is by nature conservative, and Aristophanes and all other writers of comedy tend more or less to be conservatives. Unlike tragedy, comedy has always celebrated the fact that despite all our individual defeats, life does nonetheless continue on its merry way. Or, as Christopher Fry once put it, "Comedy senses and reaches out to that . . . angle of experience where the dark is distilled into light: . . . where our tragic fate finds itself with perfect pitch, and goes straight to the key which creation was composed in." Comedy, then, celebrates man's capacity to endure; such capacity is ultimately conserving in spirit and quality.

This in large measure explains why love is always central to comedy. The basic comic plot can be reduced to the following elements: (1) boy meets girl; (2) boy falls in love with girl; (3) there is an obstacle to the fulfilling of that love (this obstacle is usually parental); (4) the obstacle is overcome and there is a reorganization of society. The persisting regularity of this pattern has led Ben Lehman to observe, quite correctly I think, in his essay "Comedy and Laughter" that the "obstacles to the hero's desire, then, form the action of comedy, and the overcoming of them the comic resolution." * But it must be noted that the reconciliation at the end of comedy always involves the preserving of the social context. Opposition, frustration, malice, lust, prejudice, and greed can and do inhabit the world of comedy, but these divisive powers are always overcome and then assimilated into the lovers' happy world. Comedy always ends in fusion and with a sense of social union. To quote Lehman once again: "The vision of comedy fixes its eye on separateness, on diversity, even on oppositions, but it insists at last on togetherness for lovers and on the restored social fabric, on solidarity for the group." †

As a satirist, rather than a writer of comedies,‡ Aristophanes has plenty of sex in his plays, but no love. First and foremost, the writer of satire must have the gift of turning our eyes inward in hilarious scorn of ourselves. But his purpose is always corrective. In showing us the immensity of our follies, the satirist is either seeking to restore values and patterns of behavior which he believes have been lost, forgotten, or debased, or he is urging us to discover new ideals and ways of living. Therefore, all of his gibes—no matter how bitter or radical they may appear—are ultimately directed at the restoration or preservation of the social order.

In each of his plays, Aristophanes is attacking the manifestations of political, social, and moral corruption which he believed were the direct result of the Athenians' shift away from an agricultural to an artisan and mercantile economy, their adoption of a more imperialist "foreign policy," and their willingness to accept the validity of new forms of thought and art. All his life, Aristophanes shared the attitudes of the rapidly disappearing landed aristocracy, whose religion, morality, ideals, and patterns of social organization were

* Ben Lehman, "Comedy and Laughter," University of California Publications, *English Studies*, Vol. 10, 1954. Quoted from Robert W. Corrigan, ed., *Comedy: Meaning and Form* (San Francisco, 1965), p. 166.
† *Ibid.*
‡ It should be understood that for the Greeks in the fifth century, any play with an invented plot and subject matter drawn from contemporary life was called a comedy, and therefore was presented during the afternoon portion of the Dionysian Festivals.

based upon an agricultural economy and a closed, heroic view of society. He resisted all that was modern. He condemned innovators or any who would seek to change or reform the traditional ways of doing things because they were old or outmoded. Euripides, Socrates, the Sophists, the orators, the early scientists Empedocles and Pythagoras—all were characterized in Aristophanes' plays as charlatans and subversives who were destroying the national fiber and upsetting the traditional patterns of government, thought, art, and everyday behavior. The Delian League (the classical Greek equivalent to the United Nations) was a striking instance of government waste and a good example of the evils of the new policy of Greek "internationalism." The increased number of people depending upon the government for support was seen by Aristophanes as a maneuver on the part of the central government to gain greater power, as well as another symptom that the old value that each man should earn his own way was rapidly breaking down. One could continue this list of his grievances at some length.

To be sure, Aristophanes had a point and his position was not without justification. He lived and wrote in one of the most turbulent periods in the world's history. It was a time of war, expansion, and rapid, radical change, and the breakdown of the traditional ways of doing things can be seen in every aspect of Greek life, from architecture to the worship of Zeus. As a larger and more centralized government became necessary, it was easier for the demagogues to gain power and widespread graft soon came to be commonplace. New religions from foreign lands, and especially the Orient, were introduced into the country by the merchants, traders, soldiers, and slaves with the result that new moralities did begin to emerge. As the Athenian people began to produce a great deal more than they consumed, the acquiring and accumulating of wealth (not to mention the social problems that the acquisition of capital wealth creates) tended to become the central concern of more and more people. Aristophanes, then, lived in a volatile atmosphere and he was deeply disturbed by the many changes that were taking place and the effects they were having on Athenian life. He was determined, like so many of our Southerners today—although for different reasons—to do all he could to resist this erosion of the time-honored Greek traditions. He would fight till the death for the old order, and he did.

To those who might consider this evaluation of Aristophanes' position to be either erroneous or too harsh, I call attention specifically to the following plays. In *The Birds*, probably the greatest of Aristophanes' three "Utopia" plays, the ideal society (Cloud-Cuckoo-Land) will be established by the farmers who will then run their brave new world like a large farm. Certainly, this solution is exaggerated and fanciful, but there is little doubt that Aristophanes did believe that things would be much better in Athens if the old values, as embodied and propounded by Peithetaerus, were restored to their former position of dominance. For all of its delightful (and sometimes scatological) grotesquerie, *Peace* celebrates the same values. Only the farmers, of all the people in Greece, are shown to be strong enough and capable of working together long enough to pull Peace out of her underground prison so she can once again rule the earth. Not only do the farmers save Greece from the horrors of war, but Trygaeus, who is clearly Aristophanes' mouthpiece, states explicitly that peace is the opportunity for the farmers to work in their fields. In *The Plutus* the solution to all the misuse of wealth in the world is to give Plutus, the god of wealth, to the honest, hard-working farmers. They will solve all of the problems: no more corruption, no more injustice, no more crime. If only it were so, even in fourth-century Greece! Finally, behind all the sexual fun of *Lysistrata*, Aristophanes is really trying to solve the question of Panhellenic unity and the problems of war. After the women have overcome the old men who were guarding the treasury on the Acropolis, Lysistrata begins the long *agon* (the most significant one in the play) with the Commissioner. As her arguments become increasingly persuasive she finally gets to the central issue: "How can we have peace?" I should like to quote this passage at some length, because I believe it makes my point so clearly.

> COMMISSIONER: And how, on the international scale,
>    can you straighten out the enormous
>    confusion among all the states of Greece?
>
> LYSISTRATA: . . . Very easily.
>
> COMMISSIONER: . . . How? Do inform us.
>
> LYSISTRATA: When our skein's in a tangle we take
>    it thus on our spindles, or haven't you seen us?—
> one on this side and one on the other side,
>    and we work out the tangles between us.

And that is the way we'll undo this war,
> by exchanging ambassadors, whether
you like it or not, one from either side,
> and we'll work out the tangles together.

COMMISSIONER: Do you really think that with wools
> and skeins and just being able to spin you
can end these momentous affairs, you fools?

LYSISTRATA: With any intelligence in you
> you statesmen would govern as we work wool,
> and in everything Athens would profit.

COMMISSIONER: How so? Do tell.

LYSISTRATA: First, you take raw fleece
> and you wash the beshittedness off it;
just so, you should first lay the city out
> on a washboard and beat out the rotters
and pluck out the sharpers like burrs, and when
> you find tight knots of schemers and plotters
who are out for key offices, card them loose,
> but best tear off their heads in addition.
Then into one basket together card
> all those of a good disposition
be they citizens, resident aliens, friends,
> an ally or an absolute stranger,
even people in debt to the commonwealth,
> you can mix them all in with no danger.
And the cities which Athens has colonized—
> by Zeus, you should try to conceive them
as so many shreddings and tufts of wool
> that are scattered about and not leave them
to lie around loose, but from all of them
> draw the threads in here, and collect them
into one big ball and then weave a coat
> for the people, to warm and protect them.

COMMISSIONER: Now, isn't this awful? They treat
> the state like wool to be beaten and carded,
who have nothing at all to do with war!

Lysistrata's arguments make such very good sense. She's so logical, and therein lies the play's great appeal. But such a solution to the problems of achieving world peace is too simple; it assumes that the tightly wound and complex strands of world affairs can be worked like a skein of wool. It also assumes that once the skein has been untangled it will stay that way. It is this desire for a simple solution to complex problems, and more important, the belief that the use of time-tested patterns of the past makes such solutions possible, that prompted me to link Aristophanes with Goldwater at the beginning of this chapter.

For better or worse, Aristophanes failed in his attempts to change the patterns of Greek history. Quite predictably, the Greeks did not follow his advice and go back to the good old days. Nor have his condemnations of Euripides and Socrates held up; as a teacher of literature and philosophy, Aristophanes was a failure. But in one very important area of the history of ideas he has had a profound and lasting influence: namely, the judging of poetry. Quite correctly, Aristophanes can be called the "father" of Greek literary criticism, and his belief that the chief function of poetry is to teach morality is an idea which is still very much with us. Euripides is condemned in nearly all the plays because Aristophanes believed that the tragedian's poetry corrupted the youth of Athens, poisoned patriotic spirit, and advanced the cause of immorality everywhere. Aeschylus is set up as the model for tragedy in *The Frogs*, not because of his ability with language (even Aristophanes admitted that Euripides was the best versifier of all writers of tragedy), but because his plays—like "all genuine poetry"—helped to make us better human beings. Aristophanes was the first Greek writer to insist that the basic aim of the arts and all culture should be education. This idea was developed more fully by Plato in *The Republic* and *The Laws*, and it was finally expanded in its fullest (although somewhat compromised) form in Horace's *Art of Poetry* in the dictum that art should both delight and teach. The idea was militantly reasserted in the eighteenth and nineteenth centuries by Lessing, Herder, and the Schlegels in their criticism of Greek drama; and it is fascinating to note that even Nietzsche's description of the decay of Greek tragedy is nearly identical to the one put forth by Aristophanes more than two thousand years earlier. And this view has lost none of its virulence today, ranging in scope and significance from the controversy over awarding the Bollingen Prize to Ezra Pound to local obscenity trials.

I have no intention of getting involved in this argument here, but

I believe that Aristophanes must finally be seen as a romantic reactionary who refused to give up what was already lost. Instead of
welcoming the new, he mourned the loss of the old. History has
shown that he (and all like him) was wrong in his moral objections
to change. The traditional code is never the *only* morality; there is
always the possibility of another sanction. The fact that men oppose
traditional values and appeal to other and new authorities does not
make them troublemakers, nor immoral. What Aristophanes either
did not see or refused to recognize is the fact that as long as a new
idea of what is right is held with conviction and is not just an isolated sentiment, it may be fully as moral as obedience to established
laws or customs.

However, thus far I have presented only one side of the case.
Aristophanes may have been a reactionary but he was certainly no
weepy sentimentalist. As I said earlier, he lived in a volatile atmosphere when life was wide open, and so too are his plays. All of
his work has an extravagant power and a quality of overriding
buoyancy and verve. This almost animal exuberance and vitality is
probably best seen in the wide-open use of sex in his plays. We
sense neither neurotic lust nor puritanical guilt in his use of it, and
this probably explains (differences in taste and dramatic conventions notwithstanding) why his blatant sexuality is still so inoffen-
sive when it is read or produced on our stages today. But no matter
what he took for his subject, he had the capacity as a writer to take
any idea and push it as far as it would go, and then give it one
more push. He is probably best compared in our day to such comedians as Mort Sahl, Dick Gregory, Lenny Bruce, or Shelley Berman.
(The only writer in the theatre today who even approaches Aristophanes is the Swiss playwright Friedrich Duerrenmatt, whose
grotesque ironies and biting satire in such plays as *The Visit*, *Romulus the Great*, and *The Physicists* have a certain resemblance to the
Athenian's wit.) However, with these modern satirists, unlike Aristophanes, it is difficult to know exactly what they are for—except on
the issue of civil rights—but their techniques are much the same.

Actually, a fuller understanding of the Aristophanic techniques is
the key to our enjoyment of his plays. Rather than having a comic
action, Aristophanes' plays are built upon the comic conceit (the
sex strike in *Lysistrata* or Socrates in the balloon in *The Clouds*),
which acts like a mousetrap to create the world of the play for us.
To be sure, all of the plays share certain structural characteristics

which make it possible for us to talk of an Aristophanic structure, and such giants of classical scholarship as Gilbert Murray, F. M. Cornford, and Jane Harrison have shown that his structure originated in the rituals of the Dionysian worship. But such discussions, while undoubtedly true, tend to be misleading for they force upon early Greek comedy a terminology of dramatic criticism which is for the most part either inappropriate or irrelevant. There is really very little plot to most of Aristophanes' plays (certainly not in the sense that there is a plot in the comedies of Shakespeare, Molière, Congreve, or Shaw), only a series of episodes which serve as the occasions for his wit and satiric thrusts. His plays move from moment to moment and have a sense of spontaneity rather than structure. Such an episodic structure (if the term must be used) not only gives freedom to the ranging and wayward movements of Aristophanes' comic mind, but it also sets up the audience for the rapid-fire potshots which he takes at every kind of subject. Like our own late George S. Kaufman, or more recently Bob Hope, Aristophanes was a master of the phraseology and attitude of the wisecrack. But the basic strategy of the wisecrack is to keep the audience with you. This becomes almost impossible if the audience becomes too involved in the workings of a plot.

Aristophanes was not a subtle writer, and his plays, more than most, are a theatrical rather than a literary experience. He has little interest in the more refined phases of human absurdity, and everything in his comedy is dependent upon the immediacy of the theatrical effect. His satiric wit is, of all forms of wit, the most ephemeral. The basic comic gesture is universal in its appeal but the particularities of the form are based on immediate, topical references, usually the absurdities of current political or social behavior, and almost impossible to translate or pass on to future generations. In tone, Aristophanic comedy is much like the newspaper cartoons of a Herblock, Bill Mauldin, the early Al Capp, or Jules Feiffer; in technique, it is like the gridiron dinner show or the topical review. Almost, that is! But one important ingredient is still missing. Aristophanes wrote in verse, and it is clear that music and dance played an all-important role in the productions of classical Greek comedy. For this reason we will completely miss the essential quality of an Aristophanic play if we do not think of it as a comic musical revue. The two most significant and highly praised recent revivals of his plays were successful because they accented this musical base. The well-known Greek director Karolos Kouns won the first prize and worldwide acclaim at the International Theatre Festival in Paris in 1962 with a production of *The Birds*. Not only did he modernize the dialogue, but he had new music composed by Manos Hadjada- kis (the composer of "Never On Sunday") and the production was choreographed by the eminent Greek dancer Zouzou Nicoloudi. More recently (1964), in our own country, Herbert Blau had a similar success with the same play at the Actor's Workshop in San Fran- cisco when he presented it in a jazz version. These two productions provide sufficient proof that Aristophanes can continue to live in the theatre (and not just as a museum piece in the library or the classroom) if we understand the dynamics and techniques of his plays.

But for all of Aristophanes' vitality, what is known as Greek "Old Comedy" went into a decline shortly after the turn of the fourth century, and this decline is probably best described as a process of diminution which was finally completed in the drama of Menander. The fact that the decline had begun can easily be seen in Aristoph- anes' last preserved play, *The Plutus*, which was first performed sometime during the years 390–388 B.C. We can still discover traces of the old Aristophanes: his bias toward the farmers, the episodic structure, the open stagecraft and the presentational style of musi- cal comedy, and the too-simple solution. Yet, everything is different. The bite is gone. The comedy is generalized. Instead of dealing with the particular behavior of specific people, we find a gentle mockery of the manners of people in general. The episodes seem un- related; each of them deals with human foibles, but they lack a cumulative force. The whole play is probably best summed up by Browning in his "Aristophanes' Apology."

> Aristophanes
> Surmounts his rivals now as heretofore,
> Though stinted to mere sober prosy verse—
> "Manners and Men," so squeamish gets the world!
> No more "Step forward, strip for anapaests!"
> No calling naughty people by their names.

The final question to be asked here is "What happened?" Why in less than a century had the scope of comedy been so drastically re- duced? Obviously, we cannot know for certain, but it is very likely related to the Greeks' loss of political freedom. This had been coming for some time, and with the fall of Athens to Sparta in 404 B.C., the end was in sight. Then in 338 B.C. Athens was conquered by the Macedonians and all public occasions (including the theatre) were rigidly censored. Satiric comedy has never flourished under a dictatorship. Audiences who do come to the theatre in such times want to escape the problems of life, and more important dictators have never tolerated comedy. S. N. Behrman put it best when he wrote: "Dictators are terribly afraid of comedy and its laughter. For laughter is the most humanizing—as well as the most critical—agency in the world. The ability to laugh at his own pretensions and shortcomings is the true mark of the civilized nation, as it is of the civilized man." One need only remember what happened to the German theatre under Hitler to see the truth of these remarks. More important, we should realize that in recent times even in our own country there are some things we can no longer make fun of and laugh about. One of the most interesting documents on the subject of comedy and freedom that I know of is an essay entitled "It's Hideously True" by the cartoonist Al Capp. It was published as an article in 1952 in *Life* magazine,* and in it Mr. Capp explained why he finally decided to have Li'l Abner marry Daisy Mae. Admittedly, this was at the time when Senator Joe McCarthy was at the height of his power and an almost hysterical fear was sweeping the nation. But Capp, who had thrived for twenty years kidding hell out of all the lunacies of American life, suddenly discovered that there were some things he no longer had the freedom to kid. (He had noted "the gradual loss of our fifth freedom. Without it, the other four freedoms aren't much fun, because the fifth is the freedom to laugh at each other.") When the comic writer loses his freedom, he invariably turns from broad, topical satire on a national level to the more gentle forms of humor found in domestic life. (It's significant, I think, that "Blondie" is the most popular comic strip in America.) And if this restricting atmosphere continues, the comic must eventually turn in upon himself, and he becomes the butt of his own humor. This is what probably happened to classical comedy, and the decline in Aristophanes' comic power is probably more a matter of political freedom than it is of artistry. Aristophanes was the Will Rogers of the classical Greek theatre; unfortunately, he wasn't able to be its Jack Benny as well.

* *Life*, vol. 32, no. 13 (March 13, 1952), pp. 100–108.

# SOME THOUGHTS ON ROMAN DRAMA

THE ROMAN theatre in its first days was one of the most vital the world has ever known. It knew and drew upon the established traditions of the Greeks; there existed in many parts of Italy lively popular customs which were theatrical in nature; numerous theatrical troupes traveled and regularly performed throughout most of the country; and early in its development (the second half of the third century B.C.), a playwright of great talent had emerged to assist the theatre in its growth. Only the English theatre of the fifteenth and sixteenth centuries had conditions anywhere near comparable. But here the similarities cease; the England of Elizabeth gave us Shakespeare, Marlowe, and Jonson; the Romans—well, Seneca. Ironically, as the Romans gave the theatre more official patronage they destroyed the popular tradition which had been the source of its vitality. The virile Atellan farces were replaced by gaudy circuses. The riotous comedy of Plautus gave way to the pretentious moralizing of would-be tragedians. Soon the histrionic sensibility went underground, and only emerged in the form of a Terence who wrote for the cultivated members of the Scipionic Circle, or a Seneca who wrote mostly for himself. The Roman audience—apparently one of the best history has ever known—was transformed into a passive Public, and the theatre ceased being entertainment (a meaningful tension between a performer and his audience—*inter:* between and *tenere:* to hold) and soon became only a

63

diversion. Great theatre always has a sense of mystery about it; no such quality existed in the Roman drama of the first century.

There are many reasons that such promising beginnings bore so little fruit, but certainly one of the most important causes for the rapid decline of this theatre was the need on the part of the Roman leaders to take every spontaneous popular involvement and turn it into a public attitude. The Augustan sensibility had a self-conscious need to institutionalize everything. It was an age of public life, public virtue, public welfare, and public works. The arts were treated in the same way. It is worth recalling that when Julius, Augustus, and Tiberius Caesar were building the first of history's "great" societies, they honored Roman artists publicly, albeit briefly, and then went back to more important matters such as war or tribute. We remember Pericles and Sophocles, Elizabeth and Shakespeare, Louis and Molière, Weimar and Goethe. Then there is Caesar and ————!

## I. *Fantasy and Farce*

When reading the plays of Plautus, one very quickly becomes conscious of what a remarkable sense of the theatre that early Roman playwright had. He seems to have known every theatrical trick, and what's more, he knew how to use them. There is something in his work which would be sure to appeal to every level of sophistication and every social class. As could be expected, much has been written about Plautus and his theatre (unquestionably the best book being George Duckworth's *The Nature of Roman Comedy*, Princeton University Press, 1952), and there isn't much we don't know about his sources, his techniques, and the conventions of the theatre of his time. But somehow this isn't enough. None of the magistral studies ever seems to get to the heart of things. Everyone admits that Plautus was a great farceur, and after describing the external characteristics and so-called conventions of farce—usually in a deprecatory manner—the subject is dropped. Q.E.D. But this is the key subject; this is what Plautus was really up to and, if one is ever to understand the spirit which courses through the plays of Plautus, he must also understand something about the nature of farce. Now, farce isn't quite a dirty word in critical parlance, but it certainly hasn't been given very much attention by our serious critics and theorists. At least not until Eric Bentley turned his fine mind to the subject; and as so often is the case, Bentley is right. Attention must be paid!

Farce, like a curse, is the expression of repressed wishes. We in the United States lack the colorful curses of Europe, particularly those of the staunchly Catholic countries such as Spain and Italy. When a Spaniard says, "I'll defecate in your mother's milk" or calls another a "son of a whore," he is in effect committing murder. (Indeed, after he says such things, he may actually be murdered in return.) All such phrases are expressions of the wish to destroy the existence of a person. Farce works in much the same way. As Bentley points out in his *The Life of the Drama,* farces are much like dreams in that they "show the disguised fulfillment of repressed wishes." I believe Professor Bentley is right in this, but I believe it would be more fruitful to use a less limiting and more inclusive idea, namely, fantasy. Dreams certainly are assertions on the part of the unconscious to express many things which our conciousness represses. But farce also concerns itself with the materials and images of our conscious fantasies. We know that fantasy and repression are inextricably linked in a dynamic tension, and the rhythm of farce is —to use a forced image—that of the cat of fantasy chasing its tail of repression. And our pleasure in witnessing farce is that our wildest fantasies can be acted out, without—as Bentley reminds us— our having to suffer the consequences.

This relationship leads us to one of the central misunderstandings about farce. Just as so many discussions of psychoanalysis are invariably reduced to the psychopathology of sex, so, too, the literature on farce, such as it is, is invariably concerned with farce as an expression of our sexual fantasies. Hence "bedroom" is the adjective most commonly associated with this whole form of drama. There is certainly some justification for this, but when we read (or even better, see) Plautus's plays, we become increasingly conscious of the fact that, although sex is present, so too are many other subjects. Think of Molière's one-act farces, or Chekhov's riotous early plays. Or think of the best known of our modern farceurs: Chaplin, Buster Keaton, the Marx Brothers, Abbott and Costello, Laurel and Hardy. Sex and slapstick have always been combined, but never exclusively, except in the old-time burlesque routines. Farce's spirit of violence and rebellion is also directed to other situations and standards of value such as wealth, social class, life in the city, and even the arts.

The essential condition for the creation of farce is the existence of strong publicly shared values and standards of behavior. The last really big-hit bedroom farce on Broadway was *The Seven Year Itch*, and I believe it is significant that it was first produced in 1952. The sexual taboos and rigid standards of sexual behavior have been dissolving (or at least are changing profoundly) so rapidly in the past couple of decades that the old-fashioned bedroom farce has just about disappeared. The *Up in Mabel's Room* and *Getting Gertie's Garter* of my youth just don't make it today, and even such a blatantly lewd piece as the more recent *Pajama Tops* was most successful in the boondocks and to my knowledge was never brought into New York. The sex farce undoubtedly still has some appeal, but usually to less sophisticated and more parochial audiences. (In this regard, it is worth noting that many so-called bedroom comedies can do very badly in New York, and still be counted upon to make money in community theatres around the country.) The Hollywood film is still a pretty hospitable medium for the sex farce, as *The Apartment* and *Some Like It Hot* will attest, but the success of a recent film like *M\*A\*S\*H* indicates that here, too, things are changing.

Eric Bentley is certainly correct in his explanation of why bedroom farce appeals to audiences. He writes:

> Farce in general offers a special opportunity: shielded by delicious darkness and seated in warm security, we enjoy the privilege of being totally passive while on stage our most treasured, unmentionable wishes are fulfilled before our eyes by the most violently active human beings that ever sprang from the human imagination. In that application of the formula which is bedroom farce, we savor the adventure of adultery, ingeniously exaggerated in the highest degree, and all without taking the responsibility or suffering the guilt. Our wives may be with us leading the laughter.*

But as more liberal sexual attitudes develop, farce has tended to move to other realms.

Not too long ago I was talking to some of my students about the subject of farce, and I discovered that they did not find the bedroom variety very funny. Sex, they said, was increasingly a take-it-or-leave-it matter for most of their generation, and they were neither outraged nor titillated by it when it was represented in the theatre. They even went on to admit that they had actually acted out most

* *The Life of the Drama* (New York, Atheneum Publishers, 1964), p. 229.

of their sexual fantasies—or at least all of those which, with even a modicum of taste, could ever be presented on the stage. Money, business, education, middle class morality, bureaucratic power, IBM-ization, and the system—these, they insisted, were the widely held values of our time, and hence the more appropriate subject matter for farce. One then thinks of the popularity of *How to Succeed in Business Without Really Trying* and *Dr. Strangelove*, *A Hard Day's Night*, and the films featuring Jean-Paul Belmondo, or such farcical contemporary novels as *Up the Down Staircase* and *Catch-22*. Perhaps the younger generation is right.

The real point, however, is that farce can and does have many masks. The theatre of Plautus is one of the first in the Western world to reveal this fact. Sex and the family, money and social caste, accomplishment and pride, are just some of the materials that this first farceur used. He seemed, instinctively, to understand the cathartic nature of fantasy. He also knew—and equally as well—that fantasy is both preceded and followed by repression.

## II. *The Tempo of Farce*

Whenever stage directors talk about the problems of producing farce, inevitably the first matter mentioned is the question of pace. Farce, they say, must be played at breakneck speed. So everything is speeded up, only to discover, more often than not, that what has been created is not art at all, only confusion. This chaos usually stems from the director's failure to understand the inner dynamics of farce. But directors are not the only guilty parties, the critics and scholars have been just as far off the mark, and nowhere is this fact more apparent than in the studies of Roman comedy.

Even those critics well disposed to Plautus cannot help but approach his plays with an air of slight superiority. We must like Plautus, they imply, because it is our cultural duty to do so; but they then go on to admit in confidential tones that his plays are really pretty thin. This prejudice against farce in general and Plautus in particular is inevitably revealed when the critics begin discussing the tempo of his plays. Farce, they say, deals with "amusing confusions rather than psychological complications." They go on to say that there is no real conflict in farce and the characters have little stature and practically no significance. Being only a drama of situation, it is peopled with passive characters who in no way determine the course of events. Finally, they argue that, since the characters lack complexity and the situations exist only to be superficially exploited, these situations have no other meaning than confusion and embarrassment for their own sake. Hence the conclusion: If a situation has no intrinsic meaning, then the playwright must depend upon variety, novelty, and uniqueness if he is to ever achieve the proper theatrical effects. Rapidity of pace is seen, then, as a means of compensating for the script's obvious insignificance. Plautus is praised as a farceur because of his ability to move from situation to situation, incident to incident, so fast that the audience never has the time to question the implausibility of what is taking place on the stage, nor to be bored by what is essentially only cotton-candy fluff. However, interspersed in the midst of all of this are numerous kind references to the author's earthy sense of humor and his boisterous animal spirits.

Such well-intentioned criticism could not be more wrong! Farce is a surrealistic art. Like the fairy tale and the dream, it is an art of flat surfaces. It is also an art of images. Like a giant collage, it is composed of violent juxtapositions, short, bright flashes, and disparate patterns having no apparent continuity. As a result, through all the external hilarity, we become aware of the childlike truth of its nature and the mysterious quality of its means. Both in its techniques and in our responses to them, the dynamics of farce are much like those of the Punch-and-Judy shows. Since the laws of logical cause and effect do not exist in such a world, the facts of our daily existence are presented in what seems to be a distorted fashion. But, as Bentley has pointed out so persuasively, farce is "always faithful to the inner experience."

"That's the way it is; that's the way it *really* is!" So the saying goes, and so it goes in farce. We may never have literally experienced the trials and tribulations of the Brothers Menaechmus, but our most profound psychic dramas certainly include an Erotium and a wife, an irate father-in-law and a Brush, and above all an alter ego among its cast of characters.

No other form of drama makes such great demands on the actor, and Plautus, being an actor, must have been well aware of it. This fact, probably more than any other, accounts for the great disparity which exists between the audience's enthusiastic response to farce and the scholar's general lack of regard for it. Its most important qualities cannot be gotten inside the covers of a book. Farce is always acted. For its effects it concentrates on the actor's body—on his facial expressions, his mimicries, and his physical gestures. (Bentley, to quote him yet again, put it beautifully when he wrote: "The dialogue of farce is sound and movement.") The critics' problem is to capture the physics of performance. This is next to impossible to do except through performance itself. But what the critics can do is to make directors and actors aware of the fact that the tempo of farce is not an external compensatory technique; it is not something a George Abbott can come in and impose upon a production that won't get off the ground. To do Plautus—or the plays of any farceur—well one must first enter into fantasy's magic realm; once there, the buoyant and violent spirit of that world will provide all the other necessary directions.

## III. *A Funny Thing Happened on the Way to the Forum*

When *A Funny Thing Happened on the Way to the Forum*, starring Zero Mostel, opened on May 8, 1962, many people were surprised to learn that this successful musical was actually a pastiche of scenes from Plautine farce. How amazing, many of them thought, that the works of an old Roman could have such vitality and be so much fun. They shouldn't have been surprised, for the authors were doing little more than updating essentially Plautine techniques. In fact, Plautus is history's first known writer of musical comedy and it is no accident that countless musicals (*Fanny, The Boys from Syracuse*, and *A Funny Thing*, to name a few) have been based on his plays.

Because musical comedy is not generally respected in academic circles, most scholars have not paid much attention to this aspect of Plautus' work. They do discuss his practice of *contamnatio* (the technique of stealing and piecing together scenes from several plays by the writers of the Greek New Comedy), and then go on to talk about the puns, racy obscenities, the many comic-coined words, and the general exuberance of his language. But the most significant aspects of Plautine theatre are the songs and the dance routines.

From the more than one hundred and thirty plays which we know Plautus wrote, we have close to sixty songs still remaining. And it is clear from these texts that the typical Plautus play was composed of forty percent songs and another twenty percent were probably chanted or recited to a flute, à la Rex Harrison in *My Fair Lady*. (One play, *Epidicus*, was eighty percent musical.)

The clue to this is the great variety of meter to be found in any one of Plautus' plays. All Roman comedy was composed in verse, but no other playwright used so many different kinds of meter and, more important, used them in such wild combinations. Terence, for instance, almost always used regular iambic meters and only occasionally shifted to regular trochees. Plautus, on the other hand, used not only highly irregular iambic and trochaic meters, but the extremely colloquial proceleusmatic and the rarely used anapestic meters as well. Even the Roman critics tended to denigrate Plautus for such impurity. Quintilian considered Terence a better playwright because he wrote with greater consistency of style rather than in the hodgepodge style of his predecessor. Horace complained of Plautus' fame, using many of the same arguments that the academic detractors of musical comedy use today. But at least one critic of great repute was on Plautus' side. At the playwright's death, Varro wrote in *De Poetis*:

> After the death of Plautus, comedy mourned, the stage was deserted, and laughter, sport, jest, and countless numbers all shed tears of sorrow.

The "countless numbers" (*numeri innumeri*) was a direct reference to both the songs and the polymetry of Plautine farce.

This raises a difficult question: It is generally believed that the source of Roman comedy was the Greek New Comedy, especially the plays of Menander. But polymetry is not a characteristic of Greek New Comedy. We find shifts of meter only in the choruses, and these follow a very consistent pattern. It is more likely that Plautus borrowed his plots from the Greeks and then infused them with the musical-comedy techniques of the Italian popular theatre, especially those of the Etruscan *satura* and the Fescennine verses of Etruria. Whatever the explanation, the medieval editor put it just right when he wrote on a Plautine manuscript, "*mutatis modis cantica*" (songs in changing measures).

It is this quality which makes Plautus' plays so devilishly hard to translate. There are frequent elisions (or else hiatuses); synizesis —the running together of separate vowel sounds within a word to create a pun or other comic effects—is common; and the songs themselves are filled with unnatural accents, obviously necessary to create the proper rhythms of song. In short, only if approached as a musical text will a Plautine play make much sense.

So, in reading Plautus, we must realize that we are reading a musical-comedy script. Not much is there. This fact certainly explains why a literary playwright like Terence became more influential than Plautus in the Augustan period and also later on in both the Middle Ages and early Renaissance. But the Renaissance theatre of both England and Spain had no real vitality until its writers began to discover Plautus; or, if not Plautus himself, at least the buoyant spirit of musical comedy that dominates his plays.

## IV. *The Beginnings of the Commedia Tradition*

Probably the most penetrating, brief description of the peculiar genius of the Italian theatre can be found in Pirandello's essay, "Introduction to the Italian Theatre." * The great playwright writes about many aspects of his country's theatre, but he is at his best when he accounts for the development and describes the nature of the *commedia dell'arte*. One passage in particular is worth noting here:

> The *Commedia dell'arte* emerged, little by little, precisely from theatrical personalities . . . who, as actors, knew the pulse of the public and, as authors, also indulged their own personal tastes and ambitions . . . But they were also well acquainted with the output of the *litterati*, and as producers took out options on those works, performing them with their own, or revising them to suit their purposes. It is absurd to imagine in this an accidental discovery of mere actors. Anyone having even the slightest acquaintance with the way an actor works on stage, with the precise directions he requires if he is to take a step to the right instead of the left, will readily see that the idea of improvising their performances could never have occurred to actors.
>
> The *Commedia dell'arte* is born, on the contrary, out of authors who are so deeply involved in the Theatre, in the life of the Theatre, as to become, in fact, actors; who begin by writing the comedies they later perform, comedies at once more theatrical because not written in the isolated study of the man of letters but in the presence, as it were, of the warm breath of the public; who then take up the task of adapting for their own performance and that of their

* "Introduzione al teatro italiano," trans. by Anne Paolucci, in Eric Bentley, ed., *The Genius of the Italian Theater*, New York, Mentor Books, 1964).

troupe the comedies of other authors, old and new, in order to supply the pressing need for repertory, constantly revising these adaptations, after having tried out on their audiences the effectiveness of
certain flourishes added as an outlet and vehicle for the particular
talents of some actor of the company. And as their fellow actors
gradually become skilled in keeping up the already-familiar repartee
of the middle episodes, they will write only the exits and the outline
of the action.

In other words those authors must have lost all their serious artistic pretensions; the transitory, impassioned life of the Theatre must
have taken such full possession of them that the only interest left to
them was that of the spectacle itself—a complete absorption in the
quality of the performance and communication with the audience.

They are no longer authors; but they are no longer even actors,
in the true sense of the word.

What are they, then?

By now each one of them has become a *type*, with a completely
defined stage life of its own; so that finally a theatrical convention
is established whereby with ten of them, ten such types—no more,
no less—a complex and varied spectacle can be put on that will provide full satisfaction for the audience—an audience already familiar
with these conventions, with the rules of the game, and passionately
interested in how their favorites carry on, how far each succeeds in
giving prominence to his part.

Pirandello then goes on to point out that the *commedia* is uniquely
Italianate in spirit. There is no doubt he is right about this; the traditions of the *commedia* are as old as Italy itself. But one might have
wished that Pirandello had broadened his perspective a bit more,
for no man of the Italian theatre embodied those traditions more
fully than Titus Maccius Plautus. He even had a *commedia* name.

The popular Italian theatre has always been imbued with the
spirit of *commedia* and the particular genius of Plautus is that he
was the first to incorporate it into his plays. The first known theatrical performances in Italy were the *Fabulae Atellanae*, developed
by the Oscans in the town of Atella in Campagna. The *Fabulae*
were short (three hundred lines) satiric parodies of life in the country. They had such titles as "The Sick Boar" or "Daddy, the Farmer,"
and occasionally they were parodies of heroic figures, as can be
gathered by a title like "Hercules, the Tax Collector." These
sketches were filled with riddles and obscenities and were played
by companies of touring actors. It is interesting to note that the
actors played them *planipes*, with bare feet, and not in the *cothurni*

of tragedy nor in the *socci* of comedy; indicating that, from the beginning, the *fabulae* were farcical in nature.

However, the most significant thing about them was the fact that their casts were composed entirely of the "stock" or type characters which Pirandello referred to in his essay. The first records tell us of only four characters (*Maccus*, the clown; *Bucco*, the glutton or braggart; *Pappus*, the foolish old man; and *Dossemus*, the hunchback trickster), but this number was gradually increased, and by the middle of the third century B.C. there were at least eight. And all of them can be found in the plays of Plautus.

Plautus began as an actor, and from his name it is obvious that he played the clown. He was not the first known Roman dramatist (both Livius Andronicus and Gnaeus Naevius are known to have preceded him), but it is clear that he was the first to incorporate the native comic traditions of the *Fabulae* into the framework of the literary comedy which his predecessors had borrowed from the Greeks. And very soon Plautine farce came to dominate the Roman theatre.

The first thing one notices about Plautus' plays is how insignificant the plots are. In fact, the plot is usually revealed in the prologue. The audience was not concerned with what happened; their interest was in how things were worked out and the form of the performance itself. For this reason, type characters are ideally suited for Plautine drama. A type character is one who needs no explaining and whose future is predictable no matter what his situation might be. Such a character is, as Bentley describes him, a creature of habit, and he brings a great energy to the theatre. He has the characteristics essential for farce; these also happen to be the same qualities which Pirandello ascribed to the characters of *commedia*.

No one, to my knowledge, has ever referred to Plautus as the father of the *commedia dell'arte;* and one would probably be in error to do so now. But the *commedia* did not come into being *de novis* either. Ruzzante and his colleagues may not have known it, but Titus the clown was out there on the platform with them.

## V. *The Limitations of Understanding*

It seems almost inevitable that when we discuss authors of the past—especially classical authors—we tend to link together writers who have so little in common that, if we were to do it with our own contemporaries, we would be dismissed with derision. Such, however, has nearly always been the case with Plautus and Publius Terentius Afer, better known as Terence. True, they lived at approximately the same time (Plautus: *c.* 254–184 B.C., Terence: *c.* 195–159 B.C.), and they both wrote comedies based upon the plots of Greek New Comedy. But the similarities stop there, and our understanding of how the Roman theatre developed (or, perhaps, failed to develop) has been severely limited by our failure to realize how different in style, tone, and technique these two dramatists actually are. Plautus, as I have indicated, was a man of the theatre. His plays are imbued with that sense of immediacy which popular performance demands. He was no *littérateur*, but a theatre craftsman who knew what his boisterous audiences liked and wanted, and he happily gave it to them. Terence, on the other hand, was first and always a writer—a writer who happened to write plays. His work belongs in the library and is best appreciated when read. (I know of no major revivals of a Terence play in the twentieth century.) The vast difference between these two writers is certainly one of temperament and sensibility, but it is also much more than that.

Unlike his predecessor, Terence wrote his plays to be read (and occasionally performed) for the cultivated members of the Scipionic Circle. I doubt if there have been many literary circles in all of Western history whose membership could be compared to that of this august group. (Dr. Johnson's circle is the only one which readily comes to mind.) Regularly, the members of the Circle would meet at Scipio's to discuss ways in which the Roman language and literature could be refined and improved. Terence was an important member of this group, and his plays reflect its linguistic interests much more than they reveal any sense of theatrical vitality.

Today, Terence is best known for his numerous neat and polished maxims, and it is certainly true that without his plays *Bartlett's Familiar Quotations* would be much impoverished. One immediately thinks, for example, of such lines as: "A word to the wise is sufficient," "Fortune favors the brave," "The very flower of youth," and "The quarrels of lovers are the renewal of love." But quotable lines, although many of them have been used by playwrights, are not the stuff out of which great plays are made, and Terence as a great writer was not much of a playwright.

Actually the cause of his failure can probably be attributed to the most famous of his maxims: *"Homo sum: humani nil a me alienum puto"* (I am a man: I consider nothing human foreign to me). This is a profound view of life, and it is no doubt true that a playwright (not to mention all other men) must be receptive to all of man's possibilities. But when, as it is in Terence's case, this capacity for understanding is carried to the point of absolute compassion, to that point where the playwright can "forgive all" that his characters may do, it becomes exceedingly dangerous. The limitations of the stage, and more particularly the demands of comedy, require that the dramatist have a partial view of life in his attitude toward his characters. This Terence did not have. His characters are always attractive, his plots are intricate and carefully worked out, and the dialogue is polished to a glossy brightness; but somehow as a whole his plays lack substance. Like Chinese food, they are never fully satisfying. We can admire his wisdom, respect his compassion for his fellowmen, and praise him as a master of literary style, but as a writer of plays Terence was too gentle and kind to exist for long in the knockabout and violently partial world of the theatre. His work has long been a source of inspiration for other playwrights, but his natural habitat was, and still is, the library.

## VI. *An Ecstasy of Madness*

Whenever something intended to have great dramatic significance takes place in one of Seneca's plays, it is sure to be either preceded or followed by the stage direction, "In an ecstasy of madness." Scholars usually explain this direction by going on at great length about Seneca's belief in the supernatural and its role as the motivating force in his plays. While such an interpretation may well be correct, it is not the whole story. The long history of tragic drama shows us that, when the most important events in a play do not spring from the characters themselves, it is a sure sign that the playwright has not presented a dramatic action, but only a recounting of dramatic deeds. Such is the case with Seneca. For all of his concern with dramatic motivation—both natural and supernatural, the characters in a play like *Medea* have little or no life of their own. They are flat and two-dimensional; and, like pawns in a grandiose stage chess game, they have no choice but to move forward. Psychological explanations are not enough to make a play, as many of our contemporary playwrights have discovered, especially if, in its crucial moments, we do not believe the characters are responsible for what they do.

T. S. Eliot, in his important essay "The Three Voices of Poetry," reminds us that the fact that lines in a play are spoken by many characters does not necessarily make them dramatic. To be dramatic, characters must speak for themselves; and it is the playwright's job to extract the language out of the characters rather than impose it on them. Nor is complexity of character essential, so long as we believe that communication between the characters is taking place. In the end, drama is concerned only with human relationships, with what men do to each other. Aeschylus' characters in the *Oresteia*, for instance, are not very well developed psychologically; in fact, they are so simple they could be described as monolithic. But we always believe them as characters, because they are individuated parts of an action. They have an existence, independent of the playwright, within the action. We do not experience Seneca's characters in this way; rather, we feel that he, much like Browning, was always speaking for himself through the characters.

This failure to achieve a dramatic idiom is in large measure due to the fact that, as far as we know, Seneca composed his plays for private readings rather than public performances on the stage. But it can also be explained in terms of the entrenched Roman oratorical tradition, which we know had a strong influence not only on Seneca's style, but on his whole approach to the dramatic event. The most revealing evidence of this influence is to be found in Seneca's continued use of *sententiae* (wise sayings) in his dialogue. These pat verbal solutions and moral clichés first appeared in the plays of Euripides, but there is some justification for the Greek tragedian's use of them. There were some problems and dramatic issues which Euripides could not resolve, nor did he believe they ever could be resolved; the meaning of several of his plays resides in this very lack of a resolution. However, since the play as a theatre piece had to come to an end, Euripides resorted to the use of the *deus ex machina* (a plot device) and the *sententiae* (a device of language) as means of resolution. There is no doubt that this is a shortcoming in Euripides' work, but it is an understandable, and even justifiable, one. But in the Roman drama the use of *sententiae* was not a strategy of despair. Because of the state-oriented nature of Roman life, virtue, and artistic expression, its writers were not given to private utterance. And the *sententiae* were an essential part of Rome's long and well-established oratorical tradition. Every guest speaker from Demosthenes and Cicero to Kennedy and Stevenson is considered effective because of his ability to express complex issues in a meaningful but brief statement. (Loftiness of tone is another essential characteristic of great oratory, and it is interesting to note that the early investigations on the sublime were seldom concerned with the drama.) But the substitution of statement, no matter how apt or lofty, for dramatic process inevitably reduces the range of the theatre. Nowhere in the history of drama can this reduction be more clearly observed than in the plays of Seneca. He consistently aborted his dramatic situations with the persistent maxim. Note for example:

> MEDEA: [My crimes] are yours, they are yours, indeed! The one who profits by a crime is guilty of it.

and in Act V:

> MESSENGER: Ruin, total ruin! Our royalty is annihilated. Daughter and father are one low heap of ashes.
> CHORUS: How are they trapped?
> MESSENGER: As kings regularly are, by gifts.

A similar debilitating tendency can be found in the bloody images Seneca uses to describe death. For all the gore, these passages are purely ornamental. They are a substitute for both dramatic and moral significance, and while they may be horrifying they are never horrible. They lack the sharp bite of a conscience which is involved in human suffering. The passion of these rolling speeches is only a *declared* passion; it does not involve developed feelings. It is merely a pose, a passion of attitude.

Again, the public nature of Roman life at the time of the Caesars may account for this tendency in Seneca's drama (Eliot, for one, argues that "the ethic of Seneca's plays is that of an age which supplied the lack of moral habits by a system of moral attitudes and poses"), but it must finally be attributed to Seneca's failure to understand the demands of the theatre. In the plays of Seneca everything is in the word, but his words are not supported by any other concrete reality. They neither require nor imply an actor, a stage, nor a specific emotional actuality. His plays, as Eliot observed, are, in effect, radio plays "full of statements useful only to an audience which sees nothing." Such plays are not without qualities, but they are qualities which find the stage an inhospitable medium.

Thus, in reading Seneca today, we cannot help but feel his significance is only of an historical nature. This does not mean his plays do not have value. They do, for instance, embody—probably better than anything else in Roman literature—the qualities of Roman Stoicism. Also, there is no doubt that the rhythms of his language especially as they were translated into English in the sixteenth century, had a profound influence on the development of the blank verse which reached its fullest flower in Elizabethan drama. No one should deny the importance of these facts; but, finally, Seneca has been kept alive by the scholars and not by the theatre. And one cannot help but wonder if this is not one of the reasons that classical literature has declined as a meaningful force in the imaginative lives of modern men.

# PART TWO

# THE MODERNIST DILEMMA

# THE MODERN THEATRE

AFTER VISITING the United States, Alexis de Tocqueville prophetically described the kind of literature which he believed an industrialized democratic society would produce. "I am persuaded," he wrote in *Democracy in America,* "that in the end democracy diverts the imagination from all that is external to man and fixes it on man alone. . . . It may be foreseen in like manner that poets living in democratic times will prefer the delineation of passions and ideas to that of persons and achievements. The language, the dress, and the daily actions of men in democracies are repugnant to conceptions of the ideal. . . . This forces the poet constantly to search below the external surface which is palpable to the senses, in order to read the inner soul. . . . The destinies of mankind, man himself taken aloof from his country, and his age, and standing in the presence of Nature and of God, with his passions, his doubts, his rare prosperities and inconceivable wretchedness, will become the chief, if not the sole theme of poetry." Any examination of the arts of the past century would seem to indicate that Tocqueville's prophecy has been fulfilled, and it is certainly clear that the theatre's general pattern of development during this time can be best described as a gradual but steady shift away from universal philosophical and social concerns toward the crises and conflicts of man's inner and private life. It is possible to discover foreshadowings of this change in direction and emphasis in the works of early nineteenth-century romantics—Buechner, Hebbel, Kleist, Gogol, Musset—but it is not until Ibsen that the theatre's revolutionary break with the past becomes clearly discernible. In fact, Ibsen's development as a playwright, beginning with his large philosophical dramas (*Brand* and *Peer Gynt*), through the plays of social protest and reform (*Pillars of Society, A Doll's House, Ghosts, An Enemy of the People*), to the autobiographical and almost pathologically introspective plays of his later years (*Rosmersholm, The Master Builder, When We Dead Awaken*), to a large extent embodies in a microcosmic way both in form and theme the modern theatre's increasing tendency to be more concerned with the conflicts of the individual's interior world than with the significance of his public deeds.

The causes of any revolution are always as difficult to untangle as its consequences are to assess, and any attempt on the part of the critic to describe them will inevitably result in oversimplification. But it is possible to discover certain basic changes in attitude which had been evolving in Europe since the time of Luther and had begun to crystallize in Continental thought by the second half of the nineteenth century. And the works of the revolutionary playwrights—Ibsen, Strindberg, Chekhov, Shaw, and Hauptmann—were the first to express in the theatre certain of these radical shifts in the way man had come to think of nature, society, and himself. What follows is an attempt to set forth briefly some of the more important aspects of this revolution in the drama which Ibsen referred to as "a war to the knife with the past."

Probably no force in the nineteenth century did more to destroy man's belief in an established norm of human nature, and hence begin the process of internalization in the theatre, than the advent of psychology as a systematized field of study. In his book *"Modernism" in the Modern Drama,* Joseph Wood Krutch argued that the basic issue confronting all the dramatists of the past one hundred years was the problem of "modernism." Briefly, modernism involves both the conviction and practice that to be modern is to be, in many important ways, different from anyone who ever lived before. This does not mean that man has changed; human nature is the same, but man's way of looking at himself has changed in a way that is significantly new. It is this new view of man that creates the problem for the dramatist.

Good examples of this changed perception can be found in Ibsen's *Hedda Gabler* (1890) and Strindberg's *Miss Julie* (1888). Hedda and Julie have the distinction of being the first fully and consciously developed neurotic heroines in dramatic literature. By neurotic we mean that they are neither logical nor insane (in the sense of being random and unaccountable), but that the aims and motives of each of them have a secret personal logic of their own. Both are motivated as dramatic characters on the premise that there is a secret, and sometimes unconscious, world of aims and methods —a secret system of values—which is more important in human experience than rationality. The significant difference is that neither of these characters can be explained or judged by a common standard; the actions of each dramatic character (and, by extension, each human being) are explicable only in terms of that peculiar combination of forces, frustrations, and desires which is unique to himself.

For us, living in the middle of the twentieth century, there is nothing very new in these psychological ideas; but, coming when they did, they were quite revolutionary, and they have created problems for the playwright that have not yet been solved. By convincingly demonstrating that normal people are not as rational as they seem, and that abnormal people do not act in a random and unintelligible way, psychology has made it difficult, if not impossible, for the dramatist to present his characters directly. In earlier times, when it was believed that there was a sharp distinction between the sane and the insane, the irrational "aberrations" of human behavior were dramatically significant because they could be defined in terms of a commonly accepted standard of sane human conduct. It seems clear, for instance, that in Shakespeare's presentation of them, Lear on the heath is insane while Macbeth at the witches' cauldron is not. But, for the modern dramatist, deeds do not necessarily mean what they appear to mean, and in themselves they are not directly revelatory of the characters who commit them. Like Othello, Miss Julie, Hedda Gabler, and Kostya Treplev of Chekhov's *The Sea Gull* are suicides; but, in the case of these three, the meaning of each death cannot be clearly ascertained from the actions that preceded it. The plight of the modern dramatist in this regard becomes apparent when we realize that without Strindberg's Preface to *Miss Julie* or Ibsen's Notes for *Hedda Gabler*, we could never know for certain what, in each instance, the significance of the heroine's death really was. And the ambiguity of almost every interpretation of *The Sea Gull* is largely due to the fact that Chekhov never made the meaning of Treplev's suicide explicit.

All drama of the past is based upon the axiom "By their deeds shall ye know them." The significance of the dramatic hero was re-

vealed by his deeds, and there was a direct relationship between
the hero's overt acts and his inner spiritual condition. The significance of Oedipus, for instance, is revealed by what he does, not by
some explanation that he is suffering from an Oedipus complex;
and there is a direct relationship between the act of tearing out his
own eyes and his solving the riddle of the Sphinx. Even when a
character commits a dissembling deed, it is to deceive the other
characters in the play, not the spectators. Certainly one of the chief
functions of the soliloquy in Elizabethan drama was to keep the audience continually informed as to what was going on. Hamlet may
put an antic disposition on, but not before he tells the audience he
is going to do so. However, beginning in the nineteenth century,
the drama began to reflect man's growing distrust in the ability of
his senses to comprehend the true nature of reality. Appearances
are no longer believed to be direct reflections of ideal reality, like
the shadows on the wall of Plato's cave; rather, they are thought of
as a mask which hides or distorts reality. And by the time of Pirandello, particularly in such plays as *Right You Are, If You Think
You Are* (1916), *Six Characters in Search of an Author* (1921), and
*The Emperor* (*Enrico IV*) (1922), appearances not only do not express reality, they contradict it, and the meaning of these plays is
not to be found in appearance or reality but in the contradiction
itself.

One of the great achievements of the Elizabethan dramatic form
was its ability to express several levels of experience simultaneously.
The world of *Hamlet* is both public and private, a world in which
personal and familial relationships, fantasy and mystery, and political and psychological conflict coexist in a state of constant dramatic
tension. One of the main reasons why the Elizabethan dramatic
form works so successfully is that appearances can be taken at their
face value. But when the dramatist begins to distrust the validity
of the information yielded by his sensory perceptions, it becomes
difficult, if not impossible, for him to dramatize the complex totality
of experience in a single form. Reality must be broken down into its
component parts, and each part can only be expressed in a form
peculiar to itself. Admitting the existence of individual differences
in the work of each dramatist writing in any given period, it is nonetheless possible to describe with some accuracy the dramatic form
employed by the playwrights of the fifth-century Greek theatre,
the Elizabethan and Restoration theatres of England, and the French

neoclassic theatre of the seventeenth century. But in discussing the modern theatre we must always speak of forms, for there is no single, dominant form in the serious theatre of the past hundred years. It is for this reason that the evolution of the drama since the time of Shakespeare has been so aptly described as a process of fragmentation.

It is very likely that every serious dramatist believes that it is his artistic duty to be true to his presuppositions about the real nature of the world in which he lives. However, once a playwright believes that the meaning of every human action is relative and intelligible only in terms of a unique and subsurface combination of forces, the dramatic events of the plot cease to have meaning in themselves, and they take on significance only as the secret motivations of the characters who participate in them are revealed. (The technique of earlier drama is just the reverse: the motivations of the characters are revealed by the events of the plot.) But how does the dramatist objectify the hidden and unconscious, and what happens to the theatre when he feels obligated to explain and probe into his characters' hidden lives? Explanation is always a dangerous business in the theatre (since the time of the ancient Greeks, exposition has always been the dramatist's most difficult problem), but the moment a playwright assumes that if he explains his characters he has written a play, that danger becomes mortal. All too often the writers of the modern theatre have forgotten that a dramatic situation requires not that we should *understand* a character but simply that we should *believe* in him. Dramatic action always leads to a judgment; it requires that something shall happen to and through the characters—something that is embodied in the events of which the characters are a part. Whenever the personality of the character, rather than the action of which the character should be a part, becomes the playwright's chief concern, dramatic process dissolves into explanation; and when that occurs, the range of the theatre is drastically reduced, if not unalterably damaged.

One has only to compare the plays of the mid-twentieth century with those of Ibsen, Shaw, or Strindberg to realize just how much the scope of the theatre has been narrowed. However, evidence of the gradual loss of belief in dramatic heroes, who needed no explaining, can initially be found in the sentimental bourgeois drama of the eighteenth century. For the first time a character was no longer noble, responsible, or morally significant—and, therefore, dramatically interesting—just because of his birth, position, power, or wealth. As a result, the dramatist was obliged to justify both his choice of characters and the situations in which they are engaged. The Romantic drama of the eighteenth and nineteenth centuries resisted a break with the past and attempted unsuccessfully to perpetuate the forms and figures of earlier times. Certainly, the revolt of Ibsen and his contemporaries in the last quarter of the nineteenth century was at least in some measure due to their conviction that the dramatic conflicts of the Romantic drama were inflated and without significance, and that the nobility of its characters was artificial and contrived. In rejecting these artificialities the modernists changed the theatre in many ways; but nothing that they could do would forestall the attrition of belief in the possibility of heroic characters who needed no explaining.

This was largely due to the fact that, as a literary movement, nineteenth-century naturalism was so closely related to nineteenth-century biology. Darwin's theories of evolution (*The Origin of Species*, 1859) and the discovery of new genetic laws had convinced many writers that man's existence, including his personality, was a phenomenon that could be explained in terms of scientific laws. As a result, increasingly, man's complex biological needs rather than his capacity to make moral choices were thought to be his most significant characteristic. Once such a view was accepted, however, the exceptional man, who because of his position and power had the greatest freedom of choice, ceased to be the fullest embodiment, and therefore the best representative, of those conflicts and choices that most clearly define the human condition. Instead, the lives of the poor, where the role of natural necessity is most readily observable, became the playwright's most suitable subjects. The drama of the common man, then, did not happen by accident, nor did it evolve because some dramatist or group of dramatists wanted it to. Given the problem of creating in a world in which all human actions tend to be explained in terms of some kind of psychological or sociological cause and effect, a world in which the possibility of deliberative and moral choice is doubted if not rejected outright, it is difficult, if not impossible, for the playwright to fashion a character of traditional heroic stature.

While the advent of psychology as a systematized field of study may have been the most powerful single force to shape the modern theatre, actually the process of internalization had begun much earlier. For instance, it is clear from Hebbel's essays on the drama that the despair of old Anton's "I don't understand the world anymore" in the final scene of *Maria Magdalena* is much more than an expression of the age-old frustration of the parent who does not understand the behavior of his children. It also reflects his dimly understood but tremendously painful realization that it is no longer possible for him to comprehend what the world has become or to imagine what the future will be like. Until the Industrial Revolution, patterns of life were passed on from father to son with the confidence that these patterns would satisfy the needs and desires of each new generation. Such confidence was justified, for life changed so gradually and imperceptibly that when changes did occur they were easily assimilated into the shared life of the community. But by the middle of the nineteenth century the effects of the Industrial Revolution had begun to be felt on all levels of society. Technology, with its ever-increasing capacity to transform man's way of living, not only made the future so unpredictable that it soon became impossible for him to imagine what his life would be like twenty years hence, but in its singular concern with the individual's functional qualities technology tended to isolate him from his fellows and invalidate his spiritual values and metaphysical concerns. At the same time, the discoveries of the nineteenth-century archeologists and the ensuing interest in anthropology tended to break down provincial and absolutist attitudes concerning human nature. Early anthropologists like Mannhardt, Robertson-Smith, Tylor, and the great James Frazer made it clear that human nature was not something fixed and unchanging but only that kind of behavior exhibited in each culture. In fact, as early as 1860 scholars were demonstrating that human nature is so plastic that it can, as Frazer was later to point out in the Preface to the first edition of *The Golden Bough* (1890), "exhibit varieties of behavior which, in the animal Kingdom could only be exhibited by different species." Furthermore, by the middle of the century, democracy was finally beginning to be established both as a way of life and as a form of government. Today we tend to forget what a revolutionary idea democracy is and the shattering effects that it had upon the values of eighteenth- and nineteenth-century Europe. We also forget what Tocqueville told us long ago: "Not only does democracy make every man forget his ancestors, but it hides his descendants and separates his contemporaries from him, it throws him back forever upon himself alone and threatens in the end to confine him entirely within the solitude of his own heart." In short, by the middle of the nineteenth century, every established view of God, human nature, social organization, and the physical universe was beginning to be seriously challenged if not invalidated. And this revolutionary climate had a profound effect on the theatre.

Of all the Arts, theatre is the only one which has always concerned itself with human destinies. Dramatic action is historical in the sense that the perpetual present of each moment on the stage is created out of past events and is directed toward a definite, if yet unknown, future. In previous ages the destiny of any dramatic action was significant because the everchanging events in the lives of dramatic heroes could be meaningfully related to eternity—that is, to some permanent value or idea such as Fate, the Gods, or Heaven and Hell—which transcends the human condition and which is believed in by the dramatist, or his audience, or both.

In the plays of Buechner and Hebbel we discover the first indications in the theatre of that sense of alienation both from God and from Society which underscores the fact that man's belief in eternity had been shaken. And one of the most significant aspects of Ibsen's work (at least after Peer Gynt, 1867) is that the realm of ultimate value has either disappeared or has become so mysterious that it has ceased to have dramatic relevance. In its place we find instead a belief in some form of social ideal or societal structure, first as the agent of some unknown Destiny and then as Destiny itself. But when Society begins to assume the role of Destiny—that is, is thought of as the determining force for good or evil in the lives of men—man cannot help but feel eventually that the meaning of his Destiny has been drastically reduced. For Society, as Robert Bolt writes in the Preface to his A Man for All Seasons, "can only have as much idea as we have what we are about, for it has only our brains to think with. And the individual who tries to plot his position by reference to our society finds no fixed points, but only the vaunted absence of them, 'freedom' and 'opportunity'; freedom for what, opportunity to do what, is nowhere indicated. The only positive he is given is 'get and spend' . . . and he did not need society to tell him that. In other words we are thrown back by our society upon ourselves, which of course sends us flying back to society with all the force of rebound."

Any mind capable of spiritual aspiration seeks in the actions of the dramatic hero that which affirms the vitality of the free will in any given situation. Man's free will may be defeated by the forces of Destiny—in fact, the great plays have always testified that the destroying forces of Destiny are as much a part of the hero's character as his free will; it may be paralyzed and thus incapable of action; it may be submerged by the battle in such a way as to become part of that Destiny; it may even turn out to be an illusion; but it must always be an active force if we are to believe that we are partaking in human greatness. Such a Destiny must be greater than an aggregate of human beings or an expression of social patterns.

Ironically, the revolt of Ibsen and Shaw against the conventional nineteenth-century drama was motivated by a desire to enlarge the range of Destiny in the theatre. In their attempts to present man in his total historical and social setting, they were rebelling against the narrow and private worlds that had been dominating the stage since the Restoration. But in spite of their efforts, nothing could change the fact that in the two hundred years since Shakespeare the world of the spirit had greatly diminished. The Ekdals' attic and Mrs. Warren's drawing room were not—and never could be—the same as Elsinore or Cleopatra's barge.

Nonetheless, the pioneers of the modern drama had revitalized the theatre precisely because they believed that significant social issues should be dealt with there. Thus for nearly three decades the theatre had a vitality of spirit and a forcefulness of manner which it had lacked for better than a century, for the very reason that its context had been reduced. To the playwright writing at that time, the human and social problems, which were the source materials of the naturalistic play, appeared capable of solution if only man and society would learn to use their common sense. This usually meant one of two things: the acceptance of a less rigid standard of social morality or the espousal of some form of socialism. But with the collapse of the established social order in the First World War, the validity of these too-easy solutions was impugned, and, beginning with the plays of the early German Expressionists (written between 1912 and 1916), the positive optimism of the Edwardian era gave way to a sense of bewilderment, exasperation, and defeatism, only occasionally tempered by the slim hope that the war had brought man to the threshold of a "New Age." The theatre reflects these changes from confidence to doubting and despair; from complacent faith in cherished values to an anxious questioning; from a rigorous, but rigid, morality to the mystic evangelism, the fanatical polemics, and the frivolous apathy of a disintegrating world. These changes are most apparent in the Jekyll-and-Hyde theatre of the German Expressionists, whose nerve-shattered playwrights alternated between militant idealism and grotesque nightmares. But one need only compare Shaw's *Heartbreak House* to *Major Barbara*, Pirandello's *Right You Are, If You Think You Are* to *Liola,* or Hauptmann's *Winter Ballad* to *The Weavers* to realize that the effects of the collapse of the old order were widespread and were reflected in the works of established writers as well as those of the new generation. Immediately after the war the theatre on the Continent was dominated by attitudes of emotionalism and cynicism, but these gradually gave way to feelings of frustration, futility, and despair, and by the middle of the 1920s the serious drama of Europe had become almost totally introspective and psychological in its orientation.

Because they were essentially isolated from the main currents of European history in the first two decades of the century, the Irish and American theatres were not immediately affected by the spreading paralysis that was transforming the rest of modern drama. But it is clear from O'Casey's *The Plough and the Stars* ( 1926) and *The Silver Tassie* (1927) that the Abbey Theatre could not withstand for long the theatre's introspective tendencies, and there was no serious American drama until O'Neill's plays were first produced right after the war. In the twenty years between *Beyond the Horizon* (1920) and *The Iceman Cometh* (1941) the American theatre repeated the Continental cycle in its own terms, and by the beginning of the Second World War all of the Western theatre had reached that no-man's-land between comedy and tragedy, between pathetic aspirations and ridiculous bewilderment, between neverbeginning action and never-ending talk.

Obviously, this tendency toward paralyzing introspection has by no means been accepted by everyone writing for the theatre. In fact, a large segment of the modern theatre might be best described as a reaction against the despair and dehumanizing implications of the modernist position. These "resistance movements" have sought to discover the means, both formal and substantive, whereby the possibility and validity of selfhood and human integrity, personal responsibility, and morally significant judgments could be reasserted in the theatre. The first of these groups are those playwrights like Eliot, Fry, Betti, and Claudel who have used some form of orthodox Christian belief to provide the metaphysical basis for their drama. Each of these playwrights understands the despair of modernism, and they are fully conscious of man's sense of isolation and estrangement. But, unlike most writers in the modern theatre, they believe that man's alienation is spiritual and not social or psychological; for them the modern condition is one of estrangement from God. As a result, almost all of their plays are intended to lead us to a state of spiritual awareness; they are attempts to envisage some form of the Christian community by dramatizing the need to recognize and accept the supernatural in experience. This is a mysterious realm, and it is this area of mystery that Eliot is describing in his essay "Poetry and Drama" when he writes:

> It seems to me that beyond the nameable, classifiable emotions and motives of our conscious life when directed toward action there is a fringe of indefinite extent, of feeling which we can only detect so to speak out of the corner of the eye and can never completely focus; a feeling of which we are only aware in a kind of temporary detachment from action.

The reason this kind of theatre has not been very successful in counteracting the debilitating effects of modernism—apart from the crucial fact that it does not seem relevant to a large segment of the modern audience and, therefore, has had only a very limited impact on them—is that the theatre is an art form which deals with the nameable and classifiable. An action that is a "detachment from action" does not find the theatre to be a very hospitable home, and only the "true believers" are satisfied by such plays—and this, probably, for theological and not theatrical reasons.

A second group might be called the "folk dramatists." They are writers such as Lorca, Synge, and, to a certain extent, Betti and the early Pirandello, who write out of the traditions and value systems of premodern hieratic societies. There is no doubt that they succeed artistically. Lorca's tragedies of Spain and Synge's plays of the Aran Islands are among the most moving and effective pieces in the modern repertoire. They are filled with human significance, and they celebrate affirmatively man's greatness, his inevitable defeat, and the possibility of spiritual victory. But as much as we are moved by these plays, we must ultimately reject them as irrelevant to our times. For most people living in highly industrialized urban situations, these rural dramas can at best evoke only nostalgia. And all attempts by more recent writers to imitate them have been self-conscious, precious, and sentimental. This is quite understandable, for the world of Synge's and Lorca's plays is, by contemporary standards, a comparatively simple one. It is a world in which the individual insists upon making every relationship a personal one—an heroic society based upon the feudal aristocratic values of honor, generosity, and revenge. These are values which we, in our economic society, have chosen to deny. We may admire or sympathize with a Yerma, a Christy Mahon, or a Maurya, but it is impossible for us to identify ourselves with them. After our brief experience of uplift and exaltation (and for some it is boredom), we return to our city and suburban homes having enjoyed these folk dramas but not having been nourished by them. (In this regard, I believe it is significant that, in spite of the praise of the critics and scholars, neither Lorca nor Betti has ever been successfully produced on Broadway, and there certainly hasn't been a successful New York production of Synge since the Abbey Theatre's visit in the 1930s.)

The third and last group is by far the largest and probably the most important one: those who have sought to escape the deadly strictures of modernism by turning to classical mythology. The use of myth in modern art has become commonplace. It has been successfully employed in poetry and the novel by Yeats, Pound, and Joyce. T. S. Eliot, in his famous review of Joyce's *Ulysses*, pointed out its great value when he wrote: "In using the myth, in manipulating a continuous parallel between contemporaneity and antiquity, Mr. Joyce is pursuing a method which others must pursue after him. . . . It is simply a way of controlling, of ordering, of giving shape and a significance to the immense panorama of futility and anarchy which is contemporary history. . . . It is a step toward making the modern world possible for art." Myth used in this way provides the playwright with a form for the expression of his experience, rather than the subject matter itself. In a world seen as constantly changing, myth orders the chameleon-like present with a calculable objectification of reality. It permits the modern dramatist to present the here and now in terms of the universal and historical. The use of myth makes it possible for the dramatist to create a theatrical world that has a meaning which he is unable to find in the world outside the theatre, and thus he is able, temporarily at least, to communicate with the disparate world that his audience represents. In a sense, by playing with the themes and forms of a now nonexistent ordered world, the playwright has solved the problem of the artist in modern society. However, the fact that he *plays* with these themes and forms reminds the audience all over again that it does not live in such an ordered world. As a method, then, the use of myth has often been very successful, and some great plays have been written in that form. But the universality of such achievements is finally artificial, and the use of myth as a means of dramatic expression, while attractive to the playwright, is usually employed with fear and trembling. It is too obviously a compensatory technique, a substitute for that community of belief which most dramatists find lacking in the modern world.

All these "resistance" writers shared one common and fundamental attitude: Each of them was in some way rebelling against the conditions of the modern world. They were not only conscious of that lack of a sense of community which inevitably occurs in an increasingly democratic society; more important, they were aware of man's growing sense of his own isolation. In the end, however, all of those playwrights who have rebelled against modernism have not been completely successful, because in their attempts to construct a system that would provide a meaning for their lives and a validity to their art they have more often than not had to deny the realities of the modern world in the process. By insisting upon values that we may once have cherished but which no longer in actuality exist, the playwrights of the resistance have not been able to revitalize the theatre or its audiences. And most important, they have not succeeded in stretching the imaginations of men in order that they might conquer that sense of isolation and despair which pervades the modern world. And this brings us to the playwrights of the mid-twentieth century.

In an age dominated by space orbits and artificial satellites, the fear of nuclear war, the tension of cold-war diplomacy, and the insecurity of a defense economy, our greatest uncertainty is whether or not, in the midst of epochal disorder, man has any good chance (to borrow Faulkner's phrase) of prevailing; and if he does, what kind of man will prevail.

This atmosphere has had a profound effect on our theatre, and if there is one thing that characterizes the work of almost all our serious playwrights of the last two decades, it is that their plays express the contemporary theatre's tremendous concern to find a metaphor for universal modern man as he lives on the brink of disaster. We sense that our condition is much like that of those helpless travelers described by Kafka in his *Notebooks:*

> We are in the situation of travelers in a train that has met with an accident in a tunnel, and this at a place where the light of the end is so very small a glimmer that the gaze must continually search for it and is always losing it again, and, furthermore, both the beginning and the end are not even certainties. Round about us, however, in the confusion of our senses, or in the supersensitiveness of our senses, we have nothing but monstrosities and a kaleidoscopic play of things that is either delightful or exhausting according to the mood and injury of each individual. What shall I do? or: Why should I do it? are not questions to be asked in such places.

The train of our national and international—indeed interglobal—life seems to be wrecked, too; and as a result, in despair and desperation, our writers have become increasingly preoccupied with finding a metaphor of the theatre that is symbolic of the inalienable part of every man; they are searching for a metaphor of man left face to face with himself.

But what happens to the theatre when our dramatists believe that their chief obligation is to reveal man in a condition of isolation? One of the reasons that the works of our new playwrights seem so difficult to audiences and critics alike is the fact they are so different. Until recently—Chekhov, of course, is the notable exception—we went to the theatre expecting to see a story about someone doing something; "character in action" is the way our critics put it. This story also usually involved some kind of "message" or "statement" about an aspect of human experience. In short, one of the things we expected of a dramatic action was that it express some kind of completion to the statement: "Life is . . . !" But increasingly the modern dramatist has come to doubt that "Life is something"; and all of their plays are expressions of the proposition that "Life is."

Such an idea of the theatre has tremendous implications for the drama, and we are just now becoming aware of them. First of all, it abolishes the traditional linear plot, because our contemporary playwrights are not interested in presenting an action in any Aristotelian sense. They are, rather, dramatizing a condition. Whenever one asks what the central action of a Beckett, Ionesco, or Pinter play is, he comes a cropper; "action" for the contemporary playwright is an artificial concept. He is concerned with showing life as it is, and in life there is no central action, there are only people, and the only thing that is basic to each individual is the ontological solitude of his being.

But such radical shift in intention has brought with it equally revolutionary experiments with dramatic form. Earlier, we said that these plays were not imitations of an action in any Aristotelian sense. Most serious contemporary playwrights are dramatizing a condition, and therefore they need a dramatic form which, as Ionesco put it, "progressed not through a predetermined subject and plot, but through an increasingly intense and revealing series of emotional states." Such a drama must from the beginning, then, dispense with the traditional linear plot. The traditional plot is sequential; it starts at a certain moment in time and then moves through a series of events to a conclusion. Everything that occurs in this kind of play—each speech, every action, any symbol—is a part of the play's forward movement and is causally related to the sequence of events. It is this sequential nature of dramatic action, of which plot is the first form, that Aristotle was referring to when he said that tragedy is an imitation of an action "which has a beginning, a middle, and an end."

But the new playwrights—first in Europe, and now in the United States—are not interested in "imitations of actions"; they want to show "life as it is," and life as it is lacks direction, the external causality, the cathartic effect of completed events. Like so many painters, composers, poets, and novelists before them, our dramatists are aware that the crises which are so neatly resolved by the linear form of drama are not so neatly resolved in life. To be alive is to be in a continual state of crisis; in life, as one crisis is resolved another is always beginning. Today the playwright wants his plays to express the paradox, the contradiction, and the incompleteness of experience; he wants to suggest the raggedness, the confusion, the complexity of motivation, the "discontinuous continuity," and the basic ambiguity of all human behavior. The contemporary playwrights have rejected the traditional forms of theatre because they are convinced that these forms, ruled by the destructive tyranny of a sequential and chronological structure, are incapable of expressing the "is-ness" of experience. So they have developed a form (Chekhov was the first to use it fully) which might be called, to use the terminology of the new criticism of poetry, *contextual* or *concentric*. The structure of these plays, then, is epiphanic; its purpose is to reveal, literally "to show forth," the inner lives of the characters. In such drama the plot has been twisted into a situation that is to reveal the psychic lives of the characters. There are many dramatic situations in a plot; in these new plays a single situation has been stretched to take the place of the plot. This inflation of the situation into the source of the dramatic action so that it replaces the plot is the vital secret of the dramaturgy of the new theatre. The new playwrights, in an attempt to capture "the aimless unclimactic multiplicity" of their characters' lives, have created a form of drama based on what Marvin Rosenberg has called "the tensions of context, rather than direction, of vertical depth, rather than horizontal movement." *

But once you assert that the meaning of life is absurdity, that the laws of logic are spurious, that action is meaningless, that individuality is illusory, that social interaction is unimportant, and that communication is impossible, you have denied every assumption upon which the art of the theatre as we have known it in the Western world is based. The playwrights of the Absurd did not really set out to destroy the modern theatre; they maintain, to the contrary, that they are seeking the means to revivify it. Rather, they are pursuing to their fullest and most logical conclusions the premises of modernism. These dramatists are facing the "facts of life." If the dramatic meaning of their plays is that drama is no longer possible, they would contend that any other meaning would be artificial, illusory, false; if the dialogue in their plays consists of meaningless clichés and stereotyped phrases, they would insist that this is the way we talk; if their characters are constantly changing their personalities, these playwrights would point out that no one today is really consistent or truly integrated. If the people in their plays seem to be helpless puppets without any will of their own, the Absurdists would argue that we are all passively at the mercy of blind fate and meaningless circumstance. They call their theatre "Anti-Theatre," and this they insist is the true theatre of our times. If they are correct, so be it! Then history has again followed its own inexorable laws. The very forces which gave life and strength to the modern theatre have caused its decline and death.

But the theatre is always dying, and with equal regularity, like the phoenix, it is resurrected. No one can say with certainty what

* Marvin Rosenberg, "A Metaphor for Dramatic Form," *Journal of Aesthetics and Art Criticism,* Vol. XVII (December, 1958), pp. 174–180.

its new form will be, although it would seem that the increasing influence of Brecht on the work of new dramatists all over the world indicates that the conflicts of men living in industrialized collective societies will provide the themes for the theatre of the future, and that the narrative structure of epic drama is the most appropriate form within which to embody these conflicts. But no matter what the future of the theatre will be like, that there will be a future is certain. First, largely because of the development of college and university theatre programs in this country, and the large increase in the number of professional repertory theatres here and abroad, there are more people who have experienced good theatre than ever before. And this enlarged audience wants and needs theatre, and it will not be satisfied for long with the maimed rites of psychological and moral cliché, or impassioned jeremiads from prophets of doom, or the meandering contemplations of writers who are morbidly consumed in introspection and self-analysis. Fortunately, audiences still go to the theatre in the spirit of expectancy, in the hopeful anticipation that the stage will be capable of accommodating all of the terrible-wonderful emotions and insoluble dilemmas of our shared life together. This demand bid made by our new and increasingly informed and aware audiences for a drama that deals with the significant issues and concerns of our public life will, I believe, force our playwrights to open up new frontiers in the drama and thus extend the boundaries of the theatre. The second great hope of the theatre is that, in spite of the overriding temper of despair and the current dominance of anti-theatricality, our playwrights still find human action significant, still find it necessary to write plays, and in the very act of writing attest to the miracle of life that contemporary despair would deny. We live in one of the most dramatic ages in the history of mankind, and if the past is any kind of reliable guide to what the future of the theatre will be, we have good reason to believe that the theatre of tomorrow can be as dramatic as the world in which we live today.

# 9

# IBSEN'S GHOSTS
# AS TRAGEDY

*What profit has man of all his labour wherein
he laboureth under the sun? One generation
passeth away, and another generation cometh; but the earth abideth forever. . . . The
sun also ariseth, and the sun goeth down,
and hasteth to the place where he arose.*

ECCLESIASTES

HENRIK IBSEN's biography is a study in conflict and contradiction.
The gadfly of bourgeoisie morality was helplessly bourgeois; the
enemy of pietism was a guilt-ridden possessor of the worst kind of
"Lutheran" conscience; the champion of the "love-life of the soul"
was incapable of loving; the militant spokesman against hypocrisy
and respectability was pompous and outraged at any breach of decorum. Ibsen's life is the contradiction of those values affirmed in
his plays. This should not confuse us, however, if we will look even
briefly at some of the significant events in a life that was really quite
dull.

Ibsen was born into an atmosphere of fairly prosperous parochial
respectability. His father was a small-time shipping tycoon in the
little town of Skien. In 1836, when Ibsen was eight years old, his father went bankrupt and was accused of embezzlement and forgery.
The charges were never proved, but the family was ostracized and
reduced to a grubbing kind of poverty. When Ibsen was sixteen he

left his family, amidst bitter renunciations on both sides, never to see or correspond with them again. Even when his parents died he failed to return or write. He wrote to a friend on the occasion of his father's death that he was "unable to offer assistance of any kind." So at sixteen Ibsen went to the dismal town of Grimstad as an apprentice in pharmacy. Here he had an illegitimate son, Hans Jakob, and once again was "run out of town." He left Grimstad, leaving mother and child stranded, and never took the slightest interest in them. He went to Christiania (now Oslo) to begin his career as a writer and failed. In 1851 he was hired as director and dramaturg of the new Bergen National Theatre. Again, Ibsen was a failure. Letters and memoirs of actors in his company show him to have been incompetent both as a director and as a manager; and the plays written expressly for the theatre in his role as dramaturg were all disasters. Furthermore, he must have felt failure in his personal life. He fell in love three times in Bergen, and in each instance the girl's father broke off the affair because Ibsen was not suitable as a son-in-law. By 1857 he was on the verge of being fired; friends stepped in and got him a job as director of the newly organized Norwegian Theatre in Christiania. But failure followed him and by 1862 the National Theatre was bankrupt both artistically and financially and Ibsen was bitterly denounced by the press. Once again, friends came to his aid and he was given a small dole in the form of a literary scholarship to study abroad.

The story of Ibsen's success as an international playwright is well known and in 1891 he returned to Norway as a celebrity. In Christiania, where he settled for good, he became something of a national institution and was far from disliking such a status. All the frustration, humiliation, and rejection he had endured in youth and early manhood were now amply compensated for. He was wealthy and internationally famous. As if anxious to do full justice to his literary and social position, Ibsen increased his air of excessively dignified respectability, so much so that in all his external habits he was even more strict and methodical than those philistines whom he had ridiculed so aggressively in his plays. Immaculately dressed in his frock coat and silk top hat, he took his daily walks along the same streets, sat at the same table in the same café (where the customers all respectfully rose whenever he entered), and went home at the same time, with the regularity of clockwork. He was also fond of displaying his numerous decorations and medals, which he used to collect and covet with the relish of a *nouveau riche* enjoying all the external insignia of his own importance.

In short, Ibsen became a pillar of society in his last days; he was a regular speaker at the Norwegian equivalents of the Rotary Club, the AAUW, labor unions, and the Better Business Bureau. In his speeches he praised all of these groups and gratefully accepted their adulation and honors. His study walls were covered with plaques and certificates from civic organizations and only a bust of Strindberg—a bust that captured the penetrating and demonic quality of Strindberg's gaze—acted as an antidote to this display of middle-class self-righteousness. On March 15, 1900, Ibsen had a stroke, and another in the following year. These paralytic strokes were followed by amnesia and for six years he lay helplessly senile. He died on May 23, 1906, at the age of seventy-eight.

The clue to the meaning of all Ibsen's plays lies in this strange biography. Ibsen's plays are a continuous act of expiation. Certainly, it is significant that bankruptcy and the resultant rejection by society appears in four of his plays; the desire to restore the family honor is central to two more; and there are illegitimate children in eight plays. Thematically, the plays are, almost without exception, patterned in a similar way: a hidden moral guilt and the fear of impending retribution. Structurally, the plays are epilogues of retribution. All of the plays after *Peer Gynt* begin on a happy note late in the action. In each case the central figure has a secret guilt which is soon discovered. As the play progresses, by a series of expository scenes (scenes which delve into the past and are then related to the present condition of the characters), a sense of the impending retribution envelops the action and each of the plays ends with justice, in the form of moral fate's having its way. And finally, beginning with *Ghosts*, Ibsen introduces the theme of expiation. In every play following *Ghosts*, at least one of the central characters feels the need to exorcise his guilt, doubt, or fear by some form of renunciation.

Perhaps more important is the fact that as Ibsen's art developed these themes and attitudes changed in tone and form. The guilt, which had been specific in the early plays—Bernick's lie, Nora's forgery, Mrs. Alving's return—becomes more and more abstract, nebulous, and ominous as best evidenced in the nameless guilt of Solness and Rosmer. The fear, which in the early plays had been the fear of discovery, becomes a gnawing anxiety. Self-realization, which in

*Brand* is presented in terms of the Kierkegaardian imperative of either/or, is achieved in the later plays in an ambiguous kind of self-destruction. And finally, significant action on the part of the characters has tendencies toward becoming a frozen *stasis* of meaningless activity and contemplation.

Ibsen's life and his work are closely interwoven. Ibsen, rejected from society as a young man, had good reason to see the blindness of bourgeois respectability in his exile. And yet his sharp criticism of society is always balanced by his desire to be a part of that very society he saw and knew to be false. Over and over again in his plays and letters he condemns the hypocrisy, the intellectual shallowness, and the grim bleakness of his Scandinavian homeland. But he returned to it in pomp and circumstance. Herein lies the crux to an understanding of Ibsen's art in general and *Ghosts* in particular. More and more we see that both in Ibsen the man and in the characters of his plays the basic struggle is within.

Ibsen lived in a time of revolution; he was a maker of part of that revolution; and he knew full well that all the things he said about bourgeois society were true. But despite his rational understanding, his intellectual comprehension of this fact, he was driven by deeper forces within him not only to justify himself to that false society, but to become a part of it. It is this struggle within himself between his rational powers and the Trolls of the Boyg that best explains his life and work. Ibsen's plays are his attempts to quell the guilt he felt for desiring values which he knew to be false. In support of this point, I call attention to two important bits of evidence: the first is a letter written by Ibsen to Peter Hanson in 1870:

> While writing *Brand*, I had on my desk a glass with a scorpion in it. From time to time the little animal was ill. Then I used to give it a piece of soft fruit, upon which it fell furiously and emptied its poison into it—after which it was well again. Does not something similar happen to us poets? The laws of nature regulate the spiritual world also. . . .

The second is a short poem entitled "Fear of Light" (presently, I shall relate the significance of that title to *Ghosts*):

> What is life? a fighting
> In heart and brain with Trolls.
> Poetry? that means writing
> Doomsday-accounts of our souls.

I contend that Ibsen's plays were attempts—attempts that were bound to fail, just as Mrs. Alving's attempts were bound to fail—to relieve Ibsen of his guilt and at the same time were judgments of his failure to overcome the Trolls (which first appear as Gerd in *Brand*), those irrational forces and powers within man over which he has no control.

Keeping these facts in mind, let us now turn to *Ghosts*. One does not have to be a very perceptive student of the theatre to realize that the "ghosts" Ibsen is talking about are those ghosts of the past that haunt us in the present. In fact, Ibsen has often been criticized for using his ghost symbolism with such obviousness, such lack of subtlety, and so repetitiously. Certainly, when reading the play we feel this criticism is justified. Oswald's looking like Captain Alving; his interest in sex and liquor; his feelings toward Regina; his syphilitic inheritance; Pastor Mander's influence over Mrs. Alving, the orphanage, and the fire are only a few of the "ghosts" that Ibsen uses as analogs to his theme. Alrik Gustafson puts it this way:

> Symbols are, of course, a commonplace in Ibsen's dramas, but in his early plays before *The Wild Duck* he uses symbolistic devices somewhat too obviously, almost exclusively to clarify his themes. Any college sophomore can tell you after a single reading of *Pillars of Society, A Doll's House,* or *Ghosts* what the symbols expressed in these titles mean. The symbols convey *ideas*—and little else. They have few emotional overtones, are invested with little of the impressive mystery of life, the tragic poetry of existence. They tend to leave us in consequence cold, uncommitted, like after a debate whose heavy-handed dialectic has ignored the very pulse-beat of a life form which it is supposed to have championed.*

But *Ghosts* is concerned with more than the external manifestations of an evil heritage. In those oft-quoted lines that serve as a rationale for the play, Mrs. Alving says:

> I am half inclined to think we are all ghosts, Mr. Manders. It is not only what we have inherited from our fathers and mothers that exists again in us, but all sorts of old dead ideas and all kinds of old dead beliefs and things of that kind. They are not actually alive in us; but there they are dormant, all the same, and we can never be rid of them. . . . There must be ghosts all over the world. . . . And we are so miserably afraid of the light, all of us . . . and I am here, fighting with ghosts both without and within me.

* Alrik Gustafson, "Some Notes on Theme, Character, and Symbol in *Rosmersholm*," *The Carleton Drama Review,* vol. I, no. 2, pp. 9–10.

The ghosts of plot and symbol are the manifestations of Mrs. Alving's struggle with the ghosts within. It is this internal conflict, a conflict similar to Ibsen's personal struggle, that is the play's central action.

To define this action more explicitly, I would say that Ibsen is imitating an action in which a woman of ability and stature finds her ideals and her intellectual attitudes and beliefs in conflict with an inherited emotional life determined by the habitual responses of respectability and convention. As the play's form evolves it becomes apparent that the values Mrs. Alving affirms in intellectual terms are doomed to defeat because she has no control over her emotional inheritance—an inheritance of ghosts which exists, but which cannot be confined to or controlled by any schematization of the intelligence.

Every significant choice that Mrs. Alving has ever made and the resultant action of such a decision is determined by these ghosts of the past rather than by intellectual deliberation. To mention but a few instances: Her marriage to Captain Alving in conformity to the wishes of her mother and aunts; her return to her husband; her reaction to the Oswald-Regina relationship; her acceptance of Manders after she has seen and commented upon the hypocrisy of the scene with Engstrand; her failure to tell Oswald the "straight" truth about his father; the horror of her reaction when Oswald is indifferent to his father's life; and finally, the question mark with which the play ends. All of these scenes are evidence that Mrs. Alving's ideals of freedom and her rhetorical flights into intellectual honesty are of no use to her when it comes to action. Perhaps I can make my point clearer by briefly developing two of the above-mentioned episodes.

As the second act opens, Mrs. Alving comes to a quick decision about Oswald's relationship with Regina: "Out of the house she shall go—and at once. That part of it is clear as daylight." I will return to the relationship of light to enlightenment, but for the moment we see that Mrs. Alving's decision is based upon an emotional response determined by her inheritance of respectability. Then, Mrs. Alving and the pastor begin to talk; and Mrs. Alving always talks a good game. After better than four pages of dialogue, Mrs. Alving is finally able to exclaim: "If I were not such a miserable coward, I would say to him: 'Marry her, or make any arrangement you like with her—only let there be no deceit in the matter.'" The pastor is properly shocked when Mrs. Alving gives him the "face the facts of life" routine; but her liberation, which is only verbal, is short-lived! Manders asks how "you, a mother, can be willing to allow your. . . ." This is Mrs. Alving's reply: "But I am not willing to allow it. I would not allow it for anything in the world; that is just what I was saying."

Or to take another situation. In Act I, Mrs. Alving tells Manders what her husband was really like: "The truth is this, that my husband died just as great a profligate as he had been all his life." In Act II, she is telling Manders of all the things she *ought* to have done and she says: "If I had been the woman I ought, I would have taken Oswald into my confidence and said to him: 'Listen, my son, your father was a dissolute man.'" In the third act circumstances have forced Mrs. Alving to tell Oswald the truth about his father: "Your poor father never found any outlet for the overmastering joy of life that was in him. And I brought no holiday spirit into his house, either; I am afraid I made your poor father's home unbearable to him, Oswald."

When we come to see the big scenes in this way, we then recall the numerous small events that create the network of the action and give the play its texture. Such things come to mind as Mrs. Alving's need of books to make her feel secure in her stand, and the neat little bit in the first act where Mrs. Alving reprimands Oswald for smoking in the parlor, which Ibsen then underscores by making it an issue in the second act.

Ibsen's plays are filled with such incidents; those little events that tell so much. I am of the persuasion that Ibsen is not very good at making big events happen; as appealing as they may be to a director, they tend to be theatrically inflated; they are melodramatic in the sense that the action of the plot is in itself larger than the characters or the situation in the play which create such events. Ibsen is the master of creating the small shocking event, or as Mary McCarthy puts it, "the psychopathology of everyday life." Nora's pushing off the sewing on the widow Christine; Hjalmer letting Hedwig do the retouching with her half-blind eyes as he goes off hunting in the attic; his cutting of his father at Werle's party and the moment when Hedda intentionally mistakes Aunt Julia's new hat for the servant's, are all examples of this talent. These are the things we know we are capable of! This is the success (and the limitation) of the naturalistic convention "which implies a norm of behavior on

the part of its guilty citizens within their box-like living rooms."
But to return to the main business at hand: the conflict for Mrs.
Alving, then, is not how to act. She just acts; there is no decision,
nor can there be, for she has no rational control over her actions.
Herein lies the conflict. Just because Mrs. Alving has no control
over her actions does not mean she escapes the feelings of guilt for
what she does and her inability to do otherwise. Her continual
rhetoricizing about emancipation and her many acts of renunciation
are attempts to satisfy these feelings of guilt. For example, and I
am indebted to Weigand here,* the explicit reasons she gives for
building the orphanage do not account sufficiently for her use of the
expression, "the power of an uneasy conscience." There is a big
difference between fear that an ugly secret will become known and
an evil conscience. Mrs. Alving's sense of guilt is the result of an
intellectual emancipation from the habits of a lifetime; it is an
emancipation from those values which she emotionally still accepts.
It is precisely for this reason that her attempts at expiation are
never satisfactory—they are not central to and part of her guilt.

To put it another way, Mrs. Alving's image of herself as liberated
from outworn ideas is at odds with what in fact she is, a middle-
aged woman bound by the chains of respectability and convention.
It is for this reason, in a way similar to Sartre's characters in the
hell of *No Exit*, that she suffers. She is aware of the disparity between image and fact: "I ought" is a choric refrain that runs through
her conversation; and she constantly looks for ways to affirm her
image and assuage her guilt. And yet, the very fact that she accepts
the image of herself as free, when experience has proven otherwise
time and time again, explains why she is defeated in every attempt
at atonement.

The sun finally rises. Ibsen has been preparing for this from the
beginning. As the past is gradually revealed in the play and as the
issues of the action come into sharper focus, "light" becomes more
and more important in Ibsen's design. The play opens in the gloom
of evening and rain; Mrs. Alving, at least according to Ibsen's stage
directions, plays most of her important revelation scenes at the
window, the source of light; as Mrs. Alving decides to quell Oswald's "gnawing doubts," she calls for a light; Oswald's big speech
about the "joy and openness of life" uses the sun as its central metaphor; the light that reveals—tells the truth—how impossible it is for

* Hermann Weigand, *The Modern Ibsen* (New York, Henry Holt, 1925), p. 82.

Mrs. Alving to atone for her guilt has its source in the flames of the burning orphanage; and, finally, it is the sun, the source of all light, that reveals the meaning of the play's completed action. Mrs. Alving is still trapped within the net of her own inheritance. She, as she has already told us and as Ibsen tells us in his poem "Fear of Light," is afraid to face the real truth about herself. This fear is something over which she has no control.

If we can empathize with Mrs. Alving, and I think we can, we have been led to feel, as she believes, that as the light comes out of darkness, as the pressures of reality impinge upon her with unrelenting force, she will be capable of an act of freedom. We want to believe that she will affirm the image that she has of herself as a liberated human being by an action that is expressive of that freedom, even if that action is the murder of her own son. We want to feel that the light and heat of the sun will have the power to cauterize the ghosts of her soul. But if we have been attentive to the developing action, if we but recall what events followed the "lesser lights," then we realize that there can be no resolution. Mrs. Alving can give only one answer, "No!"

Mrs. Alving, like Oswald, who is the most important visible symbol of the ghosts, is a victim of something beyond her control. We are reminded of Oswald's famous speech in the second act: "My whole life incurably ruined—just because of my own imprudence. . . . Oh! if only I could live my life over again—if only I could undo what I have done! If only it had been something I had inherited—something I could not help." We have known all along that Oswald is a victim, so Ibsen is telling us for a purpose. The reason, as a study of his other plays will attest, is that for Ibsen the external is always the mirrored reflection of what's within. Mrs. Alving is also a victim! Like Oswald, she is doomed just by being born. And since she never comes to understand herself, since she never realizes and accepts the disparity of her image of herself and the truth about herself, she can never—in a way that Oedipus, a similar kind of victim, can—resolve the conflict.

For Mrs. Alving the sun has risen and just as she cannot give Oswald the sun, so the light of the sun has not been able to enlighten her. This, I believe, is the conflict in the play and the developed meanings of this conflict form the play's central action.

But is this action tragic? How, if at all, is *Ghosts* a tragedy? It seems to me that there are two possible answers to these questions and the answer will depend largely on which interpretation of the play one accepts. The prevalent interpretation is the one which claims that this is a play of social protest and reform. The adherents of such a view can gather together a great deal of evidence in support of their case: all of Ibsen's plays from *League of Youth* to *The Wild Duck;* passages from the play themselves, like Oswald's speech on the freedom of Europe; many of Ibsen's public speeches, and several of his letters. With this interpretation the play is saying that if man would only see how hypocritical and outmoded his values were then the disasters that occur in the play need never have taken place. This view has as its fundamental premise that social evils can be cured and that when they are man is capable of living with a "joy of life." But if this is true, if all you have to do is be honest with yourself—and such a view assumes this is possible—and if men would see the falseness of social conventions and change them, then it seems to me the eternal elements of tragedy are dissolved in the possibility of social reform. However, tragedy is concerned with showing those destructive conflicts within man that exist because man is a man no matter what age he may happen to be a part of, and no matter what kind of a society he may live in.

In some ways, I think Ibsen did intend *Ghosts* to be a play of social reform, but if this is the case, he created more than he planned. In all of his early plays, the plays we think of as the social reform plays, Ibsen is much like Mrs. Alving; he believed intellectually in freedom and wrote and talked a good deal about it, but is this the whole story? The discrepancy between the *ideals* men live by and the *facts* of their living is a central theme in Ibsen's work, but it is interesting to note that even in *Ghosts* the possibility of the "happy illusion" is presented. It is a hint that Ibsen is coming to feel that the conflict between truth and ideals can never be reconciled. By the time of *Rosmersholm,* even the free souls are tainted, the reformers are corrupt, and the man trying to redeem himself is shown to be capable only of realizing that he cannot be redeemed. Rosmer's death is an act of expiation, but suicide is decided upon only after Rosmer discovers the impossibility of redemption within society by means of freer and more honest views and relations.

Thus, while it is true that Ibsen, both in his public pronouncements and in his plays prior to *Ghosts*, gives us evidence that he believes optimistically in the possibility of social reform; that he believes that finally the sun will rise and continue to shine if man works long and diligently at facing the truth, he may be in fact whistling as he walks in the night through a graveyard. I wonder if Ibsen, even as early as *Ghosts*, isn't being a Mrs. Alving. Certainly this passage from a letter written during the composition of *Ghosts* permits us to wonder:

> The work of writing this play has been to me like a bath which I have felt to leave cleaner, healthier, and freer. Who is the man among us who has not now and then felt and acknowledged within himself a contradiction between word and action, between will and task, between life and teaching on the whole? Or who is there among us who has not selfishly been sufficient unto himself, and half unconsciously, half in good faith, has extenuated this conduct both to others and to himself?

The alternative interpretation of *Ghosts* is the one which I have outlined in this essay. Mrs. Alving is a victim in a conflict over which she has no control. What are the implications of such a view to tragedy?

In 1869 Ibsen wrote a significant letter to the critic George Brandes. In this letter he says:

> There is without doubt a great chasm opened between yesterday and today. We must continually fight a war to the knife between these epochs.

What Ibsen meant in this letter was that to live in the modern world is to be, in many important ways, different from anyone who ever lived before. Joseph Wood Krutch pursues this problem in his previously mentioned book, *"Modernism" in the Modern Drama*. Krutch develops his argument by pointing out that since Greek times the Aristotelian dictum that "man is a reasoning animal" had been pretty universally accepted. This view did not deny man's irrationality, but it did assert that reason is the most significant human characteristic. Man is not viewed as preeminently a creature of instincts, passions, habits, or conditioned reflexes; rather, man is a creature who differs from the other animals precisely in the fact that rationality is his dominant mode.

The modern view assumes the opposite premise. In this view men are not sane or insane. Psychology has dissolved such sharp distinctions, and the dramatist of our age has had to face the assumption that the rational is relatively unimportant; that the irrational is the dominant mode of life; and that the artist must realize, therefore, that the richest and most significant aspects of human experience are to be found in the hidden depths of the irrational. "Man tends to become less a creature of reason than the victim of obsessions, fixations, delusions, and perversions." *

It is this premise that all of the great dramatists at the end of the nineteenth century, beginning with Ibsen, had to face. How is one to live in an irrational world? How is one to give meaning to life in a world where you don't know the rules? How are human relationships to be meaningfully maintained when you can't be sure of your feelings and when your feelings can change without your knowing it? Ibsen's plays, beginning with *Ghosts,* dramatize man destroyed by trying to live rationally in such a world. But to accept irreconcilable conflict as the central fact of all life; to make dissonance rather than the harmony of reconciliation the condition of the universe is to accept as a premise a view of life which leads in drama, as in life, to a situation in which men and women, heroes and heroines, become victims in a disordered world which they have not created and which they have no moral obligation to correct.

It is this process, which began in the drama when Ibsen came to see man as victim of irrational powers, of the Trolls, over which he has no control, that leads to the sense of futility that so completely dominates a great deal of modern drama. This is the kind of futility that is expressed in the epigraph from Ecclesiastes with which I began this chapter (as it is expressed in Hemingway's novel, *The Sun Also Rises*); but is this sense of futility generative of what we traditionally associate with tragedy?

The traditional forms of tragedy are affirming in the sense that they celebrated man's ability to achieve wisdom through suffering. Such tragedy saw man as a victim, to be sure, but it also saw man as having those heroic qualities and potentialities which permitted him to endure his suffering and be significantly enlightened by them in such a way that victory was realized even in defeat.

The central conflict of *Ghosts* is not peculiar to the modern world. The disassociation of fact and value is a common theme in all tragedy. But there is a significant difference when this theme is used before Ibsen. Traditional tragedy celebrates the fact that, although most of us are incapable of it, the values men wish to live by can, if

* J. W. Krutch, *"Modernism" in Modern Drama* (Ithaca, New York, 1953), p. 22.

only for a moment, be realized through the actions of the tragic hero. It celebrates the fact that man's capacity for greatness is often expressed in the committing of an action which is horrifying and ought not to happen and yet which must happen. In this way the possibility that man's actions and his values can be in harmony is realized. This is the affirmation of tragedy; this is the meaning of the sun that resolves so many traditional tragedies. In this kind of tragedy the hero goes through the "dark night of the soul" with all its pain, suffering, doubt, and despair; but man is viewed as one responsible for and capable of action, even if that action is a grasping for the sun. Because of this fundamental difference in view, in traditional tragedy the dark night passes away and the sun also rises on the rebirth and affirmation of a new day.

This sunrise of traditional tragedy, which celebrates the "joy and meaning of life," is not the sunrise of futility. It is not the sunrise which sheds its rays as an ironic and bitter joke on a demented boy asking his equally helpless mother: "Mother, give me the sun. The sun—the sun!"

Perhaps Mrs. Alving is more tragic than Oedipus, Hamlet, or Lear; but if she is, her tragedy must be evaluated by new canons of judgment; for she differs from her predecessors in kind and not degree.

# 10

# STRINDBERG
# AND THE ABYSS

AUGUST STRINDBERG (1849–1912) is the most frequently misunderstood of all modern dramatists. It has been said of him that no writer "had a shorter distance from the blood to the ink," and it is true that in reading Strindberg we are always conscious of the terrible subjectivity of his work. His plays seem to be eruptions out of his very entrails, as if the word and the experience were one. But for all the immediacy of his style, Strindberg is an enormously complex figure, and no fixed critical formula will work when one attempts to analyze and evaluate his plays. Unlike Ibsen, who is always predictable, Strindberg is full of surprises, and one can never tell in which direction this Swedish genius is going next. He wrote over fifty plays, but there is no pattern to his development as an artist.

His career is usually broken down into three major divisions: the period 1870–1880, when, like all Scandinavian apprentice playwrights, he wrote mostly romantic historical plays; the period 1885–1890, in which he wrote his brutal contemporary naturalistic plays, works in which a tough naturalistic dialogue is combined with the poetic language of madness; and his post-Inferno and so-called expressionist period, which began in 1898 after his longest bout with insanity. But such divisions are artificial, for there is little consistency within any of these periods and no direct inner relationship among them. The only constant in the works of this man so full of paradoxes and contradictions was his terrifying intense vision. He always looked at life without blinders, but he was never able to find a completely satisfactory dramatic form in which to express this vision. All his life Strindberg sought the final answer to the meaning of life, but this quest was pervaded with a skepticism that doubted the validity of such a search.

By all odds the most interesting period in Strindberg's full career is the last. But because of its eclectic, almost schizoid nature the critics have tended to shy away from it, content to dwell on the easier plays of the middle period. And no wonder! Even a brief examination of his sixteen plays written between the years 1898 and 1902 reveals the problem for the critic. During this period he wrote the most brutal of his naturalistic dramas (*The Dance of Death,* Parts I and II), six of his greatest history plays (including *Gustavus Vasa* and *Eric XIV*), his most important religious play (*Easter*), several folk fantasies (including *The Bridal Crown*), a fascinating, almost Chekhovian melodrama of indirection (*There Are Crimes and Crimes*), and his monumental dream plays (*To Damascus,* I and II, and *A Dream Play*). There is no doubt that this was the most productive time of his career, but we are not conscious of any apparent order or progression in his writing, and there seems to be little or no formal or thematic relationship among the plays.

Probably the best known and most often related plays of this last period are *A Dream Play* (1902) and *The Ghost Sonata* (1907). That the two plays are invariably mentioned together is one of those strange quirks of literary history, since they are so profoundly different in theme, form, and technique. Of the two, *A Dream Play,* while better known, is the less effective experiment in psychic expressionism. Because of its symbolic character, the play is devilishly difficult to pin down; but it is clear that in it Strindberg is presenting, through the use of dream patterns, a picture of almost unrelieved sadness, in which the inextricable relationship of guilt and suffering is revealed as the basic condition of human existence. The play begins with the Daughter of Indra leaving her Father's side on high in order to discover the true nature of the human condition. She becomes involved with many aspects of life, and in episode after episode she has the same conclusion: "Human beings are such pitiable creatures!" The play builds up, piece by piece, tone on tone, jagged line over line, until, with a mosaic-like blend of unity from disintegration, it becomes an entirety of character, theme, and form which is held taut, at least most of the time, by a pervasive tension of mood. But the play never really comes off because the techniques of symbolism are continually in conflict with the play's single, over-riding theme. Strindberg's symbols are—and they are meant to be—allusive and elusive; and this open-ended suggestiveness is the source of the play's best moments: for instance, the poignant image of the Officer waiting year after year for a Victoria who never comes, or the stifling picture of the servant girl Christina stuffing all the cracks to keep out the cold as we witness, at the same time, the suffocation of the human spirit. These are two of the most effective scenes Strindberg ever wrote. But this jewellike quality is shattered by the author's constant reiteration of his theme.

Most critics contend that the horror at the heart of Strindberg's later plays is the existential horror of nothingness. While this idea might legitimately apply to the Chamber Plays, nothing could be more misleading when dealing with A Dream Play. There is a cause for man's pitiable condition and Strindberg not only names it, he judges it. We are not guilty just because we are born; we are guilty because we are born of woman. Always a misogynist, Strindberg's most brutal (but subtle) indictment of women appears in the final scene of A Dream Play. Just as the Daughter of Indra is preparing to return to her father, she has a brief but crucial bit of dialogue with the Poet. I am going to quote much of it here, because it is usually passed over unnoticed:

DAUGHTER: It's no easy matter being a mortal.

POET: Do you really understand that now?

DAUGHTER: Yes.

POET: Tell me, wasn't it Indra who once sent down his Son to hear the complaints of men?

DAUGHTER: Yes. And how was He received?

POET: How did He fulfill His mission, if I may answer with a question.

DAUGHTER: And I shall reply with another question. Wasn't the estate of Man bettered as a result of His visit?

POET: Bettered? Yes, a little—very little. But instead of all these questions, won't you tell me the answer to the riddle?

DAUGHTER: Yes, but what use would it be to you, since you don't believe me?

POET: I will believe you, because I know who you are.

DAUGHTER: All right, I'll tell you. At the beginning of time, before even the sun shone, Brahma, the Divine Primal Force, permitted His own seduction by Maya, the World Mother. This union of the

Divine Substance with the Substance of Earth was the Fall from Heaven. And therefore the world, life, and Mankind are no more than a mirage, an empty illusion, a dream.

POET: My dream.

DAUGHTER: A true dream—But in order to free themselves from this earthly substance, the children of Brahma sought renunciation and suffering . . . the eternal idea of suffering as the deliverer. But this impulse for suffering came into conflict with the desire for joy, for love. And now you understand what love is: the supremest joy in the greatest suffering, the sweetest contained in the most bitter. But do you understand what woman is? Woman, through whom sin and death entered into life?

POET: I understand. And the end of it all?

DAUGHTER: You already know that. The struggle between the pain of joy and the joy of pain . . . between the torment of the penitent and the pleasure of the sensualist.

POET: And the struggle?

DAUGHTER: The struggle of opposites produces power just as the struggle between fire and water brings forth steam.

POET: But peace? Rest?

DAUGHTER: Shhh. You must ask me no more, nor may I answer.

Here, in this passage, Strindberg's mother, his three wives—Siri von Essen, Freda Uhl, and Harriet Bosse—and characters like Laura (*The Father*) and Alice (*The Dance of Death*) have all been transformed into a mythic earth mother in whom the playwright finds the source of all human suffering. It can be argued that this scene has been tacked on and, thus, in no way invalidates the vision of life which informs the rest of the play. But either way, it is a flawed play; and, as we shall see presently, it suffers from an even more important structural weakness.

*The Ghost Sonata*, on the other hand, is one of the finest and most beautifully composed plays in the modern repertoire. The play was written in March of 1907 as "Opus Three" for the Intimate Theatre which Strindberg and August Falck, a young director, opened in Stockholm several months later. Following the lead taken by Max Reinhardt with his *Kammerspielhaus* in Berlin, the two men hoped to produce many of Strindberg's plays and particularly a new kind of highly concentrated, lyrical play which had the characteristics of chamber music: *Storm Weather, The Burned House, The Ghost Sonata, The Pelican,* and *The Black Glove.* The first four are closely related in theme, and *The Ghost Sonata* is certainly the greatest of them.

I doubt if anyone has characterized the Chamber Plays more succinctly and accurately than Erich Kahler has in his monumental book *Man the Measure*. There he wrote: "In the plays of the other great Scandinavian, Strindberg, especially in the Chamber Plays . . . ethical problems have been dissolved in the stagnant mire of a forced life together. Guilt can no longer be fixed, can no longer be attributed to one person or another. It is a permanent state of whole families. Individual relations and characters have lost their individual values and flow apart in a general mist of psychic decay. Even the spook of the abysses is no longer embodied—it has become omnipresent." This, then, is a disembodied drama: bizarre in its techniques, hallucinatory in style, and nerve-shattering in effect. Wordsworth called poetry "the spontaneous overflow of powerful feelings," but in the Chamber Plays we have something else: the spontaneous overflow of powerful disturbances. In them we find no value judgments, no police officers, no law courts; all that Strindberg seems to be concerned with is the creation of a drama which is capable of expressing a meaningless yet profoundly meaningful people. The characters are hollow men who cry out for help at the very moment that they reveal the insufficiency of all human solutions.

On first reading the theme of the play seems to be the struggle of good and evil. The vampire, Hummel, is presented as a power-mad demon who sucks life from others in order to sustain his own, while the student, Arkenholz, appears to be on the side of the good. He is a truth seeker, a "Sunday child," endowed with psychic perceptions, who is identified with the Milkmaid if not with Christ. But such a reading of the play is too easy. For in truth everyone is guilty, and each of the characters, not just Hummel and the Cook, is a vampire who derives sustenance from the common decay of their forced life together. There is no such thing as "the good" in the world of *The Ghost Sonata;* there is only uncharted anguish, indefinite hope, and insurmountable despair.

The play also communicates an overwhelming sense of alienation. One of the most dramatic examples of this is to be found in the ghost supper of the second scene, in which the cadaverlike guests sitting in silence and crunching in unison on their biscuits are as much an avant-garde comment on noncommunication as is

Ionesco's meaningless, mundane chatter in *The Bald Soprano*. Time and time again, Strindberg shows the limitation of words as a means of communication. Either they cannot approximate the feelings they are supposed to convey (as in the final scene with the Student and Adèle), or they are *too* successful in expressing truths that people are not ready to hear (as the Student's father must have discovered as he was being carted off to the madhouse). How can people communicate if words are, on the one hand, too ineffectual for the job, or, on the other hand, too upsetting to the sleepwalkers who prefer their illusions to the truth?

Finally, however, the real theme of the play, insofar as it can be reduced to such simple terms, is death. Everything that happens is built upon the occasion of death, and the characters are mummified creatures who move about, trancelike, in a world of absolute psychic and physical decay, a world pervaded with the stink of guilt and the rancid taste of impotence. Actual death is the only step not yet taken, but its specter hovers over the scene; and when the Mummy cries out, "Oh God, if only we could die!" we know the end is imminent. But this death is more than a release from the agony and anguish of having had to live; it is also the moment when all accounts are settled. Writing in his *Notebooks,* Strindberg states his belief: "It does indeed seem true that one doesn't get out of this life until everything has been settled, the small along with the big." But such a settling of accounts should not be misunderstood; it is not a judgment. When something is judged as evil, such a judgment involves the acceptance of a good somewhere. But everything in *The Ghost Sonata* is hopelessly evil. All of the characters are inextricably bound together by both the evils they themselves have committed and the evil which is the world. When Amelia finally condemns Hummel, her judgment belongs not to some moral world of the gods nor to the realm of some logical natural law. She speaks only as a mummy with a momentary moral aspiration dredged up from moldering memories. Her words have nothing to do with life; they have been evoked by the horrible pressures exerted by Hummel, who has briefly roused her from a state of stinking putrefaction. His guilt is hers, the Colonel's, everyone's. It is everywhere and nowhere, unidentifiable yet omnipresent.

The characters of the play are equally difficult to pin down. Ibsen's characters, like the playwright himself, achieve a tolerable accommodation with existence. Generally speaking, they pay only a nominal psychic fee for the license to exist. The characters in the Chamber Plays, on the other hand, are guilty of being alive. In some respects, as Evert Sprinchorn has pointed out, *The Ghost Sonata* is actually *Miss Julie* carried to its ultimate fulfillment. Hummel has much in common with Jean, the valet of Miss Julie's father. Both are servants who have a ruthless kind of energy which enables them to dominate the psychically crippled members of the aristocracy. Adèle is a kind of enervated Julie. Both are degenerate, and while it is true that Julie, in the virulence and vitality of her sado-masochism, is the more impressive character, the two girls are daughters of the same household. Just as Hummel is a Jean after a long career, so Adèle is the wasted counterpart of her perverted predecessor. This hyacinth girl is spiritually dead (Strindberg always equated the hyacinth with the death of the soul), the victim of her parents' sins. But she is not the only victim; all the characters, including the vampires, are the victims of the inexorable processes of dehumanization. Hummel may appear to be the villain, but he is in reality no different from the other inhabitants of the disintegrating house. Like them, he perpetuates the lie and crime of existence, and he too is destroyed. His actions make up the fabric of life, but he is caught in its web as well. In the end, each of the characters is crucified by the human condition.

On the surface *The Ghost Sonata* is deceptively simple. It is written in the naturalistic style of Strindberg's pre-Inferno plays, and in spite of the tone of unrelieved pessimism, it seems to move in a straightforward and predictable fashion. But as we experience the play more deeply, we become increasingly conscious of the fantastic complexities and intertwined incongruities which are developing within the play's simple external form. Seemingly commonplace conversations grow deeper and fouler and more perverted until finally all of the characters are blended and inextricably fused in the quagmire of their "forced life together." The play is a combination of impressionist transiency and northern light; it is made up of silences akin to Thelonious Monk's, of romantic chiaroscuro, and of blinding, bright flashes. But for all the dazzling individual effects, we must never forget the utter simplicity of the play's overall form. (Most modern productions of *The Ghost Sonata* have been failures because of a tendency on the part of directors to turn the play into a surrealistic fantasy.) Not only do the other four Chamber Plays make this point clear but, moreover, Strindberg himself does so. In a 1907 letter he wrote that a chamber play was to be "intimate in form; a simple theme treated with thoroughness; few characters; vast perspectives; freely imaginative; but built upon observations, experiences, carefully studied; simple. . . ." He went on to say in "Notes to the Members of the Intimate Theatre": "If one were to ask me the intention behind a chamber play, I would say that it is to search out the single, significant, and dominant theme and handle it with restraint. In treating it we avoid all tricks, all deliberate effects, all applause-getters, bravura roles, and set numbers." Finally, then, it is the creation of a dramatic form capable of expressing such a simple-complex vision of life which makes *The Ghost Sonata* Strindberg's great masterpiece.

What is the nature of that form?

After reading the Strindberg canon, one conclusion overshadows all others: Strindberg's whole career as a playwright was an unending quest to create a form capable of expressing his profoundly subjective concerns. And while it is true that this is a problem for every dramatist, none ever had Strindberg's difficulties because, to my knowledge, no one wrote so directly from his own insides as did this bedeviled Swede. Dramatic form is a mimetic expression, it objectifies subjective experience, and Strindberg was seeking means which were more directly expressionistic. In plays like *Miss Julie* and *The Father* he tried to achieve such directness by compressing the naturalistic form, and the Preface to *Miss Julie* describes these attempts, but he was soon dissatisfied. During the decade of the nineties he continued his search, and finally in 1901 he found a solution: the dream play. He announced his discovery in his now famous Author's Note to *A Dream Play*. This, then, was Strindberg's new aesthetic; the structure of the dream would provide a subjective organic form which would enable him to express meaning with greater immediacy.

Presently, we shall examine his two most celebrated attempts at creating this kind of play, but first we must deal with some of the larger issues related to all dream literature. To begin, we must make a clear-cut distinction between the dream as a psychical phenomenon and the dream as an art form. And further, we must realize that while a dramatist may use the techniques and contents of a dream in any fashion he chooses, he must adhere to the form of the psychical dream if the resultant play is to succeed as art. Perhaps

Freud can help us here.* In his *General Introduction to Psycho-analysis,* Freud pointed out that the psychical process which transforms subconscious images into actual dreams incorporates four stages of activity which when combined constitute dream work. These stages are condensation, displacement, visualization, and secondary elaboration. Condensation is the process in which the dreamer combines numerous apparently unrelated thoughts and people into a single complex image. "Such a composite figure," Freud wrote, "resembles A in appearance, but is dressed like B, pursues some occupation which recalls C, and yet all the time you know that it is really D." † However, this joining together of disparate images in dreams is an actual and not a metaphoric process. In a dream there are no hierarchies of significance, no levels of meaning as there are in literature. All meanings are equally literal; furthermore, a dream image, unlike a literary symbol which is open-ended and allusive, carries within itself all its meaning (including its contradictions). The second stage of dream work, displacement, involves the transfer of significance within the dream. It is the process by which the dreamer shifts the accents of his subconscious images from important to unimportant elements or vice versa, thereby giving the dream its distorted and surrealistic facade. Visualization is the process whereby all words, sounds, smells, tastes, and feelings are translated into visual images or sight responses. Finally, secondary elaboration is that aspect of dream work which provides the dream with its organic unity. It is the process, as Freud put it, whereby images combine into a "single and fairly coherent whole." In effect, what this means is that every dream is an organic psychical act which *engenders its own form.* As in a work of art, there is nothing accidental or haphazard about a dream. Dreams may or may not be expressive of external reality, but they are always completely expressive of the dreamer's own inner reality. This is not to say that the meaning of a dream may not radiate out beyond itself; but whether it does or not, finally the dream itself is a

* While it is unlikely that Strindberg knew Freud's work on dreams, I believe that most scholars of the modern theatre would agree with Eric Bentley's conclusion that "The same forces which at the close of the nineteenth century drove Freud to the study of dreams in the psychiatric field drove Strindberg toward the same study in his investigation of tragic experience." (*The Playwright as Thinker,* p. 70.)
† *General Introduction to Psychoanalysis,* p. 179.

coherent statement of what it is. Form and content are inseparable, identical, one. A dream is not a representation of something other than itself; more accurately, it is a structure of relationships in which meaning is a function of form, and form is its own meaning.

Now, when we reduce these elements of Freud's theory to their simplest terms, we see that the processes of dream work are very similar to those techniques used by the dramatist in writing a play, just as the finished play (at least ideally) will have an organic unity much like that of a dream. The playwright, like the dreamer, selects from his immediate experience, alters its contents and patterns of emphasis to fit his intention, translates it into images, and orders it into an organic whole for the stage.*

This perception brings us back to Strindberg. What is the nature of his achievement in *A Dream Play* and *The Ghost Sonata?*

So long as dreams and dream work and plays and playwriting are considered analogously no difficulties arise, but any attempt to combine these two worlds by writing dream plays (it is clear that in these plays Strindberg was interested in the dream as an art form and not as a psychic phenomenon) is a courting of disaster. And these two plays reveal both the perils and the possibilities of such attempts. In fact, I think one can go so far as to say that *A Dream Play*, although it contains some brilliant moments, fails completely as a dream play, while *The Ghost Sonata* is an eminently successful example of the form. Let us look at the two plays more closely to see if such a sweeping judgment can be substantiated.

Earlier, we said that the playwright must adhere to the form of the psychical dream if the resultant play is to succeed as art. But this is precisely what Strindberg did not do in *A Dream Play*. Although the play resembles a dream on the surface, Strindberg has actually deceived both us and himself; what we have are the techniques and events of a dream without the necessary corresponding form of a dream. Characters merge and split, age and grow young; scenes shift in kaleidoscopic fashion; symbolic leitmotifs are intricately interwoven throughout the play. But these are dream events and in transcribing them not only did Strindberg link them

---

* Freud, recognizing the similarity between these two processes, wrote: "Dreams form the raw material of poetic production; for the writer, by transforming, disguising, or curtailing them creates out of his day-dreams the situation which he embodies in his stories, novels, and dramas." (*General Introduction to Psychoanalysis*, p. 183.)

in a haphazard fashion,* but even more importantly he failed to follow the rigorous *internal* form of a dream.

In his Author's Note to the play, Strindberg stressed the fact that although many bizarre and seemingly unrelated and illogical things can take place in a dream play, it was essential that "one single consciousness governs them all." He was correct in his theory, but he failed in practice. *A Dream Play* finally fails aesthetically because there is no governing single dreaming consciousness. The form of the play is at odds with itself and the source of the trouble resides in the play's central character, the Daughter of Indra. She is first of all an observer of what is happening on earth (the dream), and therefore outside the dream; but she is also a participant in the dream events. And Strindberg is never consistent in his treatment of her, with the result that as a character she flipflops back and forth between the two roles. Conceivably, Strindberg could have split her dual function, and thereby solved his problem, by making the Daughter the objective observer (the "single consciousness") in a prologue (which he did write) and an epilogue (which he did not) that would serve as a frame for the actual dream, in which she would be a participant only. As the play now stands, however, whenever the dream content seeks to evolve its own form and enforce its coherence, it is shattered by the intrusion of the Daughter's objective point of view which immediately relates the dream world to the waking world. As long as the play's dream sequences can develop on their own terms the drama is successful, but the Daughter's constant refrain that "human life is pitiable" compels us to judge the symbolic structure objectively with the result that the symbolism loses all of its significance, and in some cases becomes downright absurd.

Because the Daughter of Indra is always shifting between her objective and subjective roles—between waking and dreaming—the play never achieves a single point of view. Furthermore, such alternation constantly calls to our attention the conflict between the objective form of her presence and the play's subjective dream content. Hence, *A Dream Play* is confusing and unbelievable, sometimes ludicrous, and most often forced. Strindberg hoped to escape

---

* This failure is in part due to Strindberg's inadequate understanding of the nature of dreams. In his Author's Note he states that "Anything can happen, everything is possible and probable" in a dream. Freud insists, and I think correctly, nothing that occurs in a dream is accidental; even the most haphazard events are organically related.

the crippling restrictions of the naturalistic theatre by moving into the freer and more expressive realm of the dream. However, in his first two attempts—*To Damascus* being the other—he succeeded in giving us only the images of dreams (the dream content) without also creating an organic, progressing, self-contained form which would make those images meaningful and relevant to our waking life. He wanted to dream, but unfortunately his sleep was continually interrupted by fits of insomnia.

In *The Ghost Sonata*, however, Strindberg employs the form as well as the contents of an actual dream and in so doing he wrote a powerful play which expressed his deep-seated subjective concerns. The major difference between this play and *A Dream Play* is the absence of a character like the Daughter of Indra. The Student Arkenholz's awareness (waking up) at the end of the play fulfills the drama, as our waking up ends our dreams, because it grows out of the play's action rather than being imposed on it. The Student brings nothing to the play except his ability to understand the dream he is about to participate in. The form, therefore, is not burdened by a waking character who constantly shatters the evolving dream narrative. The form of *The Ghost Sonata* is its content.

This form is a series of images progressing in such a way as to reveal their coherent importance to Arkenholz by the end of the play. In writing the play Strindberg uses all of the elements—condensation, displacement, visualization, and secondary elaboration— of actual psychical dream work to develop and define each of the characters, and since they are organically related within the play's dream form they have an internal and external reality about them which makes them believable. Because they do not call attention to themselves, the characters and their actions have a much greater impact upon us. Finally, fantastic and downright unbelievable things occur in *The Ghost Sonata* and we accept these exaggerations (as we cannot in *A Dream Play*) because they emerge out of the play itself; they are aspects of its form.

As Arkenholz becomes aware of what is happening in the action (actually why it is happening), he comes to understand the form of the play-dream and can, finally at the end of the play, analyze it. He says to the dying girl:

> . . . I stood there on a Sunday morning looking in. I saw a Colonel, who was no Colonel. I had a benefactor who was a thief, and had to hang himself. I saw a mummy, who was not a mummy; and I saw

a virgin . . . but tell me, what about virginity? Where does one find beauty? Where does one find honor and faith? In fairy tales and in children's fancies. Where does one find anything that fulfills its promise? In my imagination. Your flowers have poisoned me now and I have given you back the poison. I asked you to become my wife and to make a home for me—we recited poetry, sang, we played—and then the cook entered . . . *Sursum corda!*—Try just once more to strike fire and glory out of your golden harp! Try, I beg you. I implore you on my knees—but I will do it myself. (*He takes up the harp, but the strings do not sound.*)—It's deaf and dumb.—Yes, it's true: the most beautiful flowers are poisonous . . . are the most poisonous. The curse lies over all creation, over all life. Why won't you be my bride?—Because you're sick at the very source of your being. I feel that vampire in the kitchen beginning to suck at me too. She's a demon who sucks children's blood. The children of this house will always have their innermost beings corrupted in the kitchen . . . unless it has already happened in the bedroom. There are poisons that weaken the senses, and poisons that open men's eyes. I was born with open eyes, for I can't see the ugly as beautiful nor call what is evil good. I can't! Jesus' descent into hell was his wandering upon the earth, his visitation to this madhouse, this char-nelhouse that we call the earth. And the madmen he came to free have murdered him. But the thief has been freed, for one always sympathizes with thieves. Woe! Woe to us all! Savior of the world, redeem us, for we perish!

The Student is coming out of his own dream, the dream of the play, and he realizes that the dream play images are life itself and that the experience he has just had is a dream truth, not of this world, but about it. He has discovered that the events he has dreamt (seen) are the symbolic representations of what is. Thus, at the end of the play, Arkenholz has achieved the same kind of objectivity that the Daughter of Indra had, but his objectivity is not something god-given; it has been earned by his dreaming. The moment he has this kind of objectivity toward the events of the play, the dream is over—the play ends. Arkenholz's perception is the analysis of his own dream.

Thus by following the form of the psychical dream, Strindberg wrote a great play. The psychical dream rises out of the uncon-scious mind of the dreamer and represents to him in a series of sym-bolic images the problems and wishes most central to him. As such, the dream is the essence of subjective concern. Since this was the chief concern of Strindberg as a dramatist, it was probably inevitable, Strindberg being the genuine artist he was, that in his development as a playwright he would eventually discover that the form of dreams was the only one capable of adequately expressing the subjective concerns of all men at all times. All his life Strindberg was both consciously and unconsciously trying to write a dream play. He finally discovered a way to do it in his Chamber Plays, and without a doubt *The Ghost Sonata* was his greatest single achievement as a dramatist.

# THE PLAYS
# OF CHEKHOV

In our times no playwright is more respected and less understood than Anton Chekhov. For most theatre people he is like Faulkner's Miss Emily, "a tradition, a duty, and a care; a sort of hereditary obligation." His plays are thought to be moody, complex, soulful, vague, and impossible to do successfully on the American stage. For the most part, readers and audiences have agreed with that critic who, on seeing the famous Cornell-Anderson-Gordon production of *The Three Sisters* in 1942, remarked that she "could not see much sense in three adults spending four acts in *not* going to Moscow when all the time they had the price of a railroad ticket." But since then conditions have changed, and today Chekhov's plays seem to have a startling and refreshing contemporaneity; they reflect as few plays do the spirit of our time. What accounts for this belated popularity? Why, a hundred years after he was born, do we think Chekhov has something significant to say to us today?

Part of the answer lies in the fact that all of his plays reflect the mood of spiritual discouragement which permeates the anxieties of the mid-twentieth century. The conditions of our world are such that the sturdy optimism of the nineteenth and early twentieth centuries—say of a Tolstoy, for example—strikes us as an outmoded stance, if not an imposture. Most of us wonder what, if anything, can be done to resolve the apparently insoluble problems of life. All his life Chekhov, too, despaired of the fact that he was unable to answer life's important questions. "Life," he said, "is an insoluble problem." At the end of the first act of *The Sea Gull*, Dorn—one of the many doctors in Chekhov's plays—is trying to comfort the distraught and unhappy Masha, but all he can find to say is "But what can I do, my child? Tell me, what can I do? What?" This question, "What can I do?" runs like a leitmotif through all of Chekhov's works. This is the clue to Chekhov's great modernity.

Chekhov more than any dramatist of the late nineteenth and early twentieth centuries was very conscious of the existential loneliness of the human condition. In fact, the central theme of all his plays is estrangement. He was conscious of man's helplessness before the overpowering forces of circumstance; he was aware of man's littleness, his insignificance in a gigantic and impersonal universe; he knew that no matter how closely men huddled together they could never really communicate. In short, he was aware of the fact that the very conditions of life doom man to failure and that there was nothing anyone could do about it. He knew the utter impossibility of finding an answer to the question "What can I do?"

In their ontological solitude, Chekhov's characters are like those helpless travelers described by Kafka in his *Notebooks.** The train of their lives has been wrecked too; there is no continuity upon which they can depend; everything seems ludicrous and absurd, painful and hopeless. Ivanov cannot extricate himself from the morass of his lassitude; nobody succeeds in finding love in *The Sea Gull;* no one achieves his goal in *Uncle Vanya;* the sisters do not go to Moscow (and it would not have solved their problems if they had); and the cherry orchard is not saved. In short, there is nothing one can do in such a situation, and we notice increasingly, as Chekhov matures, nothing is even attempted. Ivanov's and Treplev's suicides are at least solutions, albeit negative ones, to their problems. Uncle Vanya is incapable of even such a negative solution. In *The Three Sisters* the nearest attempt is Irina's and Tusenbach's decision to get married and at least try to make a new life. But even this fails, for despite man's best efforts, a meaningless and mocking fate will destroy him even before he begins. (And we must remember that the couple's approaching marriage was not anticipated joyfully, for Irina did not love Tusenbach.) Finally, in *The Cherry Orchard* nothing is attempted. The sending of Gaev to the auction is little more than an afterthought, a pitiful reminder that

* See above, Chapter 8, p. 94.

nothing can be done, for the cherry orchard, the symbol of their lives, is doomed, no matter who owns it, from the beginning.

But this is not the whole story. If it were, Chekhov's plays would be little more than unrelieved pictures of gloom, and this we know they are not. This is so because Chekhov, in spite of his realization that man was alone and doomed to failure in all of his attempts to find meaningful relationships and meaningful action, never abdicated his sense of responsibility for human life. Even though Chekhov knew there were no solutions, all his life he sought to find an answer, and his plays are a record of that quest. Thomas Mann, in his perceptive essay on Chekhov, in *Last Essays*, was conscious of this when he wrote:

> One has to face the fact that man is a failure. His conscience, which belongs to the spirit, will probably never be brought into harmony with his nature, his reality, his social condition, and there will always be "honorable sleeplessness" for those who for some unfathomable reason feel responsible for human fate and life. If anyone ever suffered from this, it was Chekhov the artist. All his work was honorable sleeplessness, a search for the right, redeeming word in answer to the question: "What are we to do?" The word was difficult, if not impossible, to find.

This, I believe, was the central and creative tension in all of Chekhov's life and work. His own life was filled with the kind of experience that made him ever aware of the inevitability of failure and the absurdity of a man's attempts to triumph over his fate. All of his early years—and he did not have many years to live—were spent in an erosive struggle against poverty, and only shortly before he died did he achieve any kind of personal and financial independence. Finally, after years of hard work, he succeeded only to discover, before he could enjoy the fruits of his labor, that he was dying as a young man of tuberculosis. All his life was a constant and quiet search for love, and he finally seemed to have found it in his marriage with the great actress Olga Knipper. But their happiness was at best sporadic—their careers kept them apart much of the time—and was never free of the engulfing shadow of his approaching death, a death which came less than three years after they were married. The same characteristic was true of his relationship with Stanislavsky and Danchenko at the Moscow Art Theatre. Without the encouragement and support of these two men, Chekhov very likely would never have succeeded as a playwright; in fact, it is doubtful that he would have written his last three plays. But his relationship with Stanislavsky was never a happy one and was a constant source of frustration to him, for Stanislavsky never understood what Chekhov was trying to do in the theatre and "ruined" his plays in production. Finally, his approaching death itself, which Chekhov as a physician was the first to diagnose, and the reality of which, because he was a physician, he could not escape in the mists of illusion, made the playwright ever aware of the loneliness and absurdity of his own existential nature. Death, and therefore, as we shall see, life also, was not an abstraction for Chekhov. He, like all men, was born to die; but unlike most of us, Chekhov lived his life with the full awareness of his unique, dying self.

Yes, Chekhov had good reason to know that life is loneliness, failure, and absurdity, but as I said earlier, that is not the whole story and this second aspect of his life is the source of strength for the other half of that creative tension which informs his plays. Chekhov countered the reality of his death with an equally powerful weapon—his own life. He met his dying life with honesty, reserve, integrity, and simplicity; and above all, as an artist, a doctor, and a man he had great sympathy for others and an abiding respect for the dignity of human life. Chekhov's career both as a dramatist and a physician took its nourishment from a single source: his great capacity to observe and cherish life; not life as an abstraction or as an ideal, but as a doomed phenomenon of which he was a part. His tolerance, sympathy, wisdom, and his hardheaded vision made it possible for him to achieve, as few writers do, an unflinching but generous perspective on life; a perspective which is a victory over our absurdities, but a victory won at the cost of humility, and won in a spirit of charity and enlightenment. Maxim Gorky, Chekhov's younger colleague, caught some of this when he wrote of Chekhov:

> I think that in Anton Chekhov's presence every one involuntarily felt in himself a desire to be simpler, more truthful, more one's self. . . . All his life Chekhov lived in his own soul; he was always himself, inwardly free, and he never troubled about what some people expected and others—coarser people—demanded of Anton Chekhov. . . . Beautifully simple himself, he loved everything simple, genuine, sincere, and he had a peculiar way of making other people simple.

And thus we find in his plays, as in his life, a regard for his characters' pathetic destinies, and a nobility in their attempts to change or overcome that destiny. Goethe once wrote: "It occurs to me that the hope of persisting, even after fate would seem to have led us back into the state of nonexistence, is the noblest of our sentiments." And this is the quality that informs Chekhov's characters. Vanya is a ridiculous, fumbling, grumbling, ineffectual, self-pitying man, and yet we take him and his plight seriously (we must or the play would collapse); we do, I think, because for all his weakness he never loses his sense of dignity. Tusenbach is a funny little man with his three names, his ugly appearance, his pampered childishness, and his ridiculous talk about the brickyards. He knows this, and he also knows that life has no meaning and will not change. But this does not keep him from making the effort, from asserting the validity of life in the face of death. In his last speech, when he knows he is going to be shot in the duel with Solyony, when he is fully aware that just as all his dreams are about to be realized he will be deprived of them, he is still able to say:

> Really, I feel fine. I feel as if I were seeing those pine trees and maples and birches for the first time in my life. They all seem to be looking at me, waiting for something. What beautiful trees—and when you think of it, how beautiful life ought to be when there are trees like these! (*Shouts of "Halloo!" are heard.*) I've got to go. . . . Look at that tree, it's dead, but it goes on swaying in the wind with the others. And it seems to me that in the same way, if I die, I'll still have a part in life, one way or another. Good-bye, my darling. . . . (*Kisses her hands.*)

We could continue this catalogue: the three sisters themselves, Nina, Lyubov, Gaev, in fact, just about every character Chekhov ever created. But the point is this: the creative tension of Chekhov's work springs from his recognition that in all men there is a great disparity between the facts of their animal existence and the aspiring ideals by which they attempt to live. But he accepted both, and he saw the life of a man as the meaningful and at the same time pathetic, ludicrous, and tragic attempt to bridge this gap. In Chekhov's plays this conflict is seen in his characters who embody both a terrible earnestness of purpose and an awkward and ridiculous acting out of that purpose. In his own life this conflict is reflected in the very act of writing itself. For Chekhov, as Thomas Mann has pointed out:

> Work, pursued relentlessly to the end with the awareness that one has no answers to the final questions, while one's conscience pricks

one for throwing dust in the eye of the reader, remains a strange obligation in spite of all. It comes to this: One "entertains a forlorn world by telling stories without ever being able to offer it the trace of a saving truth." To poor Katya's question (in "A Tedious Tale"): "What am I to do?" one can but answer: "upon my honor and conscience, I don't know." Nevertheless, one goes on working, telling stories, giving form to truth, hoping darkly, sometimes almost confidently, that truth and serene form will avail to set free the human spirit and prepare mankind for a better, lovelier, worthier life.

One of the reasons that Chekhov's plays seem so difficult is the fact that they are so different. Until recently, at any rate, most of us went to the theatre expecting to see a story about someone doing something. In presenting that story the playwright usually makes some kind of judgment about one or more aspects of human experience: Life can be good if we are honest with ourselves (*Pillars of Society*); life is always doomed because our irrational drives are at variance with our conscious aims (*Ghosts* and a host of other plays); one's marriage is doomed if as a husband you act and react like a soldier (*Othello*), and from these judgments we are able to distill his "message." I doubt if any significant dramatist ever thought or worked in this way, but the fact is one of the things that most audiences expect of a dramatic action is that it express some kind of completion to the statement: "Life is ———!"

Shortly before he died, Chekhov's wife asked him what he thought the meaning of life was. He replied: "You ask me what life is? It is like asking what a carrot is. A carrot is a carrot, and nothing more is known." Herein lies the basic secret, both in meaning and form, of Chekhov's drama. He did not believe that "life is something"; all of his plays are expressions of the proposition that "life is." This is what he meant in his often quoted and usually misinterpreted remark about what the nature of the theatre should be:

> A play ought to be written in which the people should come and go, dine, talk of the weather, or play cards, not because the author wants it but because that is what happens in real life. Life on the stage should be as it really is and the people, too, should be as they are and not stilted.

As I pointed out in the opening chapter of this section, such an idea of the theatre has tremendous implications for the drama, and we are just now becoming fully aware of them. Chekhov, like the many who have followed him, sought to dramatize a condition; he was not interested in presenting an action in any Aristotelian sense. What is the central action of a Chekhov play? Is it Treplev's suicide? Vanya's attempted murder? The three sisters' attempt to go to Moscow? The sale of the cherry orchard? The answer in each case must be no, for these are only small parts of the plays and everything that happens in the plays is not directly related to these events. Chekhov was concerned with showing life as it is, and in life there is no central action, there are only people, discrete, isolated, and lonely people. As a result, Chekhov was the first playwright in history who sought to create in his plays a situation which would reveal the private drama that each man has inside himself and which is enacted every day in the random, apparently meaningless, and undramatic events of our common routine.

But because Chekhov is more concerned with the inner lives of his characters and is not interested in presenting an action, his plays seem lifeless, timeless, static. Such plays of "wrecked travelers" are bound to be the antithesis of an Aristotelian action. Like the characters in the novels of Kafka, Proust, and Joyce, the people in Chekhov's plays talk and plan a great deal, but they do nothing. In fact, part of each play's meaning derives from this disparity between language and action. And we notice that as he develops as a playwright, Chekhov increasingly seems to doubt the possibility of meaningful action (even negative) at all. Ivanov, Uncle George, and Treplev are able to commit suicide, but Uncle Vanya fails in his attempt at murder; in The Three Sisters and The Cherry Orchard nothing happens, and in the latter play not even a gun is fired and no one dies. All of the traditional ingredients of dramatic action—love, murder, suicide, revenge—are present in the Chekhovian drama, but they are used differently, used to serve different ends. They are not ends in themselves or plot devices to further the action but are used as indirect means of focusing our attention on the inner lives of the characters themselves.

Or again, we notice the quality of timelessness in the plays. This is a strange effect, for all of the plays are structured within a variation of an arrival-departure pattern and there is a great specificity of time in each of the plays; we are conscious of dates, ages, the passage of years, the time of day, the seasons. We know that the cherry orchard is to be sold on August 22; Irina, Masha, and Olga are respectively twenty, twenty-two, and twenty-eight at the beginning of The Three Sisters, they are twenty-four, twenty-six, and thirty-two at the end; the carnival party will be coming at nine; and the daily routine of the Serebryakov estate with "tea at eight, dinner at one, and supper in the evening" has been upset by the Professor's arrival. And yet, in spite of this frame of a time pattern, we have no real sense of time passing. Chekhov for all his apparent attention to temporal concerns has been interested only in revealing more and more fully the continually shifting and changing state of consciousness within each of the characters. And when the characters, if they do, come back momentarily to temporal reality, they shout painfully as Vanya does:

> But, my God! Why are my thoughts so entangled? Why am I so old? Why won't she understand me? I despise all that rhetoric of hers, that indolent morality, that absurd talk about the destruction of the world. . . . (*A pause.*) Oh, how I have been deceived!

Or they sob with Irina:

> Where . . . Where has it all gone? Where is it? Oh, God! I've forgotten. I've forgotten everything. . . . Everything's so confused . . . I don't remember the Italian for "window" or for "ceiling". . . . Every day I'm forgetting more and more, and life's slipping by, and it will never, never return. . . .

"Where has it all gone?" and in between these moments of painful discovery, they have not been concerned with time. Most of Chekhov's characters are like the three sisters, ageless and no age at all. Only those characters whose inner life Chekhov was not interested in revealing are conscious of time and change. The Natashas, Lopahins, and Yashas for the most part live only in the world of events and appointments to be kept; they make things happen, they are interested in time. Natasha asks what time it is; Lopahin is constantly looking at his watch. But most of the characters in Chekhov's world have no sense of time; as Kulygin points out to the three sisters, their clock "is seven minutes fast."

Further, Chekhov made it quite clear that what his characters do want in time is really nothing at all, only an illusion: Astrov's planting of forests, Nina's achievement on the stage, Serebryakov's articles, Irina's desire for work and dreams of true love, Vershinin's happiness in two or three hundred years, the trip to Moscow, finally the cherry orchard itself. If the orchard means so much to Lyubov, why does she do so little to save it? The fact is that Lyubov loves the orchard and at the same time does not care about it at all. It is her life, but her life is meaningless. The orchard is at once the great cause, and nothing at all. All of Chekhov's characters finally arrive at that point where their most deep-felt needs are nothing, that existential nothingness which confronts Kafka's wrecked travelers. They want to be free of time; in fact, they wish to be free of life itself.

Finally, what it all boils down to is this: for Chekhov to show "life as it is," each of his characters must be defined by his solitude and estrangement from life and not by his participation in life. Each man's existence is ultimately solitary, and his unique self can only be known, if it ever can, only after all of his social contexts have been stripped away. And yet, although this may be true, no man can exist in the vacuum of self, albeit Chekhov's characters try to. Each of them attempts to build and then operate in his own little world, with no sense of social responsibility, totally unaware of the sufferings of others. Each character has his own thoughts and problems with which he is usually morbidly consumed. As a result, the people in Chekhov's plays never seem to hear or notice one another. Each has room only for himself and each acts in a social vacuum. And yet it is not always easy to keep the walls of these private worlds from breaking down. We notice that Chekhov generally sets his characters in restricted areas. The interiors are always closely confined rooms; the exteriors are usually attached to the house or are nearby. For this reason, if none other, Chekhov's characters are always in contact with each other and it is sometimes difficult to maintain a complete self-centeredness. As a result, each of his characters must have one or more protective escapes to which he can resort if too much is demanded of him. The plays are filled with escapes from social reality; for some it is drinking, for others, like Sonya, it is blind religious belief; for Vanya it is sleep; for Astrov it is beauty; for Gaev it is billiards and gum drops; for Andrey it is his violin, his books, his gambling; and for many it is work. No matter what the nature of the escape may be, they are all means whereby Chekhov's characters can return to their own little private worlds when outside demands become too great.

But Chekhov did not stop here. If he had, his characters would be little more than selfish and unattractive. And although we know this is true of them, we also know they are more than that. Chekhov's most profound insight was that in addition to knowing that each man is alone and that he seeks to maintain his solitude, he also knew that for each man solitude is unbearable. Man is aware that finally he is alone in the universe and that he is incapable of being alone. The essential drama of the human condition as it is expressed in Chekhov's plays lies in this tension between the uncertainty of each man's relationship to others and the uncertainty of his relationship to himself.

As we indicated earlier, Chekhov's plays are different from most plays we are accustomed to seeing or reading, and we suggested that this was because he was attempting to say something different and this required new dramatic forms and techniques. Therefore, we must now say something about certain dominant aspects of Chekhov's dramaturgy. From the very beginning we are faced with a difficult problem: it is impossible to use any of the usual procedures of dramatic criticism—narrating the plot line, describing the characters, thematic analysis—because the texture and density of a Chekhovian play defies such methods. The structure of a Chekhovian play is epiphanic; its purpose is to reveal—literally, "to show forth"—the "is-ness" of the inner lives of his characters. In such a drama the plot is replaced by a single situation. Chekhov then takes this situation and develops it concentrically, like a series of inscribed but tangential circles. For example, in *The Cherry Orchard* the situation at the beginning of the play is simply that Lyubov has arrived home because the cherry orchard is to be sold; at the end of the play the orchard has been sold and everyone leaves. Nothing happens really, the situation is single and static; but in the four acts in which the situation takes one, and the only one, forward step, Chekhov has revealed a great deal about the way "life is" for twelve people as they are related to that situation. It is, in short, a drama of context, not direction.

This is a new kind of drama and the devices which Chekhov used to create it and achieve meaning through it will appear by traditional standards to be untheatrical or, to use the language of his present-day followers, "anti-theatrical." And yet, as we pointed out earlier, Chekhov does use the techniques of the earlier realistic drama; only he uses them for different reasons and in different ways. It is quite proper, therefore, that his plays have been called "dramas of indirection."

Before examining the techniques of indirection, however, I should like to make one more point. In discussing the use of time in the plays, we noticed that there was a great specificity about time. This is but one example of the great specificity which informs Chekhov's drama, and this fact does much to account for the enduring quality of his art. The biggest danger that faces an artist when he is dealing with man's inner life is that in his presentation of that life he will of necessity become too private, too personal, too subjective, since such a life is the ultimate in subjectivity; but subjectivity tends to cancel out all communication. If, as Chekhov maintains, all men are solitary and ultimately unknowable, how can the equally solitary reader or member of an audience enter into the private worlds that are being presented on the stage? How and why should they have relevance for us? Who really cares, except perhaps our psychiatrist, about the *psyche* of another, and even if we might care, how can we ever comprehend it? I believe Chekhov does much to overcome this problem—and it is a lesson that many contemporary playwrights would do well to learn—by enclosing his subjective "actions" in an objective frame of specific external details. He was trying to capture the private inner lives of each of his characters, but he did it by means of those everyday events, objects, and expressions that as human beings, in all places and in all times, each of us shares. Chekhov was the great observer, and his plays are filled with the details of his observation. As a man Chekhov cared deeply for all of his fellow human beings; as an artist he always maintained complete objectivity. It is the fusion of these two characteristics that makes his plays great and, more important, makes them work as plays.

Keeping in mind, then, that all of Chekhov's plays are framed in great specificity of detail, what are some of the techniques of indirection which he employed to reveal the inner lives of his characters? The most obvious was his refusal to use the big scene, the stereotyped dramatic situation. There are no "obligatory" scenes or great dénouements in a Chekhov play. Traditionally, such scenes were used to reveal through action the truth about a play's central characters. But for Chekhov, the truth is not dramatic in this way nor is it necessarily full of consequence; more likely, it is quite commonplace. We are accustomed to the "big" scenes and have come to expect them; when Chekhov refuses to give them to us we feel cheated. But Chekhov was not trying to fulfill our conditioned expectations and responses, he was showing "life as it is." We are moved by Othello's "Soft you; a word or two before you go" as his universe crashes down upon him, but in life our universes, if they do cave in, do not usually do so quite so dramatically; rather such times are hushed and of no great consequence to most people. So *The Sea Gull* ends with Dorn taking Trigorin aside and quietly telling him: "The fact is, Konstantin Gavrilovich has shot himself. . . ."

But the very muted and underplayed quality of the scene is precisely what gives it its effect. It may not be as theatrically exciting as Hedda Gabler's suicide, for instance, but it is much truer to life and in the long run its impact upon us is probably more lasting and horrible. Chekhov had a great distrust of the artificiality of the conventional big curtain scenes of the well-made play, and his work shows that he gradually discarded it altogether. In his early plays (*Platonov, Ivanov,* and *The Wood Demon* are for the most part structured according to the conventions of the well-made play) he uses the big curtain. For example in *Ivanov,* Act I ends with Anna's decision to follow her husband to the Lyebedevs', Act II ends with her discovery of Ivanov and Sasha in each other's arms, Act III with Ivanov's brutal revelation to his wife that she is soon to die, and Act IV with Ivanov's suicide. But Chekhov gradually came to see that such scenes were phony and while he was working on *The Wood Demon* he wrote:

> The demand is made that the hero and the heroine should be dramatically effective. But in life people do not shoot themselves, or hang themselves, or fall in love, or deliver themselves of clever sayings every minute. They spend most of their time eating, drinking, or running after women or men, or talking nonsense. It is therefore necessary that this should be shown on the stage.

*The Sea Gull* is the first play to manifest this change of attitude. The suicide is still there, but, as we have shown, it was used in a very different way. The only "dramatic" event in *Uncle Vanya* is Vanya's botched attempt to shoot Serebryakov near the end of the third act. In *The Three Sisters* Tusenbach is shot by Solyony in a duel, but his death is off stage and the shot is muffled. Finally, in *The Cherry Orchard* none of the traditional dramatic events take place and even the sad departure of Lyubov and Gaev is undercut by the final appearance of the bumbling Feers. But more important than the gradual elimination of such theatrically effective scenes is the fact that when Chekhov uses them they are no longer ends in themselves but rather they serve as pointers to the more powerful, albeit less theatrical, drama that is taking place within the characters who are on the stage. By underplaying the big, exciting, dramatic events we are better able to see the drama and the complexity of the seemingly trivial, the inconsequential, and the simple that is the very tissue of the human situation. Chekhov had learned well the wisdom of *Hamlet:* "By indirections find directions out."

Chekhov's use of obligatory scenes, then, was ironic, and this leads us to another aspect of his dramaturgy. Throughout his life Chekhov constantly made the statement that "the truth about life is ironical," and since he was showing "life as it is," almost all his dramatic devices were ironic. This is best seen in the disparity between what his characters say and what they do. Thus we find in all of his plays characters making brilliantly incisive remarks about themselves and other people, and yet they are said in such a way and are put in such an incongruous and ludicrous context that we do not stop to take them seriously when we hear them. The force of these statements is driven home cumulatively; we are suddenly aware as the play ends that the characters have done just the opposite in their actions to what they have expounded they should do in their dialogue. These flashes of self-revelation have been more than static, isolated, and disconnected statements of opinion; despite all their apparent ludicrousness, they have become ironically true. Thus, Yelena says to Sonya in the second act of *Uncle Vanya:* "You mustn't look at people that way. It isn't right. You must trust and believe in people, (*pause*) or life becomes impossible." Even at this point in the play we know that this is precisely what Yelena does not do. We tend to laugh at the incongruity of the situation; but as we leave the theatre our stomachs begin to squirm as the truth of her statement begins to sink in. Look at Yelena and one can see in dramatic terms just how impossible life can really become. But Chekhov has achieved his effect indirectly.

We find something similar in the third act of *The Cherry Orchard,* when Trofimov is telling Lyubov: "You mustn't worry, and above all you mustn't deceive yourself. For once in your life you must look the truth straight in the face." To be sure, Trofimov has spoken the truth about Madame Ranevsky, but it tells us very little about the Russian equivalent to our perpetual graduate student. After all, it is easy for almost anyone to make that observation about Lyubov (Lopahin has been telling her the same thing from the beginning of the first act); what is more important in the scene is how Trofimov reacts when Lyubov rebuffs him: "This is dreadful. . . . I can't stand it. I'm going. . . . (*Goes out, but returns at once.*) Everything's over between us!" By exaggerating (one of Chekhov's chief ironic techniques) his reaction, Chekhov points up the melodramatic quality of his exit and in so doing shows Trofimov as a comic butt. He underscores this by having Trofimov run out of the room and fall down the stairs in the midst of a chorus of laughter.

Or, to take a final example of this kind of ironic disparity between speech and action, let us look briefly at Treplev in *The Sea Gull.* Treplev is a typical adolescent writer; today we find his counterpart taking courses in creative writing and going to "writing workshops" in the summer. (Chekhov makes this clear by contrasting him to Trigorin, who, although not great, is a good craftsman.) We learn of Treplev's ideals when he attacks the theatre:

> But in my opinion our theatre's in a rut. It's nothing but clichés and shopworn conventions. When the curtain opens on those three-walled "living rooms," and I see those famous and talented actors, those high priests of that sacred art, parade about in their costumes in front of the footlights showing the way people eat, drink, make love, and walk about; when I hear them try to squeeze a moral out of commonplace phrases and meaningless events—some cliché that everyone knows and is suitable for home consumption; when they give me a thousand variations of the same old thing over and over again. . . . I have to leave! . . . we need new forms, and if we can't have them, then it's better to have nothing at all!

Now all this may be true, but the fact that he says it does not make him a playwright. That Treplev is a bad writer is made very clear when his own play is produced:

> Men, lions, eagles, and partridges, horned deer, geese, spiders, and the silent fish of the deep, starfish and creatures which cannot be seen by the eye—all living things, all living things, all living things, having completed their cycle of sorrow, are now extinct. . . . I am alone. Once in a hundred years I open my lips to speak, and then my voice echoes mournfully in the void, unheard by all. . . . You, too, pale spirits do not hear me.

This is drivel (it seems to foreshadow the plays of the bad expressionists) and the disparity between what Treplev says about the theatre and what he writes for it is part of Chekhov's point. I think, as much as anything, it is Treplev's recognition of this fact that drives him to suicide. (But already I am aware that such analysis

as this has falsified the significance of his death, for it tends to reduce the many interlocking meanings of the play to a single action.)
We notice just before Nina's final appearance that the young writer
is struggling over a description of moonlight:

> And the description of the moonlight is no good either. Trigorin's
> worked out his own techniques, so it comes easily for him . . . He'd
> just mention the neck of a broken bottle glittering in a mill stream
> and the black shadow of the mill wheel—and he's got a moonlight
> night. But for me it's the shimmering light, the silent twinkling of
> the stars, and the distant sounds of a piano, dying away in the still,
> fragrant air . . . It's terrible!

We know from a letter written by Chekhov to his brother Alexander
in 1886 that the playwright approved of the "Trigorin method," for
in that letter he uses word for word the example of the moonlit
night that appears in Konstantin's speech. And, finally, as Nina
leaves him, she not only confesses that she still loves Trigorin but
she also goes out the door reciting the lines of Treplev's ill-fated
play. The final truth about Konstantin Treplev is very sad and
pathetic, but it has been revealed to us indirectly by the ironic devices of Chekhov's method.

We have already indicated that Chekhov often achieves his irony
by the use of an undercutting speech. Such a device does much to
give the plays their comic quality (we shall discuss the nature of
Chekhov's comedy presently), but it also is a means whereby Chekhov can reveal some truth about the inner lives of his characters.
For instance, in the first act of *Uncle Vanya*, Vanya has been argu-
ing with his mother and he is finally shut up. An awkward pause
follows, and to relieve the tension of this pause Yelena remarks:
"What a fine day! Not too hot." Vanya self-pityingly replies: "Yes,
a fine day to hang oneself!" This line is immediately followed by
Marina's coming in to look for the chickens. She says: "Here chick,
chick, here chick." In her world, in which she is doing her job, this
is a perfectly logical line; however, coming as it does immediately
after Vanya's ironic self-dramatizing, it is not only immensely funny
but it acts as a commentary on Vanya's line. The result is a kind of
grotesque humor which makes us laugh with a lump in our throat.
It is funny until we realize the total implications of our laughter.

We find much the same thing in the opening of *The Cherry
Orchard.* Lyubov has just arrived and she is gushing about her "dear,

beautiful nursery," Gaev is talking about efficiency, and exactly at this point Charlotta, in a conversation with Pishchik, announces that "my dog eats nuts, too." In short, all this talk is just so much gabble. Or to take a final example, in the opening scene of *The Three Sisters* Olga and Irina are talking about how wonderful it would be to go back to Moscow. Tusenbach, Chebutykin, and Solyony are carrying on their own conversation in the adjoining room; we catch only snatches of their talk, but notice how Chekhov uses it:

> OLGA: I wanted so much to go home again. Go home to Moscow!
> CHEBUTYKIN (*sarcastically to* SOLYONY): A small chance of that!
> TUSENBACH (*also to* SOLYONY): Of course, it's nonsense.

A few lines later the dialogue goes as follows:

> IRINA: Go to Moscow! Sell the house, leave everything here, and go back to Moscow.
> OLGA: Yes, to go back to Moscow! As soon as possible.
> (CHEBUTYKIN *and* TUSENBACH *laugh.*)

No more need be said; from the beginning of the play the sisters' talk of returning to Moscow is an idle dream, but it has been shown to us by the ironical device of the undercutting speech.

I should like to point out one more ironic device. It is a commonplace that Chekhov's characters are addicted to making speeches. Gaev makes a speech to the bookcase; Trofimov is constantly carrying on about the "brave new world" that is approaching; Vershinin and Tusenbach, when they have nothing better to do, philosophize; Vanya is continually making speeches; and so on. But, beginning with Stanislavsky, many interpreters of Chekhov have missed the point of this speechifying. T. S. Eliot was very perceptive on this point when he wrote in his essay "Rhetoric and Poetic Drama":

> Speechmaking in a play can serve useful dramatic ends. Genuine rhetoric is a device of great effect when it occurs in situations where a character in a play *sees himself* in a dramatic light. In plays of realism we often find parts which are never allowed to be consciously dramatic, for fear, perhaps, of their appearing less real. But in actual life, in many of those situations in actual life which we enjoy consciously and keenly, we are at times aware of ourselves in this way, and these moments are of very great usefulness to dramatic verse. They are valuable because they give us a new clue to the character, for we discover the angle from which he views himself.

"We discover the angle from which he views himself"—not the way we see him, or the other characters see him, or the playwright sees him. Thus by contrasting the way the characters see themselves with what they do and with the way the other characters view them, Chekhov, again by indirection, is able to reveal the way life really is.

A few words should probably be said about Chekhov's use of symbols. It has often been noted that the modern drama, beginning with Ibsen, has been increasingly dependent upon nonverbal symbolism and the imagery of inanimate objects (what Cocteau refers to as "poetry of the theatre") to achieve emotional depth within theatrical conventions which are, for the most part, committed only to external reality. Ibsen, beginning with *A Doll's House* and *Ghosts*, and most explicitly in *The Wild Duck*, used symbols to give a metaphoric meaning that a predominantly naturalistic theatre denied him. Chekhov also used this kind of symbolism, but in a fashion different from his contemporaries (or, indeed, those that followed him). Unlike Ibsen's "ghosts," Chekhov's symbols are never abstractions, nor are they simply analogous to the play's action; they are always concrete, they are a part of the life of the people in his plays; in a word, they are organic to the texture and meaning of the play. Nor, like the "wild duck," are they bizarre superimpositions on the action. (I believe the wild duck symbolism works, but the Ekdal attic stretches conventions of naturalistic verisimilitude almost to the breaking point. What is more crucial, one has the feeling that the wild duck metaphor existed prior to the writing of the play, as a kind of symbolic framework, and that Ibsen then created an action to fit the frame.) There are big, almost all-inclusive symbols—the sea gull, Astrov's forests, Moscow, the cherry orchard—in a Chekhovian play, and these symbols do give meaning and depth to large segments of the plays of which they are a part. But these extending symbols are effective because they grow out of the action and are not imposed upon it, and, more important, because they rest upon the less noticeable but more significant symbolic underpinning of the whole play. For example, Moscow is the symbol of the three sisters' dream of happiness. This we know is an illusion and their belief in this illusion shows how out of touch with reality they are. And yet the play is filled with less obvious symbols that make it clear that everyone in the play, with the exception of Natasha, has to some degree lost touch with reality. These lesser symbols support the overarching Moscow symbol and, what is more, give it its organic quality. To point out but one instance, as the play opens Irina is celebrating her birthday (more exactly the anniversary of her baptism) and old Dr. Chebutykin, who perhaps more than all the others has lost touch with reality, with great ceremony brings Irina her present—a silver samovar. Everyone gasps, and with protestations of "you shouldn't have done it" and "it costs too much money," the incident is dropped as quickly as possible. The point is that in Russia a silver samovar is the traditional gift of a husband to his wife on their silver wedding anniversary. Nothing could have more effectively nor more completely shown just how out of touch with reality the doctor had become; nor, we might add, have revealed the lifetime of pain and disappointment that was the result of Irina's mother's decision to marry Brigadier General Prozorov rather than young Dr. Chebutykin.

In *Uncle Vanya* we notice how Chekhov uses a symbol to achieve another effect. Several of the plays have references to the watchman's rattle or stick. In nineteenth-century Russia the watchman would go about the estate clacking his sticks, much as our present-day night watchmen make the rounds with clock and key; the purpose of this was both to frighten any prowlers that might be about and to let the members of the household know that they were being protected. But Chekhov did not include this effect for verisimilitude alone; he also used it as a thematic symbol.\* Such is the use of the watchman at the end of the second act of *Uncle Vanya:* Yelena and Sonya have just had an honest talk with each other and because of it they are capable of feeling. The windows are open, it has been raining, and everything is clean and refreshed. Yelena thinks she can play the piano again; as Sonya goes to get permission, the watchman's rattle is heard: Yelena has to shut the window—the source of refreshment—and Serebryakov says "no." Their whole life of feeling has been so protected by the "watchmen" of their lives that they have no feelings left.

There are countless examples such as these in the plays. All of Chekhov's symbols have this same kind of organic quality; they

---

\* Chekhov did not believe in verisimilitude for its own sake. He was constantly quarreling with Stanislavsky over just this point. The famous director was always trying to introduce realistic touches—the croaking of frogs, the barking of dogs, crying children—that served no organic function in the play. When Stanislavsky defended his actions by saying that such effects did occur in real life, Chekhov replied: "Quite true, but the stage demands a certain amount of convention. You have no fourth wall, for instance. Besides, the stage is art; the stage reflects the quintessence of life. Nothing superfluous should be introduced on the stage."

deepen and enhance the play's meaning, but more importantly they too serve as a means of pointing, indirectly, to that inner drama which is at the heart of each of the plays.

There is one more aspect of Chekhov's art which I should like to discuss: the tendency on the part of his characters to aestheticize life. All of the people in Chekhov's plays are shown to be either consciously or unconsciously aware of their own inadequacies as people. They realize that in one way or another they have failed as human beings, and they therefore attempt to make their lives like the more perfect world of art. This desire to identify with art manifests itself in various ways. The most obvious is the tendency on the part of several of the characters to identify with great artists of the past or with great heroes from literature. Serebryakov as he suffers from the pains of old age and a life of retirement (not to mention the probable realization that his life and work as a scholar may have been as meaningless as Vanya says it was), identifies with Turgenev, when he says at the opening of the second act of *Uncle Vanya:* "They say Turgenev got heart trouble from gout. I'm afraid I'm getting it too." In *The Three Sisters,* Solyony is constantly insulting and antagonizing people because he feels inferior to them. In a quiet moment with Tusenbach, whom he later kills, he confesses: "When I'm alone with someone, I'm all right, I'm just like everybody else. When I'm in a group of people, I get depressed and shy, and . . . I talk all sorts of nonsense." This shy captain wears the mask of Lermontov—he is always quoting the Russian Byron; he has been in several duels; and he will brook no rivals in love. Vanya, unable to stand the final disillusionment of his life's work, shouts: "My life's ruined! I'm gifted, I'm intelligent, I'm courageous. . . . If I'd had a normal life, I might have become a Schopenhauer, a Dostoyevsky. . . ." Finally, in *The Sea Gull,* Treplev, out of the despair of his mother's rejection, identifies himself with Hamlet.

This aestheticizing tendency is also seen in the way Chekhov's characters are more conscious of *how* they say things than what they say. In the third act of *The Cherry Orchard,* Epihodov says to Varya: "I wish you'd express yourself more delicately." He does not care what is said so long as it is said beautifully. Or, in *The Three Sisters,* Vershinin has just made one of his typical speeches about how beautiful life will be in two or three hundred years, and Irina, oblivious to the meaning of what he has said, says with a sigh: "Really, someone should have written all that down."

The desire for beautiful expression is directly related to the many quotations and literary allusions which we find in the plays. There are quotations from Shakespeare, Pushkin, Krylov, Lermontov, and Gogol, to name but a few, and allusions to Ostrovsky, Balzac, Batyushkov, and Turgenev. Chekhov's characters are always quoting and talking—in short, finding comfort in words. They are attempting to give a meaning to their otherwise empty and meaningless lives through words by giving their words artistic form.

Finally, and most profoundly, the aestheticizing of life is carried to its limit by those characters who seek to make their own lives into works of art. Consider Astrov's remarks about Yelena in the second act of *Uncle Vanya:*

> In a human being, everything ought to be beautiful: face and dress, soul and thoughts. She is very beautiful, there's no denying it, but, after all, all she does is eat, sleep, go for walks, fascinate us by her beauty and—nothing more. She has no duties, other people work for her.

Later, he says to Sonya:

> I am old, tired, unimportant; my feelings are dead. I could never care for anyone again. I don't love anyone, and I don't think I shall ever love anyone. The only thing that appeals to me is beauty. I just can't remain indifferent to it. If, for example, Yelena wanted to, she could turn my head in a day.

Finally, he forces the affair with Yelena; his outburst is not one of physical passion but a reaction to her beauty which culminates in his asking her to keep a tryst in a beautiful forest arbor. We are reminded of Hedda Gabler's request that Lovborg shoot himself beautifully—through the head. Thus the man who has failed, who is incapable of loving anyone, attempts to substitute an erotic picture of idyllic love for a mature and demanding relationship. It is a relationship that is symbolized by the "autumn roses" Vanya brings to Yelena; such roses, like all the love affairs in Chekhov's plays, are very beautiful, but they discolor and disintegrate the moment they are touched.

This tendency is most fully developed in Trofimov in *The Cherry Orchard.* Like Astrov, he has become a walking vegetable, an emotional turnip. He loves life and the beauties of nature, but he hates anything animal or physical. Thus his whole relationship with Anya is vegetative. He wants to look at her, but even the slightest trace of physical desire is repulsive. "We are above love," he says. He cannot accept the responsibility of human animal existence and must escape into the ideal world of art which is bloodless but extremely beautiful. This, then, is but another of the dramatic processes of indirection which Chekhov employs to reveal the absorbing drama of "life as it is," as opposed to the tendency toward statement which is so prevalent in the modern theatre.

Finally, something must be said about Chekhov and comedy. Critics are continually telling us that Chekhov is funny, and also we know that both *The Sea Gull* and *The Cherry Orchard* were called comedies by their author, and that he conceived none of his plays (despite Stanislavsky's interpretations) as tragedies. But Chekhov's plays are so unlike most of the comedies we know that we are not sure we should trust even the author's assurances that they are. Perhaps a better way of understanding what is meant when Chekhov is referred to as a comic writer is to recall that he was writing a drama that was to show "life as it is." Another way of describing "life as it is" is expressed in Santayana's already quoted statement that "Everything in Nature is lyrical in its ideal essence, tragic in its fate, and comic in its existence." This provides a very important insight into the form of Chekhovian drama, and it also accounts for the complex overtones that are present in the plays, for Chekhov's characters respond to all three of Santayana's levels with an especial intensity. They are comedians by necessity, smitten with a tragic sense of life, lyrically in love with the ideal in a world poorly equipped to satisfy such aspirations.

The essential quality of the "is-ness" of life is, as we said earlier, its absurdity, its futility. Some would argue that this is tragic, perhaps the most tragic condition of all, but as Dorothy Sayers has wisely pointed out: "The whole tragedy of futility is that it never succeeds in achieving tragedy. In its blackest moments it is inevitably doomed to the comic gesture." Thus, when man comes to see his existence as absurd, that it is governed by the irrational, the inexplicable, and the nonsensical, he moves into the realm of the comic. For comedy presupposes such a world, a world being made and turned upside down. As Gautier put it, "Comedy is the logic of the absurd," and thus it can admit the disorderly and the improbable into the realm of art. Chekhov was aware that the fragmentary, schizoid life that each of us lives is an existential comedy. His plays suggest that man lives in the midst of so many irreconcilable forces, both within and without, that the only way life can be given form in art is in comedy. But it is a special kind of comedy, a grotesque kind of comedy, which makes us, as I said earlier, laugh with a lump in our throats. This is so because for all its awareness of the absurdity of experience, it is also extremely conscious of the suffering, struggle, and failure of experience. Christopher Fry wrote in his essay "On Comedy," previously referred to in Part I:

> I know that when I set about writing a comedy the idea presents itself to me first of all as tragedy. The characters press on to the theme with all their divisions and perplexities heavy about them; they are already entered for the race to doom, and good and evil are an infernal tangle skinning the fingers that try to unravel them. If the characters were not qualified for tragedy there would be no comedy, and to some extent I have to cross the one before I can light the other. In a century less flayed and quivering we might reach it more directly; but not now unless every word we write is going to mock us.

Chekhov, I think, would have seen the applicability of Fry's remarks to his plays, for they too contain such a vision of life. And yet, somehow, I am not content to stop here. Traditionally, we think of tragedy as a form which celebrates man's capacity to suffer and aspire even though he is doomed to destruction by the inexorable workings of fate. Comedy, on the other hand, celebrates, as I have said, man's capacity to endure. It is *terribly* conscious of the resilience of the human spirit. Fry, in the essay just quoted, distinguished the two forms in this way:

> The difference between tragedy and comedy is the difference between experience and intuition. In the experience we strive against every condition of our animal life: against death, against the frustration of ambition, against the instability of human love. In the intuition we trust the arduous eccentricities we are born to, and see the oddness of a creature who has never got acclimatized to being created.

Perhaps this explains the mysterious quality of affirmation that we sense in Chekhov's plays. There have been many playwrights in the modern theatre who were conscious of the doomed nature of human experience, but I know of none who accepted this fact and still had such trust in the enduring qualities of those "arduous eccentricities we are born to" as did Anton Chekhov.

# 12

# CHARACTER AS DESTINY IN HOFMANNSTHAL'S ELECTRA

As AN artist Hugo von Hofmannsthal was always violent in his reaction against materialism in philosophy and naturalism in art. Even
as a young man, living in the morally debilitated pre-World War I
city of Vienna, Hofmannsthal saw the limitations of an art which
was committed to an external view of reality. Naturalism in the
drama, with its convention of environmental credibility, from the
time of Hebbel, Becque, Hauptmann, and Ibsen (up to *The Wild
Duck*) had tended to show life as it existed on the surface; it was
all too often sociological in its orientation and failed to capture the
multiple complexities of man's inner life. It was because of this very
ordinariness, this exactitude of truth to life, that Hofmannsthal
turned to Symbolism, the shrine of all the disenchanted young poets
and dramatists of his time.

The symbolists' ideal was a poetry of *Stimmung*. Their poetry
was often exotic and usually esoteric, but so long as it was inward
and cultured, and avoided contamination with the rawness and
crudities of the external social milieu of the time, it served the symbolists' purposes. Their aim was to recapture that musical intensity
which is present to some degree in all art, but which was completely lost in the arid and sterile atmosphere of the sociological

plays and novels. Walter Pater was the leading critic and spokesman of this movement in its rebellion against naturalism. His dictum about all the arts "aspiring towards the conditions of music" sprang from his sensitive diagnosis of the condition of art at that time, and it became the credo of many artists. Hofmannsthal was one of them. Like Strindberg, he was moved by the music of Debussy and influenced by the paintings of Gauguin and Van Gogh. In a similar way the symbolist poets, particularly Mallarmé, Valéry, and Stefan George influenced the young Viennese playwright. Hofmannsthal came to believe, under these influences, that human experience is so complex that words can never express and explain it; that life can only be approached obliquely by the indirect method of symbols. As a result, Hofmannsthal rejected most of Ibsen's drama as too exact and precise for symbols and sought in his own plays to achieve the lyrical suggestiveness of music.

Hofmannsthal's early lyric dramas fit very well into this atmosphere of *Stimmung*. But all too often critics have mistakenly held that symbolism is the predominant characteristic of his drama and that his plays, therefore, are more lyrical than dramatic. This is a mistake, for Hofmannsthal thought of the theatre primarily in dramatic and not symbolical terms. By the turn of the century he had realized that although symbols could be used to heighten and deepen the implications of naturalistic drama, they also led to an ambiguity, an abstractness, and an allusiveness which the theatre could not control and express. In this connection one is reminded of Hedwig's words to her mother at the end of the second act of *The Wild Duck:*

> GINA: Wasn't that queer talk about wanting to be a dog?
> HEDWIG: Do you know, mother, I believe he [Gregers] meant something quite different by that.
> GINA: Why, what should he mean?
> HEDWIG: Oh, I don't know; but it seemed to me he meant something different from what he said—all the time.

If what Hedwig says is true, if everything that is explicit really means something else, then the drama either loses touch with reality or it becomes so diffuse that it can communicate only in a private and personal way rather than in the communal way that the theatre requires.

It is for this reason, despite his lyrical tendencies and the fact that he was strongly influenced by the symbolist ideals of verse, that Hofmannsthal ultimately broke with many writers of his generation who included a social art like the theatre in the world they rejected. After *Death and the Fool* (1893), in which he repudiates the aestheticism of the symbolists, Hofmannsthal's work is a continuing effort to achieve a theatrical form which would combine the symbolists' rich and colorful language with an action that was dramatically rather than lyrically conceived.

In his quest for a new dramatic form Hofmannsthal was never attracted to naturalism. In fact, in his *Book of Friends,* a collection of aphorisms from his notebooks, he defined the weakness of naturalistic writers with great clarity. "Naturalism distorts Nature because by copying the surface it has to neglect the wealth of inner relatedness—Nature's real mysterium." Hofmannsthal more fully describes his attitude toward objective reality as it affects the theatre in a brief essay entitled "The Theatre as Illusion." The principal thought expounded in this essay is not that the external world is "unreal" in any Platonic sense, but that it is, while real enough, too insipid, too uninspiring, too barren to be portrayed on the stage.

This attitude toward the theatre had already been strongly advanced by Strindberg. The Swedish dramatist, in advocating "sensational naturalism," believed the playwright should dramatize those moments of greatest crisis and tumult in people's lives in order to see how such people really acted. In his Preface to *Miss Julie,* Strindberg writes: "Misunderstood naturalism believed that art consists in reproducing a piece of nature in a natural way. But, the greater naturalism seeks out the points where great battles take place." By using only the moments of "crisis" in the lives of his characters as his dramatic material, Strindberg's naturalistic plays were filled with sensational episodes. But this is a sensationalism of convention. Certainly, Strindberg and Hofmannsthal would be the first to admit that all the events which take place in *The Father* or *Electra* could never occur in the twenty-four-hour period covered in each play. It is by packing in these events that the playwright is able to show that "inner relatedness" which is "Nature's real mysterium." Both Strindberg and Hofmannsthal were more concerned with those mysterious forces which drive people, even to destruction, than they were with the events that these people experienced.

With this concept of theatre in general, Hofmannsthal of necessity manifests very definite views concerning the function of character in his drama. An understanding of this conception of character

will help to untangle the complicated and tortured people of his
first mature and probably finest play, *Electra*. In an essay written
in the form of a conversation, entitled "On Characters in Novels
and Plays" (1902), Hofmannsthal discussed the kind of characters
he believed belonged in the drama. Since this essay was written
shortly before he began the writing of *Electra* it provides many
valuable insights to understanding the complex characters in that
play. Some excerpts:

> B.: Characters in the theatre are nothing but contrapuntal neces-
> sities. The stage character is a contraction of the real one . . . I
> don't see people, I see destinies. The power of the erotic for him
> who is the slave of love. The power of weakness for the weak. The
> power of glory for the ambitious. No, not just love, just weakness,
> just glory; but the love by which man is enslaved, his individual
> weakness, his specific glory.
>
> H.: What! You want to set such narrow, such sad limits to your
> genius? The atmosphere of existences consuming themselves patho-
> logically, the hideous, blind, devouring mania—are these the sinister
> and constricted subjects you want to choose instead of plunging
> into the colorful variety of human life?
>
> B.: I don't know what you call "pathological"; but I know that
> every human existence worthy of presentation consumes itself, and
> that to maintain this flame it absorbs out of the whole world nothing
> but the elements expedient to its burning. Yes, the world which I've
> fetched forth from my brain is peopled with madmen. . . . My crea-
> tures are obsessed by their fixed ideas, are incapable of seeing any-
> thing in the world which they themselves do not project into it with
> their feverish eyes. But they are so, because they are human. For
> them experiences do not exist, because there is no such thing as ex-
> perience; because the inner core of man is a fire consuming itself.

From this passage it is clear that Hofmannsthal conceived of
character in drama as a complex of conflicting and contrapuntal
foils which will reveal, in the midst of life's greatest catastrophe,
what its destiny, over and above the actions of the here and now,
really is. Since Hofmannsthal was concerned with showing those
passionate powers which are the greatest realities in human beings,
he had to conceive a dramatic context in which his characters and
their actions could collide in such a way as to reflect or express that
power which motivates both the character and the action.

Thus, the function of the theatre, Hofmannsthal believed, is to
show that sublime and true moment in a man's life when the moti-

vating passion-power of his existence is expressed. To Hofmannsthal this moment is more real than any external reality. To many critics, including the imaginary critic in Hofmannsthal's "Conversation," this necessitates creating characters who appear to be pathological cases. The playwright agrees; for he knows that in life, although the process may be slower and less apparent, man is ultimately destroyed by that very passion which gives him the power to live. It is that moment when man's motivating passion-power drives him to the conflict of life and death that must be captured in the drama.

When viewed in this way we see that Hofmannsthal's Electra is more than a depraved and wild beast. In the conflict of what she says and what she does, the playwright is able to present that which is most real in Electra: her Destiny. He dramatizes that consuming and passionate power of vengeance which destroys every attribute of Electra's womanhood, and, as the play ends, kills not only Aegisthus and Clytemnestra, but herself as well. We may complain that she is a mad woman, but she is real; and if, Hofmannsthal seems to say, we could each know our own reality, we too would be thought of as mad. Hofmannsthal's plays may be filled with demons, but they are demons who reveal, at the moment they are consumed, man's destiny.

It is this sensational quality inherent in Hofmannsthal's conception of character together with the impact made on him by modern painting, especially the works of Van Gogh, which accounts for the stark theatricality of his work. Upon reading *Electra*, one discovers that Hofmannsthal has endowed each element of the dramatic production with rich and contrasting colors. Hofmannsthal helps us here, for not only has he given explicit stage directions, but he also published a fuller account of his ideas concerning the play's production in a short essay published at the printing of the play. In the beginning of this essay entitled "Szenische Verschriften Elektra," we find the following injunction:

> Shun any suggestion of Hellenic architecture! This avoidance of classic Greek symmetry in theatre design is then carried over and consistently applied to all the other stage properties, props, costumes, even affecting the attitude and behavior of the characters themselves. In place of the Attic peninsula, the stage represents an Oriental potentate's back courtyard, where are located the hovels that house the slaves. One senses that within the enclosure an atmosphere of bleak despair prevails. It is like a cage with no possibility of flight.

Hofmannsthal is equally exact in his expressionistic description of the lighting. It is planned in such a way as to contrast the two predominant tones of the play: the black of the House of Atreus and the red of the blood which has flowed in the past and will flow again. Electra "comes out of the house. She is alone with the red flickerings of light which fall through the branches of the fig trees and drop like blood stains on the ground and on the dark walls." The color of the light is used to symbolize the density of the play's central character. It is like a Wagnerian motif; large patches of crimson are immediately associated with Electra; they grow more intense and actually glow when she makes her initial entrance and begins her monologue.

As the sun disappears from the horizon, Electra and her sister are in the shades of dusk. The pall-like quality of their existence is thus expressed and it becomes increasingly more painful as torchlights within the palace shine out through the barred windows, casting flickering striped shadows across the girls' prison.

As Clytemnestra enters, in a procession of a thousand lights, we are not only aware of Clytemnestra's great need of light, but we are even more conscious of the great darkness that surrounds Electra. Clytemnestra, the queen with phantasmagoric nightmares, cannot stand the dark and, as Electra gradually forces her into a living nightmare, the lights disappear until "only a faint light falls from inside the house across the inner court, and casts bars of shadow over the figures of the two women." This is the only link to Clytemnestra's protective yet destructive palace.

The powerful *agon* between Clytemnestra and Electra is played in the eerie shadows of this light. Just as Clytemnestra is about to go insane and that light is flickering out, she is saved and her first reaction is to call for "Lights!" Then:

> Serving women with torches come out and station themselves behind Clytemnestra. She beckons more lights! More come out and station themselves behind her, so that the court is full of light, and a red-gold flare floods the walls. Now the features of Clytemnestra slowly change, and their shuddering tension relaxes in an evil triumph. She lets the message be whispered to her again, without taking her eyes off Electra. Then the Waiting Woman lifts her staff, and leaning on both, hurriedly, eagerly, catching up her robe from the step, she runs into the house. The servant women with lights follow her, as if pursued.

Electra is left in a "Cimmerian gloom," a portentous darkness.

Electra remains in this gloom until the revenge is completed. When all the women run out into the court with their bright torches, Electra begins her dance of death in this light of flickering red and gold. The lights symbolize not only the triumph of Electra's vengeance, but in their burning heat they are expressive of that consuming fire within Electra which destroys her at the moment of victory.

Hofmannsthal describes the costumes with the same care. Electra and the slave women are miserably clad in the threadbare rags of the most menial slave. Clytemnestra wears a scarlet dress. Here is not the Queen of Argos, but a barbaric ruler from some oriental past. She is "bedecked all over with precious stones and talismans. Her arms are covered by bracelets, her fingers glitter with rings." She leans on an ivory staff encrusted with precious stones. Her two ladies-in-waiting are no less striking in this procession of exotic grandeur. The one is dressed in dark violet; and the other, like a snake of the Nile, is clad in yellow, her hair pulled back in Egyptian style. As Hofmannsthal tells us: "These three women must be taken as a unit, a brilliant antithesis to the impoverished-appearing Princess."

The playwright has conceived of the play in theatrical terms. Coming as he did at the beginning of the twentieth century Hofmannsthal was faced with the problem of how to express and communicate his feelings about human destiny in a fragmented theatre. His answer was twofold: to return to Greek mythology in an attempt to find a universal situation (a method so often used in contemporary French drama); and to seek a theatrical unity by blending all the elements of stage production into his dramatic conception. It is here that we see Van Gogh's profound effect upon Hofmannsthal; not only visually, but structurally as well. We see in the *Electra* the intensity and contrast (the use of bright colors, particularly red and yellow, sharply contrasted with black) which characterizes Van Gogh's painting. Hofmannsthal intends his play to be lighted and costumed in a very definite way and without these effects his play will suffer greatly.

To some literary purists this is the failure of the play; for it does not stand on its own feet. Hofmannsthal would admit that his drama needs the stage directions, but he would insist that only a total theatrical production can bring that unity of expression which, as Wagner advocated before him, the dramatist needs if he is to communicate in any meaningful way to his audience.

In short, Hofmannsthal's theatrical sense is an essential element of his drama; he has made everything count: color, lighting, props, costuming. The very physical appearance of the characters is so deeply symbolic that every feature, each trait, the slightest gesture has its meaning, its relationship to all the other traits, features, and gestures. Nothing is wasted here; everything is utilized with the utmost economy, to heighten an effect here or diminish a detail there. Deliberately departing from the spirit of classical antiquity, the poet has in his profound attention to detail created so perfect and flawless a stage effect to harmonize with the characters and the plot that a definite harmony and unity almost in the Hellenic sense are the result.

A fuller understanding of how all these elements of Hofmannsthal's dramaturgy are fused can best be demonstrated by a more detailed analysis of the play. The opening scene of the play is one of indirect exposition. The setting is the courtyard of the palace, but it is suggestive of a cage for wild animals. From the slave women we discover that this is the dwelling place of Electra and that her behavior is much like that of a wild cat. She "howls" nightly for her father and when we see her for the first time her actions are those of an animal. From the very beginning Hofmannsthal's heroine is presented as a pathological case. Electra is left alone; but her loneliness is of a different kind than that found in Greek dramatizations of the myth. In her passion for a bloody revenge she is beyond the pale of human relationships. A wild animal cannot exist with people in society. Unlike Sophocles' Electra, who is alone because she stands for a course of action which demands more than anyone else is capable of giving; unlike a Euripidean heroine, who is alone because she is not accepted, Hofmannsthal's Electra is alone because her driving destiny for vengeance has destroyed all her humanity and the society which surrounds her cannot tolerate her.

Her monologue is a primitive ritual. This ceremonial invocation of her father occurs daily. We are reminded of those primitive savages who attempt to control reality by ritualistic means. She goes into her trance and the ghost of Agamemnon returns. The significance of the first part of the monologue is twofold. Not only does Electra believe that she can control reality ritualistically, but as she calls for the bloody death of all those associated with the murderers in addition to Aegisthus and Clytemnestra, we become aware that vengeance has taken such a hold on Electra that it is more real than she. It is not the revenge of a murdered father, but an all-consuming vengeance which includes everyone. The whole household is to be sacrificed so Agamemnon may resume his legal role in the other world.

The ceremony is about to end, and like the close of all primitive rites, the clairvoyant Electra breaks into a dance. She sees herself, Chrysothemis, and Orestes joyfully dancing in the bloody haze that exudes from the many corpses. Their horrible victory dance ironically prefigures her own dance of death.

Her sister enters calling for her. Chrysothemis' reaction is one of fear; Electra has become a wild animal even to her own family. Hofmannsthal's intention is greatly different from that of his Greek predecessors. Chrysothemis is not the weak-kneed sister; she sees that Electra has destroyed herself and would destroy all others about her because of something which has only dubious value. We learn in this scene that Hofmannsthal is not primarily interested in justice; he is showing what happens to a person whose destiny is revenge. Agamemnon's death and the need for revenge of that death has long since been forgotten except as the excuse which feeds Electra's revengeful spirit.

Chrysothemis has discovered the plot to imprison Electra and has come to warn her sister. In Electra's reply we learn why Hofmannsthal has introduced the warning. It is not to heighten our sympathy for Electra, nor is it to prompt Electra to action. In her rejection of Chrysothemis, she states her own position:

> Do not prowl about.
> Sit on the ground, like me, and wish for death.
> And judgment upon her and upon him.

These lines are remarkable for they could only be spoken by someone in the witch-doctor era of humanity's evolution. The dramatist has shown here an amazing familiarity with primitive thought and practice, for what most characterizes the savage mind is its unshakable conviction that it can impose changes and modify phenomena in the concrete world through the exercise of will and the practice of magic ritual (mimicry). That this is what Hofmannsthal intended is made incontrovertible when Electra learns that Clytemnestra has had a horrible nightmare that Orestes had come and strangled her. Electra shouts:

> It is I,
> I, that have sent him to her. From my breast
> I sent the dream to her.

As Electra goes on, trancelike, describing the ghastly dream that she has envisioned, it is realized with the entrance of Clytemnestra. With this entrance Hofmannsthal has pulled all the theatrical stops: the colorful procession, the torches, the slashing whips, and the muffled cries of the slaves. He has used every theatrical technique available in order to create a peak of emotional tension which will control the mother-daughter scene.

Clytemnestra's opening speech shows in another way how different Hofmannsthal's intentions are from those of his Greek predecessors. When Clytemnestra says:

> What do you want? See it now, how it rears
> Its swollen neck and darts its tongue at me!
> See what I have let loose in my own house.
> If she could only kill me with her eyes!

We see that Hofmannsthal has transferred the snake image of the Greek versions from Orestes to Electra, and as Electra writhes in the courtyard it becomes clear that the dream image has been given human embodiment. It is more evidence that Hofmannsthal was intent upon showing the animal destiny of his heroine who is consumed with the fire of revenge.

The witch-doctor quality of Electra's character is further emphasized by the mystical cure which Clytemnestra seeks, and which Electra offers. The importance of this scene is once again to contrast Hofmannsthal's dramatic conception with that of his predecessors. In all the Greek versions of the theme great pains are taken to show the similarity between Electra and her mother; that Electra, too, is capable of taking justice into her own hands and thus bringing upon herself the same guilt and fear as that suffered by her mother. The purpose of this scene, the longest of the play, is also to show the similarity of the daughter to her mother; but it is a similarity of an entirely different nature. In terms of their outward actions and language the two women are different. They are alike in that they are driven to destruction by a great passion that is their destiny. Just as Electra's humanity is destroyed by her passion for vengeance, so too has Clytemnestra, who is described as a walking corpse, been destroyed by her all-consuming guilt and fear. Hofmannsthal has realized his idea of character as destiny most clearly in this scene of paradoxically contrasting similarity.

As the scene develops, Electra's destiny is seen to be the stronger of the two. With speeches of great rhetorical lyricism, Electra literally forces her mother up against the wall and is moving in, like the wild animal she has become, for the kill, when a messenger comes out to tell of Orestes' feigned death. Clytemnestra is saved, for the moment, and in her salvation Hofmannsthal foreshadows the tragic irony of the play's conclusion. Electra's destiny will overcome that of her mother, as it has in this scene, but Electra will be deprived then, as she is now, of joining in the final kill.

The next scene moves rapidly. The almost comic banter of the cook and the two servants is a much needed lessening of the tension which Hofmannsthal has created. Its purpose, however, is not totally comic, since even in their banter these servants give us another view of those conditions which have helped to mold Electra's destiny.

The following scene between Chrysothemis and Electra is the second crucial scene in the play. Electra, determined to do the murder alone now that she believes Orestes is dead, asks her sister to help her. She is refused. The purpose of the scene is not to contrast Electra heroically determined to act for what she believes is more important than living, with Chrysothemis pathetically clinging to life at all costs (as in Sophocles). Rather Hofmannsthal uses it to show the effects of destiny upon Electra as it consumes her; this is best achieved by contrasting Electra with a girl who is not a coward, but who is repulsed by an existence which has no other aim than a constant brooding for revenge.

As the destiny of revenge consumes Electra it destroys her as a woman. Her attitude toward sex is distorted by her continuing belief that her mother's relationship with Aegisthus is adulterous. As a result all normal sexuality is obscene and guilt-ridden. Yet her denial of sex as the result of this aversion has caused her to be obsessed with it. Her language is highly charged with sexual images and all that she does has a sexual referent. The effect of this sexual denial, combined with her perverted and obsessive attitude toward love, has been to create in her marked lesbian tendencies which become overt in this scene:

You! For you are strong. (*Close to her.*)
How strong you are! To you
Have virgin nights given strength. How lithe and slim
Your loins are. You can slip through every cranny,
Creep through the window. Let me feel your arms;
How cool and strong they are! What arms they are
I feel when thus you thrust me back with them.
Could you not stifle one with their embrace?
Could you not clasp one to your cool firm breast
With both your arms until one suffocated?
There is such strength about you everywhere.
It streams like cool close water from a rock,
It flows in a great flood with all your hair
Down your strong shoulders.

Hofmannsthal, a master in his use of primitive psychological phenomena, creates here a scene which vividly shows us how completely his heroine has been destroyed as a woman by her passion
for vengeance.

Chrysothemis, as we have pointed out, cannot accept Electra's
endless cries for vengeance. She is aware, as the Sophoclean counterpart is not, that the destiny of revenge has had a dehumanizing
effect upon her sister and she cannot accept it for herself. Chrysothemis is motivated by more normal human instincts; she desires
marriage and the pleasures and fruits of such a union. She has the
capacity to care and feel for others (most clearly seen, in contrast
to her sister, in her reaction to the report of Orestes' death) and
must reject that destiny which withers all human feelings. But Hofmannsthal is not asking us to sympathize with Chrysothemis, attractive as she is. Hofmannsthal's intention is to show the reality of
Electra's destiny and the destructive effects that it has on her humanity. The function of Chrysothemis in this scene is to put into
sharper focus the dehumanizing process which is taking place in
Electra's character.

Left alone Electra plans to carry out the murders by herself. Like
the wild animal which we know she is, she begins to dig in the
earth, like a dog for a bone, for the battle-ax which had been used
to murder her father. It is while she is digging for the means to
achieve, almost ritualistically, the purification of the House of
Atreus, that she is discovered by her brother. The recognition scene,
although similar in construction to Sophocles', has lost much of its
traditional importance. Hofmannsthal stresses three elements. First,

he heightens Orestes' horror at what has happened to Electra over the years while he has been absent in order to drive home with finality the process of dehumanization which has taken place in the heroine. Second, as Electra concludes her description of the horrors of being caged in the palace for years, she says: "Speak to me, speak! Why your whole body trembles." Orestes replies:

> My body? Let it tremble. Do you not think
> That he would tremble otherwise than this
> Could he but guess the way I mean to send him?

The significance of this speech (hardly noticed by most critics) is to state explicitly Hofmannsthal's belief that one's physical being is separate from that force which drives human action. Third, Hofmannsthal makes it clear that the gods do not demand vengeance. This radical change in the tradition underscores the fact that there is no motivation for the revenge except that Electra must have revenge. We really do not know why Orestes has come and what motivates his acceptance of the duty to wreak vengeance on the slayers of his father. There is only an intentional vagueness. Since Hofmannsthal is concerned with showing the destiny of revenge in Electra, and not with the ethical problems which result from matricide and murder, revenge for the sake of revenge is motivation enough for the play's external action. It is only when we see the play as an expression of Hofmannsthal's concept of the reality of destiny that this apparent "motiveless malignancy" does not cause trouble in the interpretation of the play.

From this point on the play moves quickly to its conclusion. Orestes enters the house, and while he is preparing for the murders, Electra paces back and forth "before the door with bowed head, like a wild beast in its cage." Suddenly she remembers the battle-ax. This is the final irony of her destiny. In her excitement at seeing her brother she forgot to give him the ax. Both murders are successfully accomplished without a struggle. At the moment of Aegisthus' death there begins a gigantic demonstration in which the entire populace, Chrysothemis included, participates. The echoing noise from the demonstrators swells into a mighty roar and the flickering beams cast by a thousand torches accompany this crescendo. In the midst of all the commotion one person appears motionless, unable to join the throng: Electra. Then with superhuman effort she rises and plunges into a weird, unrestrained dance. But Electra is no longer of this world; her mission on earth is fulfilled, and she no longer has a will to live. She whirls on and on until exhausted, she falls into a lifeless heap. The prophetic vow to her mother has been consummated.

This final moment, one of great theatrical power, is symbolic of Hofmannsthal's conception of the character of Electra. It is the dance that earlier in the play gave Electra ritual control over her hated captors; and yet, as the play ends, *she* is controlled by the dance to the point of death. The dance is symbolic of the victory of her destiny of vengeance; and yet it is her defeat. It is fulfillment which is empty. The dance, in its orgiastic quality, is symbolic of a kind of sexual realization, but the fruit of that realization is destruction. This is the "sublime and true moment" of Electra's life; this is the moment when her destiny, that passion and power which has sustained her through all the years of hardship, destroys her. Electra is that incendiary figure whose spark ignites Orestes to action. But the fire, like the dance, her chief weapons against her enemies, could only be turned in upon herself once they have done their work and her enemies are no more. Hofmannsthal realizes his intention that the drama "must capture that moment when man is destroyed by the very passion which gives him life!"

What is the tragedy? The more obvious answer is that Electra was engaged in a struggle that proved futile; Electra sacrificed all that she was as a human being for nothing. This futility is symbolized by the fact that Orestes succeeded without the aid of the battle-ax Electra had so carefully buried for this sacred moment. Electra failed to share even symbolically in the fulfillment of her life's dream. These ironies, however, are but symbols of the greater tragedy. The tragedy of Hofmannsthal's *Electra* is that men are destroyed by the very forces which give them life.

Hofmannsthal used the Electra theme in a new way. He was not concerned with justice, with self-realization and rebirth through suffering, nor with the helplessness of the human situation. He gave this traditional theme new life, by using it to express the tortured reality of human existence in a time when man could not live by any other means than by those passions which so molded his life as to become its destructive destiny.

# 13

# THE COLLAPSE OF
# THE SHAVIAN COSMOS:
# A STUDY OF THEME
# AND DRAMATIC FORM

*Heartbreak House is not merely the name of
the play which follows this preface. It is cultured, leisured Europe before the war. . . .*

WITH THESE words George Bernard Shaw begins his Preface to
*Heartbreak House.* The rest of the preface is a description of how
some of the basic assumptions of the Western world were all too
rapidly disintegrating and how they were finally destroyed in the
First World War. The most important of these assumptions to go
was that the rational rather than the irrational is the dominant mode
of human existence. Shaw, though he fought the good fight, was of
that legion of iconoclasts who realized that man is not so much a
creature of reason as a victim of irrational and unconscious forces
which exist and operate both within and outside himself. It is in
*Heartbreak House* that he first came to grips without equivocation
with those questions which had haunted Ibsen, Strindberg, and
Chekhov before him. How is one to live in an irrational world? How
is one to give meaning to life in a world where one doesn't know
the rules? How are human relationships to be maintained meaningfully when one cannot be sure of his feelings and when one's feel-

ings can change without one's knowing it? How can man live without being destroyed when irreconcilable conflict is the central fact of all life?

The world of *Heartbreak House* is one that has permanently misplaced the life, vitality, and victory of *Major Barbara*. The people who whirl before us in this mad "dance of death" rapidly lose whatever veneer of virtue they may have had and stand revealed as vain, insipid, blind, and vapid men and women who have made their society into "an economic, political, and as far as practical, a moral vacuum. . . ." In the years between these two plays the world was radically changed by the war, and Shaw, always sensitive to changes in moral climate, was certainly not immune to it. In postwar Europe man seems to have lost his faith in himself, and without this faith there can be no truth. This is the theme of *Heartbreak House* as it has been the theme of so many of Shaw's plays: How does man find a faith in himself that will lead to the truth? The big difference between this play and those written before it is that man not only does not succeed in *Heartbreak House*, but the possibility of his ever succeeding is flatly rejected. In the first act (written before the war) there still seems to be the possibility of salvation, but in the remaining two acts man's stupidity and evil—the nothingness of the characters and their philosophy, their inability to live in the modern world, their unworthiness to be preserved—are revealed.

But here the Shavian "true believer" will rise up in godly wrath and cry, "Nay, 'tis not so! It is easy enough to dismiss Mangan, Mazzini, Hector, Lady Utterword, and even Hesione, but have you forgotten that magnificent old man, Captain Shotover and our Ellie, so fine and true? How can you condemn them along with all the rest? It is they who will save the world. They are our hope." Captain Shotover, delightful as he is, cannot be a candidate for the man to whom one could say: "What must we do to be saved?" First of all, his life has been spent and he has accomplished little for his fellowman. His philosophy of life, in his own words, is one of self-interest above all: "A man's interest in the world is only the overflow from his interest in himself." His main activity is working out a means of destroying his fellowmen with a dynamite that explodes by thought. He, in fact, cancels out the hope some have found in *Major Barbara*. "You are going to let the fear of poverty govern your life; and your reward will be that you will eat, but you will not live." Undershaft's solution will not work in Shotover's world. Money will not save men—not even Ellie. Shotover not only sees clearly what Heartbreak House has become, he knows that it has already been judged. And he has been judged most severely, although he has found an escape of sorts. "I cannot bear men and women," he says. "I have to run away. I must run away now." There is no tranquility in his old age. "I can't remember what I really am. I feel nothing but the accursed happiness I have dreaded all my life: the happiness that comes as life goes, the happiness of yielding and dreaming instead of resisting and doing, the sweetness of fruit that is going rotten." Shaw has denied this society even the hope of a peaceful old age that can await a heavenly home. The Captain fears and hates sleep, so he drinks to keep awake and away from death.

Captain Shotover does, however, do one thing no one else in the play can do: he speaks the truth. In this he is an essential partner for Ellie. The two of them must provide answers no matter how despairing they may be. Ellie turns to him for guidance from the first. She is that person in each of us who asks the eternal questions: "What is truth and reality? How can I exist in this futile world?" In the beginning we feel that perhaps she will find the answer, but gradually as more and more deception, cruelty, and emptiness are revealed to her, she too becomes embittered. "What a vile world it is!" she cries. But Captain Shotover only replies: "It doesn't concern me. I'm nearly out of it!" Ellie comes to realize that the things she had first looked for in Heartbreak House cannot be found, even in the Captain. She turns to him as the best of those available, but her attitude in doing so is negative: ". . . I feel now as if there was nothing I could do, because I want nothing." Captain Shotover understands that she is clinging to something that does not exist. When she says, "Your own spirit is not dead," he replied, "Echoes: nothing but echoes. The last shot was fired years ago." And clinging to the old man, Ellie moves further and further from any solution to her questions, until at the end of the play she is lost—callously disappointed at the shortness of the bombing attack. Her future is the most despairing of all, for when Hesione says: "But what a glorious experience; I hope they'll come again tomorrow night." Ellie (radiant at the prospect) answers, "Oh, I hope so." Is this Shaw's answer? Could there be anything more ironical than his choice of words—"radiant" and "I hope"—as symbols of future salvation applied to a request for more war and death. Nothing is left, nothing is real or true in Heartbreak House. Ellie states her own failure and that of those around her.

> There seems to be nothing in the world except my father and Shakespeare. Marcus's tigers are false; Mr. Mangan's millions are false; there is nothing really strong and true about Hesione but her beautiful black hair; and Lady Utterword's is too pretty to be real. The only thing that was left to me was the Captain's seventh degree of concentration; and that turns out to be. . . .
>
> CAPTAIN SHOTOVER: Rum!

No one has ever questioned that *Heartbreak House* is one of Shaw's masterpieces, but today, as we look back on his career as a dramatist, this play takes on a new significance: it is clearly a pivotal play. The staunch believer in the Life Force has come to believe that the laws of navigation can never be learned. In all the plays up to, and including, *Major Barbara*, Shaw seemed to insist that salvation was possible if only we are bold of heart and clear in mind. But with *Heartbreak House* that hard-won optimism disappears never again to return. The optimism of the later plays is, as Joseph Wood Krutch puts it, "more a matter of temperament than of philosophical conviction." With *Heartbreak House* the British theatre entered the Continental mainstream and the only difference between Shaw and the Ibsen, Strindberg, and Chekhov he so admired is that he was able to take the loss of hope more cheerfully.

But much more than Shaw's belief in the redeeming power of the Life Force went up in smoke with the bomb that falls at the final curtain of *Heartbreak House*. His sense of dramatic form was also destroyed. Because Shaw was such a vital figure in the world of letters until the day he died in 1950, we have had a tendency to consider him as a contemporary rather than as a man of the nineteenth century. But in actual fact he has much more in common with Ibsen, Nietzsche, Darwin, Marx, and Zola than he has with Joyce, Kafka, Pound, Sartre, Camus, Beckett, and the numerous other great innovators of the twentieth century. This is particularly true of Shaw the playwright. Indeed, I believe one can say without equivocation that he was the last of the great nineteenth-century melodramatists.

I am sure that to many people such an assessment of Shaw's remarkable achievements will seem unfair. It would certainly appear to be assigning him to Limbo, for throughout all of England's long and illustrious theatrical history, one period, the nineteenth century, is invariably dismissed by critics and historians of theatre as unworthy of their effort and attention. Examining the stage histories, one finds pretty much the same recurring pattern: a scant mention will be made of the century's vigorous but allegedly meaningless theatricality; somewhat more space will be devoted to the numerous nondramatic entertainments which emerged during most of the second half of the century; and the lion's share of attention will be given to those actor-managers who dominated the British theatre at that time because they believed so firmly in their right to remake plays to serve their own narcissistic ends. But compared to the glories of the Elizabethan theatre, the wit and style of the Restoration, the balance and nobility of the Augustan age, and the probing, questioning, and rebellious spirit of the twentieth-century playwrights, the British drama of the nineteenth century is quickly passed over as little more than so much tinsel. This, say the critics with an air of superiority, was the age of melodrama! And since we all know that melodrama deals with externals, is simplistic in its attitudes, is sensational and sentimental in its effects, and, worst of all, appeals to the lowest level of public taste, the less said about it by serious-minded people the better. Fortunately, during the past few years, the myopic nature of this prejudicial view of one of the theatre's oldest forms has been vigorously and intelligently exposed. So the time is ripe for a reconsideration of melodrama, and particularly of that manifestation of it which flourished in the nineteenth-century British theatre, and of which George Bernard Shaw was the foremost practitioner.

Let me repeat some remarks from the essay on tragedy which begins this book. All drama is built upon catastrophe (literally, a shift in direction)—any event which overturns the previously existing order or system of things. As such, catastrophe is itself devoid of moral meanings, and is equally capable of producing joy and happiness or sadness and grief depending upon the context in which it occurs. The first important characteristic of melodrama, and it is this which finally distinguishes it from all other dramatic forms, is the fact that all the significant "catastrophic" events which occur are caused by forces outside the protagonists. *King Lear* and *The Duchess of Malfi* have many things in common, but, because Lear is clearly brought low by the dividedness of his own nature while the Duchess in spite of her inner conflicts, is ultimately destroyed by external forces, we consider Shakespeare's play a tragedy and Webster's a melodrama. The same distinction can be found in classical Greek drama; certainly there is as much suffering in *The Trojan Women* as in *Oedipus the King*, probably more; but because the King of Thebes is responsible for his own suffering in a way that the victimized women of Troy are not, we correctly believe that the difference between the two dramas is one of kind and not degree. Making these distinctions is not just academic nit-picking or an exercise in pedantic labeling. Rather it is the insistence that tragedy and melodrama are two fundamentally different structures of experience, and each must be considered on its own terms.

Perhaps we could make these distinctions clearer by temporarily dropping the term "melodrama" (which has acquired so many negative connotations) and using in its place the "drama of disaster." Disaster in its purest form means "that which happens because of the stars," and as such it is an apt metaphor for the unhappiness and suffering that come to men from without, i.e., from nature, society, or other individuals. It should be pointed out, however, that the literal meaning of "disaster" does not have such negative connotations. Plays as diverse as Euripides' *Helen* and Shaw's *You Never Can Tell* have disastrous but happy resolutions. (One of the most interesting characteristics of nineteenth-century melodrama is the ready willingness with which the playwrights alternated painful and fortunate events of disaster.) Such unhappy events can be just as painful and as capable of moving us as are the events of tragedy, but they are profoundly different. Unlike tragedy, in the drama of disaster the protagonist is a victim who is acted upon; his moral quality is not essential to the event, and his suffering does not imply an inevitable related guilt—in fact, there need not be any meaningful relation between the suffering of the protagonist and the cause and nature of the disastrous event.

This probably accounts for the overriding tone of paranoia which informs melodrama. When catastrophic events occur in our lives for which we are not responsible and over which we have no control, we cannot help but feel persecuted by a blind, meaningless, and hence absurd fate. Try as we may to fabricate rational explanations for such catastrophes, there is always the hovering shadow of the boogeyman. This fact does much to account for melodrama's strong hold on the imagination, particularly the popular imagination, and it also explains the overpowering sense of reality that the form of melodrama engenders even when on the surface it seems so patently unreal. For melodrama's greatest achievement is its capacity to give direct objective form to our irrational fears. Why else the compelling appeal of Richard III or Iago, Dracula, or Frankenstein? Because these characters have been endowed with the authentic power and energy of irrational fear. Why else the great popularity of horror movies at midnight? Because our most savage superstitions, our most neurotic fantasies, our most grotesque childhood imaginings are given uninhibited, yet harmless, expression. Even the wild and threatening landscape in which most melodramatic actions are set enhances this paranoiac effect. All of these elements prompted Eric Bentley to write in his *The Life of the Drama:* "The success of a melodramatist will always depend primarily upon his power to feel and project fear."

But this paranoiac aspect of the melodramatic vision is related to another quality which is almost unique to this form. Invariably, whenever people discuss melodrama, it doesn't take very long for the subject of "ham acting" to come up. In fact, every account of the nineteenth-century theatre moves to this point very quickly and dwells on it almost *ad nauseam.* Historians are only too ready to quote remarks such as Henry Labouchère's:

> An actor must, in order to win popularity, have mannerisms, and the more peculiar they are, the greater will be his popularity. No one can for a moment suppose that Mr. Irving could not speak distinctly and progress about the stage after the manner of human beings, and stand still without balancing to and fro like a bear in a cage, if he pleased. Yet, had he done all this he would—notwithstanding that there is a touch of real genius about his acting sometimes—never have made the mark he has. He is, indeed, to the stage what Lord Beaconsfield was to politics. . . . Were Mr. Irving at present to abate his peculiarities, his fervent worshippers would complain that their idol was sinking into the commonplace.

Or Martin Harvey's response when he was reproached for altering texts:

> My game is acting, and not necessarily the exploitation of literature. Material is chosen because it gives opportunities to practice my art— the art of acting.

Or finally Henry Irving's own account of the function of the stage:

To the common, indifferent man, immersed as a rule in the business and socialities of daily life, it brings visions of glory and adventure, of emotion, of broad human interest. To all it uncurtains a world, not that in which they live and yet not other than it, a world in which interest is heightened and yet the conditions of truth are observed, in which the capabilities of men and women are seen developed with a curious and wholesome fidelity to simple and universal instincts of clear right and wrong.

There is no doubt about it, melodrama, like its twin sister in music, opera, is a grandiose theatrical style. In fact, the characters of melodrama conceive of themselves constantly in histrionic terms; the source of their vitality and appeal is visceral and not intellectual. But a strongly marked style doesn't emerge without a cause. All literature of disaster, from Homer to Hemingway, deals with man alive in a universe of danger. The realm of disaster, as we have just indicated, is one dominated by irrational fears; it also encourages self-pity. As long ago as Aristotle we knew that whenever we shift from feeling sorry for pain received to fear of pain given, we move from the sense of disaster toward the tragic sense. In melodrama neither the characters nor the audience make such a shift, with the result that the dominant style (as opposed, but nonetheless related, to the underlying tone of paranoia) is one of grandiloquent self-pity. This combination is alien to us today—at least when we go to the theatre—but it is at the core of every successful melodrama from *Iphigenia in Aulis* to *Under the Gaslight*.

It is for this reason that from the theatre's earliest beginnings the basic plot form of melodrama has been the good guys versus the bad guys. However, it is a more sophisticated structure than such a simple formulation of it may seem to indicate, and it has been consciously used by such "tragic" dramatists as Euripides, Shakespeare, Webster, Ibsen, Tolstoy, Synge, and O'Neill, to name but a few. In the structure of melodrama, as Robert Heilman has described so persuasively in his book, *Tragedy and Melodrama: Versions of Experience*, "man is essentially 'whole.'" Professor Heilman goes on to point out that such wholeness is morally neutral and implies neither greatness nor moral perfection; rather it indicates an absence of the kind of inner conflict which is so significant that it *must* claim our first attention. (The protagonist of melodrama may be humanly incomplete, indeed he usually is; but his incompleteness is not the issue of the drama.) Wholeness, then, is the central structural characteristic of melodrama. And whether he win or lose, the action of melodrama is essentially that of an undivided protagonist facing an outer conflict. The issue is not self-knowledge and the reordering of one's relationship to the universe (as it is in tragedy), but rather the maintenance of self in a hostile world and the reordering of one's relations with others. For this reason the resolution of the melodramatic conflict is always clear-cut and simple: The protagonist is engaged in a conflict which finally is either won or lost. The resolution of tragedy, on the other hand, is always complex and ambiguous: in his struggle with necessity man always wins in the losing and loses in the winning.

Traditionally, then, melodrama has been dismissed as second rate because it lacks tragedy's broader moral dimension. However, even if tragedy is accorded a greater significance on these grounds, it should be hastily added that the very fact that the majority of the plays ever written has been melodrama underscores a basic truth of the human condition: most of the crises and conflicts in which each of us have engaged in our daily lives lack tragedy's moral dimension as well. Melodrama is the form which expresses our human reality as we experience it most of the time, a fact which Robert Louis Stevenson knew well when he wrote:

> There is a vast deal in life where the interest turns, not upon what a man shall choose to do, but on how he manages to do it; not on the passionate slips and hesitations of the conscience, but on the problems of the body and of the practical intelligence, in clean openair adventure, the shock of arms or the diplomacy of life. This is the realm of melodrama.

While it is true, then, that the structure and spirit of melodrama is as old as the theatre itself, we, nonetheless—and quite correctly—think of the nineteenth century as *the* Age of Melodrama. This was particularly so in England. Somehow the characteristics of melodrama seem to be a true reflection of both the vast number of social changes that took place during the period and also of the sturdy Victorian morality which maintained itself, at least until the very last years of the century, like a Gibraltar in the midst of those changes. Melodrama, as Michael Booth pointed out in his admirable Introduction to *Hiss the Villain,* "is a simplification and idealization of human experience dramatically presented. For its audiences melodrama was both an escape from real life and a dramatization of it as it ought to be." But its chief appeal is that, then as now, one always knows where one is in melodrama. Moral principles are clearly established, and so, too, are the rules of proper conduct (factors which in large measure explain the stereotyped characters and rigid moral distinctions which are so characteristic of the form). Motives and psychological explanations were irrelevant, at least until Ibsenism hit the country in the nineties, because to the Victorian mind actions were believed to speak for themselves and were readily and easily judged. In melodrama, as in no other dramatic form, to quote Professor Booth once again, "the wages of sin is death." The action may be full of violence, but these terrible catastrophes are all accepted, as Booth says, because they are known to be "signposts along the road to ultimate happiness, the triumph of virtue, and defeat of evil." English audiences knew this, and their pleasure was in large measure due to their knowledge that no matter how dire the circumstances, all would turn out right.

But as important as the Victorian morality is to an understanding of the nineteenth-century British theatre, it is an inadequate explanation, since, in truth, Victorianism was not so much a causal force as it was symptomatic of a broader revolution of thought and sensibility which was sweeping over all of Europe.

The nineteenth century is almost unique in the history of Western culture in that the dominant concerns of its most advanced and profound thinkers and its most sensitive and expressive artists corresponded so closely with the needs, attitudes, and tastes of the public at large. As I said, such a close relationship has seldom existed in history. We know that Socrates and Euripides probably came as close as any to revealing the tonalities of Greece at the end of the fifth century B.C., but we also know that each of them was not very popular in his own time. Shakespeare's unique genius was, among other things, that he spoke to all levels of people in a highly stratified society. But during his lifetime he was not regarded so highly by the intelligentsia as was Ben Jonson. The great dramatists—and the philosophers as well—of the seventeenth and eighteenth centuries wrote for relatively small and specialized aristocratic audiences, and therefore their works reveal very little to us about popular taste. But in the nineteenth century, at least for a good part of it and especially in England, there is an almost direct correspondence between the great revolutions of thought, the major trends in the arts, and the life and conditions of the majority of the population. In short, not only was melodrama the prevailing form of popular entertainment, it was the dominant modality of all nineteenth-century British life and thought.

No one has written more brilliantly on this subject than has Wylie Sypher in his superb essay "Aesthetic of Revolution: The Marxist Melodrama," and because his ideas apply so directly to my present point, I quote the following extensive passage from his essay to support it:

> The thesis that melodrama is a characteristic mode of nineteenth-century thought and art becomes clearer when we attempt to identify contrasting modalities in the eighteenth and twentieth centuries. Although the eighteenth century played its own incidental melodrama, we may say that the characteristic mode of enlightened thought and art was the mental fiction—those abstract and summary concepts erected inside the mind and harmoniously adjusted to each other within the rationalized order of Nature. These mental fictions where the substructure of the distinctive eighteenth-century performances in every direction: the rights of man, the literary rules, the state of nature, the deistic world order, the coherent Newtonian universe with its fictions of absolute space and absolute time, the perfectibility of mankind, the theoretical codes of the encyclopedists, the generalizations of the heroic couplet, the regularity of the sonata, the balances of Augustan and Georgian architecture, the precise articulations of the formal garden, the nobility of the savage, the simple economic motives of enlightened self-interest. All these modes of the eighteenth-century mind could enlist the emotions, and often did; yet their substratum was the purely intellectual construct, the beautiful and coherent simplification that was not dramatized because it stood detached, without opposition or polarity, as an absolute assumption or idea, and because it was not animated or mythologized. The eighteenth-century sensibility moved freely and remotely in the clear atmosphere of the mental fiction.
>
> Also in contrast to the nineteenth-century melodrama, the authentic twentieth-century modality has abandoned the "event" and the theatrical act. We bear with us a sense of the conditional, of interrelationships, that the nineteenth century did not. We cannot isolate events. Our interpretation is less personal. We are more scientific and skeptical. For us the universe is denser—a continuum, in fact, without the vacuums and intermissions necessary to distinguish the individual events. Our recognition of complexities is so involved that we cannot with assurance locate an event in its isolated status; we cannot separate it from its antecedents and con-

texts. Our novels have fewer emphatic moments and are devoted to close interconnections, uninterrupted impressions, multiple approaches. As Whitehead has put it, the whole is part of every event, and every event occurs only within the structure of the whole. Thus an event is for us a hypothetical occasion. Indeed, we have so far abandoned the melodramatic view that we have often withdrawn to impersonal, abstract representation of our perceptions. The disintegrations of cubism suggest our pictorial view. By a determined analysis or "destruction" of the object we reduce it to a study of intimate and manifold relationships, a fragmentation within a continuum of forms until the definition of the "subject" remains equivocal. In narrative the disintegration began as early as Chekhov, and has continued within Proust, Joyce, Stein, and Woolf. Melodrama has become, for us, an inappropriate and incredible modality.

But

. . . for the nineteenth century the modality is melodrama, the oversimplification into polarities and oppositions that may be animated by emphatic instances. To the nineteenth-century mind the very iron laws of science operate with melodramatic fatalism—the pressure of population against subsistence, the dynamics of supply and demand and the wages fund, the struggle for existence in a nature red in tooth and claw, the unalterable majestic course of matter and force mythologized by Hardy and the biologist Haeckel, the brooding malign policies of Egdon Heath and the awesome tyranny of power in geology and physics, with men and generations of men sealed within the grim and dusty hills of the Mongolian desert.

All this is melodrama, not tragedy: and certainly not science. The view of the world as a diagram of polar forces encourages not only a melodramatic ethics (the strong and the weak, the hard and the soft, the good and the bad) but also emotive history and emotive science, which, as Huxley confidently assumed, can satisfy the spiritual longings of man. . . . By a confusion of categories the inevitabilities of matter and motion and political economy assume a moral sanction, just as in melodrama chance assumes the tenor of poetic justice, just as the impersonal "naturalism" of Zola and Ibsen always moves toward moral conclusions. The world becomes a theatre of tensions between abstractions. Melodrama has become social, if not cosmic. . . . Therefore the aesthetic category of melodrama becomes a modality of the nineteenth-century mind, which emancipated itself only with difficulty from oversimplified premises, a fatalism theatrically effective, and a displacement of moral responses into the universe. The declamatory language, the violent and symbolic gestures, the animation of polar opposites to the point of caricature are evidence of a psychic crisis. . . . Melodrama cannot admit exceptions, for they would immediately involve the action too deeply within the context of actuality and trammel the gesture. The types must behave with a decorum of extremes; the resolution must be vividly schematic. The tensions must concentrate toward a last overwhelming tableau, a final stasis beyond which one must not think. The aesthetic values of melodrama are the values of crisis, the event accepted as consummation.*

Clearly, the emergence of melodrama as the dominant dramatic form in the nineteenth-century theatre corresponds directly to the rise of a new and significantly different audience. We tend to forget that a century ago the theatre was the only form of popular entertainment. In the decade between 1850 and 1860 the number of theatres built throughout England was doubled, and in the middle of the sixties, in London alone, 150,000 would be attending the theatre on any given day. Only when we realize that the theatre was to Victorian England what television is to us today will we be able to comprehend both its wide appeal and its limited artistic achievements. Because of the Industrial Revolution a new audience was created which demanded entertainment. Neither the Augustan theatre nor the bourgeois theatre which had emerged by the end of the eighteenth century could meet this demand. Shakespeare was too literary (unless he was hoked up), and the efforts of serious writers to write for the theatre were rejected because they in no way satisfied this new audience which came to the theatre to escape the drabness and squalor of everyday life. As a result the theatre became increasingly both anti-aristocratic and anti-middle class. And when Archer introduced Ibsen and the "new" drama, it was aimed not at the dominant popular audience, but rather was for those serious-minded people who had been driven out of the theatre two decades earlier. We cannot appreciate the achievements of the nineteenth-century British theatre unless we understand the contradictions inherent in this divorce.

And this brings me back to Shaw, for it is in his work that we see the contradictions most clearly. No one attacked the old-fashioned melodrama more violently than did the master of Ayot St. Lawrence.

---

* Wylie Sypher, "Aesthetic of Revolution: The Marxist Melodrama," *The Kenyon Review*, vol. X, no. 3 (Summer, 1948), pp. 431–444. This excerpt is quoted by permission of the author.

In his early reviews of the nineties and in numerous prefaces and plays he was vitriolic in his abuse and parody of this kind of drama "which pandered to the lowest and worst elements of mankind." And yet as Eric Bentley has pointed out (and convincingly substantiated), Shaw is the "supreme melodramatist." For all of G.B.S.'s moral, philosophical, and social concerns, his plays can be successfully produced only if they are approached melodramatically. As Bentley puts it, "If Shaw hated the morals of melodrama—the projection upon the world of our irresponsible narcissistic fantasies— he loved its manners." Once when Granville-Barker was having trouble with a production of *Androcles and the Lion,* Shaw gave him this advice: "Remember that it's Italian opera."

A final contradiction, this too involving Shaw: As I said earlier, melodrama was the most appropriate and most expressive form of the Victorian drawing room. It was the true social reflection of its times. Shaw as a playwright, essayist, and Fabian social reformer attacked violently and eloquently every manifestation of Victorian morality and manners. He was, in short, opposed to the modalities of melodrama. But as a writer, his protests notwithstanding, he was totally dependent upon the stability and values of the Victorian drawing room. Even in his diatribes against it, Shaw counted on the drawing room; it was his cosmos as much as the Olympian deities or the Great Chain of Being was the cosmos for an Athenian or an Elizabethan dramatist. And when, in *Heartbreak House,* Shaw finally acknowledged the collapse of this sturdy edifice, something collapsed in his plays as well. He achieved some great moments after 1920, but his sense of structure was gone and it was never to be restored. Thus, while Shaw and his colleagues were trying to create a new theatre, a theatre free from the moral flabbiness and psychological simplifications of nineteenth-century melodrama, they succeeded only so long as they could incorporate the morality of Victorianism and the methods of melodrama into their protest.

# 14

# LORCA'S
# TOGETHERNESS

In subsequent chapters I will have occasion to discuss the battle
which a number of contemporary playwrights, particularly the Absurdists, have been waging against the tyranny of words in the theatre. Up to a point, these writers have a very valid argument and
no one can deny that many of the better Absurdist plays have
proved to be a much needed antidote to the wornout and expressionless language and structure of the well-made, naturalistic play
which had come to dominate most of the contemporary theatre. But
legitimate as the Absurdists' case may have been, it is full of dangerous implications and one need only examine the achievements of
the avant-garde in the past few years to see how quickly the theatre
can degenerate once the playwright no longer feels that his primary
responsibility is to the creation of words for performance. History
shows us that all of the really important revolutions in the theatre
have finally had the nature and quality of dramatic language as
their central concern. This fact leads me to believe that only those
rebels in the modern theatre who have had a commitment to language will create works which will become part of the permanent
repertoire.

Whenever I turn my attention to the subject of language in the
modern and contemporary theatre, I invariably think of Federico
García Lorca. No one was ever more conscious of the power of
words in the theatre than he, and an examination of his all too brief
career as a playwright reveals his constant efforts to wed the lan-

guage of poetry with a powerful and expressive dramatic form. Indeed, the playwright's brother, Francisco, wrote in the preface to the American edition of the plays: "Any interpretation of his [Lorca's] theatre made from a viewpoint other than a poetic one will lead to wrong conclusions." Now, the dramatic gesture of poetry is the metaphor. A metaphor links two antagonistic or disparate worlds together by finding some similarity between the two which permits the soaring of the poet's imagination toward a clearly conceived picture image. A metaphor, then, implies an imaginative perception on the part of the poet of a similarity, or a common power, which exists between two dissimilar worlds. Furthermore when a given metaphor is repeated often enough, symbolic image patterns are created, and these metaphoric configurations are used by the playwright to express the meaning of the dramatic action. We know from Lorca's essay "Gongora" that he conceived of language for the theatre in this way. A few quotations from this essay make this point quite clear: "At the basis of all language is the image . . . and metaphor alone gives a semblance of the dramatic." Or, "Metaphor is always ordered by (the playwright's) vision of the action; it links two antagonistic worlds by an equestrian leap of imagination." Finally, "the poet fuses details of the infinitesimally small with astronomic intuitions; he enters what may well be called the universe of each thing . . . for this reason, the apple and the sea evoke the same response; for he knows that the world of the apple is as infinite as the world of the sea. The span of the apple, from the time of its flowering till it falls from the tree to the grass in a burnish, is as great and mysterious as the measured rhythms of the tides."

It is in this sense of "togetherness" that I want to discuss Lorca, in the hopes that we shall more fully understand the meaning of the plays and also with the hope that I can indicate how Lorca's language can serve as a model—for many reasons it can never be imitated—for others who would revivify the language of our theatre.

One can see Lorca's use of imagery patterns as a way of creating meaning more clearly in *Blood Wedding* and *Yerma* than in *The House of Bernarda Alba* because the first two are clearly poetic plays while the last is intentionally naturalistic. To indicate the nature of this difference, let me say a few words about *Yerma*. *Yerma* means the barren one and the play is about a woman who more than anything else wants children. Her husband will not and presumably cannot give her any and because of the Spanish code of honor (a subject I shall deal with presently in terms of *The House of Bernarda Alba*), she cannot have a child by another man, although the opportunity presents itself. Finally, in despair and because of a sexual overture by her husband, she kills him and in so doing insures her barrenness. To use her words, the last of the play— "Barren, barren, but sure. . . . Don't come near me, because I've killed my son. I myself have killed my son!" The focus of the drama then is on procreation and the frustration of barrenness. But the full meaning of the action can only be understood through the image patterns.

The dominant ones are of vegetation and water. In the first, he uses flowers (primarily roses), fruits, vegetables, and wheat. In employing these images Lorca not only compares the world of man to that of vegetation in terms of an idea or sensation common to both, but he fuses both worlds into one by making the idea or sensation more important than either world taken separately. For example, in such speeches as: "But when he's close to me his eyes tremble like two green leaves," or

> Through night skies he comes,
> my husband to bed.
> I like red gillyflowers,
> he, a gillyflower red.

Lorca compares human sexuality to certain characteristics of flowers in such a way that a particular quality of the sex act itself becomes important, namely reproduction. (Or when Yerma says to her husband, "These bed clothes smell of apples," the playwright creates a metaphor of fertility by joining the world of sheets and pillowcases to that of the orchard.) Thus by fusing the human and vegetative elements, Lorca creates an overriding image of fertility which he then equates with Yerma.

Lorca achieves the reverse effect within the same metaphoric configuration by using weed and thistle imagery. Or we can see it with equal clarity in the water-dryness imagery. His use of these two patterns is a particular case in point in the formation of metaphors that create the complex effect of frustration and procreation simultaneously. He does this by giving water a sensual quality:

> Men have to give us pleasure, girl. They've got to take down our hair and let us drink water out of their mouths. So runs the world.

So later, Yerma says:

But you must come, sweet love, my baby, because water gives salt, the earth fruit and our wombs guard tender infants just as a cloud is sweet with rain.

But in this land where mountain streams flow continuously, "and children come like water," Yerma is barren and badly needs the rain. So, at the end of the play when she refuses the offer of another man, she says: "I'm like a dry field . . . and you offer me a little glass of well water." Thus, the imagery becomes more complex, for the effect created is one of thirst (Yerma expresses herself in terms of how thirsty she is all through the play), and the immediate object of this thirst is moisture for the purpose of procreation.

I could go on with this, but suffice it to say that all these image patterns are focused on reproduction or those forces which frustrate it. But not only do we get the frustration but also the reason for it, so the imagery acts as a restatement of the plot, more fully expresses the characters, and helps to reveal to us the meaning of the overall action.

In *Yerma* the metaphoric configurations are an integral part of the play; in fact, I would go so far as to say that both the plot and the characters are metaphorically conceived. Such is not the case in *The House of Bernarda Alba*.

It has been often pointed out that this play is more like an Ibsen play than anything else. In a sense this is true, and Lorca intended it that way. He says "that these Three Acts are intended as a photographic document," and it is reported that when he first read his script aloud to friends, he remarked after each scene: "Not a drop of poetry! Reality! Realism!" But naturalism in the theatre, with its insistence on environmental credibility, has limited conventions of language, and metaphor has little if any place. For this reason most modern dramatists since Ibsen have sought to compensate for that depth which in earlier drama could be achieved by a richness of language by using inanimate symbols to heighten and deepen the implications of the external action and at the same time stay within the restricting limitations of the naturalistic convention. Such is the case with *The House of Bernarda Alba*.

Beginning with the names of the characters we see that Lorca has radically changed his techniques. In the early plays, most of the characters had no names, but they were nonetheless richly delineated by the playwright's poetic language as well as by the action created by that language. But in *The House of Bernarda Alba*, names become overtly and narrowly symbolic; they literally define the characters: Angustia means anguish, misery, sorrow; Magdalena, who continually weeps, reminds one of Mary Magdalene and her tears; Martirio means martyr; Adela, the lone rebel, means "to move forward"; Bernarda, Bernardine nun, and so on. Then there is the white setting to suggest heat, sterility, and purity. In the earlier plays, the settings were more neutral, and the qualities of the action were expressed directly by the language; in this play meaning is expressed indirectly by means of inanimate objects. In addition an ironic contrast is achieved by having on the walls of this prison-nunnery pictures of landscapes filled with nymphs.

We notice the same technique in Lorca's use of stage properties. We tend to forget that in the Greek, Elizabethan, or French Neoclassic theatre there is very little dependence on stage properties. They are fewer in number—in some cases almost nonexistent—and are completely functional. There was no need for them to be anything else. But in *The House of Bernarda Alba,* Adela's rebellion is expressed by her fan with green and red flowers and her green dress. The symbol of Bernarda's tyrannical authority is her cane, and Adela's revolt against this authority is symbolized by her breaking of the cane.

Or to move to another element of the plays—the songs. In *Blood Wedding* the Wife and Mother-in-law's lullaby of the big horse who didn't like water is both naturalistic and metaphoric. In this song Lorca fuses the human qualities of blood with like human qualities given to water to create a metaphor for Leonardo. The horse-Leonardo doesn't like water because he doesn't understand the meaning of a stream. Bleeding and crying, with a dagger stuck deep in his eye, he goes down to the river:

> And how his life's bloods teeming
> Of more than the rivers streaming

The whole of Leonardo's later actions are thus prefigured. He cannot withstand or understand the current of the blood-water stream, and in the forest scene this image recurs when the woodcutters tell us that perhaps the Bride and Leonardo have relieved the overbearing repression damming their blood streams:

> But by then they'll have mingled their bloods.
> They'll be like two empty jars, like two arroyos.

Thus, their frustration is expressed in terms of its being stopped up, either by the forces of life (such as not being able to yield to desire) or by definite human objects such as breasts or veins swollen to the bursting point.

We see a similar use of song in the songs of the Laundresses at the opening of the second act of *Yerma*. Here the song is used as a direct expression of the fertility-sterility, moisture-dryness action of the play. It functions organically in the developing action and has a direct relationship to all the other elements in the play.

But in *The House of Bernarda Alba* song is not used in this way. The "Song of the Reapers" with all its sexual imagery is outside the action and seems almost tacked on. Its function is not to express anything in the play's action but to heighten by contrast the sense of sexual imprisonment and frustration that exists within the house of Bernarda Alba. One last example would be to compare the use of the stallion in *Blood Wedding* and *The House of Bernarda Alba*. In the earlier play, Leonardo and his horse are fused metaphorically so they become almost a new character with the attributes of both man and stallion. But the stallion in Bernarda's corral is used primarily to heighten the atmosphere of frustration. To be sure it does represent, in addition to repressed sexuality, masculinity trying to break down the walls of the house, and later, when Adela describes the horse standing in the moonlight, it is identified with Pepe. The stallion is also used ironically, for Bernarda is immediately aware of what must be done to satisfy the horse's needs, but she is totally blind to the desires of her daughters. But in each instance, the stallion functions as an external, analogous symbol—like the burning of the orphanage in Ibsen's *Ghosts* or the infected baths of his *An Enemy of the People*—rather than as a defining metaphor through which and in terms of which the play's action is directly expressed.

But Lorca, for all his attempts to write a naturalistic play, was at times a poet in spite of himself, and the best moments of the play are those when the language of gesture asserts itself. The most obvious instance is the already mentioned symbolism of the black and white of a photograph. Lorca is obviously making a conscious effort to make the play a "photographic document." Not only are the black costumes set against white walls, but the dark stains of the walls themselves have been whitewashed, and the house and everything in it is scrubbed and polished. Not only must honor be untarnished, but virginity must be maintained. However, the black-white symbolism is not as simple as this. For in contrast to the whiteness of sterility, we also have the whiteness of fertility. The stallion, the male archetype, is white and is described as standing in the moonlight "in the middle of the corral. White. Twice as large. Filling all the darkness." Pepe, too, is pictured as a man who "likes to walk around in the moonlight." This symbolism finally becomes metaphoric in the third-act speeches of Maria Josefa, Bernarda's deranged mother, who utters strange truths out of her lunacy. In these speeches is to be found that fusion of man and nature and even elements of the supernatural and the subconscious which is so prevalent in *Blood Wedding* and *Yerma*:

> It's true. Everything's very dark. Just because I have white hair you think I can't have babies, but I can—babies and babies and babies. This baby will have white hair, and I'd have *this* baby and another, and this *one* other; and with all of us with snow white hair we'll be like the waves—one, then another, and another. Then we'll all sit down and all of us will have white heads, and we'll be seafoam. Why isn't there any seafoam here? Nothing but mourning shrouds here. . . . Now I have to go away, but I'm afraid the dogs will bite me. Won't you come with me as far as the fields? I don't like fields. I like houses, but open houses, and the neighbor women asleep in their beds with their little tiny tots, and the men outside sitting in their chairs. Pepe el Romano is a giant. All of you love him. But he's going to devour you because you're grains of wheat. No, not grains of wheat. Frogs with no tongues!

Here we have a total fusion of all the play's images. The whiteness of coldness, sterility, and death is also the white of the sperm, seafoam, and life. These speeches function metaphorically, for the waves of life which Maria Josefa vainly yearns to maintain in uninterrupted motion become doomed to stagnation. The whiteness of the house, the white sterility has triumphed over the white foam of life and productivity. There remains only the whiteness of silence, the whiteness of death.

Another successful use of metaphor in the play is Lorca's identification of Adela with St. Barbara, the virgin martyr. In the third act, as the time of blood is about to come again, the family is sitting about and the girls are watching the sky with its "stars as big as fists." Adela turns and asks:

> Mother, why when a star falls or lightning
> flashes, does one say:

Holy Barbara, blessed on high
May your name be in the sky
With holy water written high.

Now, Holy Barbara, according to tradition, was shut up in a tower by her father because she wanted to marry a Christian. He later killed her, and it is reported that he was struck down by lightning. When Amelia says she closes her eyes so she won't see the shooting stars, Adela replies, "Not I. I like to see what's quiet and been quiet for years on end, running with fire." Adela is fascinated by the night sky and the fire of the shooting star is similar to that fire which she feels in her legs and mouth. This image is picked up a short while later when Poncia tells Bernarda: "Who knows, lightning might strike suddenly. Who knows but what all of a sudden, in a rush of blood, your heart might stop." And indeed it does. The lightning of a sudden rush of blood does strike, and in so doing the action's catastrophe, the characters, and the language of the metaphor all fuse in a perfect meaning.

Another example of Lorca's poetic conception of action can be found in the opening scene when the women are returning to the house after the funeral. In a stage direction Lorca says: "*The two hundred women finish coming in.*" Obviously, Lorca didn't mean literally two hundred women (the fact that only one tray is brought on further confirms this); rather he envisioned the entire female population of the village at once. In addition to creating this effect it is also expressive of the village's tendency to prying watchfulness and the resultant sense of fear and guilt. We are never allowed to forget the continual presence of people waiting outside the house for the opportunity to find dishonor. There are the two hundred of the first act, a crowd in the second, and the large, invisible, but very real crowd that Bernarda shouts to at the end of the play. And, of course, finally, the house itself is an omnipresent symbol. The play is, after all, entitled *The House of Bernarda Alba*.

But in the final analysis, Lorca's use of language in his last play is essentially external. The imagery is used to create an atmospheric pressure for the action rather than to create the action itself. It is a poetic atmosphere that enlarges the naturalistic theatre without breaking any of its conventions. In *Blood Wedding* and *Yerma* I believe Lorca has done infinitely more than this. In these plays, because of his effective use of metaphor, Lorca has not only perceived a common power in two dissimilar worlds, he has fused them so they become a new one. As a result, the *effect* which the metaphor creates becomes far more important than the similarity itself. The effect moves the audience in such a way that the original similarity between two worlds is forgotten, and the effect itself is thought of as belonging to a single new world. This, then, is the first thing that I mean by Lorca's "togetherness." This togetherness of language is probably his most important contribution to the modern theatre, and I believe if there is to be a revitalization of language in the contemporary theatre, our playwrights must follow those paths that Lorca has blazed for us.

Thus far I have been primarily concerned with Lorca's poetic techniques. While such discussions are always helpful, they have real significance only if they enhance our understanding of the plays themselves. So we must turn now to a discussion of the other "togetherness." What is it that Lorca has photographed in *The House of Bernarda Alba* and what does it mean?

Spain has always wanted her children to prefer honor to life at every moment. For the Spaniard honor traditionally is the one value greater than the living of life. This doesn't mean there is never any conflict between honor and individual human desires; but since this sense of honor defines man's place in the community, the recognition of its code will determine personal feelings and impose a discipline which has positive value. In this way, life has meaning because in living it we affirm, perpetuate, and celebrate those values that are worth dying for. But when men lose that sense of integration in life which holds honor and desire in fruitful tension, the world trembles and comes apart.

Whenever I compare *The House of Bernarda Alba* with *Blood Wedding* and *Yerma,* the first thing that strikes me is the radical change in Lorca's attitude toward honor. It is like moving from the plays of Corneille to those of Racine. In *Blood Wedding,* as the moment of blood comes again, the Mother is torn by her personal desire to save her son's life and the demand to preserve the family honor. There is momentary hesitation, but the choice is clear:

> Go! After them! No. Don't go. Those people kill quickly and well . . . but yes, run, and I'll follow.

We find the same thing in Yerma. She wants a child more than anything else in the world, but when the Old Woman suggests that Yerma go off with her son, Yerma replies:

Do you imagine I could know another man? Where would that leave my honor? . . . Look at me, so you'll know me and never speak to me again. I'm not looking for anyone.

In these plays there is a conflict between principle and feeling, a struggle to fit the experience of the individual into the framework of the community life. But because honor is an attitude of virtue which is believed in, it enables man to dominate the life of instinct and accomplish actions which order the whole of his being instead of destroying it by placing him at the mercy of his conflicting desires. This does not mean there is no suffering, for the Mother and Yerma are clearly suffering, but there is a sense of meaning in painful reconciliation.

But in *The House of Bernarda Alba*, honor is the keeping up of appearances. It is not a reality, but an attitude to be maintained. It is an attitude in which the positive idea of virtue has been sacrificed; and when this happens, conduct becomes a series of postures which no longer correspond to any moral feelings. The result of this—and for more evidence we could also point to Victorian England or any other age of respectability—is the complete divorce between the public and private life of the individual. Such a divorce inevitably leads to moral anarchy and the destructive victory of unchecked passions. People become wild beasts, and the only morality is the morality of the jungle. This is what I believe to be the central action of Lorca's last play: the conflict between the hypocritical and sterile norms of conformity and regimentation and the overpowering desire for sexual release and expression. This play, Lorca says, is a "photographic document in three acts," but in the making of it he has used a slow motion camera which he has focused on the passions of a horrible "togetherness."

Bernarda is that character who would maintain this artificial honor. Hers is a belief in hypocritical respectability in which there is a complete disassociation between what one does and what one feels. As she says:

Each one knows what she thinks inside. I don't pry into anyone's heart, but I want to put up a good front and have family harmony.

For the most part, this attitude is accepted by the rest of the family, and it is best expressed by Martirio's "Wanting isn't doing."

But to maintain these sterile norms of respectability in the midst of her daughters' ever-growing passions and frustrations, Bernarda must be constantly on watch; her eyes are always open. Furthermore, as long as outward appearances are preserved she is satisfied and has an amazing ability to rationalize away those indications that her world is crumbling. Immediately after she enters in the first act, we learn that all the girls were desirously watching Pepe at the funeral. As if saying it will make it so, Bernarda authoritatively declares that it wasn't Pepe at all but Darajali the widower. We see the same characteristic in the third act, when in answer to Prudencia's question about Angustia's pearl engagement ring, Bernarda says: "With pearls or without them, things are as one proposes." Bernarda is the boss and will be, she says, until she is carried out by her feet. Finally, she is best characterized by her remark: "I don't merely believe it. It's so!" But this is easier said than done. One cannot live forever on the assumption that if a thing isn't known, somehow it doesn't exist. When Bernarda says, "Don't try to find out," I cannot help but be reminded of Olga's "Don't tell me, I'm not listening!" in the third act of Chekhov's *The Three Sisters*. The belief that if things are not said, although we know full well they exist, they won't be so is one of our greatest delusions.

Bernarda through most of the play is successful and fairly self-confident, but she too has her moments of doubt. When Poncia tries to warn her of the impending disaster, Bernarda shouts: "There you go again! Sneaking up on me—giving me bad dreams." Even for Bernarda there are unconscious fears that can never be completely repressed.

However, the most interesting manner in which Bernarda's dominance is dramatized is the way Lorca has made her almost a man. In this respect she is very similar to the Clytemnestra of Aeschylus' *Oresteia*. The references to her masculinity are numerous. Bernarda says: "I've always loved a good fight." She runs her property like a man and in particular handles the stallion and his breeding like a man. When Prudencia says: "You have to fight like a man," Bernarda replies, "That's it." It is only by the denial of her essential nature that Bernarda is able to keep up appearances. In the end she is unsuccessful, for the walls of respectability are not strong enough to withstand the kicks of desire.

Bernarda's house is a prison-nunnery in which she would lock up her daughters' passions. But prisons have never been able to contain desire. As Adela says: "For I'd leap not over you, just a servant, but over my mother to put out this fire I feel in my legs and my mouth." Desire and life are always bursting to get out, and this is best seen in Bernarda's mother, Maria Josefa. Bernarda keeps her locked up, but the old crone is always getting out. As the Servant says: "I had a hard time holding her. In spite of her eighty years, your mother's strong as an oak." The old mother knows that all the forces of desire drive these women to the fertility of the sea. And if desire has no release, it rots inside and turns back in on itself with poisonous destruction.

Now, it is one of the paradoxes of despotism that the attempt to impose complete uniformity on the common life defeats its own end, encourages a revolutionary individualism, and promotes a subterranean hostility between the individual and the artificial group which it tries to set up in place of the natural community of the people. In this play Adela is such a figure of revolt. Bernarda has not been able to control her desires, and Adela stoutly maintains that she "will not get used to it" and that she will do whatever she wants with her body. She is, in short, as Martirio calls her, "an unbroken little mule."

Adela's desire for Pepe is always expressed in terms of thirst, and we notice that throughout the play she is always getting a drink of water to slake her desire. She says: "Looking in his eyes I seem to drink his blood in slowly." Adela's desire—and all of the other girls have it too—is "something bursting in your breast, trying to come out." Adela says: "I didn't want him to [touch me]. It's as if I were dragged by a rope." In Lorca there are no poetic interludes on the spirit of love "whose capacity receiveth as the sea." Love is no game, but as in Racine, a mortal disease. How remote this is from Romeo's

> It is the east and Juliet is the sun!
> Arise, fair sun, and kill the envious moon.

In a world of artificial norms and despotic authority, if desire ever gets out of control it is bound to end in catastrophe. The servant, Poncia, knows this. She is a strange combination of servant, confidante, Cassandra-like warner, Chaucerian wife of Bath, and Greek chorus. Poncia knows trouble is coming. First she tries to persuade Adela to wait for Pepe, since Angustia will surely die in childbirth. She also tries to keep the other girls in check. When this fails, she warns Bernarda:

Who knows, lightning might strike suddenly.
Who knows but what all of a sudden, in a rush
of blood, your heart might stop.

Bernarda insists that "Nothing will happen here," and goes out.
There is nothing more Poncia can do:

I can do nothing. I tried to head things off, but now they frighten
me too much. You feel this silence?—in each room there is a thunder-
storm—and the day it breaks, it'll sweep all of us along with it. But
I've said what I had to say.

Poncia knows that things have gone too far and that once the dam
breaks "you're powerless against the sea" of pent-up desires. Adela
will "stand forth stark naked," and the river will carry her along to
her destruction. Bernarda believes she can resist this. She says:

Silence, I say! [Note that "silence" is Bernarda's key word] I saw
the storm coming but I didn't think it'd burst so soon. . . . But I'm
not old yet—I have five chains for you, and this house my father
built . . . I'll have to let them feel the weight of my hand.

But as the Servant says later:

Bernarda thinks nothing can stand against her, yet she doesn't know
the strength a man has among women alone.

And Poncia knows that

They're women without men . . . and in such matters even blood
is forgotten.

And indeed it is, for just a little later Martirio and Adela openly admit their love for Pepe, and Martirio shouts:

Don't put your arms around me! Don't try to smooth it over. My
blood's no longer yours, and even though I try to think of you as a
sister, I see you as just another woman.

Soon the dam does break, and from this moment on the action
rushes headlong to the catastrophe and Bernarda is helpless to stop
it. In fact, her failure is beautifully expressed by a single line which
captures all the strands of her previous dominance. She goes out to
shoot Pepe; after the shot she comes in, and Poncia says: "Did you
kill him?" Martirio replies: "No. He raced away on his mare!" and
Bernarda says: "It was my fault. A woman can't aim."
So the torrents of spring break through, but this river of desire

does not produce ripe fruit; it only drowns. Adela says just before she commits suicide:

> There's no way out of here. Whoever has to drown—let her drown. Pepe is mine. He'll carry me to the rushes along the river bank.

And this I think is the meaning of a "togetherness" that is based upon an honor which is in reality "the keeping up of appearances." There is no outlet, no hope of sanity and freedom for the hysteria of these frustrated women, women controlled by false honor and caste. There is only erotic frustration and perverted power. Even when desire successfully rebels, it is doomed to death, for the arms of the lover turn out to be the arms of death.

Thus, Lorca's "togetherness" in *The House of Bernarda Alba* consists of tying up and twisting the strands of people's passions so tightly that only the "tiny knife" can probe the center of the conflict. That tiny knife

> that barely fits the hand,
> but that slides in clean
> through the astonished flesh
> and stops at the place
> where trembles, enmeshed,
> the dark root of a scream.

Bernarda's final "Silence!" will always be mocked by the corpse of Adela hanging in the shadows.

# PART THREE

# THE THEATRE
# IN A COLLECTIVE
# SOCIETY

# THE TRANSFORMATION
# OF THE INDIVIDUAL
# IN THE MODERN THEATRE

THE ONE thing that characterizes the work of almost all contemporary playwrights is the fact that their plays express the theatre's profound concern to find a metaphor for universal modern man. Each of them seems to be looking for a metaphor that is symbolic of the inalienable part of every man—that irreducible part of each of us which exists after all the differences have been stripped away, and which is beyond and beneath all that is social, political, economic, religious, and ideological. In short, they are searching for a metaphor of man left face to face with himself.

I suppose Jack Gelber's *The Connection* was one of the first American plays to reflect this concern. I happen to think that this play, which is apparently about dope addiction, is a bad play and that its success was largely due either to the sensationalism of its subject matter or the morbid curiosity of our audiences. Nonetheless, it is a significant play because somehow, in spite of its monosyllabic language, it is an articulate expression of one of our contemporary world's deepest concerns: man's need to make a connection, with his own divided self, his fellowman, his society, and with God. Each of the characters in the play is looking for a "fix" which will help to bridge the great gulf that separates him from the others. Only

Harry, the mute record player, succeeds, and his success in its isolation only heightens the sense of man's ontological solitude.

We were strangely moved by *The Connection*, as we were by the many plays like it which soon followed, and yet when we left the theatre we were dissatisfied. Somehow it is a theatre without commitment; it is existential without being engaged. It is a theatre which reveals man detached from the machinery of society, and it presents an image of man having no historical situation or function. In short, it is a theatre showing man defined by his solitude and estrangement, not by his participation.

So, blame the world! Estrangement is the human condition and only a Pollyanna will ask the theatre to provide more. But, somehow, the very act of going to the theatre is to demand more. It is an assertion that underneath everything that divides us there are certain feelings and responses, anxieties and fears, hopes and joys that we all commonly share. And from its earliest beginnings the theatre has been a celebration of this community of spirit. Thus, a theatre which denies the validity of man's social context is bound to fail its audiences.

There is a growing awareness of this failure among our theatre's most serious practitioners, and this accounts for the numerous attempts in the modern theatre to establish some kind of communion with its audience. Now, the concept of communion is not new in the theatre. Ever since the time of Goethe we find playwrights and directors trying to create for themselves the lost audience. The most magnificent attempt was undoubtedly Wagner's temple-theatre at Bayreuth; but the same impulse was the motivating force in the work of Appia, Craig, Fuchs, MacKaye, Hofmannsthal, Yeats, Copeau, Gheon, and Claudel. And today it manifests itself with great intensity in the popular theatre movements both here and in Europe. Finally, however, all of these noble efforts have either failed or fallen terribly short of their much-to-be-admired aims. And I believe the reason for this is the simple but frightening fact that the kind of communion they are looking for cannot exist in the modern world; it is a lingering phantom from a world long since lost. All the searchers for communion have either forgotten or have refused to accept the truth of what Tocqueville told us long ago, that "not only does democracy make every man forget his ancestors, but it hides his descendants and separates his contemporaries from him; it throws him back forever upon himself alone and threatens in the

end to confine him entirely within the solitude of his own heart."
Only Brecht, sensing the failure of the theatre to satisfy modern
man's deepest concerns, realized that our playwrights had to take a
new direction. He faced the grim realities of estrangement and
ontological solitude in his first plays, and as early as 1926 he wrote:
"When one sees that our world of today no longer fits into the
drama, then it is merely that the drama no longer fits into the
world." * I believe what Brecht meant by this statement is that the
drama had ceased to be relevant to modern audiences because it
was based upon outmoded premises. He was the first playwright to
be fully aware of the fact that since the Renaissance and the Industrial Revolution, with their insistence upon the "self-sufficient finitude" of man, we no longer live in a communal world, but rather in
a collective society—a society in which the traditional concept of
community is as obsolete as the one-horse shay. Therefore, if the
modern dramatist is to "communicate" with his audience it cannot
be within the traditional framework of the individual living in community.

Now, to many this is a frightening idea. The term collective
"smacks" of communism (and to be sure, Marx and Engels were
among the first to understand clearly the collective nature of an industrial society), so perhaps we should first define our terms. I suppose at its simplest level, a community is a group in which all the
members can communicate directly with one another. But more
significantly, in communities people are linked together by common
origins. A community is a group which *precedes* its individual members and the individual's place in it is clearly defined from the moment he is born into it. For this reason, in a communal society all
human relationships tend to be personal, because those forces which
bind men together—values, attitudes, customs, traditions, rituals, and
habits—are handed down as a common heritage from generation to
generation. Certainly, many communities still exist in rural and isolated areas of the world; but in an age of spreading urbanization and
increasing industrialization they are rapidly disappearing, and socio-
logically and economically I believe it is safe to say that they exist
only anachronistically.

A collective, on the other hand, is post-individual. It is a group
brought into being by previously existing individual members who
have gathered together because they share common ends. Thus col-

* *Brecht on Theatre*, John Willett, ed., p. 17.

lectives—political parties, labor unions, great business corporations, educational institutions, and even churches—unlike communities, are not derived from the past, but are directed toward the future by the aims of its individual members.

Any economy based upon the dynamic process of the productive circulation of goods necessarily involves the expansion of public life and collective cooperation. Pluralistic industrialism is the most fully developed form of such an economy and it is rapidly coming to dominate the whole world. Kerr, Dunlop, Harbison, and Myers in their important book *Industrialism and Industrial Man* go so far as to say:

> In our times it is no longer the spectre of Communism which is haunting Europe, but rather emerging industrialization in many forms that is confronting the whole world. The giant of industrialization is stalking the earth, transforming almost all the features of older and traditional societies.

But industrialization, based as it is upon the premises of production and profit, has as its first principle specialization. And specialization inevitably leads to functionalism, standardization, anonymity, or interchangeability, and finally alienation. Victor Thompson describes the effect of this process on the individual in his book, *Modern Organization:*

> The microdivision of work, by making the goal of activity invisible, deprived work of any meaning for the individual. He was no longer engaged in a "worthwhile" task. He became alienated from his work, and at the same time his work lost its social identity. It had no meaning for significant persons beyond the immediate work group. The industrial worker lost status and function.

Finally, and perhaps most important of all, the dominant characteristic of industrial collectivism in all its forms is manipulation: the manipulation of nature, material things, ideas, and people—people as objects. (The best definition of bureaucracy that I know of is "the organization of people as objects." And I think it is significant that all over the world a new technology of management is being developed. It is best known as industrial or business administration, and its chief concern is with the recalcitrance of people, rather than the hardness of materials.)

The implications of this shift from a communal to a collective social organization for the institutions of our society are almost frightening in their enormity, but in the context of this chapter I am most concerned with the effects it has had upon the individual. In a collective economy the individual comes to represent only a specialized function within the larger objective function of the particular collective of which he is a part. Specialization does not make demands upon the individual as a human being, only on his specific technical abilities. It is only concerned with the individual's functional qualities. And as the individual is increasingly absorbed by the collective, his human qualities tend to atrophy and his personality undergoes severe psychic and moral changes, and eventually he comes to lose all sense of his own identity. Erich Kahler, to whom I am greatly indebted for my understanding of this whole problem, goes so far as to say in *Man the Measure:*

> the average individual of a modern metropolis is no longer a real person. He is a focus, an intersection point of various collective interests, collective activities, collective inclinations and reactions. His personality consists almost wholly of the specific combination of collective interests that meet within him.

If this is true, then man in a collective society is no longer an individual in the Renaissance-humanistic sense of the word. Rather he has become a collective social personality. Etymologically, individuality means that quality in man which cannot be divided, that which is indivisible. But industrialization, as we have indicated, does just that; it divides man. It is indeed capable of invalidating man's sense of his own individuality. Again, I should like to quote from Professor Kahler's *Man the Measure:*

> ... individuality does not mean personal interests and their pursuit, but an inner, personal way of thinking and feeling that suffuses the whole person's existence and permeates all of its manifestations and forms. In other words: to have individuality is not so much to have a mind of one's own, as to have one's own mind. A person can live utterly for God, for another, for his work. He can forget himself completely in his devotion or preoccupation and still be a shining example of individuality, provided that what he lives for is his personal relation to God, his personal love, his personal work—a work that bears his features, that reflects the meaning and content of his own life. The work of the artist who achieves a creation complete in itself, of the thinker whose vision interprets the world, of the craftsman of earlier times who wrought an object from beginning to end and put into it the experience of years, of the farmer who saw

his labor whole within the circle of the seasons, the work of such a person is literally in his own hands, he is literally at home in it and with it; work is a function of his personal life, not the function of an alien, overwhelming enterprise that imposes the rules for working and even for living. Because his work is such that he can put himself into it, he can take from it what he gives to it—meaning, knowledge, purpose—and in this interplay of two wholes each builds and informs the other, each, in fact, gives individuality to the other. But the specialized work of today does not concern the whole human being, it requires and develops only partial and peripheral skills. The division of labor has divided man as well as his work, divided him from himself as well as from his work. And as man loses his wholeness, his indivisibility, he loses his individuality.

But as soon as man loses his sense of individuality, and since the demands of industrialism make impersonal relationships inevitable, he not only comes to lose his sense of identity, he comes to think of himself only as a commodity.

The effects that the full-blown emergence of a collective society and the social personality in the twentieth century have had on most aspects of modern life have been widely recognized; but their effects on the arts—and they have been tremendous—have not been fully acknowledged, and this is particularly true of the theatre. First of all, they have to a large extent been responsible for that sense of helplessness which pervades the modern world, and hence its theatre. We hear all the time that our world is getting smaller and smaller; it is a time of "one world" diplomacy with "direct distance dialing," jet travel, communication satellites, and moon walks. But there is little comfort in all these technological advances which appear to have made the world smaller. On the contrary, increasingly we sense that the world is greater, not smaller, than we had ever supposed. We are overwhelmed by the new data and phenomena of complexity which besiege us daily. And more important, we are overwhelmed by the needs of humanity which seems greater as we become increasingly more aware of them. What about the uprooted? The refugees? The wounded and the maimed? The spiritually and mentally disturbed? How do we meet successfully the struggles of race, class, hunger, poverty, and rising nationalism? And what about such problems as public education, the care of the aged, and on and on? In a recent interview, Samuel Beckett was asked why he was so concerned with human distress. He replied: "Yes, my plays deal with distress. Some people object to this in my writing. At a party an English intellectual—so-called—asked me why I write always about distress. As if it were perverse to want to do so! He wanted to know if my father had beaten me or my mother had run away from home to give me an unhappy childhood. I told him no, that I had had a very happy childhood. Then he thought me more perverse than ever. I left the party as soon as possible and got into a taxi. On the glass partition between me and the driver were three signs: one asked for help for the blind, another help for orphans, and the third for relief for the war refugees. One does not have to look for distress. It is screaming at you even in the taxis of London."

But our awareness of these problems and the seeming impossibility to do much about them tends to paralyze us; it creates in us a pervasive sense of helplessness. We are aware of this in our leaders as they try rather unsuccessfully to face national and international crises. How much more so for the rest of us! "Who am I?" we ask; and "What can I do?" But how can the dramatist create a meaningful action or significant characters in a "What-can-I-do?" kind of world? Our world, it would seem, has become almost too big for the playwright, for only what the mind can comprehend and the eye can take in can be made visible in art. Compare, for example, the achievement of a Lindbergh (our last "lone" hero) to that of Colonel Glenn, who was interchangeable with five other astronauts. Or, how can the power of a Napoleon be envisioned today? In our times power is so enormous that it is barely visible and those who govern are little more than incidental and easily replaceable expressions of that power. (Allen Dulles, for instance, as head of the Central Intelligence Agency, had the power to secretly raise and train within our own borders an army to invade Cuba; and yet he was replaced shortly after that ill-fated invasion with little, if any, public notice.) Power, then, is like an iceberg; the largest part is submerged in abstraction, anonymity, and bureaucracy. Government, like modern physics, has lost its physical reality and can be expressed only in statistics and formulae. But what are the implications of this for the theatre? Who are the true representatives of a world whose tragic heroes are nameless? After all, a theatre of reports and statistics is a contradiction in terms. As the Swiss playwright, Duerrenmatt, put it: "Any smalltime crook, petty govern-

ment official, or policeman better represents our world than a senator or president. Today art can only embrace victims if it can reach
men at all; it can no longer come close to the mighty. Creon's secretaries close Antigone's case." In short, can you have heroes at all
in a world of social personalities?

It would seem that a collective society not only does not need
heroes, but it actually suppresses or perverts our need of them. In
their book *Industrialism and Industrial Man,* Kerr and his colleagues convincingly demonstrate that:

> Like ideologies, the great personality—the one great figure around
> whom historians so frequently weave their story—began to seem less
> important. Instead of ideologies and dominant personalities, we be-
> came increasingly attentive to the inherent nature of the particular
> industrializing system and the basic strategy and forces at work
> within it.

Only the system, then, is important, and it fills men's remaining
need for heroes by promoting celebrities, those heroes of the surface
who play their constantly shifting roles well.

Furthermore, specialization—the key operative principle of an industrial society—not only produces pluralism in our economic system, but also a pluralistic deviation of heroic types. However, when
there are and can be so many heroic types—one cannot even begin
to count all the heroes of the popular imagination—you begin to
get a leveling: and with that leveling not only is the stature of heroism diminished, but the individual's sense of his own identity is
actually invalidated.

In this regard I should like to mention one final consideration
which I believe has had a significant effect on the modern theatre.
As I indicated earlier, one of the functions of the hero, both in art
and life, is to supply those images, values, and ethical standards
which people aspire to and which they would like, if possible, to
incorporate into their own lives. Traditionally, the hero is always
best described in terms of those forces which urge him to spiritual
redemption. Maxwell Anderson once wrote that "from the point of
view of the playwright, the essence of a tragedy, or even a serious
play, is the spiritual awakening, or regeneration, of his hero." But
the one thing that characterizes the hero of surfaces—and this is
certainly in large measure due to industrialization and bureaucracy
—is precisely the fact that he lacks the dimensions of spiritual

awareness, personal morality, and social responsibility. Paul Tillich wrote in his *The Religious Situation* that "the fundamental value in ethics of a capitalistic society is economic efficiency—developed to the utmost degree of ruthless activity." Such an ethical standard is hardly conducive to the creation of great heroes in the drama. (Even the negative heroes of earlier ages, the heroes of evil, affirmed indirectly a standard of order and value to which all men could aspire.) It can only produce the morality of the Eichmann defense, the Nuremburg Trials, the General Electric price-fixing scandals, the TV quiz-show investigations, and the ethical dichotomy inherent in the attitudes of so many of our atomic physicists.

That we live in an antiheroic age is a commonplace. Carlyle proclaimed its coming in the nineteenth century when he said "we shall either learn to know a hero . . . when we see him, or else go on to be forever governed by the unheroic." This transformation has occured; we have accepted it; we are even used to it. Whatever nostalgia we may still occasionally feel is more than adequately taken care of by television. In the place of the hero we have the celebrity, that triumph of the ordinary. In our time, hero worship has become horizontal; indeed, we even look down to a "man like myself."

Many modern artists have rebelled against the conditions of growing collectivism. They see that the Renaissance and industrialism have not only freed the individual, but also have deprived him of a metaphysical basis for his universe. The modern world paradoxically tends to throw man back upon himself while at the same time it increasingly tends to destroy the individual's sense of his own selfhood. This creates an impasse which the modern dramatist, for the most part, has been unable to overcome. Joseph Warren Beach, in analyzing the problems of modern fiction, describes the reaction of many writers to this condition:

> One of the hardest things for man to bear is spiritual isolation. The sense that he stands alone in the universe goes terribly against his gregarious instincts. He has an overpowering impulse to construct a system which will enable him to feel that he does not stand alone but is intimately associated with some force or group infinitely more powerful and significant than himself.

But all attempts on the part of the artist to construct such a system inevitably fail, for the one thing these compensatory systems cannot supply us with is a sense of self. Robert Bolt, in his introduction to

*A Man for All Seasons,* describes this failure in brilliant terms when
he writes:

> We no longer have, as past societies have had, any picture of indi-
> vidual Man (Stoic Philosopher, Christian Religious, Rational Gen-
> tleman) by which to recognize ourselves and against which to meas-
> ure ourselves; we are anything. But if anything, then nothing, and
> it is not everyone who can live with that, though it is our true
> present position. Hence our willingness to locate ourselves from
> something that is certainly larger than ourselves, the society that
> contains us.
>   But society can only have as much idea as we have what we are
> about, for it has only our brains to think with. And the individual
> who tries to plot his position by reference to our society finds no
> fixed points, but only the vaunted absence of them, "freedom" and
> "opportunity"; freedom for what, opportunity to do what, is no-
> where indicated. The only positive he is given is "get and spend"
> ("get and spend—if you can" from the Right, "get and spend—you
> deserve it" from the Left) and he did not need society to tell him
> that. In other words, we are thrown back by our society upon our-
> selves at our lowest, that is at our least satisfactory to ourselves.
> Which of course sends us flying back to society with all the force
> of rebound.

However, there is an increasing number of contemporary playwrights—and Bolt is one of them—who have gazed unflinchingly at
our collective modern world and can still affirm their belief in both
the individual's sense of his own selfhood and also in the vitality of
the free will to assert itself in any given situation. These writers
insist that as individuals we are not only conscious of our existential
condition, but that implicit in this awareness there is also a sense
of the organic totality of our being. We certainly experience this
sense of coherence, correspondence, and cooperation—this sense of
wholeness—biologically; but more important, we also have a sense
of psychic coherence. For each of us there are times when we are
aware of the silent but continual presence of every moment of our
past life, of the immeasurable avenues of memory; and as we move
into the future, we are conscious of the fact that we carry this interior world with us. And this realization not only gives us a sense
of self-coherence, but also a sense of being able to cope with our
lives. In the works of many of the contemporary authors whom I
have discussed in this volume we discover an expression of its au-

thor's conviction that any mature human being is capable of living, at least in times of crisis, in a state of fully unfolded consciousness. In such a state, the individual is conscious of the fact that his present has been created out of the past, and furthermore, he senses that both the present and the past are creating his future. In short, he is capable of living with a sense of his own destiny. And it is this sense of our own destiny that makes us capable of spiritual aspiration and also validates for us our belief in the power of the will to meet in direct struggle the conflicts of our daily existence. As I have already pointed out, man's free will may be defeated by the forces of Destiny—in fact, the great plays have always testified that the destroying forces of Destiny are as much a part of the hero's character as his free will; it may be paralyzed and thus incapable of action; it may be submerged by the battle in such a way as to become part of that Destiny; it may even turn out to be an illusion. But the great dramas in the history of the theatre have always affirmed that the will must be an active force if we are to believe we are partaking in human greatness. To be sure, none of us are conscious of our lives in this way all the time we live them. The fact that we are not is what Eliot probably meant in the *Four Quartets* in his line: "humankind can't bear very much reality." But the plays of many of our dramatists celebrate the fact that each human being is capable of it. This capacity is the source and strength of selfhood, and from this sense of self we engage in combat—sometimes in triumph, more often in defeat—with the collective world in which we live.

# THE DISAVOWAL
# OF IDENTITY IN
# THE MODERN THEATRE

*We live too variously to live as one.*
J. ROBERT OPPENHEIMER

FEW AMERICAN plays in recent years stirred up quite so much controversy as Arthur Miller's *After the Fall.* I have no intention of recalling the arguments here, but I believe the situation is worth
noting for it was symptomatic of one of the central problems facing
the theatre of our times. Most of the furor was a reaction to the
ways and means that Miller had embodied and developed his hero's
attempts to justify his integrity in terms of the search for his own
identity. And the play and the author were either attacked or defended in terms of this search. In fact, if we are to believe Mr.
Miller and his critics (and they are certainly not alone in this), the
search for identity is the chief preoccupation of the contemporary
theatre.

Now, in a way the theatre has always been centrally concerned
with the question of "Who am I?" Beginning with Orestes' mad
journey to the Earth's navel in the opening scene of *The Eumenides*
in Aeschylus' *Oresteia,* this quest has been a dominant theme in the
drama. *Oedipus the King* is probably the prototype of such a search
in the theatre; and just about every great play ever written has
touched upon the problem of identity in some way.

202

At the same time that the theatre has concerned itself with the subject, each of us has had a tendency to talk about the crises involved with the individual's search for his own identity. Each of us desires to know who we really are, as distinct from what others—our parents, siblings, friends, associates, even our enemies—believe or desire us to be. The need to establish a sense of our own identity is a very creative force in our lives (although it is demonstrably destructive, as well), and I am sure that one of the theatre's great appeals is its very concern for identity. In the process of our own search, we are moved by a representation of the search fulfilled. However, when we reflect upon this fulfillment, we discover that the great dramas of identity usually end immediately after the search has been completed; and that ending, though it may be noble and affirming, is more often than not catastrophic. And when we think about it further, we realize that although the theatre can show the hero discovering his identity, in life this can never happen.

What we call our identity is, in fact, only a convention, a labeling that is descriptive of one or more aspects of our selfhood, but not expressive of our total self. To identify is to fix, or as the dictionary puts it, "to make to be the same; to consider as the same in any relation." Scientists tell us that it is inaccurate for us to think of matter in this way; we know we cannot think of ourselves or others in this way, although at times we may desperately attempt to do so. Personality is always in a state of gradual change. The single being may be compared with other organisms that it resembles; it may be classified, accounted for statistically, subsumed under a type, but its individuality can only be *felt*. Whatever unity, if there is a unity, the human organism maintains at the base of its transformations is something mysterious. To the human being himself, his own coherence is, as Herbert Read once put it, "an organic coherence intuitively based on the real world of sensation."

In life as we experience it, we are conscious of our physical natures, our social situations, and our unique psychic existence; and we live on all three of these levels simultaneously. For this reason it is impossible for us to act or make a choice without some element of human behavior—what we do out of physical necessity or because of social habit—playing a significant role in our decision. At the same time, because of the simultaneity of our being, it is impossible for us to understand completely the individuality of our actions. But in the theatre we see life as pure deed, that is, life in which the arbitrariness of human behavior has been eliminated and in which the mysterious transformations of individuality have been fixed. Thus, in contrast to a person in life, who is recognized by the continuity of his being and finally can only be known through intuition, a character in a play is an "identity" who is defined by the coherence of his acts. The term "identity," then, represents the human individual as an actor, as opposed to the organic concept of personality, which sees a man's actions as only an attribute of, a clue to, a being who can be known only through intuition.

As I said earlier, all drama of the past is based upon the axiom "By their deeds shall ye know them." I believe it is beyond question that traditionally the significance of the dramatic hero was revealed by his deeds, and there was a direct relationship between the hero's overt acts and his inner spiritual condition. For this reason the deeds of a dramatic action were always public, and the characters best suited to drama were men and women who, either by fate or choice, led a public life and whose deeds were of public concern. This explains why traditionally kings, princes, and nobility have been the most suitable subjects for drama.

However, beginning in the nineteenth century the drama began to reflect man's growing distrust in the ability of his senses to comprehend the true nature of reality. Appearances were no longer believed to be direct reflections of ideal reality, like the shadows on the wall of Plato's cave; rather they were thought of as a mask that hides or distorts reality. And as the machine has become an increasingly dominant force in modern life, the direct relation between a man's intention and his deeds has dissolved still further, and public figures have ceased to be our most appropriate heroes because, as W. H. Auden points out in *The Dyer's Hand*, "the good and evil they do depends less upon their characters and intentions than upon the quantity of impersonal force at their disposal."

The growing awareness of this condition has tended to make the modern dramatist, particularly those writing since the Second World War, reject the realm of deeds as the most significant sphere of human action. However, if this is true, and I believe it is, then, no matter what all the critics may say to the contrary, the fact is that the mainstream of the comtemporary theatre has not really concerned itself with the search for identity at all. If anything, our playwrights have either underscored the *lack* of modern man's search for identity or they have openly denied the value of such a search. Beginning with the Father's agonizing refusal to be judged by what he had done in the brothel with his stepdaughter in Pirandello's *Six Characters in Search of an Author*, we can trace the modern theatre's increasing tendency to reject the validity of identity. In the most impassioned moment of that play, the Father cries out:

> For the drama lies all in this—in the conscience that I have, that each one of us has. We believe this conscience to be a single thing, but it is many-sided. There is one for this person, and another for that. Diverse consciences. So we have this illusion of being one person for all, of having a personality that is unique in all our acts. But it isn't true. We perceive this when, tragically perhaps, in something we do, we are as it were, suspended, caught up in the air on a kind of hook. Then we perceive that all of us was not in that act, and that it would be an atrocious injustice to judge us by that action alone, as if all our existence were summed up in that one deed.

In short, the Father—like the other characters in the play—does not want to be a character; he does not want to have his personality fixed, and he rebels against the injustice of being identified. Pirandello, like so many modern novelists, and especially Proust, Mann, and Joyce, believed that the traditional concepts of action and character were artificial because they were incapable of expressing the essential flow and change of being. And an increasing number of playwrights have followed suit, so that today most of our serious dramatists seem to sense that Kafka best described modern man's true condition with his metaphor of "man in a tunnel." Thus trapped, one does not ask himself the question, "Who am I?" and get a very meaningful or helpful answer.

It is a commonplace that there are no great figures (one can't even think of using the word "hero") in most of the plays of our new writers. But it hasn't been pointed out strongly enough that perhaps the chief reason for this is the fact that these writers are not interested in describing personal histories. The reason there is no Oedipus, Lear, or Macbeth is because, in his concern to show us life as it is, the contemporary playwright has no use for seeing particular men in particular world systems. His only concern is to create in his plays a situation that will reveal the private drama that each man has inside himself and that is enacted every day in the random, apparently meaningless, and undramatic events of our common routine.

"History," said Stephen Daedalus, "is the nightmare from which I must awake." The rapidity of historical change and the apparent powerlessness of the individual to affect collective history has forced most of the theatre's best talents into a retreat from history. Instead of tracing the history of an individual who is born, grows old, and dies—instead of presenting identities—many modern playwrights have devoted their attention to the timeless passionate moments of life, to states of being, with the result that their plays are revelations of a condition and not dramatic actions in the Aristotelian sense of *praxis*.

In rejecting the fixity of identity for the flux of personality, the theatre has followed—as it almost always follows—directions already taken by the other arts. For this reason the innovations in dramatic form that have occurred in recent years were fairly predictable. But since only the dramatist is compelled to deal exclusively with human beings, there is one aspect of the modern theatre's disavowal of identity that is not so readily apparent, but that must be recognized if we are to understand today's drama. Perhaps, the reason the modern theatre no longer dramatizes the search for identity, in spite of all our talk about modern man's search for it, is that as human beings we have already reversed the process—we have, in fact, tended to become identities in life. Perhaps the dehumanizing forces of industrialized collectivism have shaped our lives in such a way that in our daily existence we have no personality, but have actually become "characters" without our even realizing that such a transformation has occurred.

One of the most difficult roles to play in the Shakespearean canon is Iago. He has baffled actors and critics for better than three hundred years, and he continues to do so. Coleridge attempted to explain him in terms of "motiveless malignity," and at the other end of the spectrum of *Othello* criticism, E. E. Stoll attempted to resolve the difficulties of the part in terms of the convention of the "calumniator credited." But both of these explanations, and the countless number in between, fail because it is impossible for an actor to play either a "motiveless malignity" or a convention. However, if the actor tries to find the human wants, aims, and motives of Iago's character that will provide a consistent explanation for his actions, he discovers, if he is honest, that he cannot succeed. And the reason for this is that Iago is not a character in the traditional sense at all; rather, he is a particular kind of personality. A genius like Shake-

speare can make him credible, or at least nearly so; but as a type
he is difficult, if not impossible, to dramatize adequately. And yet,
Iago may well be the prototype of modern man, and if this conten-
tion is correct, it may help to explain one of the most difficult problems confronting the contemporary playwright.

In the preceding chapter I discussed the idea that the central issue facing the theatre of our times is the fact that the traditional
drama of the West is based upon the idea of an individual's living
in community, and that today such a relationship no longer exists.
I pointed out that since the Renaissance and the Industrial Revolution we have been moving toward a collective society and that
collectivity tends to destroy man's sense of his own individuality.
In fact, I went so far as to say that I believed that the average individual of a modern metropolis is no longer an individual at all, but
is rather a combination of the various collective interests that meet
within him. He is, in short, a collective social personality. I should
like to develop this idea further.

Many commentators on the contemporary social scene have
noted the various ways in which specialization, the cornerstone of
all forms of industrialization, has tended to divide the individual.
But they usually stop short of pointing out that once this process has
begun, it ultimately invalidates any sense the individual may have
of his own identity, for within the collective system only a man's
specialty is of value, and his function tends increasingly to be the
only source of his identity. (One need only recall the number of
times that the first question asked when meeting a stranger is "Who
are you with?" Or how, when we introduce even our best of friends,
we invariably say "Meet Mr. X, he is a butcher," "a baker," or what-
have-you.) But a sense of identity based on function alone inevitably leads to impersonality. And, in fact, our lives are, for the most
part, made up of impersonal relationships of mutual interdepen-
dence.

The implications of this shift from a communal to a collective
social organization for the institutions of our society are indeed
vast, but here I am most concerned with the effects that the emergence of the social personality has had upon the theatre.

If it is true that our image of ourselves is to a large degree expressed through our popular heroes, then one of the most significant
effects that the emerging social personality has had upon the contemporary imagination is to have changed our popular heroic mod-

els. All those heroes of previous ages who supplied us with the images, values, and ethical standards that we sought to emulate and incorporate into our own lives have ceased to have any relevance to the world in which we live today. Already they have, for the most part, become nostalgic monuments to the remembrance of things past. The Horatio Algers of our grandparents' time are now thought of as slick operators. Similarly the popular imagination has rejected the great work heroes—Franklin, Carnegie, Edison—of the past. In their places, we have substituted (at least currently) Mick Jagger, Johnny Carson, Joe Namath, Jacqueline Kennedy Onassis, Bobby Fischer and Ronald Reagan. Specialization has tended to create a new type of hero. Instead of the "whole man" or the rugged individualist, we now have the hero of surfaces, those sandwich-board leaders and celebrities without morality or principle, who are unusually susceptible to corruption, but who are nonetheless fantastically successful in a society where mass communication, audience acceptability, and role-playing skill are the new obligations to greatness.

This shift in heroic types cannot be attributed to a loss of national moral fiber. It is an inevitable consequence of collectivism and a corporateness of specialists. Such a system demands role playing. But it should be pointed out, as many others have already done, that since role playing is not a genuine commitment, it cannot be a strong and durable social bond, however much it looks like one. Nothing characterizes the social personality more accurately than his lack of commitment (even in marriage and friendship); but for the most part we don't notice this shallowness of relationship because of the profusion of superficial feelings, and the ease with which relationships are established in our time. Modern man has become an expert at generating the appearance of fellowship, even with strangers.

For this reason, I suppose Fred Demara, "The Great Impostor," may well be the perfect symbol of the social personality, and his explanation of his success may well describe the condition that produces the social personality. He remarked: "If you act like you belong somewhere, even people who know you don't belong are hesitant to call you on it. People are so insecure. Deep in their souls they don't feel they belong either." In such a world, success and domination depend upon one's ability to outmanipulate, as it were, others in every situation. And in this sense we are all becoming social personalities. Like Iago, mid-twentieth-century man tends to be an actor whose only reality is the particular role he happens to be playing.

But if this transformation has, in fact, taken place, then the theatre has lost its natural subject. It can no longer celebrate the anguish and the pain, the celebration and the triumph, of a man's search to know who he is and what his place in the universe may be. Rather, our modern playwrights note with increasing horror that modern man has become an actor who is all too willing to have an identity thrust upon him. It is a corporate identity, designed by whatever industrialized collective he happens to be a part of, but it is clearly not his own.

Thus, the central concern of most contemporary dramatists is *not* man's search for his own identity, but rather the sense of helplessness that the individual must feel if he seeks to face and combat the conflicts of the collective world in which he lives. The great man of our times has ceased to be the doer of heroic deeds, but is the one who is capable of withstanding some of the pressures of a mass society and still manages, somehow, to maintain a face and stance more or less his own. And probably no playwright in the twentieth century comprehended the nature and significance of this condition more fully than did Brecht.

# 17

# BERTOLT BRECHT: POET OF THE COLLECTIVE

BERTOLT BRECHT was a Marxist and the prophet for the theatre of a collective society. But he never wore his prophet's mantle with ease, nor was he ever fully comfortable with his Marxist posture. He was, however, the first playwright of the modern theatre to comprehend fully the effects of industrialization and collectivism upon the structures of society—not to mention how they transformed man's sense of his own individuality—and he realized that these forces were creating new kinds of conflicts which were not being dealt with in the theatre.

To understand Brecht's development as a dramatist, and particularly the significance of the influential theories of his later years, it is important to realize that he was born of quite well-to-do middle class parents and that his imagination was shaped by definitely bourgeois attitudes. He had served in World War I as a very young man, and while he experienced the war deeply he was not politicized by it. He returned to Augsberg as a kind of renegade hipster—anarchic, without political convictions, and still very middle class. His great hero was Frank Wedekind and, like him, Brecht wrote poetry and songs, played the guitar, and began to get interested in the theatre. His early poems had all of the verbal extravagance of the Baroque lyric. In them one finds an overwhelming obsession for death and decomposition which is somehow miraculously transformed into a wild, yet vegetive, greed for life. His first theories of the theatre began to appear in 1918 when he became the drama critic for the Augsberg *Volkswille*. It is interesting to read the reviews that he wrote during this period (1918–1921) because they reveal that while he had a probing and in some ways a radical mind, his basic orientation to the theatre was quite traditional. He admired Ibsen and Hauptmann; he was particularly attracted to Shaw (an affinity that will become quite significant in later years); he rejected the great German classics for their lack of contemporary relevancy; and he was negative about the work of most of the expressionist dramatists who were then in vogue. (With the exception of Kaiser, whose cinematic sense of form he admired, Brecht dismissed the expressionist theatre as "proclamations of man without man.") More significantly, these reviews reveal that Brecht's own sense of the theatre was very much in the modernist mainstream. Words such as "soulfulness," "inwardness," "gripping," "touching," "fourth wall" appear often and show that Brecht's vision of the theatre was essentially naturalistic, illusionary, and psychologically oriented. This background is important because I believe that the ambiguity and complexity of the great works of his maturity can only be comprehended when we realize that Brecht came to the theatre essentially as a poet and that as a theorist his break with the naturalistic theatre was an act of apostasy.

In some ways Brecht's first play, *Baal* (1918), provides the clues which will help us understand everything else he was to write. This remarkable play seems to spring parthenogenetically out of nowhere. Like Buechner's *Woyzeck* (with which it shares so much in common), *Baal* represents a complete break with the dominant modes of the theatre of its time. It is not so much a play as it is a poetic revelation of the seething inner spirit of the man who was, more than anyone else, to reshape the theatre of the twentieth century. Baal is a wild and wonderful character who has a death-haunted greed for life. He is rapacious and homicidal, swinish and bacchanalian, and underneath his wild posturings there is an orgiastic joyousness. He exists having stripped himself of all the trappings that society creates and demands. But finally, for all its energy, the play is about ontological solitude. Baal, like his creator, is lost and alone. His is an immense existential loneliness that nothing can fill. Meaningful contact with another human being is illusory; social structures are impersonal and dehumanizing; even the natural world, with which Baal seems so attuned, has some meaning for him only because it is there. Using an ancient fertility myth, Brecht reveals in his first play a world in which the only reality is an immense nothingness—the void. Eric Bentley, in his insightful essay on the play, observes that *Baal* reflects Brecht's *feel of the world* before he came to commit himself to belief. This *Weltgefühl* pervades all of his work, indeed it is the very foundation of his theatre, and it reveals Brecht as a great "shut-in" who could never be known and who in spite of the efforts of a lifetime, could never really get out of himself.

But even if Brecht's "feel of the world" is that each man must forever remain unknown, he still does exist and hence has an overpowering need to make contact, somehow or in some fashion, with his fellowmen.* This is the theme of Brecht's next major play, *In the Jungle of Cities* (1923). It is the drama of two men who seek desperately to make a connection. They chase each other all over the city of Chicago (Brecht's mythic image of urban collectivity, which was, in fact, more like the Berlin of the Weimar Republic than the actual city of Chicago) and finally meet on the beach of Lake Michigan. They begin to fight, and this struggle is a despairing and violent attempt to break through their loneliness. But they break it off; what's the use? Even enmity fails. Some of the dialogue of this last scene of the play is a particularly moving expression of the condition of estrangement:

> SCHLINK: Man's infinite isolation makes enmity an unattainable goal. But even with animals understanding is not possible.
> GARGA: Speech isn't enough to create understanding.
> SCHLINK: I've observed the animals. Love, the warmth of bodies in contact, is the only mercy shown us in the darkness. But the only union is that of the organs, and it can't bridge over the cleavage made by speech. Yet they unite in order to produce beings to stand by them in their hopeless isolation. And the generations look coldly into each other's eyes. If you cram a ship full to bursting with human bodies, they'll all freeze with loneliness. Are you listening, Garga? Yes, so great is man's isolation that not even a fight is possible. . . .

---

* I believe this contradiction explains the ironic tone and detached stance of much of his later work. These are mechanisms of self-defense. Brecht wanted to touch the world; he knew he never could, but he never stopped trying.

The central fact of life is the root experience of loneliness, of a lost grublike evanescence, an experience which underlies any kind of philosophical, political, or sociological theorizing.

Today we are used to this. It became the central perception of Beckett, Ionesco, and most of the other Absurdist playwrights. But Brecht realized, as the Absurdists did not, that once you deny the possibility of conflict (when "not even a fight is possible") you have destroyed the very basis of the theatre. This impasse becomes readily apparent in a play like The Killer. Ionesco's Everyman hero, Berenger, described the nature of his estrangement in a speech delivered in "a tumultuous vacuum":

> In short, inner and outer worlds are bad expressions; there are no boundaries between the so-called two worlds. There is a fundamental impulse, obviously, which comes from us, and when it can't be exteriorized, when it can't be objectively realized, when there is no complete accord between my inner me and my outer me, the result is catastrophe, universal contradiction, the final break.

In the final scene, as Berenger is face to face with the Killer, he has a long monologue in which he gives all the reasons why he shouldn't be killed. But as he builds his case, he comes to discover that there is no reason why he should not be killed. He finally says:

> I don't know anymore. I don't know anymore. Maybe you're wrong, maybe wrong doesn't exist, maybe it's we who are wrong to want to exist. . . . Explain. What do you think? I don't know, I don't know.

The Killer's "infinite energy of obstinacy" wins over all values, even the most basic of animal drives, self-preservation. All Berenger can say as he is knifed is "what can we do?" Each of Beckett's plays reveals a similar condition, and I believe his most recent play, Breath, is, in fact, the last gasp of a theatre which is committed to the dramatizing of absolute estrangement.

There are probably many reasons—his youth, the fact that he had not yet experienced the horrors of World War II, perhaps even the giddy quality of life in Berlin in the 1920s—why Brecht did not follow the natural bent of his Weltgefühl. Had he done so, the theatre of the absurd would have been a phenomenon of the 1920s. But rather than continue in the direction of his first plays, Brecht turned his attention to reassessing the nature of the theatre. In a series of articles written in the Berliner Borsen-Courier in 1925 we find the first seeds of his soon-to-be-developed new idea of the theatre:

> Art can only express its own time. A theatre which lacks contact with the public makes no sense. Our theatre therefore makes no sense. The fact that theatre today has as yet no contact with the public results from its ignorance of what people want of it and of what the world is really like.

While it is clear that Brecht still doesn't know who his audience is, he is certain of one thing:

> When one sees that our world of today no longer fits into the drama, then it is merely that the drama no longer fits into the world.

This remark to Elisabeth Hauptmann, which I have already quoted in a previous essay, may seem rather insignificant; but it indicates that Brecht perceived that the reason the theatre had lost contact with its public was because its playwrights were not expressing the realities of the present.

And the realities of the present were deeply disturbing to Bertolt Brecht. He had believed that the "drama must be linked to individuals, to vigorous, vital personalities," but his own sense of the world was that one could never know another person, that indeed perhaps individuality as it had been experienced in the Western world had been transformed by the forces of industrialization. If this were so, how could we continue to write plays? How, in fact, could we go on living? Joseph Warren Beach described as accurately as anyone what I believe was Brecht's condition at this time:

> One of the hardest things for man to bear is spiritual isolation. The sense that he stands alone in the universe goes terribly against his gregarious instincts. He has an over-powering impulse to construct a system which will enable him to feel that he does not stand alone but is intimately associated with some force or group infinitely more powerful and significant than himself.

Brecht knew all about spiritual isolation and in his first plays he dramatizes the impossibility of communion. It would appear that he also had "an over-powering impulse to construct a system which will enable him to feel that he does not stand alone." So in 1925 and 1926 he began an intensive study of sociology which eventually led to his espousal of Marxism.

Brecht was the first modern dramatist to comprehend fully how industrial capitalism had created that kind of collective society which I described in the preceding two chapters. Further, he saw that one of the chief results of collectivism and its attendant specialization was the disappearance of the individual and the emergence of what I have called the "collective social personality." Brecht's awareness of the emergence of this new character type had a profound effect on his theatre, and we can see this in his next play, A Man's a Man (1926). This is a transitional play, but from this time onward Brecht becomes committed to those beliefs which were the generative force of his "epic" theatre. A Man's a Man is a comedy of "the transformation of the stevedore Galy Gay in the military barracks of Kilkoa in the year 1925." Its subject is "the infinite interchangeability of human beings." Galy Gay is a naïve Irish dockworker who is kidnaped while on his way to lunch by a group of British soldiers serving in India. One of their comrades is missing, so they take Galy Gay and transform him (after first killing his insignificant former self) before our eyes into a substitute soldier to be shoved into line at the next inspection. However, Galy Gay is by no means presented as a pitiable victim; he is the victor, the true hero in a collective society. In fact, Brecht makes it clear that the sergeant, Bloody Five, is the real victim—a victim because he is an individual in the traditional humanistic sense. He is defeated by his very individuality. In 1927 Brecht prepared a special introduction for a radio broadcast of the play, and in it he discusses those ideas which shaped A Man's a Man. I wish to quote extensively from that introduction, not to illuminate the play, but because I believe it indicates the nature of the Brechtian hero which will emerge in the plays of the next two decades:

> What matters most is that a *new human type* should now be evolving, at this very moment, and that the entire interest of the world should be concentrating on his development. . . . And any work that has nothing to do with him is not alive and has nothing to do with anything. This new human type will not be as the old type imagines. It is my belief that he will not let himself be changed by machines but will himself change the machine; and whatever he looks like he will above all look human.
>
> I would now like to turn briefly to the comedy *Mann ist Mann* and explain why this introduction about the new human type was necessary. Of course not all these problems are going to arise and be elucidated in this particular play. They will be elucidated some-

where quite different. But it struck me that all sorts of things in *Mann ist Mann* will probably seem odd to you at first—especially what the central figure, the packer Galy Gay, does or does not do—and if so it's better that you shouldn't think you are listening to an old acquaintance talking about you or himself, but to a new sort of type, possibly an ancestor of just that new human type I spoke of. It may be interesting for you to look straight at him from this point of view, so as to bring out his attitude to things as precisely as possible. You will see that among other things he is a great liar and an incorrigible optimist; he can fit in with anything, almost without difficulty. He seems to be used to putting up with a great deal. It is in fact very seldom that he can allow himself an opinion of his own. For instance when he is offered an utterly spurious elephant which he can resell, he will take care not to voice any opinion of it once he hears a possible purchaser is there. I imagine also that you are used to treating a man as a weakling if he can't say no, but this Galy Gay is by no means a weakling; on the contrary he is the strongest of all. That is to say he becomes the strongest once he has ceased to be a private person; he only becomes strong in the mass. And if the play finishes up with him conquering an entire fortress this is only because in doing so he is apparently carrying out the unqualified wish of a great mass of people who want to get through the narrow pass that the fortress guards. No doubt you will go on to say that it's a pity that a man should be tricked like this and simply forced to surrender his precious ego, all he possesses (as it were); but it isn't. It's a jolly business. For this Galy Gay comes to no harm; he wins. And a man who adopts such an attitude is bound to win.\*

*A Man's a Man* marks the beginning of a course of development which Brecht will follow for the remainder of his career as a playwright. Although one will still find, like an almost invisible watermark, the haunting despair of spiritual isolation, Brecht's dominant concern will be to create a theatrical form capable of expressing the conflicts of social personalities as they live within a collective society. His ultimate achievement will be *Mother Courage*. For Mother Courage is the perfect embodiment of the social personality; she is a woman whose very stature is the result of her being able to sacrifice her individual humanity to the collective system of which she is a part and which she affirms to the end. *Mother Courage* is articulate testimony that to destroy the humanist concept of

---

\* *Brecht on Theatre,* John Willett, ed. (New York, 1964), pp. 18–19.

the individual does not necessarily mean a loss of stature in the theatre, nor the disappearance of dramatic conflict. Rather there is a new kind of character and new kinds of conflict, and Brecht's theatre will provide the forms and language to express them.

The subject of Brecht's Marxism always seems to create problems. I can think of very few critics who agree, and even now so long after his death (not to mention the weakening of the battle lines between East and West) there are raging disputes. I do not wish to enter the lists. On the basis of all the evidence available to me (which, compared to others, may be relatively small), I do not believe that Brecht's temperament was political in any activist way, nor do I believe that he was spiritually attuned to the methods and practices of the Communist party. On the other hand, I am convinced that Marxism did fulfill Brecht's "over-powering impulse to construct a system which will enable him to feel that he does not stand alone but is intimately associated with some force or group infinitely more powerful and significant than himself." I see Brecht's embrace of Marxism as a strategy of despair and while the strategy may have worked successfully, it was nonetheless an act of will imposed by the intellect upon the sadness, the loneliness, the sense of emptiness which were the ground of Brecht's being. But no matter, for whether I am right or wrong, I am convinced there is only one key issue regarding Brecht's Marxism and only when we understand this will all of the controversial aspects of both his theory and practice fall into place.

The great revolution in the theatre which was begun in the second half of the nineteenth century by Ibsen, Strindberg, Chekhov, Hauptmann, and Shaw and which Ibsen referred to as "a war to the knife with the past" was essentially concerned with the role that the irrational played in human affairs. What made the plays of this period so radical was not so much their form, or even their apparent subject matter, but the fact that almost every one of them reflected its author's conviction that the irrational was the dominating force in all human experience. Now while Marx certainly played a major role in the nineteenth-century "re-evaluation of values" which brought about the modernist revolution in the theatre, the modernist view of the irrational is completely incompatible with Marxist thought. The reason Lunacharsky * could proclaim that there would

* The first Soviet commissioner of education.

be no tragedy in a communist state is because Marxists do not believe in the idea of *ananke*, the Greek term for Necessity. (As I said in the opening section of the book, for the Greeks Necessity is not some kind of social disease that those who would change the world can ignore, soften, or legislate out of existence. It is the embodiment of life's smallness, absurdity, and fragility; it is the acknowledgment of the limitation and mortality of all human experience.) "Necessity is blind," Marx said, "only where it is not understood." It is this crucial idea which Brecht picks up and it had far-reaching consequences. For Brecht, the idea that there are in nature (including human nature) hidden and uncontrollable forces which can dominate the mind has no objective reality whatsoever. Indeed, such forces have no real existence. For him the irrational is "not the chaotic, insoluble remainder, the overflowing part of reality" and therefore a part of reality. Rather he believes that this "apparent chaos exists only because our head is not a perfect one and therefore that which remains outside it we call the irrational." Since we cannot know it rationally, it *seems* chaotic; but this "remainder is irrational only in respect to the capacity of our mind for knowing." Thus, while Brecht does not believe in the perfectibility of man (Marx believed that only the powers of reason can master the natural world), he does believe that the mind's range can be stretched. This distinction is crucial because all Brecht's theatrical theories are based upon it.

For example, it is the basis of his anti-empathic theories of production and explains his controversial Alienation-effect. Here Brecht, although he was passionately antipsychological, got his clue from Freud. Just as psychiatric therapy—and I think it is very significant that psychiatrists were first known as "alienists"—seeks to detach us from ourselves so we can begin to see ourselves in a more objective way (almost as an object), so Brecht believed that if the theatre was "to stretch the mind's range" it must not encourage the spectator to identify with the action but must show it so the audience can come to know itself better.* But this experience, as anyone

* This explains Brecht's affinity to Shaw. In 1926 when he was first formulating his new ideas he wrote an interesting essay on Shaw. While everything is still tentative, it indicates where Brecht is going. "He throws our customary associations into disorder. The world of Shaw is one which comes into being through points of view. These views concerning the actors are opposed to those about the spectators. Thus, there is an alienation of the spectator from the dramatic event; the invitation to make an unforced decision is realized to a large extent in Shaw's dramatic form."

who has been through therapy knows well, is not unemotional; in fact, it can be highly charged with emotional energy. In the same way, Brecht did not think of his theatre as anti-emotional. In an interview in 1959, Jean-Paul Sartre was asked if a proper production of Brecht wouldn't be cold. He replied:

> Anti-emotionalism is not what Brecht wanted. All he wanted was for the spectator's emotion not to be blind. After all, in *Mother Courage* his wife and admirable interpreter, Helene Weigel, moved the audience to cry. The ideal would be to "show" and "move" at the same time. I don't think Brecht considered that contradiction as an insoluble absurdity.

So throughout his plays, Brecht is trying to isolate the inconspicuous moral drama, to estrange it, to set it in a sharp light, so that it is not taken for granted before it falls, dragged down by the weight of society. Brecht's own analogy for what he means by estrangement is a watch. "A watch is a familiar object. But," he says, "take it apart, and all the pieces seem strange and small: they are unfamiliar in their estrangement from the functioning timepiece, almost irreconcilable with it. There is the same strangeness, or irreconciliability, about an individual in society. To understand, we must stand at a distance and judge him; where we are powerless to help him, but we can recognize where he goes wrong."

It is this attitude which prompted Sartre to say:

> What Brecht wanted was to provoke what Plato called "the source of all philosophy" that is wonder, by making the familiar unfamiliar.

Seen in this light, *Mother Courage* is not a pacifist tract, nor is Brecht the playwright a polemicist. His most daring achievement in this play is his use of war as an all-encompassing metaphor for the modern world, and his presentation of Mother Courage, who lives off the war and continues to exist because of it, as the symbol of the ordinary human condition. However, the play is not an attack on war, but an attempt to show all aspects of that war which is the central fact of the contemporary human condition. From the ironical speech of the Top Sergeant on the "horrors" of peace in the first scene, it is very clear that Brecht is very much aware of the negative and destructive aspects of our warring condition, but other parts of the play make it equally clear that war does make money, which we hold dear; war does create courage, which we admire; war does support the established institutions of society, which we want to maintain; and war does promote a sense of love and brotherhood, which we find valuable. As the play ends, Mother Courage is seen trudging after another regiment. In her (our) circumstances she cannot do otherwise. The tragedy of the situation, indeed, if it is a tragedy, is that her perception of what is wrong cannot alter her situation as it traditionally does in tragedy. In *Mother Courage* the situation completely dominates the individual. Brecht was in all likelihood not very happy about this, but he has been one of the few playwrights in our time who was capable of facing up to the realities of life in an industrialized collective society without having to abdicate his responsibility as an artist.

For Brecht this meant developing a new kind of dramatic form. He rejected the traditional forms of the theatre because they were based upon older and now largely nonexistent forms of communal society. In the previous chapter I discussed the problem of identity in a collective world. How different Brecht is, compared say to Pirandello, when he writes in 1926: "Even if a person is involved in contradictions, that is because in two unequal moments he can never be just the same. The shifting Outside constantly induces an inner regrouping in him. The notion of a continuous I is a myth. Man is a constantly disintegrating and self-renewing atom." It is clear from this that Brecht sees that man is changed by the forces of the world outside him. And it follows that he must reject the characteristics of the traditional inner-directed drama in the Aristotelian mode. The basic assumption of Aristotle's theory was that drama was an "imitation of an action." "Action" (*praxis*) does not mean outward events or deeds, but the movement of all modes, conscious and unconscious, of the life of the spirit to a specific end. And this movement includes within itself intention, act, and consequence. The idea of *praxis*, then, presumes the existence of a motivating self and also the linear structure of beginning, middle, and end. But when you deny that the self can act in this way and see it determined by "the shifting Outside," then one must, as Brecht did, also reject those techniques of characterization and structure which grew out of this older way of thinking. In 1929 he makes his break with what he calls the "classical dramatic" theatre and heralds the emergence of the "epic theatre."

> Simply to comprehend the new areas of subject matter imposes a new dramatic and theatrical form. Can we speak of money in the form of iambics? "The Mark, first quoted yesterday at 50 dollars,

now beyond 100, soon may rise, etc."—how about that? Petroleum resists the five-act form; today's catastrophes do not progress in a straight line but in cyclical crises; the "heroes" change with the different phases, are interchangeable, etc.; the graph of people's actions is complicated by abortive actions; fate is no longer a single coherent power; rather there are fields of force which can be seen radiating in opposite directions; the power groups themselves comprise movements not only against one another but within themselves, etc., etc. Even to dramatize a simple newspaper report one needs something much more than the dramatic technique of a Hebbel or an Ibsen. This is no boast but a sad statement of fact. It is impossible to explain a present-day character by features or a present-day action by motives that would have been adequate in our fathers' time.*

What is Brecht's epic form? † Obviously the term alludes to epic poetry and we immediately think of Homer and Virgil, Tasso, Ariosto, and Milton. And this can be helpful when we remember that one of the significant distinctions between epic and tragic poetry is that the epic celebrates the "destiny of history" while tragedy is concerned with the dividedness of human nature. The hero of an epic poem is always placed in a specific historical context and even as he embodies his destiny he is a pawn in its working out. Achilles, for all his wrath and physical prowess, is finally a secondary figure in the larger battle between the Gods. Aeneas clearly is a culture hero who represents the fulfillment of the Roman Empire's manifest destiny. This meaning of the epic corresponds with Brecht's view that the individual is governed by external forces and that therefore a dramatic action must move from the outside in and not from the inside out. He was also thinking of the drama as episodic and narrative and, therefore, more like the structure of an epic poem than the well-made play. But I think there is a more profound reason for his choice of the term, and I believe a passage from Paul Tillich can help us understand it. In *The Religious Situation*, Tillich writes:

> Capitalist society had substituted the idea of progress for the idea of the end of the world. For the spirit of self-sufficient finitude there is no such thing as an end in the definite sense of the term, since the

---

* *Brecht on Theatre*, John Willett, ed. (New York, 1964), p. 30.
† We know Brecht took the term from his friend and collaborator, Erwin Piscator, but they did not use the term in the same way. Piscator was much more concerned with production techniques, Brecht with dramatic structure.

end means the real catastrophe of all finitude which is sufficient to itself.

Now, he wasn't talking about the theatre here, but I think it might be applicable. All of the major world views of Western Culture—Judaic, Greco-Roman, and Christian—posit the idea of the end of the world, and each man's existence, therefore, is seen as a preparation for and way to that end. Given this fact the idea of *praxis* corresponds to the *Weltanschauung* and from the time of Aristotle we have thought of dramatic form linearly in terms of beginning, middle, and end. In the 1950s the absurdist playwrights could successfully reject this idea and replace the traditional linear form of the theatre with what I have called the contextual or epiphanic form because they did not view man in a social context. But the two central ideas implicit in Tillich's statement are that progress, by definition, has no end (which explains why in an age of progress death can never be seen as an achievement as it is traditionally thought of in tragedy; it is only a cutting off, and therefore death is viewed as life's enemy and not its companion), and secondly, that in a collective society, of which capitalism is the most highly developed form, there is no beginning, middle, and end; there is only a constantly shifting series of episodes. The dramatic processes of history never do end, they only move on to the next episode. Thus the end is replaced by the process itself and the playwright does not think of "Life as a process leading to an end" but rather of "Life is a process. . . ." This shift in attitude radically alters his sense of form and it explains why the question of "how" was Brecht's only concern in his later plays. Perhaps we can see this more clearly by briefly examining *The Caucasian Chalk Circle*.

From the very outset we know what the play is about and how it will end. If most people do not know the ancient Chinese parable, they are in all likelihood acquainted with the biblical version of King Solomon. Moreover, Brecht's prologue not only gives the play a contemporary significance, it also indicates how the ensuing action is to be interpreted. The prologue prefigures the last lines of the play:

> What there is shall go to those who are good for it,
> Children to the motherly, that they prosper,
> Carts to good drivers, that they be driven well,
> The Valley to the waterers, that it yield fruit.

Brecht, then, is not interested in *what* happens, but only in *how* it happens.* The play, divided in two parts, is actually composed of three actions. The first shows *how* Grusha becomes the "mother" of the young prince Michael "because there is no longer a difference between her interests and those of the child"; the second shows *how* Azdak comes to be the kind of judge that makes it possible for the people of Grusinia to think of "the period of his judging as a brief golden age, almost an age of justice"; and the third shows *how*, given the first two, Azdak will make the decision which gives Grusha the child and also makes it possible for her to marry Simon. Each of the first two actions begins at the same time, the day of the palace revolt during which both the baby prince is abandoned and then saved by Grusha and the Grand Duke escapes and is saved by Azdak, and they are presented as independent and unrelated cycles composed of a series of episodes. There is nothing random or arbitrary about the order of these episodes (directors who cut or alter the text invariably destroy the play in production); they are arranged to show the process of the two protagonists' growth, and the play's meaning is derived not so much from what is said as it is from the order in which it happens.

Brecht's epic form, then, is his way of expressing the complexity, multiplicity, variety, and even the contradictions of a collective world while still maintaining that unity of form which is essential for art. He uses its episodic structure as a kind of counterpoint of estrangement for the purpose of stretching the limits of the audience's mind. Finally, it is a form that seeks to achieve the capacity of the novel (the literary mode which emerged out of the industrial revolution and is probably best suited to express our times) in dealing with the central issues of the modern world, without sacrificing the immediacy and force of the actor on a stage.

The epic form is also the most appropriate vehicle for the Brechtian hero. As I have indicated in the preceding two chapters industrialization has tended to transform the individual into what I have called the collective social personality. Earlier in this chapter I

---

* This is a superb example of Suzanne Langer's distinction between the suspense of plot and the suspense of form. In the first case our interest is in what will happen next; in the latter our aesthetic pleasure is derived from the fulfillment of a known form. Miss Langer argues that the second is a more satisfying experience since it enables us to enjoy a work of art several times over. It makes no difference that we know what happens in *Hamlet;* our pleasure comes from the expectancy of having what we know will happen fulfilled.

discussed Brecht's awareness of this change and his belief that the
theatre must reflect it. As a result Brecht created a totally different
(and totally new) kind of protagonist. Traditionally, in Western
drama, the hero is conceived as a man acting with virtue and courage in the face of powerful opposing forces. The modern theatre
has learned to live without such heroes. The reasons for this are
numerous—the loss of belief in permanent and widely accepted
values, the inevitable tendency towards leveling in a democratic
society, the increase of psychological knowledge, etc.—but very few
people have noticed that the disappearance of heroes in our theatre
is an inevitable result of industrialized collectivism.

Traditional heroes were not necessarily good people; but, whether
right or wrong, they always commanded our moral attention. We
take them seriously because we believe they have an heroic destiny
and because they are struggling with significant issues that are related to the fulfillment of that destiny.* Brecht rejected this kind of
hero as the necessity of an evil and now outmoded Age. ("Unhappy
is the land that needs a hero!"—*Galileo*) He did so because he believed that an industrialized society, in its open-ended concern for
increased expansion, production, and profit tends to reject the idea
of destiny and espouses the belief in progress, and is thus an inhospitable ambience for great men of destiny.† When viewed in the
context of an industrialized collective society, Brecht believed the
actions of such "old-fashioned" heroes tend to be little more than
the empty posturings of the foolish, the headstrong, or the selfish.
Genuine goodness, such as Kattrin's in *Mother Courage,* is equally
irrelevant. While her behavior in the play seems to have a mute
nobility about it, Brecht makes it very clear that her dramatic function in the play is to reveal the futility of the instinct to goodness
and the impossibility of its surviving in a world in which the ever-
growing cult of the celebrity, with its tendency to value charm without character, showmanship without real ability, bodies without
minds, and information without wisdom, celebrates the triumph of

---

* Only folk literature, with its iconoclastic wisdom, occasionally protested
against the assumption that destiny is determined by the quality of a man's
personality. More often than not in folk art, the clown or the nincompoop gets
the hero's reward by accident or sheer luck.
† This probably explains why so many modern dramatists, whether they are
conscious of it or not, tend to be more interested in man's fate rather than his
destiny, why revelation—since fate can only be revealed—has replaced action
in the contemporary theatre.

ordinariness. As Mother Courage exclaims: "Whenever there are great virtues, it's a sure sign something's wrong. . . . But in a good country the virtues wouldn't be necessary. Everybody could be quite ordinary, middling, and for all of me cowards." Thus, beginning with *A Man's a Man*, the idea that the assertion of individuality in the name of virtue is the chief cause of human failure in a collective society is a recurring and dominant theme in almost all of Brecht's plays. However, it should be pointed out that the Marxist playwright Brecht never completely represses the lonely poet Brecht. For we obviously don't live in a good country and the messenger doesn't come riding in nor does the Grand Duke always save the judge at the last minute. Once again, Brecht's basic duality manifests itself. For while it is true that he sees such characters as Bloody Five (*A Man's a Man*), the Young Comrade (*Measures Taken*), Joan Dark (*St. Joan of the Stockyards*), Puntila (*Puntila and His Servant Matti*), Kattrin (*Mother Courage*), and even Grusha * (*The Caucasian Chalk Circle*) as failures because they give in to their human feelings and good instincts, paradoxically, he also believes that to be overwhelmed by the gratuitous impulse to do a good act is the beginning of freedom.

It is a fact that when Brecht returned to East Berlin to become the director of the Berliner Ensemble for the Communist government, he retained both his Austrian passport and his Swiss bank account. This is probably the best insight of all into the nature of the Brechtian hero. His protagonists have learned that the best solution is to hedge your bets, be as clever as you can, and play it safe in the middle. The famous "Song of the Center" in *The Caucasian Chalk Circle* is repeated in various forms in the majority of his later plays.

> When you go to war as now you do
> When you fight the foe as soon you will

* We must remember that as Grusha waits for the trial to begin she says, "I *need* luck right now." She gets it when the grand duke's messenger comes in and saves Azdak at the last minute. But we know that in life this doesn't usually happen. In his production notes to the play, Brecht writes: "There is an American word, 'sucker,' which expresses what Grusha is when she takes on the child. . . . Her motherly instinct exposes Grusha to persecutions and labors which almost kill her. She wants nothing from Azdak but the permission to go on toiling, that is, to 'get the short end of the stick.' Plainly, she loves the child. She derives her right to the child from her readiness and ability to work. After the trial, she is no longer a sucker." *The Drama Review*, Vol. 12, No. 1, Fall, 1967, pp. 95–96.

> Don't lead with front line
> And don't push with the rear line
> At the front is red fire
> In the rear is red smoke
> Stay in the war's center
> Stay near the standard bearer
> The first always die
> The last are also hit
> Those in the Center come home.

Michael, we must be clever. If we made ourselves as small as cock-roaches, the Sister-in-law will forget we're in the house, and then we can stay till the snow melts.

Brecht's heroes are of a new breed. Like Iago, their actions lack consistency of motivation unless they are viewed as social personalities. But unlike the Shakespearean prototype they are not villains, but are presented as representations of the only positive attitude toward good possible in the modern world. Brecht may use his audience's habitual responses concerning the nature of heroism as a foil to achieve his effects, but finally if they do achieve a kind of new world heroic stature, it is precisely because they, as I said earlier of Mother Courage, are willing and able to sacrifice their humanity and their individuality to the collective system of which they are a part and which they affirm to the end.

It is in the realm of language, however, that I believe Bertolt Brecht made his greatest contribution to the modern theatre. The problems of language have been a central issue in the theatre for the past one hundred and fifty years and every one of its revolutions and counterrevolutions has sought to revitalize the language of the theatre and at the same time deal with the tendency of words to tyrannize a medium whose most appropriate language is a fused and indivisible combination of the verbal, the visual, and the aural. I shall treat these problems at greater length in subsequent chapters, but I should like to close this essay by discussing Brecht's unique handling of this difficult problem.

Any discussion of the use of language in the German Theatre must begin with the realization that Germany (like Italy) has spoken languages and *a* literary language. Political unification came late in Germany and as a result it has a language of many and widely diverse dialects. These differences were perpetuated, in fact enforced, by the efforts of each of the many states to preserve its own autonomy. As a result, any writer who had ambitions to communicate to the public at large could not consider using one of the regional dialects; * rather he employed the idiom and structure of the national literary language which had emerged out of Luther's translation of the Bible. As Dante had done earlier in Italy, Luther created a style of language which cut across all regional boundaries. The other unifying force in the German language, and it is closely related to the first, were the hymns and chorales that were the central elements of the religious celebrations of Lutheran Protestantism. Because of both these factors the German literary language was celebratory in nature.

This fact is important if we are to understand the nature of Brecht's achievement. As I said at the outset, Brecht began his career as a poet and his early poems are very much in the established tradition of German verse. While one can notice the direct influence of Stefan George and the symbolists, it is clear from his first published volume of poems, *Die Hauspostille* (The Book of Prayers) that his greatest debt is to Luther. This influence never really diminishes throughout his career, and it is interesting to observe that many years later, when Brecht comes to elaborate his influential theory of "gestic language" in the theatre, he acknowledges Luther as the source of his inspiration. At the same time the poet was tremendously influenced by the singing, guitar-playing, and life style of Frank Wedekind, and Brecht's ironic use of the ballad tradition can be traced to this source. Furthermore, we must remember that American Jazz became enormously popular in Berlin in the 1920s and Brecht assimilated the percussive rhythms of this music into his work. Finally, much like T. S. Eliot who was also first recognized at this time, Brecht was striving to create a poetic idiom that expressed contemporary reality in the concrete images of the city. In short, when the poet Brecht came to write for the theatre he brought with him a number of wide-ranging, even eclectic, traditions.

After he turned to Marxism Brecht's interest in language as a poetic medium diminished and his chief concern was how to revitalize the theatre so it could, in fact, stretch the minds of its audiences. He believed that art, life, politics, science, and religion were inseparably related, and that it was the playwright's responsibility to force audiences to an awareness of this fact. To this end,

* In this regard, Hauptmann's *The Weavers* is a remarkable exception.

language was seen as the means of prodding the audience into a condition of comfortless detachment and critical reflection. But in spite of his increasingly didactic purpose, Brecht remained a poet and he realized that the language of the theatre must be much more than a means of conducting characters through a plot. He was powerfully conscious of the fact that drama is, as George Steiner put it, "language under such high pressure of feeling that the words carry a necessary and immediate connotation of gesture." Gesture is not a decorative addition that accompanies words, it is the source, the cause, and the director of language. But Brecht developed this idea further. He saw that gesture also carried with it the quality of "bearing," "carriage," "mien." Thus *gestus* is not simply gesture but a combination of gesture and attitude.*

The primary significance of Brecht's gestic style of theatre is not theoretical, however. Many modern dramatists have reached similar conclusions. But in their work they have actually tended to impoverish the language of the theatre, for not only do they dislocate the mechanisms of language, they actually tend to dislocate the very syntax of rational discourse. This Brecht did not do. As a poet he put his trust in words. He believed in the power of verse to deal with the contradictions of reality. He knew that by virtue of elision, concentration, and obliqueness, poetry can create an image of life which is far denser and more complex than that of prose. And, finally, he was aware that his new vision of reality as dialectical had to be expressed in poetry, for only poetry can advance discordant persuasions simultaneously and still retain that gestural quality which is essential to the theatre. Thus it may very well turn out

---

* "It must be remembered that the bulk of my work was designed for the theatre; I was always thinking of actual delivery. And for this delivery (whether of prose or verse) I had worked out a quite definite technique. I called it 'gestic.' This meant that the sentence must entirely follow the gest of the person speaking. Let me give an example. The Bible's sentence 'Pluck out the eye that offends thee' is based on a gest—that of commanding—but it is not entirely gestically expressed, as 'that offends thee' has a further gest which remains unexpressed, namely, that of explanation. Purely gestically expressed the sentence runs 'If thine eye offends thee, pluck it out' (and this is how it was put by Luther, who 'watched the people's mouth'). It can be seen at a glance that this way of putting it is far richer and cleaner from a gestic point of view. The first clause contains an assumption, and its peculiarity and specialness can be fully expressed by the tone of voice. Then there is a little pause of bewilderment, and only then the devastating proposal." *Brecht on Theatre*, John Willett, ed. (New York, 1964), pp. 116–117.

that Brecht's greatest contribution as a poet in the theatre was to create a poetry of the collective.

In his Production Notes for *The Caucasian Chalk Circle* Brecht tells us that the only way to make the play work is for the actors to play its contradictions. This could be said of all his plays, and finally, it is the best insight I can think of regarding Brecht himself. His life and his work were always in a state of dialectical tension. He rejected nature and emotional feelings overtly expressed and yet the most moving and powerful scenes in his plays are pervaded by the sense of them. He once told Max Frisch that he liked the large picture window in his home which looked out onto the Alps only because it gave lots of light; nonetheless, he chose to live in a house that had a magnificent view. Brecht in his last years was the high priest of collectivist drama, but he never genuflected to communism and as long as he lived he never allowed his theatre to become a shrine. His spiritual makeup always had enough heresy in it to permit the poet in him to work against the grain of orthodoxy. There is no doubt that he embraced the realities of a collective society and sought to find the language, forms, and characters that would best express such a world; but everything he wrote reveals a profound kind of rebellion against such acceptance. Perhaps George Steiner captures this quality of contradiction as well as anyone, when he writes in *The Death of Tragedy*:

> Brecht stands midway between the world of Oedipus and that of Marx. He agreed with Marx that necessity is not blind, but like all true poets, he knew that she often closes her eyes. And when she has closed them, she lies in ambush, for the coming of man along the road from Corinth.

# 18

# THE PURGATORIAL
# THEATRE OF
# UGO BETTI

UGO BETTI, after Pirandello, is generally regarded as the most important dramatist to write for the modern Italian theatre. In fixing Betti's position within the broader perspective of modern drama, it is possible to note the influence of Pirandello, Ibsen, Chekhov, German expressionism, and the postwar French dramatists, but finally through the use of emblematic techniques he created a symbolic style of theatre that was uniquely his own. Certainly few writers in the twentieth century have come to grips with great moral issues more directly, forcefully, and imaginatively than did Betti in the twenty-five plays he wrote from 1926 until his death in 1953. With a flinty moral integrity, he spent a lifetime creating dramatic situations which forced his characters to face unflinchingly the problem of evil. Unlike so many modern plays in which moral issues are dissolved by psychological explanation or by those mists of fantasy which are at one with the spectator's moral evasions, Betti's plays affirm both man's need to struggle with real alternatives and his capacity to do so. The dominant themes of all his work are justice and the individual's need for judgment (Betti's lifelong interest in this theme was certainly to a large degree occasioned by his own adult career as a chief justice in the Italian courts), the redemptive and transforming power of love, and a belief in the power of the human imagination to transform the quality of life. But in dealing with

230

each of these themes there is no attempt to whitewash man's sense of his own guilt, nor the attendant need to avoid moral responsibility. Betti's attitude in this regard is best expressed in a newspaper article he wrote shortly before his death: "It is not very popular these days to attribute responsibility to oneself; the general practice is to blame others, history, laws, parents, etc. The fact is, the vast picture of our life has an author, carries a signature: Our own! We are responsible for it."

In a sense, throughout his whole career as a playwright, Ugo Betti was writing the same play.* In it the individual is searching for a meaning in life and the faith to believe in that meaning. This search is always conceived as a trial in which the protagonist(s) is viewed as the defendant. The charge is not a moral transgression in the criminal sense, but rather the individual's failure to love, to keep faith, to be responsible in human relationships. "At the root of this trial," says Betti, "is a yearning for a lost innocence which rises beyond a sigh of nostalgia to become a scream of attention, a demand to be acknowledged as worthy of love, a salvation." As a judge Betti was conscious, as few men have ever been, of the impossibility of achieving justice in human society; but he also understood man's need to search for it constantly. This is clearly seen in a play like *Corruption in the Palace of Justice.* In developing the action of the play Betti shows his acute awareness of the insufficiency of all forms of human justice, the inevitability of corruption in men and society, and the irreparable loss implicit in human relationships. The three justices—Vanan, Croz, and Cust—are all guilty; and as they judge others, they too are judged by a Grand Inquisitor. It is the death of the innocent Helen that finally precipitates these confessions, and yet the action has been moving inexorably toward this moment from the beginning. This sense of the inevitability of a just reckoning is the result of Betti's belief that there is a "spark of goodness" in all fallen men, and the light of this spark attracts and leads all men up the purgatorial mountain. In this Betti is clearly a Catholic writer in the tradition of Dante. It is for this reason that Betti does not discard the forms of human justice, inadequate as they may be, for he sees that man's quest for justice is, in fact, a quest for God. This

* Betti was very aware of this and said as much in a radio interview in 1951. "I am always writing the same play . . . the situations and characters are as diverse as possible, but they all come upon certain problems and certain sentiments that are always the same."

is his most powerful perception: Betti could affirm the sanctity of the individual not because of his capacity to act justly, but because "all of my heroes are seekers after God; and to seek after God means to have found Him." And divine justice is not retributive or corrective, but purgative and redemptive. Hence his drama celebrates the fact that under all the abdications of our selfhood, there reigns the small but powerful force of "yes." Life is continually renewed and rebuilt on these affirmations. There are in men, Betti wrote in his famous essay, "Religion and the Theatre,"

> inexplicable needs. But in the soul of the unjust man, and even in the soul of the judge who betrays justice, we will discover that, in the end, he, himself, cannot breathe or survive without justice. Underneath the most hardened bitterness we will, at a certain point, discover in the cruel, selfish, lost souls, a need for mercy, harmony, solidarity, immortality, trust, forgiveness, and, above all, for love: a mercy and a love which are far greater than the pale imitations offered by this world. This is a thirst which all of the fountains of the earth cannot quench. Each of these mysterious needs is one side of a perimeter whose complete figure, when we finally perceive it, has one name: God.

The spirit of affirmation which courses through all of his plays is neither sentimental nor simplistic because it has its roots in Betti's belief that man's most distinguishing characteristic is his capacity for choice. Perfect justice, abiding love, enduring fidelity may be impossible to achieve and/or maintain, but man is always free to choose as if they are and the characters in each of Betti's plays are pushed to those frontiers of the spirit where a confrontation with choice is inescapable. (It is interesting to note that many of Betti's plays actually have mountainous frontier settings. It is as if his characters have been forced to those barren outposts on the heights where the making of choices is necessary for survival. These settings thus express both the frontier and the purgatorial qualities of his vision.) For example, Agata, alone on the goat island, having succumbed to her desire for Angelo, chooses to murder him because it is better to choose damnation than lead the "trimmer's" life of equivocation. As she makes her decision to leave Angelo trapped in the well, she says: "There is a point when we choose what we are to be. It is at the very beginning: when nothing so far exists, and everything is free for us to choose; and our eyes turn both upwards in joy and thanksgiving. Or downwards . . . that is the starting point.

However, there is always a kind of peace in being what we are, and being it completely: the condemned man has that blessing. I accept." *

However, these lines, taken as they are out of the context of the play, may make it appear that we have only one choice to make in our lives. This is misleading, for it is clear from the body of Betti's work that he had a much more existential view of choice. Man has the freedom to choose, whether it be redemption or damnation, to the last moment of his life, but the choice will always be judged by God's will. It will never be easy and no one else can make it for him. As he says in *Troubled Waters:*

> It is childish to hope that whoever gives us specific duties will turn around and relieve us of them, will make the decision for us, and then arrange for the conditions necessary to carry out that decision! No, it's up to each one of us alone to choose; and then to act. Not tomorrow, not sometime in the future. But now. On a narrow ledge where there's barely room to put your feet!

The main movement in the Bettian theatre is towards atonement (at-one-ment). It is a drama of reconciliation based upon our capacity to choose and then to act. However, before his protagonists can begin this arduous climb up the Mount of Purgatory it is absolutely essential that they accept, with full consciousness, their own guilt. Even the victim must come to understand that "deep within himself he is not innocent." Characters such as Agata (*Crime on Goat Island*), Argia (*The Queen and the Rebels*), Cust (*Corruption in the Palace of Justice*), and Giovanni (*The Burnt Flower Bed*) finally reach the condition of atonement, and are thereby fulfilled, because they can accept the responsibility for their guilt. On

---

* Betti confirms this interpretation in his "Notes for *Crime on Goat Island*," where he writes: "Agata . . . 'I believe in justice because I feel it within me. I believe that I deserve to be punished, and, in the end, the only joy for the damned lies in being true to oneself, without hypocrisy, and in almost loving one's damnation, which is the most satisfying condition.' (Agata's savage and calm credo.) It is a mysterious truth: the guilty one accepts his damnation, and it is from damnation that he derives a real pleasure; it is damnation that guarantees him what he wants, what he has chosen, for all eternity. Can you imagine the embarrassment, the boredom, the sadness of one of the damned sent, by mistake, to sing Hosannahs in paradise for all eternity? For Agata, the result is that she wants to be damned in order to salvage something: her daughter, certain things which she herself has thought, felt: compassion, tenderness." *Tulane Drama Review*, vol. 8, no. 3, p. 85.

the other hand, Nina and Danielle in *The Fugitives* are fugitives, and hence alienated, to the very end because they cannot.*

The capacity to respond, then, is central to the action of atonement. The failure to respond is to deny that guilt which we must accept if we are to make meaningful choices. (The great negators in Betti's theatre are those who know this and are nonetheless indifferent; this is particularly true of the Doctor in *The Fugitives* and Commissar Amos of *The Queen and the Rebels*.) This accounts for the unique role of children in Betti's plays. Unlike Anouilh, who bewailingly sees the child as the symbol of man's lost innocence, Betti views the child as the agent of innocence. For him, innocence is our capacity to respond and this explains why children invariably prompt the protagonist to accept his or her guilt and thereby be capable of those choices which make them fully alive. This is the "piece of good news" which everyone, and especially children, has inside himself. The presence of children (Sylvia in *Crime on Goat Island*, Helen in *Corruption in the Palace of Justice*, Rosa in *The Burnt Flower Bed*, the Queen's son in *The Queen and the Rebels*) provokes repentance (literally "to re-think one's situation") and thus assures the possibility of atonement. In those plays in which there are no children (one thinks particularly of *Struggle Till Dawn* and *The Fugitives*) there is no reconciliation.†

* The nature of this form of alienation is described in an interesting way by Thomas Merton in his preface to *The Prison Meditations of Father Delp*: "Modern Man has surrendered himself to be used more and more as an instrument, as a means, and in consequence his spiritual creativity has dried up at its source. No longer alive with passionate convictions, but centered on his own empty and alienated self, man becomes destructive, negative, violent. He loses all insight, all compassion, and his intellectual life is cruelly perverse. Or else his soul, shocked into insensitivity by suffering and alienation, remains simply numb, inert, hopeless. In such varying conditions, man continues in 'blind conflict with reality' and hence his life is a repeated perpetration of a basic untruth. Either he still hopes in matter and in the power he acquires by its manipulation, and then his heart is one which God himself cannot find access, it is so hedged around with insurance. Or else, in abject self contempt, alienated man believes more in his own unworthiness than in the creative power of God."

† Gino Rizzo explains the central role of the child in Betti's plays somewhat differently in his essay "Regression-Progression in Ugo Betti's Drama," where he writes: "He has chosen consistently and coherently to employ the child as the *irrational third* that can reconcile the opposites of life and provide a link between a primordial past and an unknown future. He has found in the child the most appropriate vehicle for the fusion of biological impulses, psychological manifestations and spiritual needs thus transcending the limitations of clinical case-histories through the metapsychology of religious myth." *Tulane Drama Review*, vol. 8, no. 1, pp. 128–129.

This leads us to the second major theme in all his plays, the redemptive power of love. Love is perfect justice, and Betti believes in the transforming power of love. Man cannot live without love, but love must be genuine. For Betti, to love another person perfectly is to love him as oneself and not as an object. (One of the reasons sexuality plays such an important role in his plays is because in the sexual relationship it is so easy to corrupt love, i.e., think of the partner only as a thing.) Again, Thomas Merton can be helpful, this time in his book *Disputed Questions,* where he wrote in this regard that:

> to love another as an object is to love him as a "thing," as a commodity which can be used, exploited, enjoyed and then cast off. But to love another as a person we must begin by granting him his own autonomy and identity as a person. We have to love him for his own good, not for the good we get out of him. And this is impossible unless we are capable of a love which "transforms" us, so to speak, into the other person, making us able to see things as he sees them, love what he loves, experience the deeper realities of his own life as if they were our own. Without sacrifice, such a transformation is utterly impossible. But unless we are capable of this kind of transformation "into the other" while remaining ourselves, we are not yet capable of a fully human existence.

This passage I believe provides an important key to the understanding of much in Betti's plays. But to it one more idea should be added: Betti's deep conviction in the power of the human imagination. For Betti, imagination is the divine attribute of all men; it is that creative force, that power within the individual which enables him to transform the quality of life. It has the power to create in man not only a sense of dignity, it endows him with the ability to live his life regally.

Each of Betti's plays reveals his abiding concern for these ideas, but none of them expresses it more forcefully than his masterpiece, *The Queen and the Rebels.* Briefly, the play is about the transformation of a common whore into a queen. The action takes place on a frontier during the revolution. A group of travelers has been stopped by the rebels because it is believed that the now deposed queen is a part of the company. The queen, though long since defeated, is the symbol of resistance for the peasants; and her very existence makes it impossible for the rebels to achieve total victory. The queen is indeed part of this group; however, the chief suspect is Argia, who is in fact a commoner-become-prostitute. Her only significant qualities are inborn pride and a love of "silly games of make believe"; characteristics which give her a simple-minded pleasure when the investigators mistake her for the queen. It is Argia, however, who recognizes the queen. The queen, it turns out, is only a frightened little old woman who wants to live at any cost. The symbol of courage and the reality of the person have nothing in common. Argia is revolted by the queen's subservience and lack of dignity. "You can't lose your dignity!" she cries out; "You are abdicating." Argia had been plotting the queen's death, but has compassion for the old woman and helps her to escape. With this act, the transformation begins. The queen gives Argia her ring, the last vestige of her nobility, and the new queen is born.

The change is immediately noticeable. Argia has a new quality of dignity and a correspondingly more refined style of behavior and rhetoric. When she realizes her captors believe she is the queen, she plays her new role to the hilt. This part of the play might be called the "rehearsal for reality." She is still acting, but the appearance and the reality are beginning to merge. However, when the reality of the role means imminent death, Argia shrinks from the dangers and responsibilities of nobility. Only after she has been betrayed by those who she believed would save her, does she unequivocally assert that, "Yes, I am the Queen." The role and the person have become one.

In the last act, as she awaits execution, Argia discovers the true meaning of nobility. In a powerful *agon* with Commissar Amos, who embodies all that says no in the world, Argia exclaims: "I think there comes a time when the only thing to do is to stand up and say why do you insult me like this? And, my God, why have I allowed you to? Get away from me! . . . Show me respect! Respect, because I am the Queen!" As she goes to her death, the common woman has become a queen; and her last words are Betti's testimony to life, dignity, and that power of the imagination which makes them meaningful: "Unquestionably, this is a seat for kings, and in it we must try to live regally."

Failure to see that the driving force of Betti's theatre is the transforming power of the imagination, will lead one, as did Kenneth Tynan, to dismiss his plays as clichéd and verbosely solemn melodramas. But, in fact, Betti has taken the techniques of traditional dramaturgy and infused them with new meanings. Religious meanings. In a radio interview two years before his death, Betti reaffirmed his lifelong aim as a playwright: "What I would like to do in my writings would be to put certain individuals and certain sentiments naked and alone on the bottom rung of a tall ladder, and see if there is in them, and in them alone, without any help or prop, the capacity, or rather the necessity, to climb. To climb: that is, to love, to believe in themselves and in others; to see in life and beyond it a harmony, a justice; to feel within themselves an immortal destiny. To be a valid proof, this ascent must start very low; from the lowest rung, just that. It is in the despairing man, the skeptic, that it is important to detect a spark of light; only then will such a spark be proof of something." That spark is the light which drives Argia to her throne.

In our time when social and economic forces tend to destroy individual integrity and the courage to accept the destiny of our own identity, many people have lost faith in the power and the possibility of heroism. Not so Betti, who has given us a powerful weapon to use against negativism and despair: imaginative style. The mid-twentieth-century theatre has tended to be a theatre of victims, sell-outs, or lucky fools. When occasionally we find characters with genuine heroic stature, we admire them for the strength and integrity of their will, but we also know the futility of emulating them—our wills lack that kind of iron. In Brecht's *The Caucasian Chalk Circle*, for example, the myth of justice and reason are equated to the mythical figure of Azdak who is only possible in such a state of chaos because a more benevolent vision of circumstances, namely, luck, is present. Azdak is able to save Grusha because he is at the same time saved by the messengers of the grand duke. Justice and goodness can exist only because luck has changed circumstances, thus making possible "a brief golden age almost of justice." Betti's heroism is of a different kind; it is based on the power of the imagination to assert itself with generative and regenerative force. Unlike the Brechtian hero who acts chiefly in response to external social pressure, Betti's heroes are driven by inner forces which urge them to spiritual redemption. We know that when an individual seizes upon something with his imagination great things can happen in spite of failures of the will. What Betti's heroes represent is neither moral boot-strapping nor pipe-dream illusions; rather they embody that kind of imaginative power which Lenin once described as the kind which "allows us to catch up with the natural course of events" and gives us "support and strengthens our energy." Success for the Bettian hero depends on spiritual awareness. Survival is considered not in terms of physical existence, but in the retention of the capacity to love, to keep faith, to assume responsibility, in short, to respond. Thus it is that while the Brechtian hero needs to be shrewd, the Bettian hero needs to be shriven.

One of the biggest challenges facing both artists and audiences is to discover ways in which our theatre can help to renew and reinvigorate those deep and interior orders of human sensibility and human feeling which give quality and meaning to life. Ugo Betti met this challenge all his life and is one of this century's most eloquent spokesmen for the cause of human dignity and freedom.

# 19

# THORNTON WILDER
# AND THE TRAGIC
# SENSE OF LIFE

OF ALL modern American dramatists, none is more difficult to pin
down than Thornton Wilder. He is thought of, together with O'Neill,
Miller, and Williams, as one of our "Big Four," and yet his reputation is based on only three full-length plays and was made on one.
And whereas reams of criticism have been written on the other
three playwrights, only an occasional article on Wilder is published.
This is all the more surprising since no one seems to agree about
his work. For some he is the great American satirist; for others he
is a soft-hearted sentimentalist; and for still others he is our only
"religious" dramatist. Furthermore, no American playwright is more
respected by contemporary European dramatists than is Wilder;
Brecht, Ionesco, Duerrenmatt, and Frisch have all acknowledged
their debt to this "great and fanatical experimenter." Therefore, it
is about time that we reevaluate his work.

From his earliest volumes of one-acts, *The Angel that Troubled
the Waters* and *The Long Christmas Dinner*, to his last full-length
play, *The Matchmaker*, Wilder has dealt boldly and affirmatively
with the themes of Life, Love, and Earth. Each of his plays is a
hymn in dramatic form affirming life. But the important question
is: What is the nature of this affirmation? It is not, as some would
have it, Christian. To begin with, Wilder has no belief—at least as
expressed in his plays—in a religion that is revealed or historical.
These are basic premises of Christianity. To be sure Wilder is deistic,

but as almost all of his critics have pointed out, he is essentially a religious Platonist; and this position must ultimately reject the historic dimension as meaningful. Francis Fergusson ties these two ideas together when he writes:

> The plays are perfectly in accord with the Platonic kind of philosophy which they are designed to teach. The great Ideas are timeless, above the history of the race and the history of actual individuals. Any bit of individual or racial history will do, therefore, to "illustrate" them; but history and individual lives lack all real being; they are only shadows on the cave wall.

Mary McCarthy approaches this another way when she writes of *The Skin of Our Teeth:*

> In other words, if George misses the five-fifteen, Chaos is come again. This is the moral of the piece. Man, says Mr. Wilder, from time to time gets puffed up with pride and prosperity, he grows envious, covetous, lecherous, forgets his conjugal duties, goes whoring after women; portents of disaster appear, but he is too blind to see them; in the end, with the help of the little woman, who has never taken any stock in either pleasure or wisdom, he escapes by the skin of his teeth. *Sicut erat in principio.* . . .
>
> It is a curious view of life. It displays elements of Christian morality. Christ, however, was never so simple, but on the contrary allowed always for paradox (the woman taken in adultery, the story of Martha and Mary, "Consider the lilies of the field"). . . . No, it is not the Christian view, but a kind of bowdlerized version of it, such as might have been imparted to a class of taxpayer's children by a New England Sunday School teacher forty years ago.

Now, I happen to believe that both Fergusson and Miss McCarthy (even in their admiration for Wilder) overstate their arguments, because Wilder, except in his preface to *The Angel that Troubled the Waters,* has never thought of himself as a Christian or a religious playwright. He best states his position when he writes: "*Our Town* is not offered as a picture of life in a New Hampshire village; or speculation about the conditions of life after death. . . . It is an attempt to find a value above all price for the smallest events of daily life." Wilder is talking about *Our Town,* but what he says applies to all of his work. In short, Wilder is a humanist, an affirming humanist, a "yeasayer to life" as Barnard Hewitt calls him.

When we examine the nature of Wilder's humanistic affirmation, what do we discover? His plays celebrate human love, the worth and dignity of man, the values of the ordinary, and the eternity of human values. From the little boy in Wilder's first play who says: "I am not afraid of life. I will astonish it!" to Dolly Levi and her cohorts in adventure in *The Matchmaker*, Wilder has always been on the side of life and life is seen to be most directly affirmed through love. Love, then, is his most persistent theme and it has been for him an inexhaustible subject. Of its worth he is convinced, but it is interesting to note that Wilder has never been able to make any commitments as to the reasons for its worth. Wilder can deal with life and love directly and concretely; but when he moves to the edges of life, the focus becomes less sharp. Certainly, Wilder deals with death—he is not afraid of it, but death in his plays is terminal. When Mrs. Soames says in Act Three of *Our Town:* "My, wasn't life awful—and wonderful," Wilder is reminding us that beauty is recognizable because of change and life is meaningful because of death. But as both John Mason Brown and Winfield Townley Scott have pointed out, Wilder never deals adequately with Death's own meaning. And as for what's beyond death? The Stage Manager in *Our Town* tells us:

> You know as well as I do that the dead don't stay interested in us living people for very long. Gradually, gradually, they let go of the earth. . . . They get weaned away from the earth—that's the way I put it—weaned away. Yes, they stay here while the earth-part of 'em burns away, burns out, and all that time they slowly get indifferent to what's going on in Grover's Corners. They're waitin'! They're waitin' for something that they feel is comin'. Something important and great. Aren't they waitin' for the eternal part in them to come out clear?

But what is this eternal part, this Platonic essence, which in our imperfect awareness of living is only a shadow on the wall of the cave? What is death's meaning? The Stage Manager has just told us:

> everybody knows that *something* is eternal. And it ain't names, and it ain't earth, and it ain't even the stars . . . everybody knows in their bones that *something* is eternal, and that something has to do with human beings. All the greatest people ever lived have been telling us that for five thousand years and yet you'd be surprised how people are always losing hold of it. There's something way down deep that's eternal about every human being.

So, we are right back where we started: Life is reality and eternity
is the perfected essence of that reality to which we are too often
blind and of which we can't stand too much.

It is this tendency, a tendency consistent with his Platonism, to
reduce the dimension of eternity so that it can be encompassed by
life itself, that has led me to believe, although he has written no
tragedies, that Wilder has essentially a tragic rather than a Christian or even religious view of life. To be sure, Wilder has not created any Ahabs or Lears, but this is not because he lacks a tragic
vision. He happens to believe, as did Maeterlinck, that there are
times in each of our lives when we are conscious of moving into
the boundary situations of the tragic realm, and that furthermore,
life's tragedies can best be seen in the drama of the everyday, in
life's smallest events. For this reason he does not dramatize great
conflicts in order to capture the quintessence of tragedy. I think it
is important to see the validity of this, although we must point out
that while this approach is tragic it is not always dramatic. And
this, I think, accounts for the fact that Wilder's plays are usually
referred to as "hymns," "odes," "songs," and so on, and most critics
feel that there isn't much conflict in their plots. It might be helpful
to take a specific example to illustrate Wilder's position on this
matter.

Over and over again in Wilder's work, the belief is stated directly
and indirectly that "life is what you make of it." The fullest discussion of the idea is in his novel *The Ides of March*, where Caesar
says: "Life has no meaning save that which we confer upon it."
Later he says:

> Am I sure that there is no mind behind our existence and no mystery
> anywhere in the universe? I think I am. . . . How terrifying and
> glorious the role of man if, indeed, without guidance and without
> consolation he must create from his own vitals the meaning for his
> existence and the rules whereby he lives.

Many of us believe this idea when stated in its simpler form: "Life
is what we make of it." But we are unaware that this is really an
existential position and that Wilder is very close to Sartre's "Man
is condemned to be free."

In fact, upon reflection, we discover that in starting from "Life is
what we make of it," Wilder is really in the mainstream of the modern drama beginning with Ibsen and Strindberg. And this is a dan-

gerous position and usually in the drama has led to despair. The image of man in this drama is an image of collapse. Certainly, Kierkegaard saw this in the already quoted passage from *Fear and Trembling*:

> If there were no eternal consciousness in a man, if at the foundation of all there lay only a wildly seething power which writhing with obscure passions produced everything that is great and everything that is insignificant, if a bottomless void never satiated lay hidden beneath all—what then would life be but despair.

Most modern dramatists have answered with "that's all!" But Wilder hasn't, even though he holds a position that should lead this way. I think he averts despair—and also tragedy, even though his view of life is essentially tragic—with a kind of Santayana-like belief in life. In fact, Wilder's Platonism can make sense only if it is seen as coming through Santayana. Wilder is, as probably most of us are, saved from despair and its paralyzing effects by what Santayana has called "animal faith." Many will admit that by the rules of logic life is little more than an irrational nightmare in which the only reality is that grotesque illusion which we happen to believe in at a given moment; but somehow our animal faith, which bids us believe in the external world, is much stronger than all the logical arguments which tend to make life seem absurd. As Joseph Wood Krutch put it: "Everybody acts as though he believed that the external world exists; nearly everybody acts as though he believed that his version of it is a dependable one; and the majority act as though they could also make valid value judgments about it." It is this belief, this animal faith, that permits Wilder to say "Life is what you make of it," and still come up in affirmation on this side of despair. All his plays might be described by that verse of Theodore Spencer's (and I think Wilder and Spencer have great affinities):

> Oh how to praise that No,
> When all longing would press
> After the lost Yes!
> Oh how redress
> That disaster of No?

But although Wilder can assert meaning to life, the meaning is almost in the assertion itself and this is not a very comfortable position to be in. One gets the feeling that Wilder has to keep saying it to make sure that it is true. The danger of this position is that it lacks the necessary polarity and tension for full meaning. This in itself keeps Wilder from being a religious dramatist. In all great religious drama—the works of Sophocles, Calderón, *Everyman*, and in more recent times the later plays of Hofmannsthal, Eliot, and even Fry—there is the backdrop of religious belief which gives meaning to and informs the hero's "life is what you make of it." There is the greater stage. The medieval theatre and the Spanish theatre of Calderón exhibit this, and this is what Hofmannsthal tried to achieve at the Salzburg festivals with his productions of *Everyman, The Great World Theatre,* and *The Tower*. In all of these plays the actors—man—are faced with a moral choice under the very eyes of God and his angels upstage. The scaffold of these multiple stage structures not only serves as a magic mirror for the visible world and its invisible order, but the invisible order is made visible. For in these plays the idea of man as a player on the world's stage becomes the very principle of the *mise-en-scène*. For God, the master, speaking from the top of the scaffold, actually orders the world to produce a play under his eyes, featuring man who is to act out his part on earth.

More important than the absence of a religious dimension to Wilder's work, however, are the many experiments he has made in theatrical technique to compensate for this lack of an ultimate perspective. It is a commonplace in talking about modern literature to comment on the loss of a community of values and the disappearance of public truths in our time. It is equally well known that writers tend to compensate for the lack of a community of belief with new techniques of expression. The problem for the dramatist is how to make a highly individual standard of values appear to the audience to be a natural objective standard. Most of the modern dramatists have attempted to meet this problem by focusing on the psychology of their characters. In so doing they leave begged the question of value by confining the world of the play to the limits of an individual character's mind and then assessing value solely in terms of the consciousness of that mind. Thus, an incident in *Hedda Gabler* may not be important by any communicable standard of human significance, but if the universe is confined to her mind and Ibsen makes us look deeply enough into it, we can at least see it as important in that tiny context. In this way psychology makes possible such a drastic limitation of context that a private world can be the subject of a tragedy. Furthermore, by new techniques of presentation that private world and its values can be made, at least for the duration of the performance, convincing.

Wilder has not been interested in psychology and has never used psychological techniques to solve the "modernists'" problems in the theatre. This accounts, I think, for his great influence on the Continental avant-garde dramatists who are rebelling against our psychologically oriented theatre. Wilder sought to achieve the sense of an ultimate perspective by immaterializing the sense of dramatic place on stage. The bare stage of *Our Town* with its chairs, tables, and ladders, together with the Stage Manager's bald exposition, are all that he uses to create the town. The same is true of *The Skin of Our Teeth;* you never really know where the Antrobuses live, nor when. This is his second dominant technique; by destroying the illusion of time, Wilder achieves the effect of any time, all time, each time. But this is risky business, for without the backdrop of an ultimate perspective to inform a play's action, it can very easily become sentimental or satirical, or even pretentious. Wilder at his best keeps this from happening, but his only weapons are wit and irony. And a production which does not succeed in capturing these qualities (as, alas, most college and school productions do not) is bound to turn out bathetic and sentimental; when technique is used as a compensation for the ultimate perspective, the resultant work of art always lies precariously under a Damoclean sword.

It is important that we see the dangers in Wilder's methods, but that a tragic sense of life informs his plays is best illustrated by his sense of destiny. In Wilder's novel *The Woman of Andros*, Chrysis tells her guests a fable of the dead hero who receives Zeus's permission to return to earth to relive the least eventful day of his life, on the condition that he see it both as onlooker and participant.

> Suddenly the hero saw that the living too are dead and that we can only be said to be alive in those moments when our hearts are conscious of our treasure; for our hearts are not strong enough to love every moment.

He quickly asks to be released from this experience, and it is the opinion of Chrysis that

> All human beings—save a few mysterious exceptions who seemed to be in possession of some secret from the gods—merely endured the slow misery of existence, hiding as best they could their consternation that life had no wonderful surprises after all and that its most difficult burden was the incommunicability of love.

Eight years later Wilder incorporated this into the last scene of *Our Town*. When Emily comes back on her twelfth birthday, she discovers that "we don't have time to look at one another. I didn't realize. So all that was going on and we never noticed. . . . Oh, earth you're too wonderful for anybody to realize you. Do any human beings ever realize life while they live it?—every, every minute?" The answer, of course, is no, and Emily must conclude with "That's all human beings are! Just blind people."

What Wilder is saying here is that human beings cannot stand to have a sense of destiny—the awareness that there is a continuity in all our acts, the awareness that every present moment comes from a past and is directed to a future. Only at moments, usually of emotional crisis, do we have this sense of destiny, this sense of awareness of the future. It is this sense of destiny that is the great human reality and the tragedy of life lies in our fragmentary and imperfect awareness of it. Wilder is aware, like Eliot, that "human kind cannot bear very much reality," but his plays fall short of tragedy because he takes the Platonic escape, he moves into a world that denies the reality and the nemesis of destiny. Nor does he have the solution of an Eliot. For in denying, finally, the reality of destiny he shuts out the possibility of ever providing the means to perfect our fragmentary and imperfect vision. He fails, to use Karl Jaspers' phrase, to go "Beyond Tragedy." That Wilder lacks this dimension is not to discredit him, however, for no other American dramatist more fully affirms that miracle of life which so much modern drama would deny.

# 20

# DUERRENMATT'S THE PHYSICISTS AND THE GROTESQUE

IN A time when so much that's written for the theatre seems tentative and small, self-conscious and undramatically reflective, the plays of the Swiss playwright Friedrich Duerrenmatt, by comparison, are marked with the grandeur of an almost Jacobean excess. When we enter his fantastic world there can be no doubting that we have come into a realm where the impossible has become probable. Like those writers whom he most admires—Aristophanes, Wycherley, Nestroy, and Thornton Wilder—Duerrenmatt is the master of the dramatic conceit. He invents a bizarre and improbable situation and exploits it for all it is worth, and then some. However, just beneath the apparently absurd lunacy of the surface conceit we discover a stern moral vision which shapes all that he writes. Like Ibsen, only with a somewhat better sense of humor, Duerrenmatt has a Lutheran conscience much like that of a Protestant pastor who has defrocked himself because he has lost his belief in the possibility of a salvation. He is a stern judge of the world, but his harshest judgments are directed against himself. Like a cynical Shaw, we sense he is ever ready to turn the stage into a pulpit from which to preach about the evils of a world turned sour. But until *The Physicists* he has always stopped short just in time. His troubled agnosticism would reassert itself at the final moment, and with awkward protestations that his sermons would be of little use, he returns to the theatricality with which he began, once more ironic and aloof.

It is this constant struggle between the zealot and the cynic which finally accounts for all the contradictions in Duerrenmatt's theatre. He appears misanthropic, but he cares deeply for humankind; he claims the world is beyond hope, while he desperately searches for the strategies of salvation; and, in spite of his insistence that art doesn't teach any lessons, he has a tendency to be hopelessly didactic. In an interview in 1958, he said: "When you write a play you don't do it to teach a lesson or prove a point or build a philosophy, because you can never force art to prove anything. I describe human beings, not marionettes; an action, not an allegory; I set forth a world, not a moral." He is sincere in this, and up to a point he is correct; and yet, no other contemporary playwright (unless it be Miller in his openly autobiographical play *After the Fall*) makes us so keenly aware of his personal presence on the stage. His usual dramatic method is to set up a grotesque fantasy world and then step back and watch with the audience as his invented fate works itself out with a ferocious inevitability. But this Olympian detachment is more apparent than real. He is, in fact, a puppeteer-god, and there are times when we sense he wants to change the script or is on the verge of getting involved in the action himself.

Duerrenmatt's chief protection against this tendency for over-involvement is his remarkable grasp of theatrical technique. His dramaturgy, like that of his fellow countryman Max Frisch, can best be described as "Biedermeier." He employs a hodgepodge of theatrical style and will try any device or theatrical convention if he feels it will work on the stage. Such disregard for consistency is not the amateur's lack of discipline, but the result of Duerrenmatt's fervent desire to put the richness and manifold diversity of the world on the stage. It is his strong conviction that the theatre should present "not the potential of a situation, but its rich harvest." The total effect of such an idea of the theatre is not confusion, but a baroque lushness. But he combines this penchant for amplification with the techniques of romantic irony, and as a result he achieves a toughness of tone as well as a richness of style. His use of bizarre and macabre situations, the chatty comments to the reader in the stage directions, the bits of buffoonery and grand guignol, and the constant employment of anachronism and irreverent parody all contribute to the creation of an ironic fairy-tale world which captures our attention, but at the same time keeps us at a distance.

Brecht talked about the effect of thoughtful alienation, but seldom realized it in his own plays. Duerrenmatt insists that such an effect is impossible to achieve in the theatre, and does it all the time.

The two major themes in all that Duerrenmatt has written are guilt and helplessness. He is painfully conscious of men's collective sense of guilt for the disasters of global upheaval, but he is perhaps even more aware of the sense of helplessness people feel living under the shadow of imminent atomic destruction in a world that seems too difficult and too complex for even the wisest or wiliest of men to control and govern. Like Kafka, Duerrenmatt describes the human condition as that of victims trapped in a tunnel (one of his most powerful short stories is called "The Tunnel") with no beginning and no end, in which there can be no meaningful action, and from which there can be no escape.

However, a view of man which sees us all as victims and believes every attempt on the part of man to shape his own destiny is inevitably doomed to failure must of necessity reject the traditional forms of heroism. There are no victors in a Duerrenmatt play, and the only survivors are those who follow the beggar Akki's advice in the closing speech of *An Angel Comes to Babylon:* "To withstand the world the weak must understand it, lest he get onto a path which leads nowhere. . . . Heroism makes no sense, it only reveals our impotence. . . . Only he remains unscathed who has nothing and who is nothing. . . . Play stupid and survive. . . . Humble your self and you breach every wall. Endure ignominy; go devious ways; if the times demand it, bury wild hopes, ardent love, sorrow, grace, humaneness under the hangman's red cloak." Much too pessimistic? Perhaps. But those characters who do not take Akki's advice and refuse to abdicate their sense of responsibility for the world suffer a worse fate. They, too, are victims: the blind king in *The Blind Man* is a victim of degrading illusions; Mr. Mississippi and Saint-Claude (*The Marriage of Mr. Mississippi*) and Claire Zachanassian (*The Visit*) are victims of their own warped desire for revenge. And even Alfred Ill (*The Visit*), who recognizes his responsibility for the evils that have come to the people of Güllen, fails in his attempt to be a hero. Like everything else, he is only another commodity to be bought and sold. There is little doubt that Duerrenmatt's world is black, but it is not passive. Here again the basic creative contradiction at the heart of his work reasserts itself. Duerrenmatt does not give up without a struggle, but his protests against the systems of the world are to no avail; it is a castrated protest that must ultimately resign itself to the image of Ubelohe pathetically attired as Don Quixote in the final tableau of *The Marriage of Mr. Mississippi*. As the curtain comes down, he cries out:

> Often cudgeled, often mocked and
> Yet defiant.
> Well, then!
> As thou raise us with thy swirling hand,
> Horse and man, wretched both,
> As you smash us against the glittering
> Silver of the glassy sky.
> Riding on my nag
> I fall
> Over thy greatness
> Into the flaming abyss of infinity.
> An eternal comedy.
> So that thy glory may shine
> Fed by our helplessness.

In *The Physicists*, Duerrenmatt brings these two major themes to their fullest development. The play is set in a mental hospital and is about three atomic physicists who apparently have been made mad by their feelings of guilt for having unleashed those forces which may well destroy the world. One believes he is Albert Einstein and spends his time playing the violin; the second pretends to be Sir Isaac Newton (he knows that he is really Einstein, but he doesn't want to upset his colleague); and the third, Johann Wilhelm Möbius, regularly listens to the voice of King Solomon for his inspiration. The plot is ostensibly built on the fact that each of these madmen has murdered his nurse because she has fallen in love with him and believes he is not mad at all, but a genius who should be set free to save the world. It is a typically bizarre Duerrenmatt situation, made even more effective by his use (for the first time) of the classical unities of action, place, and time. But, as usual, Duerrenmatt goes from irony to irony, with each new one more grotesque than the one which preceded it. After the first two killings the police inspector is completely frustrated because he cannot arrest the murderers, since they cannot be held responsible for their crimes. But when Möbius, acting on orders from King Solomon, strangles Nurse Monika, the Inspector's frustration finally gives way to relief. "For the first time," he says, "Justice is on holiday—and it's a terrific feeling. Justice, my friend, is a terrible strain; you wear yourself out in its service, both physically and morally; I need a breathing space, that's all. Thanks to you, my dear Möbius, I've got it."

But just as we are convinced that the play is about the triumph of irresponsibility, Duerrenmatt gives the plot another ironic twist. The physicists are not mad. Möbius is a great genius who has feigned madness because he cannot face the inevitable destruction which will come if his new (and world-shaking) discoveries are made known; Newton and Einstein turn out to be rival secret agents (each thinks the other is mad) who knew all about Möbius, and both of them were in the hospital with orders to abduct him at all costs. The major part of the second act is taken up with a three-way debate on the question of freedom versus moral responsibility in scientific discovery. Inevitably, Duerrenmatt's didactic tendencies begin to show, and although the long arguments are stimulating to read, they tend to become a little tedious on the stage. Newton argues that scientific knowledge must be freely pursued, and the question of how it is used is not the scientist's concern. Einstein contends that scientific experimentation must be continued, but that such work can only be responsibly undertaken if it is done in the name and for the greater glory of the state. Möbius finally convinces them both that either way they are actually prisoners, and that in any event the risks are too great, and "there are certain risks that one may not take: the destruction of humanity is one." He tells them that he took on the fool's cap and bells because "only in the madhouse can we be free," and he is convinced that "either we stay in this madhouse or the world becomes one. Either we wipe ourselves out of the memory of mankind or mankind wipes itself out."

Duerrenmatt the zealot is persuasive, and we feel relief and almost hope for the possibilities of the human race when the three physicists finally decide that if they are to be "mad, but wise," "prisoners, but free," and "physicists, but innocent," they must remain in the madhouse. But Duerrenmatt the cynic (or is he a realist?) has the last word. And it is grotesque! There can be no such thing as innocence in our time, and all of our carefully devised plans to save the world turn out to be illusory dreams doomed to failure. It turns out that the hunchback director of the hospital has known of Möbius' strategy all along and is using his discoveries to gain dominion over the whole world. The hospital really *is* a prison, and henceforth the physicists can never be innocent or free. Realizing that "the world has fallen into the hands of an insane female psychiatrist," they can only return helplessly to their cells. Now they *are* mad!

With *The Physicists*, Duerrenmatt seems to be entering a new stage in his development as a playwright. His fantastic imagination and his unrivaled powers of invention are still very much present, but they seem to be completely under control for the first time. This play has a concentration which all of his earlier plays except *The Visit* have lacked. In his important essay, *Problems of the Theatre*, Duerrenmatt bemoans the fact that the modern dramatist is incapable of achieving that tightness of form which characterizes the classical Greek theatre. *The Physicists* indicates that Duerrenmatt can, and we only hope that his achievement will persuade other playwrights that theatrical richness and a rigorously controlled form need not be considered mutually exclusive or incompatible in the contemporary theatre.

# 21

# THE THEATRE
# IN SEARCH
# OF A FIX

ONE OF the most amazing occurrences in our theatre in recent years has been the discovery and gradual acceptance by audiences and critics of the plays of Beckett, Ionesco, Adamov, Genet, and Ghelderode. With a prudishness that is just about par for the course, many people tended to reject these plays and label their authors opprobriously as avant-garde. But somehow, in spite of our rejection, these plays keep reasserting themselves; they have a mysterious hold on our sensibilities. We find ourselves going to them, being moved or amused by them, and applauding them, fully aware that we don't always know what they mean or what their authors intend. For all their seeming unintelligibility and simplicity, these plays possess a vitality we have missed, and more important, in their boldly experimental nature they are symptomatic of the unrest which prevails in the contemporary theatre. These playwrights want to "fix" the theatre, and their plays suggest ways that have been taken to revitalize it.

Each of the writers in this movement shares the conviction that the theatre must express the senselessness and irrationality of all human actions. They believe the theatre must confront audiences with that sense of isolation, the sense of man's being encircled in a void, which is an irremediable part of the human condition. In such a universe communication with others is almost impossible, and the language of these plays is symptomatic of their authors' belief in man's inability to communicate and express his basic thoughts and feelings. This has prompted Wallace Fowlie to say that "all of these plays give the impression of being autopsies of our unacknowledged, invisible manias." All that happens in them is beyond rational motivation, happening at random or through the "demented caprice of an unaccountable idiot fate." And so critics, using Ionesco's definition of the "absurd" as "that which has no purpose, or goal, or objective," have come to label the theatre of these playwrights "The Theatre of the Absurd."

But in reducing the human situation to its ultimate absurdity, Beckett, Ionesco, *et al.*, realize that the stereotyped dramatic progressions of our determinism-oriented naturalistic theatre will no longer satisfy. They are searching for a new form, new techniques, techniques that are expressive of the central fact of their world: that man's unconscious is no more help to him than his intelligence in solving time's inscrutable ironies.

Now, the revolt against naturalism is not very new; but with the possible exception of Alfred Jarry—and he had so little impact he hardly counts—none of the theatre's revolutionaries beginning with Ibsen and Strindberg have ever resolved so systematically to undermine and destroy not only the superstructure of naturalism, the elaborate settings, the contrived plot, the socially recognizable characters with their all-too-familiar problems, but the very foundation of the naturalistic vision: the laws of logic.

For the Absurdists, tragedy and comedy are both manifestations of despair, of the act which *exists*, exists alone in its own unmotivated isolation, unmeaningful and absurd. The recognizable hero, the logically motivated heroine, the well-knit plot all give *meaning* —a spurious, illusory, distorting meaning—to the act, and so rob it of its elemental import, which lies in its irreducible absurdity. For the Absurdist playwrights, as for Sartre and Camus, the absurd alone bears the stamp of truth; logic is a pattern imposed by a dishonest philosophy pandering to the comfort of those who dare not face reality.

This attitude toward the so-called natural logic of the universe has had tremendous effects on the dramaturgy of the Absurdist playwrights. The first of these is manifested in their thinking about tragedy and comedy. Tragedy doesn't seem to flourish in the world of the absurd. When man is forced to admit that the absurd is more than ever inherent in human existence, when he sees his existence as essentially governed by the irrational, the inexplicable, and the nonsensical, he moves into the realm of the comic. For comedy supposes an unformed world, a world being made and turned upside down. In our Punch and Judy world no one is guilty or responsible. As Gautier put it, "comedy is the logic of the absurd," and thus it can admit the disorderly, the absurd, and the improbable into the realm of Art. As Dostoevsky, Joyce, and Kafka have so adequately shown in the novel, the fragmentary, schizoid lives that we live are an existential comedy. They suggest that modern man lives in the midst of so many irreconcilable forces that the only way they can be given form is by religious faith or comedy. But it is a special kind of comedy, the "comedy of the grotesque." Our world is similar to the one represented in the apocalyptic paintings of Hieronymus Bosch. The grotesque is a means whereby art can encompass the paradoxical and express the form of the unformed, "the face of a world without a face." However, this grotesque comedy, so aware of the absurdity of experience, is also extremely conscious of its sufferings, struggle, and failure. It is best described as a kind of tragicomedy. It is a vision of life which Ionesco described when he wrote: "It all comes to the same thing anyway; comic and tragic are merely two aspects of the same situation, and I have now reached the stage when I find it hard to distinguish one from the other."

The most striking thing about the plays of the avant-garde dramatists is that on the surface they seem to be either unintelligible or simple to the point of absurdity. Yet these plays are the result of serious attempts to give dramatic form to all the complexities of our world. Today we must embrace the idea of paradox in our art as well as our foreign policy. As Duerrenmatt has suggested, "Our world seems still to exist only because the atom bomb exists: out of fear of the bomb."

In *Waiting for Godot*, for instance, Beckett has created an image of man searching for relationship—with himself, with his fellowmen, and with his God—only to shatter this image by questioning the validity of the quest. Is there, after all, any ultimate and objective truth? How can we know it? Is it possible that we may be wrong? Is it true for all of us? Prove it! Why bother? In short, what's the use of living anyway?

As John R. Moore has pointed out in his essay, "A Farewell to

Something," * *Waiting for Godot* ends not in a tragic resolution but in a comic impasse. This is what is so new and important about it. Beckett has rejected the heritage of the French (and probably the Western) theatre; Descartes' *cogito, ergo sum* (I think, therefore I am) has become *vomeo, ergo sum* (I retch, therefore I am); the lyric deliberations of Corneille and Racine on the wonder of the human will have been reduced to an emotionally charged short-hand; the Pascalian dialectic of reason and passion has been mocked to absurdity, or as Anouilh put it, "*Waiting for Godot* was the *Pensées* acted out by circus clowns." But Gogo and Didi, two irreducible specimens of humanity, remain comically, tragically, ambiguously alive with the courage of their hallucinations. They affirm that man can still, albeit fearfully, stick his tongue out at the universe. Like Henry James' Bostonian, they have "the ability to dare and endure, to know and not to fear reality, to look the world in the face and take it for what it is."

But for all its concern for man's ontological solitude, the Theatre of the Absurd is not a theatre of ideas. Ionesco makes this point very strongly when he writes:

> The theatre is not the language of ideas. When it tries to become the vehicle of ideologies, it can only become their popularizer. It simplifies them dangerously. . . . Every ideological theatre risks being only a theatre of patronage. What would be, not only its use-fulness, but its proper function, if the theatre were condemned to do the work of philosophy, or theology, or politics, or pedagogy? A psychological theatre is insufficiently psychological. It is better to read a treatise on psychology. An ideological theatre is insufficiently philosophical. Instead of going to see the dramatic illustration of such and such a political theory, I prefer to read my usual daily, or listen to a speech by the candidate of my party.

Rather than ideas, then, these playwrights are trying to deal directly with the themes—emptiness, frustration, change, despair, and death —that obsess them. They believe that the theatre of naturalism either does not treat such themes, or if it does, it presents man in a reduced and estranged perspective. "Truth is in our dreams, in the imagina-tion," says Ionesco. This is the clue to his theatre. All of the Absurd-ists want a theatre "which progresses not through a predetermined subject and plot, but through an increasingly intense and revealing series of emotional states."

* *Tulane Drama Review*, vol. V, no. 1, pp. 49–60.

But action, which alone can create movement and bring a play to life, is normally provided by the plot. It is the plot that unites ideas, character, and language; yet the plot depends upon the close relationship of all three. We are now dealing with a dislocated drama; its traditional elements have been given a violent wrench. So we find that the plot has been twisted into a situation that is to reveal an emotional state. There are many dramatic situations in a plot; here the situation has been stretched to take the place of the plot. This inflation of the *situation* into the source of dramatic action, so that it replaces the plot, is the vital secret of the Theatre of the Absurd. It is the most exciting and the most disturbing aspect of this theatre. Exciting because the dramatic situation is the essence of the theatre; disturbing because it has serious limitations. It is no accident that most of Beckett's, Ionesco's, and Adamov's plays are written in one act; a plot is capable of endless ramifications largely because character changes circumstances. Once you have fixed your characters, their psychological reactions are no longer of interest. The situation assumes full command.

But if this is so, then what happens to character in the Theatre of the Absurd? None of these playwrights has created a character who can stand alone as a great individual. Traditionally, one of the most successful ways for a dramatist to express a profound truth about life, philosophy, or human nature has been for him to create a great character, a great individual in whom the audience can recognize a universal truth. In the Theatre of the Absurd the characters are types; they have no individuality and often not even names. Sometimes they are interchangeable, as for example in *Godot*, when Pozzo and Lucky change roles; or the same name, in a Kafka-like manner, is used in several plays, as is the case in Ionesco's Berenger plays.

But once you do away with a character's individuality, it is impossible for the dramatist to make individual judgments, for there can be no sequence of acts, no real interaction of character and situation, leading to a judgment. We never feel that the question of whether Gogo and Didi, Hamm and Clov, the Old Man and Woman are good or evil is raised or even pertinent; they are pathetic victims of a nothing which is so much. There are no value judgments or distinctions in values in the world of the Absurd. In Adamov's *Ping-pong*, the aesthetic, economic, and philosophic implications of pinball machines are discussed with religious fervor. In Ionesco's *Jack*, *or the Submission* the whole action is to convince Jack to accept the family's chief value: "I love potatoes with bacon."

In such a world, human action and self-sacrifice have no meaning. The most horrible aspect of Ionesco's *The Chairs* is the fact that the old couple's immolation at the end of the play is so meaningless. Ionesco presents us with an inverted Messiah and the end of the world in his "salvation." As the Orator signs autographs and the Old Woman sobs, the Old Man begins his final soliloquy:

> Our existence can come to an end in this apotheosis. . . . My mission is accomplished. I will not have lived in vain, since my message will be revealed to the world. . . . Our corpses will fall far from each other, and we will rot in an aquatic solitude. . . .

Confident that their message will save the world, they dive into the sea. The professional orator, who is to deliver their message, takes the podium and turns out to be a deaf-mute; he can only squawk and write two words on a blackboard: "Angelfood" and "Adieu." Ionesco seems to be saying that enriched cake flour is a significant token of farewell for our age; it is the perverted apocalypse of our civilization.

One of the most significant results of the Absurdists' rebellion against the natural laws of logic has been their rejection of the psychologically oriented play. Each of these playwrights is vehement in maintaining that with our almost morbid concern with psychology, particularly here in America, we are denying the theatre's historical nature. For most of this century the remedy that our theatre offered for the mystery of evil was: "Change the society!" Since 1945 it has been: "Get a doctor!" Now, there is no denying that the increased concern for psychology on the part of our dramatists has had salutary effects on the theatre. But it has gotten to the point where every so-called serious play has become a clinical case history, and this is more detrimental than beneficial.

There is an old saw about no man being a hero to his valet. Neither is he one to his psychoanalyst. Nor can he be one to a playwright who views his actions as behavioral phenomena explicable in terms of some kind of laws, scientific or otherwise. Oedipus, for example, remains a hero of great stature so long as he is not suffering from an Oedipus complex. But once we learn to explain him in terms of repressed hopes and fears, traumatic childhood experiences, or a vitamin deficiency in infancy, he may remain interesting—in fact, he will gain a new kind of interest, as Cocteau's *The Infernal Machine* attests—but he loses stature. Or while, temporarily, we accept the Elizabethan attitude toward them, which of us can understand a Hamlet or a Lear? And which of us can forgive an Othello or a Macbeth? But it is precisely that they seem mysteriously beyond our powers of understanding that they remain heroes for us. And it is a belief in a mysterious quality in men which passeth all understanding that affirms the importance of man in his universe. However, if a playwright comes to believe that all human actions are in reality predictable behavorial responses, and that his moral judgments of these actions can be dissolved by psychological understanding, how can he pattern a tragedy or create characters with stature? If there can be no possibility for an appraisal of personality as such, why should Hamlet's death be any more significant than that of Rosencrantz and Guildenstern?

That there has been a shift in our attitude toward the heroic is easily seen when we examine any one of the many modern adaptations of the Greek tragedies. For example, today most people find Anouilh's *Antigone* much more compatible with their attitudes and, thus, more interesting than Sophocles' tragic working of the theme. The characters and the dilemma of their situation seem more human. Antigone is not a hard and almost inhuman girl, with such a monomaniacal fixity of purpose that she rejects all other feelings and desires. In the modern version she is, humanly, both weak and strong. She has a lover in Haemon, whom she rejects, but she is also a helpless little girl who runs to "Nanny" for comfort and strength; as she approaches death she is afraid and seeks the consolations of even the most calloused of guards. Creon is not a blind and power-mad tyrant; he is a businessman-king who is caught in the complex web of compromise and expediency which will not allow abstract moral principles to upset the business of government.

However, what the play gains in humanity it loses in tragic force. The sense of Antigone's aloneness and Creon's moral blindness has been softened. Anouilh's Antigone is not alone and unloved, and his Creon is not blind. We pity their situation in that they are two quite attractive people caught up in a situation which neither of them likes but which they cannot control. They are victims in a disordered world which they have not created and which they have no moral obligation to correct. As the play ends, we are left with an ambiguity that allows for no reconciliation.

Now, obviously, we can't return to the womb of some hypothetical pre-Freudian existence. It will be impossible for us ever again to view man without some degree of psychoanalytic prejudice; but the important issue is whether the theatre will be so dominated by psychology that it is blinded to those older and more valuable insights of a social, moral, and spiritual nature which have been the basis of theatre from the very beginning. The Theatre of the Absurd is revolting against the kind of theatre in which all action is conceived in terms of psychological plausibility, a theatre in which actions are dissolved by psychological explanation or by those mists of fantasy which are at one with the spectator's moral evasions.

But more important than the avant-garde's concern with man's ontological solitude and its rebellion against psychology is its attitude toward language. Each of these playwrights is revolting against the tyranny of words in the modern theatre. As a result, their plays, at least until very recently, have no "message"; the dialogue is not a monologue apportioned out to several characters; they are packed with symbols, but these symbols don't mean anything in particular and they suggest many things. Their characters lead their own lives, talk their own thoughts. Their speeches impinge on each other and glance away. There is none of the planted line and heavy-handed cross references we are so accustomed to. There doesn't seem to be any central theme, only many related ideas, to these dramatic St. Vitus' dances. But as the plays draw to a close—they don't end in any Aristotelian sense—each of these ideas is subtly recaptured and made to work for an overall impact. Furthermore, nearly all these playwrights feel a great affinity to the mimes—Étienne Decroux, Marcel Marceau, and Jacques Tati. It is with this impulse that they turn for inspiration to the early films of Charlie Chaplin, Buster Keaton, the Keystone Cops, Laurel and Hardy, and the Marx Brothers; and it finally explains why they are all under the influence of Jacques Copeau and Antonin Artaud. It was only with the translation into English of Artaud's book, *The Theatre and Its Double* (the earlier and more seminal work of Copeau has not as yet been translated), that most of us have been able to discover what the aesthetic of this whole avant-garde theatre movement is.

As I pointed out earlier, Artaud's basic premise is that it is a mistake in the theatre to assume that "In the beginning was the word." And our theatre does make just that assumption. For most of us, critics as well as playwrights, the word is everything; there is no possibility of expression without it; the theatre is thought of as a branch of literature, and even if we admit a difference between the text spoken on the stage and the text read by the eyes, we have still not managed to separate it from the idea of a *performed text*. Artaud and the playwrights who have followed him maintain that our modern psychologically oriented theatre denies the theatre's historical nature. For them, to quote Artaud once again, "the stage is a concrete physical place which must speak its own language—a language that goes deeper than spoken language, a language that speaks directly to our senses rather than primarily to the mind as is the case with the language of words."

It is this insistence on restoring the gestural basis to theatre that has resulted in the renascence of pantomine in such plays as *The Chairs, Waiting for Godot, Ping-pong, Endgame, The Balcony,* and *Escurial.* But how different this pantomime is from pantomime as most moderns conceive it! For most of us, pantomime is a series of gestures which represent words or sentences—a game of charades. But this is not the pantomime of history. For the great mimes, as Artaud points out, gestures represent ideas, attitudes of mind, aspects of nature which are realized in an effective, concrete way, by constantly evoking objects or natural details in a manner much like that Oriental language which represents night by a tree on which a bird that has already closed one eye is beginning to close the other.

Now, up to a point this attitude is valid and certainly it is a much needed antidote to the worn-out and expressionless language and structure of most modern plays in the well-made-play tradition of naturalism. However, as is the case with most revolutionaries, the cause is just, but they go too far.

In the first place, for all the noise, the debates, the angry articles, the thumping of the "young Turks," there is nothing really very new in this. Ionesco's essays say nothing that Mallarmé didn't say in his long essay on the theatre seventy years ago. Artaud, the high priest of the Absurdists, said very little in *The Theatre and Its Double* that Appia, Craig, and Copeau did not imply long before he wrote his book. It is all well and good to insist that we do away with stereotyped plots and concern ourselves with expressing emotional states, but Maeterlinck and the Symbolists were doing this at the turn of the century, and where did Mityl and Tityl get the theatre? It is grand to say that the theatre has a language prior to words, and so

Beckett and Ionesco write (is "write" the correct word?) Acts Without Words; but how different is this from Jacques Bernard's "Theatre of Silence" of the twenties?

More important, and we tend to forget this, is the fact that it was the desire for more expressive language that caused realistic dialogue to be introduced into the theatre in the first place. Ibsen, Strindberg, and Chekhov didn't write the way they did because they had theories about language; they wrote realistic dialogue partly in reaction to the hollow rhetoric of the romantic play, but chiefly because they had created characters who could best express themselves with this kind of speech.

The Absurdists, in turn, are reacting against the arid language of naturalism. They insist, although I am not sure what they mean by the distinction, that the real content of a play lies in the action and not in the words. As a result, in some of their plays, Beckett's *Act without Words* and Ionesco's *The New Tenant*, they have discarded language altogether. However, the answer to the problem doesn't lie in the defiant rejection of language, but rather in the revitalization of it. If the playwrights of the avant-garde are ever going to "fix" the theatre they must discover new ways (or rediscover old ones) to make the language of the theatre once again dramatic. This will not be an easy task, for apart from the tendency toward artificiality, which characterizes so much of our so-called "poetic drama," there are two other obstacles to overcome. The first is the effect that the movies and TV have had on our audiences. We must face the fact that these two mass media have stepped in between the theatre and the popular imagination. They have seized upon the daydreams of wealth, love, physical beauty, luxury, and adventure that haunt the emotionally starved and financially pinched millions of our civilization. The movies and television, while they appease these longings, at the same time create a whole mythology for them. And this world of fantasy cannot but influence the playwright, since it forms a part of the world picture which confronts the modern sensibility, and since it contributes to the patterns of speech and the reservoir of visual imagination from which the writer draws his metaphors and images. But more important than this is the audience's loss of *imaginative power*, its inclination not so much to share in a dramatic experience as to have it served up as diversion. The consequence of this dulling effect is that more and more of our audiences find it difficult to comprehend anything but the most colloquial and explicit dialogue. They tend to reject anything that demands an active effort or response. One reason for this, I suppose, is that the language of visual images is easier to assimilate but more equivocal than that of words. It allows for that blurring of emotion and situation which is so characteristic of modern plays. We are led up to some psychological climax and then the situation is left inarticulate. We are given some cliché of gesture, a shrug, and a fadeout as a substitute for an artistic solution. One is reminded of *Tea and Sympathy, Dark at the Top of the Stairs, Two for the Seesaw,* and *Look Homeward, Angel.*

This leads to the second obstacle: the firmly entrenched convention of inarticulateness in our theatre. The rebels of naturalism were right in rejecting the romantic verse drama with its purple passages, soliloquies, and asides for "real" dramatic speech. But the convention of colloquial speech may be as restricting as any other. The drama is so much more confined in time and space than the novel that it must live by finding short cuts to the imagination. If speech is limited to the flat level of "natural" conversation, the dramatist will find it hard to penetrate any distance below the surface of character and situation, and harder still to "place" his play in relation to the wider universe of thought and experience, which lies behind its physical setting. Finally, the reticence, inarticulateness, and homely idiom of our theatre is no longer a healthy reaction but a lazy abdication, an inarticulateness which is not dramatically significant but is the inarticulateness of characters who have nothing to say.

If we are to "fix" the theatre, we must make the case of articulateness and imagination, for it will be done only by the dramatist who uses metaphor and imagery, whether in verse or prose, to achieve intensity and depth of meaning. We must have plays that are essentially true to human nature, but don't attempt to convince the audience that they are watching a piece of real life. People do not rage in the phrases cf Lear or make love in the words of Romeo, though they may wish they could. Dramatic poetry or real dramatic prose is not lifelike; it is larger than life, it employs all the resources of language to illuminate the short hour of experience in which the dramatist has caught his figures and which may bring to a climax the events of a lifetime. In language what the dramatist seeks above all is concentration. Imagery and metaphor, by appealing to our memory or our senses, by relating the concrete to the abstract, are the most highly charged forms of language he can use. And more important, they enable the dramatist to solve the most difficult of his problems: those revelations of the inner life of his characters which may not relate directly to the action of the plot, but are nonetheless significant parts of the play.

It is for this reason that our playwrights need to realize again the basis of their art—the living word. Of all language, that which I've called imaginative is the fullest and most intense, and unless the theatre relates itself to the most vital expression of the modern sensibility it will become as it too often has, superficial. As I have said, such language is not necessarily lifelike, yet it offers the richest and most fully *articulate* expression of human experience; it is the only language which can give the full expression to that balance of human faculties which characterizes the art of the theatre.

In their use of language the Absurdists would deny this, and it is very possible that the theatre they would revive will turn out to be stillborn. I am sure they would counter this by saying that what they write is in accordance with the "facts of life." If the dialogue in their plays consists of meaningless clichés and stereotyped phrases, they would insist that this is the way we talk. If their characters are constantly changing their personalities, these playwrights would point out that no one today is really consistent or truly integrated. If the people in their plays seem to be helpless puppets without any will of their own, the Absurdists would argue that we are all passively at the mercy of blind fate and meaningless circumstance; that their theatre is the true theatre of our time. If that is the case, then *Hail to the Ultra-Naturalists!*

But if it is true, and I believe it is, that man is a creature of his language, that by his use of it he defines himself, then ours is a civilization that has lost its nerve. It has lost its trust in the possibility of words to communicate meaningfully. I am sure the Absurdists would agree with this, and their plays are persuasive documents of the fact. Whenever an age loses its nerve, more and more it reduces its language to the verb, that verbal expression which denotes action in its simplest and most concrete form. On the other hand, a more confident age uses nouns and adjectives, those verbal forms which express the quality of action. This is the irony and the danger of the avant-garde theatre. They would "fix" our theatre by "connecting" it with the vital theatre of former ages; but they forget that the source of vitality of this enduring theatre is in that language which they would deny.

By all means let's revitalize the theatre and its language. But we must never forget that the theatre in its most embracing form begins with the play, and if you eliminate the spoken language, the play will not exist. It can be admitted that words are limited in what they can express, but they are finally all we've got. Yes, the language of our stage has become stagnant, but the answer is not to throw it out, but rather—and this I believe is the obligation of all writers—to revitalize language so it can more fully express man's feeling. Only an increased trust in the possibility of words to communicate meaningfully will bring about the renaissance of our theatre.

The Theatre of the Absurd has done us a great service by experimenting with nonverbal techniques. In this it has broken down many of Naturalism's restrictions and in so doing has opened up the theatre. But the final irony is appropriately directed to the playwrights themselves. They are seeking ways to link the contemporary theatre with the traditional theatre, and the traditional theatre is first and foremost a celebration of life, that life which the Absurdists would deny.

The real answer to the despair of the Absurdists, and this is the affirmation of our theatre, is that our playwrights—and I include Beckett, Ionesco, and Adamov—still find human action significant, still find it necessary to *write* plays, and in the very writing attest to the miracle of life that their philosophy would deny.

# PART FOUR

# THE PRESENT
# AND ITS
# POSSIBILITIES

# 22

# ENGAGEMENT/
# DISENGAGEMENT
# IN THE CONTEMPORARY
# THEATRE

WHENEVER ANY tendency in the arts catches on to the point that it becomes an attractive commodity to be packaged in formulas, labeled as "avant-garde," and sold supermarket-style in paperbacks and college courses by those purveyors of new movements, the critics, you can be pretty sure that it is nearly dead or has been completely misunderstood. Such has been the case with that recent fashion in dramatic literature, the Theatre of the Absurd.

To hear most people talk, one would think that Beckett and Ionesco, and later Pinter and Albee, had read Camus' *The Myth of Sisyphus* and then had accomplished some kind of magical philosophic and aesthetic fusion between the content of absurdity and theatrical form. To think this way is to misunderstand both the theatre and absurdity (not to mention Beckett and Ionesco, Pinter and Albee). We tend to forget that these playwrights are using techniques as old as the theatre itself, and that absurdity, and our awareness of it as an inescapable fact of the human condition, is as old as life itself. The quality which characterizes so much of the serious drama of the past two decades is not absurdity but the despair that many writers have felt when confronted with the seemingly bleak fact that, as Simone de Beauvoir put it, "between birth and death there is absurdity." Despair is the only mortal enemy of art, and the lifelessness of so much of the contemporary theatre is not due so much to our playwrights' concern with absurdity as it is to their unnecessary capitulation to it. We are, after all, absurd whether we know it or not, and the basic challenge of existence is to live in spite of it, because of it. The same holds true for the theatre; what is crucial is not absurdity but what comes after it.

Looking back, one is almost immediately conscious of the fact that the theatre, like the victims of Hiroshima, has gone through some grotesque (although not uninteresting) permutations since the close of the Second World War. But with very few exceptions, there has not been an important play written during this period which has not been either a violent protest against the forces of dehumanization that seem to dominate our world, or else has been an attempt to reveal the isolated and alienated nature of the human condition as it exists amongst such hostile forces. Until very recently, most playwrights have had a tendency to renounce the public forum and have recoiled to the innermost privacy of unsharable moments of existence. At best, their plays have been little more than rebellious gestures; more often, they were the violent graphs of a cornered man. These writers may cry out in anguish, "Where, oh, where, can we find 'a man for all seasons' in an age of the common and dehumanized man?" but they have, in fact, denied the validity of any season but the winter of their discontent. The central actions of the contemporary theatre have been protest and retreat. It has been, as I have pointed out, a theatre which has revealed man detached from the machinery of society; one in which man is defined by his solitude and estrangement, and not by his participation; one in which man is left face to face with himself.

In a way such protests certainly seem justified. The problems of our times are so numerous, complex, and immense, that the mind, not to mention the imagination, is overwhelmed if not paralyzed by them. Samuel Beckett has said that human suffering has reached such colossal proportions that it is impossible for him to write about it anymore. Duerrenmatt, in *Problems of the Theatre*, expresses his fear that our world has grown too big for the theatre.

> For only what the eye can take in can be made visible in art. . . .
> Today art can only embrace the victims, if it can reach men at all;
> it can no longer come close to the mighty. Creon's secretaries close
> Antigone's case. The state has lost its physical reality, and just as

physics can now only cope with the world in mathematical formulas, so the state can only be expressed in statistics. Power today becomes visible, material only when it explodes as in the atom bomb, in this marvelous mushroom which rises and spreads immaculate as the sun and in which mass murder and beauty have become one. The atom bomb can not be reproduced artistically since it is mass-produced. In its face all of man's art that would recreate it must fail, since it is itself a creation of man. Two mirrors which reflect one another remain empty.

How do you dramatize the war in Vietnam? Or the starvation in India? Or the poverty and overcrowding in Harlem? Or? Or? Or? In short, the central problems of our times. As far as I know, there hasn't been a single play of national or international reputation which attempts to deal directly with any of these problems. It can be argued, and often is, that such issues, while they may be important to the artist as an individual, should not be the concern of his art. Perhaps. But the theatre, if it is to be vital, must be what Herbert Blau has called "The Public Art of Crisis." By its very nature it involves a social context, and if it is to be meaningful, it must deal with the world as it is now; it must celebrate the conflicts and crises of the individual in his life with other men. There is no question that these conflicts are difficult to cope with, but if our dramatists retreat from them, our theatre has had it. They cannot renounce the dimensions of the twentieth century just because in certain respects adjustment to them is not achieved without distress. We may suffer from exposure to the new scale, but it is necessary for us to meet it. For only complete acceptance of the world that is developing can make our lives genuinely acceptable and our art genuinely meaningful.

Generally, the artist's failure to establish an entente with the living present is defended on the grounds that the world which has developed over the past century is either inhospitable to art or is unworthy of being celebrated by the artist. And when this defense is pushed, invariably technology and its two monster children, industrialization and collectivity, are indicted as the mortal enemies of the arts. Read the critics, read the cultural historians, read many of the artists themselves, and it will be the exception who does not agree with the late theologian, Paul Tillich, when he argues that "technical society is the great threat against the person and the arts."

Very briefly, the anti-technology case is built something like this:

Our industrial collective society is, for the most part, based on technology and technological change. Technology has as its first principle specialization. Industrialized specialization inevitably leads to functionalism, standardization and interchangeability, the manipulation of people as objects, a sense of personal anonymity, and ultimately a condition of total alienation. Since specialization does not make demands upon the individual as a human being, but is only concerned with his functional qualities, his specific technical ability, the individual's human qualities quickly tend to atrophy as he is increasingly absorbed into the industrial collective. Soon his personality begins to undergo severe psychic and even moral changes; and eventually the individual comes to lose all sense of his own identity. Our highly industrialized technological society has standardized man so completely that he has come to be nameless, faceless, and readily interchangeable. So, the argument goes. And for the past two decades most serious dramatists, both in Europe and America, have been dedicated to the task of revealing the depersonalized nature of this kind of society. They, like the students in the 1960s, have been protesting against the increasing IBM-ization of our world.

All right, fair enough; so this is true. So we are alienated and estranged. So we feel like victims of a system which we weren't responsible for creating. So robotization seems to be the cause and effect of every facet of modern life from supermarket packaging to the most horrifying totalitarian atrocities. This has become a pretty fashionable position for people to take. In fact, one of the most acceptable intellectual postures of our time is to bemoan the loss of selfhood in an age of technology. And no one has assumed this position more readily than myself. *But maybe we are all wet?* Maybe those of us in the theatre who strike such doomsday poses harm the theatre more than we ever help it?

Fortunately, today attitudes seem to be changing, and with increasing frequency our artists, even in the theatre, are asking, What's wrong with an age of technology? Why must it be the enemy of art? Perhaps it is wrong to make technology our twentieth-century whipping boy? And as these questions are asked, our views about alienation begin to change.

We have become aware, for instance, how naïve much of what has been written about our contemporary alienation really is. Invariably the well-known authors on this subject tend to contrast the fragmented twentieth-century city dweller with the whole man of some earlier paradise of togetherness. But alienation—the loss or voluntary surrender of self—has been a feature of all historical societies. More important, and the arts reflect this with increasing frequency, we are discovering that the sense of alienation which technology is supposed to have created is not as widespread as our cultural commentators maintain that it is. For most people there is no basic incompatibility between one's sense of self and the many social masks which each of us must also assume. In fact, for the majority of us, the capacity to fit oneself into roles (and hence enter into a condition of alienation) is seen not as an unavoidable necessity, but as a highly desirable talent to have. We do not despair over the plurality of our condition, but rather we are intrigued, if not absorbed, by the possibilities of it. Alienation, then, is a fact of life. And thus to identify it as a universal evil characteristic of this age is neither accurate nor useful. It supports an ideology of despair; it is a sham profundity that repudiates the present and its possibilities. The present and its possibilities. That's what I believe a vital theatre has always been interested in. Rather than joining Tillich in insisting that "technical society is the great threat against the person and the arts," perhaps we ought to recognize the fact that the spirit of our industrial and electronic technologies has brought to man a maturity and a larger measure of freedom than he has ever known before in history. Actually, I believe most Americans recognize this fact; it is an awareness that is central to our national character. For most of us, and this has been true from the beginning of our history, frontiers—whether geographical, industrial, or cultural—are not thought of as limits of the possible, but rather as challenges to be overcome. The frontier spirit and its capacity for adaptation is a part of the technological spirit; it has brought with it the qualities of freedom and dynamism which characterize our nation; and it is something which we as a people know instinctively. (Perhaps this characteristic explains, at least in part, why not one important American playwright of the past twenty years has followed the various paths forged by his Continental counterparts. American audiences have not been wildly enthusiastic over most of the "significant" post-World War II European plays either. Only our "serious" critics, usually under the influence of Continental intellectuals, have been uniform in their acclaim of the diverse achievements of the new theatres of Europe.)

I know it is not fashionable these days for critics of the arts to refer to C. P. Snow, but he made an observation about the kinds of freedom that our technologies have produced which cannot be overlooked.

> We cannot avoid the realization that applied science has made it possible to remove unnecessary suffering from a billion lives—to remove suffering of a kind, which, in our privileged society, we have largely forgotten, suffering so elementary that it is not genteel to mention it. For example, we *know* how to heal many of the sick; to prevent children dying in infancy and mothers in childbirth; to produce enough food to alleviate hunger; to throw up minimum shelter; to insure that there aren't so many births that our other efforts are in vain. All this we *know* how to do.—(*The Two Cultures: A Second Look*)

Obviously, knowing how to do these things doesn't necessarily mean we do them. Disease, starvation, poverty, and overpopulation are still major problems in most parts of the world. But the fact is—and this both because of and in spite of the bomb—we have at hand the knowledge and the resources to free people from that terrible absolutistic preoccupation with survival so that with increasing frequency they can turn their energies to building a culture in which men can more nearly fulfill their greatest potentialities.

In widening the possibility of our choices, widening the possibilities for us in ways that even our parents find it difficult to comprehend, technology has freed us into a fuller measure of our selfhood, and in so doing has, I believe, begun to restore the dimension of significant moral choice to the theatre. No one questions for a moment that our mass society is fraught with problems and limitations, but it is also developing a new kind of freedom which is peculiarly appropriate to drama. Perhaps an example will clarify what I mean. A few years ago, a UNESCO team was traveling about the Middle East, and, as UNESCO teams are wont to do, they were making a survey. The team went about the hillsides asking the shepherds if they had ever considered doing something else. The shepherds were completely baffled; it wasn't a matter of not being able to answer the question, they couldn't even comprehend it. It was like asking them if they had ever considered changing their age or their sex. The identity of those shepherds was so locked into a pattern of static conformism that their imaginations were incapable of conceiving of the possibility of change. In our highly developed technological society, on the other hand, a man is able to realize his identity according to the many functional roles he fulfills. Strangely enough, I believe this gives us an elusive freedom to create a fuller destiny of our own. This freedom may be hard to bear, as Dostoevsky's Grand Inquisitor pointed out; but such burdens must inevitably attend man's emergence into his most appropriate freedom. *

In addition to its power to enlarge the range of human choice, another of the most striking characteristics of technology is *play*. Ask any man working on basic research what he is doing, and he is likely to answer: "Playing around." This response has a profound meaning. It indicates a spirit of liberation and suggests that there is an unexpected element of humanity involved in technological research. One of the dominant characteristics of all scientific research is improvisation, and I do not believe it is an accident that all of the arts, including the theatre, are moving more and more toward the improvised performance. In the past few years our artists seem to have come to a new awareness that technology is not something to be afraid of, but rather it is a great tool which the artist can use both in a technical way *and* in a spiritual way. And that quality of technology which captured the artist's attention first was its aspect of play. Play, the manifestation of delight and wonder in one's creative powers and the world that gives those powers scope. Play, that unself-conscious, ebullient homage to life itself; that uncalculated celebration of existence.

As I indicated earlier, the contemporary theatre has not, for the most part, celebrated the dimensions of the twentieth century. Rather it has tended to be in protest against them. In their manifestos these playwrights of protest claim that they want to revitalize

---

* The difficulties that such freedom imposes was certainly one of the central elements in the student revolts a few years back. Although I am well aware that the issues then were extremely complex, I cannot help but agree with Clark Kerr (the former president of the University of California at Berkeley) when he said: "The University is a disturbing place for many students but that does not mean it is devoid of meaning. One of the big advantages of a big city or a big university—as against a smaller and more monolithic closed community—is that people find those things which may mean something to them. They are given a choice. It would be terribly stultifying to find yourself in a place which has a single meaning, and that meaning is the same for everyone. The only kind of society that has only a single meaning is an authoritarian one. . . . Many tend to be overwhelmed by their opportunities; there are so many lectures to choose from, so many things to do, that they tend to become lost. They are torn too many ways and wind up condemning the whole structure."

the theatre. But history shows us that whether we are talking about discrimination and civil rights, poverty and urban renewal, or the arts, protest is never enough. There must be an embrace as well as a protest. And this means the theatre must embrace this industrialized collective world which our technologies have played such a major role in creating. In the past, whenever it was most alive and most a part of people's daily lives, the theatrical performance was an act of celebration. We must never forget that a celebration, whether it be of a birthday or the Fourth of July, a momentous victory or some great achievement of the human mind and spirit, is a joyful response to an event; it is not the creation of the event itself. A celebration is always ex post facto. Thus, only by consciously and expectantly standing within the movement of history, only by standing *within* the technological enterprise, can our playwrights ever hope to be capable of celebrating it. The theatre in its greatest periods has always been concerned with man's capacities, and it seems to me that there has never been a time in history when there was a greater potential for human capacity than right now in our high-voltage electrical age.

However, in making this hopeful prognosis of the theatre's future, I have failed to discuss a very important kind of play. In the 1950s the theatre was unquestionably dominated by the Absurdist playwrights. The major theme was alienation, and in play after play man was revealed in a condition of helpless passivity, unable to communicate, unable to cope, incapable of altering a system which was transforming him in so many profound ways. Beckett's Gogo and Didi could only wait for an unknown Godot who might not come; Ionesco's recipe for salvation was delivered by an orator who turned out to be a deaf-mute muttering something about angelfood cake; Osborne's Jimmy Porter could rail against the world with passionate rhetoric, but it all turned out to be helplessly inept. One could continue this catalogue, but it seems clear that the drama of the alienated man was as passive as it was pessimistic.

By 1965 there were signs of new vitality in the theatre. The emergence of the thrust stage as the dominant form of theatre architecture created a new kind of audience involvement. Happenings, games, improvisations instilled a new spirit of spontaneity. A willingness to mix media, especially the film, has opened up all sorts of new possibilities both in form and technique. The theatre of the present seems to be in a very unpredictable stage, but there is no denying it is full of life.

However, what about the first half of the 1960s?

Generalizations seldom, if ever, hold up for very long; but as I look back at that five-year period, the most significant characteristic which I discover in the theatre was the unflagging *drive* on the part of playwrights to deal, somehow, with absurdity. Quite interestingly, American writers approached this struggle in totally different ways than did their Continental counterparts.

I should like to substantiate this point by examining briefly the three American plays which were, in my opinion, the most significant ones written during the period 1960–1965: Tennessee Williams' *Night of the Iguana* (1961), Edward Albee's *Who's Afraid of Virginia Woolf?* (1962), and Saul Bellow's *The Last Analysis* (1964).*

Everything Tennessee Williams has written springs from his continuing preoccupation with the extremes of human aspiration and frustration. His plays deal with the war perpetually waged within the hearts of men between death and desire, the public and the private, the real and the ideal, the need for faith and the inevitability of inconstancy, the love of life and the overpowering urge towards self-destruction. But underneath these dualities we discover that each of his tormented characters is trying to touch someone in a meaningful way. Whenever people accuse Williams of being morbidly obsessed with violence and perverted sexuality, I recall a remark he made shortly after *Sweet Bird of Youth* had opened. He said then: "Desire is rooted in a longing for companionship, a release from the loneliness which haunts every individual." Williams has always been primarily interested in dramatizing the anguish of solitude, a solitude which is made increasingly unbearable as the individual feels cut off from all the old securities, as he becomes conscious of the disparity between the outer life of one way of living and the inner life of a different way of dreaming; but it was not until *Night of the Iguana* that we find him confronting directly the anguished condition of man's spiritual life with the result that in this play the continuing theme of all his work has an added dimension of depth.

All of the well-known Williams' trademarks are still present, but they have been recast. The sexuality and violence so characteristic

---

* I have intentionally omitted the plays of Arthur Miller, since I will discuss them in detail in a later chapter.

of his earlier plays have been softened and moved to the play's outer edges; and the sense of human fragility has taken on a new and steely strength. The central action of *Night of the Iguana* takes place in the world of inner disturbance and the dominant force in that world turns out to be the fantastic, that mysterious chemistry in human encounters which, to use theological terms, has the transforming power of grace. Both Shannon and Hannah, the play's central characters, have been brought to the last outpost of human possibility and in their different ways they discover and earn a moment of peace.

I believe it is worth noting that while European playwrights were protesting against the impossibility of meaningful human communication, America's leading playwright was celebrating man's capacity, admittedly hesitant and crippled, to achieve a situation in which there need be no limits, a place where a "little understanding" between two people can exist. (Significantly this union is not sexual. Nothing underscores the growth in Williams' perspectives more forcefully than the realization that Shannon and Hannah have clearly evolved from Stanley Kowalski and Blanche DuBois of *A Streetcar Named Desire*.) But there is nothing easy about this achievement, nor is the playwright sentimental in his treatment of it. The play ends at a moment of repose when all is in balance, but as Hannah speaks the final lines ("Oh, God, can't we stop now? Finally? Please let us. It's so quiet here, now.") there is panic in her heart. Like the iguana, man may briefly be set free from the "continual rush of time," but we and the characters know the still moment will not last. However, that moment surrounded as it is by perils and impermanence, nonetheless reveals not only the possibilities of human experience but also intimations of the eternal. No one writing for the contemporary theatre is more conscious of how difficult it is for people to communicate and thus discover a meaning for their lives than is Tennessee Williams. However, unlike so many of his Continental colleagues, he has not capitulated before this difficulty but rather, like the wise men of old, he has sought out new ways with the result that his work celebrates the capacity of the human spirit to triumph, if only briefly, over what had seemed to be insuperable odds.

Edward Albee has used a different strategy. In his major full-length plays he has avoided absurdity's attendant pitfalls by refusing to acknowledge them as central concerns. This has not been a matter of escapism so much as a difference in emphasis.

The initial reception to Albee's *Who's Afraid of Virginia Woolf?* was remarkably similar to the one Ibsen received upon the opening of *Ghosts*, and for a time it looked like our critics were retreating to the nineteenth century. The prestigious *Tulane Drama Review* denounced the play as a "morbid fantasy" filled with "womb-seeking weakness"; others referred to it as a "puerile dirty joke"; and in the summer of 1963, writing in *The New York Times*, playwright Joseph Hayes (*Desperate Hours*) accused Albee of destroying the American way of life, saying that he "will corrupt the taste of our theatre audiences, destroy our theatre, undermine the national morality, and bring things to a point where it will not matter if the bomb falls." Today such ludicrous strictures (certainly, only a minor talent would attribute such destructive—or constructive, for that matter—power to the arts), have been pretty thoroughly dismissed, but the play, which I believe is one of the best examples of the American theatre's new maturity, has not yet received enough serious critical recognition.

The main theme of *Who's Afraid of Virginia Woolf?*, illusion versus truth, is one of the standards in the modern repertoire, but Albee has given it a new twist. In *The Wild Duck* Ibsen denounced the need for illusion as destructive; sixty years later, O'Neill in *The Iceman Cometh* granted that illusions might be destructive, but the play finally attests that man is incapable of living without them. In *Who's Afraid of Virginia Woolf?* Albee takes what might be called a middle view: We all have illusions and need them to exist. But, nonetheless, we must strive not to confuse them with the facts, for the most disruptive conflicts in all human relations are caused by the failure to make such distinctions. This is a next to impossible task, and Albee knows it; but the play affirms the validity of the attempt:

> MARGARET: Truth and illusion, George; you don't know the difference.
> GEORGE: No, but we must carry on as though we did.

One of the remarkable characteristics of loving is the capacity to accept knowingly and with charity the illusions of those whom we love. This acceptance is the cement of life's most profound relationships, that of husband and wife, parents and children. And so long as these illusions are kept in the family, as it were, all goes well. But the moment such private illusions are treated as actual public facts, trouble begins, within individuals as well as in their relationships. This is the source of conflict in *Who's Afraid of Virginia Woolf?* When Martha tells Honey about her nonexistent son, she has taken a shared private illusion (it is clear that she and George have created a fiction which they both know does not actually exist) and proclaimed it as a public fact. Throughout the first part of the play George warns against such a revelation, but Martha, driven by frustration and an overwhelming sense of insufficiency, finally succumbs to the temptation and in so doing she triggers the explosive events of the last two acts.

No one would ever argue that George and Martha had a great relationship; but the fact is, in spite of—and perhaps because of—its sadomasochistic nature, it is still virulently alive and they have maintained it for a long time. Furthermore, as the play unfolds it becomes clear that real love exists between them. Each of them has deeply disturbing personal problems, but of equal significance is the fact that they share a common sadness: a sense of failure for their not having a child. Within this context the fictitious son is as much a bond as it is a lie.

*Who's Afraid of Virginia Woolf?* is a play in four movements—the four games—about children and childhood (and, by extension, parents and parenthood). The first game, "Humiliate the Host," is not, as so many critics contend, about George the "bog" in the history department, but about George the child. All his life he has been obsessed by the guilts, both real and imaginary, of his childhood, and the book which he wrote as a young man was an unsuccessful attempt to exorcise these guilts. Since then he has consciously and unconsciously chosen humiliation through silence and resignation as the way of atonement. The second game, "Get the Guests," reveals Honey's history of miscarriages and in so doing exposes an irredeemable emptiness in the young couple's relationship. All of the children in *Who's Afraid of Virginia Woolf?* (none actually exist, but at the same time all four of the characters have not as yet grown up) have a symbolic function: On a literal level they represent the fruit of relationship, and hence the absence of meaning in the play's two relationships, but they also underscore the need to find meaning in relationship. George and Martha are barren not only because they cannot have children, but more significantly because their own personal inadequacies prevent them from creating meaning in other ways. Nick and Honey's relationship lacks meaning because of Honey's fear of childbirth and Nick's inability to relate to anything outside himself. If the play's first movement is about guilt, the second develops the theme of sterility and in so doing extends by indirect means our understanding of the protagonists' plight. "Hump the Hostess," the third game, is one which only veteran sadomasochists are capable of playing. In it George and Martha reveal how crippled they have become. (And also how dependent they are upon each other.) George submits to the humiliation of his wife's flagrant adultery because of his overwhelming sense of inexorable guilt, a guilt which Martha is incapable of forgiving. Martha, on the other hand, must continually punish herself for her own inadequacy. Since she cannot accept herself she punishes George for his love and acceptance of her. In the anguish of self-disgust, she cries out:

> I will not forgive him for having come to rest; for having seen me and having said: Yes; this will do; who has made the hideous, the hurting, and insulting mistake of loving me and must be punished for it.

Interwoven through these three games, which reveal the nature of and reasons for George and Martha's relationship, is the story of the "son," and when Martha tells this story to outsiders a new and unexpected game must be played: "Kill the Son." Martha broke the rules. Once the private illusion becomes public, once it is stated to others as a fact, George must destroy the illusion to save what little is left of their relationship. As the play ends, all the masks have been stripped away and George and Martha are at last alone, fully conscious of their spiritual nakedness. It is a fear-laden condition, and they are still very much afraid of the bogeyman (the big bad wolf): but in facing these fears, they at least admit the possibility of redemption. In this regard, Hannah Arendt wrote in *The Human Condition*:

> The possible redemption from the predicament of irreversibility—of being unable to undo what one has done—is the faculty of forgiving. The remedy for unpredictability, for the chaotic uncertainty of the future, is contained in the faculty to make and keep promises. Both faculties depend upon plurality, on the presence and acting of others, for no man can forgive himself and no man can be bound by a promise made only to himself.

As the play ends, I believe George and Martha are aware of plurality. With the exorcism of the illusion they, for the first time, become conscious of each other as persons, and this kind of awareness makes it possible for them to forgive each other and even to make promises to each other and hence to be capable of redemption.

W. H. Auden once remarked that "it is very difficult to conceive of a successful drama without important personal relations, and of such, the most intense is, naturally, the relation between a man and a woman." *Who's Afraid of Virginia Woolf?* is such a drama of personal relations, and no one would ever argue that it lacked intensity. But more important, in this play Edward Albee has backed away from the spirit of nihilism which has dominated most of the contemporary theatre and which was certainly the governing force in his earlier work. Great drama has always shown man at the limits of possibility. In our time we may feel these limits have been drastically reduced, but in *Who's Afraid of Virginia Woolf?* Albee has stretched them some, and in doing so he has given not only the American theatre but the theatre of the whole world, a sense of new possibility.

It is Saul Bellow's leapfrog over absurdity that makes *The Last Analysis,* his only full-length play, such an important theatre work. In his first effort, Bellow revealed himself as one of the small vanguard who would lead the theatre to those frontiers beyond absurdity. Despite the fact that neither the original Broadway production nor a later revival was a great success, *The Last Analysis* may prove to be one of the most significant American plays written in a long time.

After reading the play, one thinks of Chekhov. Like the great Russian writer-turned-playwright, Bellow is a comic artist. Comic, however, not in the sense that he pokes fun at humanity's shortcomings, but in that he sees the comic as the most appropriate weapon in man's struggle for survival in an absurd world. The characters in *The Last Analysis,* and especially its hero, Philip Bummidge, like so many of Chekhov's memorable creations, are comedians by necessity, smitten with a tragic sense of life and lyrically in love with the ideal in a world poorly equipped to satisfy such aspirations. And finally, like his Russian predecessor, although more directly, Bellow reveals his belief that the only successful strategy for dealing with the absurd is to allow the actor in oneself to emerge; to play all of life's roles; to act furiously within the paradoxes of life in order to cope with our consciousness of its absurd terms.

On the surface, *The Last Analysis* appears to be a spoof of psychoanalytic methods and American popular taste; but its real subject, as Bellow indicates in his brief preface, "is the mind's comical struggle for survival." Bummidge, a popular comedian of yesteryear, now fading, nearly broke and sixty, has been struggling for self-mastery and self-definition by performing his own psychoanalysis. Playing the roles of both doctor and patient, he produces a kind of Freudian "This Is Your Life" show by reenacting all the psychic crises of his past.

The play opens as the analysis is in its final stages, and as a grand climax Bummidge is going to relive his life via closed-circuit television for an invited audience of distinguished psychiatrists using all of the people of his past—his wife, son, father, sister, girl friend, associates, friends, enemies, and even an old midwife who helped bring him into the world—as actors. The ensuing scenes are based on the archetypal pattern of life, death, and rebirth, and one would be hard put to think of a single scene in the contemporary theatre to equal the magnificence of Bummy's reenactment of his own birth. The experiment is a smash hit (it has also been witnessed by TV executives and agency directors), and Bummy is offered the world. He declines the lucrative contracts, however, and marches off to the old vaudeville theatre where he first got his start to establish the Bummidge Institute of Nonsense.

If this seems nonsensical, it is. But there is great sense in the nonsense. Bummidge wants to be God, and he has an overwhelming need to create; but in his absurdity he also knows that this passionate game can only be played in the theatre. Like all great comic writers, Bellow uses comic techniques to serve serious ends. Life as revealed in *The Last Analysis* is a grand guignol but with less sense. To live is only to make the comic gesture, or what Pirandello called the comic grimace. This is not, however, cause for despair; for it is, after all, the only way of drawing life into a stalemate in our cold war with existence.

But Saul Bellow's greatest achievement in this play is finally his protagonist. Philip Bummidge is a modern-day Hamlet, leavened with a liberal dose of the Quixotic. He is the prototype of the absurd man. The perfect society (The Bummidge Institute of Nonsense) can never exist for the absurd man, but when the final curtain comes down on Bummy as he exclaims "I am ready for the sublime," we believe that this little man, who, like each of us, can never quite trust the eccentricities he's born to, is a fitting Virgil to lead us toward the other side of despair.

While admittedly three or four swallows don't make a summer, the evidence provided by the American theatre during the 1960s indicates that we need not take a dim view of its achievements. The American playwrights of the sixties were not afraid of historical reality. For them, protest against the existential limitations of the twentieth century was not enough; there was embrace as well.

But most of the European dramatists writing during this period followed a different strategy. On the Continent the reaction against the Theatre of the Absurd was more subtle and at times more aggressive, although it was not so affirming and optimistic as the American reaction. In the fifties the protagonist in the European theatre was, as I said earlier, the alienated man. In the first half of the sixties he was the disengaged man. At first glance, the distinction between these types may appear too slight to have any significance. Certainly the behavior of both kinds is usually similar. The essential difference, I believe, is involved with a switch from the passive to the active voice, and this switch brought about profound changes in the kind of plays which were written. The image of man presented by the absurdists was one of supine helplessness. The theatre of the disengaged man, on the other hand, while it ultimately had no solutions to man's victimized condition, refused to take it any more. The new playwrights seemed to be saying that if the dehumanizing forces which seem to dominate the world cannot be changed or overcome, then "let's cut out!" It has the same change of attitude which distinguished the Diggers and the Flower People from the Beatniks. No longer was the slogan "we shall overcome"; it had become "tune in, turn on, and drop out." Alienation may be the unavoidable condition of mid-twentieth-century life, but if this is so, then an increasingly large number of people are insisting on their right to detach themselves from a society which perpetuates such a condition. But such a decision leaves these people in an ambiguous kind of position which is as strange as it is new. Their decision to be disengaged, while it is a conscious and meaningful choice, is totally dependent upon the continuance of that world from which they would be detached. They may be "cutting out," but as they move away from the scene they have to be constantly looking back over their shoulders to make sure that the scene is still there. The disengaged man is a self-dramatizing personality, and his every action is composed of two elements: he must watch himself as he acts and he must always be conscious of how those people from whom he has detached himself are reacting to his actions. In a very real sense, then, for him to act is to be the voyeur to his own actions.

It is for this reason that I believe Jean Genet was the most important single influence in the European theatre of the sixties. Almost all of the significant plays of that decade can best be understood if they are seen in terms of Genet's belief that the most effective strategy the individual can employ to deal with the absurdity of his condition is to allow the actor in himself to emerge. Each of us, Genet contends, must play all of life's roles; we must act furiously within the paradoxes of life in order to resist and withstand our consciousness of its absurd terms. In a sense, Genet urges each of us to become like Hamlet after he has learned the lesson of the players: we must become actors. This is the choice of the disengaged man. He has become an actor in an effort to accept, to tolerate, or to escape from the multiplication of paradox that defines him in his world. He has become an actor because it allows him to play at committed living within a context which provides a safe sense of definitenesses and definition. It is a condition analogous to children's games or participation in a sport. In both cases there can be great passion and involvement, and in some cases, total identification; but there are also rules and we know it. Just as the child knows that his games are played in the realm of fantasy (in fact, he is insulted if adults ever feel the need to point this out to him), so adults know that to cheat in a game is to spoil the game. It is this paradox which Diderot described so long ago, and it further explains why the disengaged man acts and at the same time is the voyeur to his actions. And this capacity for voyeurism enhances his capacity to act meaningfully. However—and this is crucial to our discussion—to choose to be an actor as a life strategy is to create a fantasy world which, while it may be self-contained, is totally dependent upon the real world it would reject. No one described this ambiguity more clearly than Hazlitt in his definition of the actor written in 1817 in "On Actors and Acting":

> Players are "the abstracts and brief chronicles of the time"; the motley representatives of human nature. They are the only honest

hypocrites. Their life is a voluntary dream; a studied madness. The height of their ambition is to be *beside themselves*. Today kings, tomorrow beggars, it is only when they are themselves that they are nothing.

The disengaged man, like the actor, succeeds so long as he is able to play at living in imaginary worlds. But the moment one of these is impinged on by the objective reality of our industrialized collective society he either reverts to his condition of helpless alienation or he is completely destroyed. Such is the fact of the disengaged man.

Hopefully, I can point out the way this attitude of disengagement is in such sharp contrast to those expressed in the American plays of the same period by examining three European plays which were either written in or were first publicly recognized in the early 1960s. They are Lars Forssell's *The Sunday Promenade* (1963), David Guerdon's *The Laundry* (1963), and Michel de Ghelderode's *Pantagleize* (an unbelievably prophetic play which was written in 1929 but was not given a major production until 1957, and was not really known about until 1960).

Lars Forssell (1928–    ) is a Swede with an American undergraduate degree. He is best known as a poet, but he has been writing plays since 1953. A number of them have received major productions in Sweden (the most important being *Mary Lou* in 1962 with Ingrid Thulin in the title role), but it was not until *The Sunday Promenade* was produced by the Royal Dramatic Theatre in the fall of 1963 that Forssell came to be thought of as a man of the theatre rather than as a talented poet trying his hand at writing plays.

Everything he has ever written for the theatre has had disengagement as its central theme. However, he gives it a special emphasis: The disengaged man is ultimately a dehumanized man and hence a betrayer of humanity. The protagonist in each of Forssell's plays— and especially his last three: *Charlie MacDeath, Mary Lou,* and *The Sunday Promenade*—has lost all faith in anything outside himself and is totally incapable of loving another human being. He sees that all ideologies have eventually failed, and he believes that disengagement from all personal loyalties and commitments to values is the only strategy for coming to terms with the absurdities of existence. Forssell, both in his plays and essays, asserts that this betrayer is the true representative of our times and should be treated sympathetically. In an interview in 1962, he is quoted as saying: "In our times the betrayer becomes a tragic person and consequently is not unsympathetic."

It is this sympathetic approach to the disengaged man which explains why Justus Coriander, the protagonist of *The Sunday Promenade*, is such an interesting and engaging character. But Forssell makes it clear in all of his plays that his hero is doomed from the start. Either the betrayer is himself betrayed by the world from which he would escape, or what is even more painful, in his distrust of all tender feelings and responses, he will cut himself off from all human sensibility, and will hence ultimately betray himself. But because Forssell is sympathetic to the impulse which leads to his disengagement and ultimate betrayal, his plays, and particularly *The Sunday Promenade*, seem to be driven by the excitement and heady energy of an impossible gamble with life rather than by the energy of vituperative disgust.

*The Sunday Promenade* is Justus Coriander's play. The opening scene sets up his flamboyant entrance; the rest of the first act and the first scene of the second act develop his character through exposition and several peripheral episodes; the second scene of the second act and the third act are concerned with his involvement in the central action of the play; and the epilogue reveals his demise. Coriander is a grocer in a small provincial Swedish town. The people who live there are small of mind and spirit; conditions are really quite shabby, and everything about existence there is abysmally dull. No could be blamed for wanting to escape its dreary confines. And Coriander attempts to do so by creating imaginative constructs. In the opening scene it soon becomes apparent that when he is not around life is pretty dull. He breaks all the rules; he makes people laugh; he is a practical joker and a master put-on artist; he feasts outrageously on life. But the most important thing about him is his creative imagination. Such characterizing phrases as "Justus is a poet"; "Justus he *creates*, he does"; "You never know what to expect with Justus"; "He's an actor. Justus is a real rascal"; "Yes, I *know* I go to extremes. It's just that when I pretend to be a gypsy, I *become* a gypsy" make it clear that for life to be bearable Justus must continually turn every situation into a theatrical event for which he writes and directs the script and in which he plays the starring role. But he does this at the expense of others. To live his fictional life he must defile and humiliate the rest of humanity. As his son says: "Why must Father's fantasies always be at other people's expense? He says the world is beautiful, and you have to use your eyes, and you have to love. . . . And yet he does everything in his power to ridicule the world and defile the people in it!"

The central metaphor of the play is the promenade of the title. The only regular custom of the Coriander household is to take an imaginary trip on Sunday afternoons by walking around the dining room table. They can go anywhere they choose, but once the journey has begun everyone must adhere to rules of the game. These trips are filled with many exciting imaginary adventures, and Justus is always urging his followers to think up more exotic episodes. But the point of this game is that it is Coriander's way of conquering a shabby reality. He creates a fictional world which is governed by laws of his own making, and so long as he controls the game he not only has a stranglehold on life, but he also controls the feelings and lives of his family. The rest of the family humors him in this—in fact, they really quite enjoy it—but they at best take it only half seriously, and they certainly do not attribute the same powers to it that the master of the house does. For Justus this fiction is reality. Without it, like Hazlitt's actor, he is nobody. As Pastor Uriksson says:

> No one is allowed to break the spell during the Sunday Promenade. Since we've come three laps, anyone who has to go back must return three laps. Those are the rules of the game. They must not be broken. Whoever breaks them is . . . dead, you might say.

During the Promenade which occurs in the play, everyone is a member of an army sitting around the campfire on the eve of a battle. The spirit of the game is catching and we see how each character begins to reveal many of his true thoughts and hidden desires. Suddenly Coriander's invalid son, Carl Michael, has a real attack. A life situation has impinged upon the game and as the family rushes to help the stricken boy, Justus struggles vainly to maintain control by keeping the fiction alive even at the expense of his son's life. He fails, because as one of the characters says: "This is no game now, Mr. Coriander," and the second act ends with Coriander weeping and apparently defeated.

It is fitting that Coriander's fictional world is shattered by the collapse of Carl Michael, for it was in the *agon* which just preceded the Promenade that the traits of Coriander as a betrayer of life were revealed by his soon-to-be-dead son. Although our sympathies are still with the energetic father during this scene, the boy says things to and about his father which we soon discover to be true. An idealistic student of Marx, Carl Michael sees the delusion of his father's isolated life within a world fabricated of dreams. "Just look at you!" he says, "You talk about Life. But you don't give a damn about the living. You talk about Death. But you've forgotten the dead. You talk about Love, but you can't love. The same is true of the poetry you read . . . drawn from a reality you talk about but have never seen! . . . And you . . . you dream in general! You don't want to hear about reality!"

The breakdown of the Sunday Promenade proves Carl Michael to be right, but at just this point Forssell surprises us and this, I believe, is his greatest achievement in the play. Justus Coriander is a tenacious gambler and rather than acknowledge the collapse of that construct which symbolizes his whole way of life, he enters into the most impossible wager of all: He will defeat death. Like the daughter of Jairus, he will bring his now dead son back to life. And he wins. However, it is this apparent victory, for his son had not actually died, which sets him up for his final downfall: In his bargain with God, Justus has promised that if the boy's life is saved he will go to Outer Mongolia as a missionary to the barbarian hordes. He will leave his safe little world and will set out "to conquer the world." No more dreams, but reality. ("I've been a dreamer, now I'm going to face reality.") He goes, but as we learn in the epilogue which takes place seven years later, he fails completely. Reality, it turns out, is dangerous and involves much more than Coriander had bargained for. He is slain by the Mongolians, and his last words before they had significantly cut out his tongue—the source of his power over life—were "I didn't know the world was that big."

For Justus Coriander the only acceptable reality is the moment of here and now which he attempts to shape and control with his extraordinary imaginative powers. The future is always to be feared because in its unpredictability it can always get out of control. Like all Romantics (and thematically the play has much in common with the poetry of Keats and Shelley), Justus attempts to conquer time: "Time is our enemy. Let's not talk about anything but *now. Now* we're alive, *now* we exist." And like all Romantics, he is doomed to failure. His end is fittingly prefigured in the midst of the Promenade. As the group sits around an imaginary campfire, Coriander asks his mother to tell him a story. She complies and relates the legend of "The Man Who Wanted to Murder Time." In the story, for the man to succeed he must finally kill himself; then he is free of all time, he belongs to eternity. So, too, with Justus; when, in the midst of his struggle with reality, he is drawn into a situation which is too large for his imagination to control he is bound to be destroyed.

In *The Sunday Promenade* the disengaged man is revealed as a betrayer who is ultimately betrayed. But there is something almost noble in his impossible quest. The only characters in the play who find love and some measure of contentment are Angelica, Coriander's deaf-mute daughter, and Abraham, his good-hearted but unimaginative clerk. In a long monologue in the third act, Abraham sums up the alternatives:

> Mr. Coriander seems to be living in a dream. He can't see how shabby and dirty and ugly life really is. He doesn't *want* to see it. The others . . . they seem aware of the shabbiness, like I am, and they live with it. That's why they're wiser and *happier* than he is, because he *wants* to be happy, he *has* to be happy, no matter what! That's why he cries sometimes . . . he cries. Did you know that? Once you realize how . . . shabby everything is . . . then you can be happy in the midst of the shabbiness. Then you're wise, Angelica. Otherwise, you're not. But I guess all this is depressing, isn't it.

Depressing, indeed! If the acceptance of life's shabbiness is the only recipe for salvation, then there will always be Justus Corianders who will search for the strategies to transcend such narrow limits even if the search ultimately leads to self-destruction and the betrayal of the human condition.

*The Laundry* by the French playwright David Guerdon is an example of still another way that the conflicts of the disengaged man were dramatized in the theatre of the sixties. The play is based on the Cretan myth of the Minotaur, and since it is quite likely that most contemporary readers and audiences will not easily remember this myth, it might be helpful to summarize briefly the legend's basic outlines before discussing how Guerdon works with it in his play.

Minos is struggling with his brothers for the throne of Crete. The god Poseidon sides with him and agrees to send a bull out of the sea as a sign of Minos' supremacy providing that Minos then sacrifices the bull on Poseidon's altar. The bull appears, Minos becomes the King, but he does not sacrifice the bull as he had vowed he would, but rather substitutes a lesser animal in its place. For a time the kingdom thrives, but Poseidon will have his revenge. The god instills in Queen Pasiphae an uncontrollable lust for the bull which she is driven to satisfy. The fruit of their union is the Minotaur: a monster with the body of a man and the head and tail of a bull. The Minotaur soon becomes a threat to the community and Minos has Daedalus, the master artist-craftsman, build a labyrinth as a prison for it. Locked in the labyrinth, the Minotaur is fed young men and women captured by the Cretans as they expanded their empire. Eventually, Theseus comes from Greece and with the help of Ariadne and Daedalus enters the labyrinth and slays the monster.

The two most important aspects of the legend, at least as far as our discussion is concerned, are: (1) Minos, himself the son of Europa and Zeus disguised as a bull, is clearly the one responsible for the monster's existence. The theme of the legend is public responsibility and Minos' failure to act as befits a true king. The birth of the Minotaur does not connote a sexual crime, but is Poseidon's punishment of Minos for his original transgression of personal greed. (2) Theseus is the hero because he acts not for himself but for the commonweal. He is the archetypal figure of the culture hero, who because of his pure spirit (and the assistance of a woman with equal purity of heart), is able to cleanse society of the stain of sin and restore it to a condition of vitality and well-being.

These are the elements of the legend which Guerdon uses in the writing of his play. But the ways he changes both their structure and incidents to create a contemporary parable of disengagement is what makes it so interesting. Everything in the legend has been perverted; indeed, one can go so far as to say that, like Genet, perversion is the basis of Guerdon's theatrical style. The cause of the monster's birth is sexual: Madame Yvonne's infatuation with another minotaur nineteen years earlier. (Her husband, the Minos figure, doesn't figure in the play at all.) While this sexual cause is used only to heighten the atmosphere of guilt in the play, the ambience of the action is, nonetheless, one of perverted feelings in a world in which love is considered a "disease." This ambience is maintained throughout the play, and the dénouement is a homosexually inspired murder. In developing this action, Guerdon uses the labyrinth—the Laundry of the title and the setting—as a grotesque metaphor of the modern world. But again there is a change of emphasis, for while the laundry does indeed house a monster, it soon becomes apparent that the members of Madame Yvonne's household, and not Daniel the Minotaur, are the real monsters. Daniel is, in fact, a sensitive, gentle, and loving soul whose chief delight in life is to take long walks in the countryside. On the other hand, Laurent, the contemporary Theseus, is a hero of hostility. With behavior ranging from the extremes of arrogance and submission, he is lazy, unfaithful, a crooked schemer, and a murderer. Driven by guilt and yearning for his lost innocence, he finally kills Daniel because the "monster's" purity of spirit makes Laurent's consciousness of his own monstrousness unbearable.

Guerdon develops the theme of disengagement in two parallel ways, one of them obvious, the other not so readily apparent and much more complex. On one level Daniel is the hero of disengagement who would prefer to return to his prison in the laundry rather than live as a hero-freak in a world which he has discovered to be tawdry and rapacious. While this is certainly a meaningful aspect of the play, I believe it is the development of the other level that is Guerdon's most significant achievement. On this level, Laurent (and to a degree all of the others in the family) is the disengaged person and his situation is revealed as the true condition of contemporary man.

The world which Guerdon shows us in *The Laundry* is one that perverts, and Laurent is its victim: He is the completely perverted man. But he in turn attempts to use perversion as a strategy of disengagement from that world. Whenever one discusses perversion he is plagued by the moralistic overtones which have become attached to the word in common parlance. But as psychologists use the word, perversion represents a compromise between the expression and inhibition of a forbidden wish. It is, as defined by the psychoanalyst Donald M. Kaplan, "The crime our guilt forbids and the deed that fulfills certain infantile ideals." It is in this sense that psychology refers to homosexuality as a perversion, and why to the neurotic personality the pervert is a hero. Herbert Marcuse explains in greater detail why this is so in *Eros and Civilization:*

> The perversions seem to give a *promesse de bonheur* greater than that of "normal" sexuality. What is the source of their promise? Freud emphasized the "exclusive" character of the deviations from normality, their rejection of the procreative sex act. The perversions

thus express rebellion against the subjugation of sexuality under the order of procreation, and against the institutions which guarantee this order . . . the perversions seem to reject the entire enslavement of the pleasure ego by the reality ego. . . . In a repressive order, which enforces the equation between normal, socially useful, and good, the manifestations of pleasure for its own sake must appear as *fleurs du mal*. [Perversions] are a symbol of what had to be suppressed so that suppression could prevail and organize the ever more efficient domination of man and nature—a symbol of the destructive identity between freedom and happiness.*

I believe this passage can help us understand Laurent's ambivalent relationship to Daniel—not to mention all of the other characters, and especially his wife—but it also helps to clarify both the nature of Laurent's relationship with Tony many years before and why he must murder Daniel. To see just how it does, I should like to examine the play's crucial scene: the confrontation of Laurent and Daniel in the second act. When they meet in the darkened laundry (at the heart of the labyrinth of personality) the intoxicated Laurent is afraid and believes Daniel wants to hurt him. Daniel knows it is the other way around, and quietly leads Laurent to reveal his true self: He is totally alone, hates women, is filled with a lacerating self-disgust, and is haunted by a monstrous guilt. As he tells his life story—especially of his love for and murder of Tony when he was twelve—it becomes clear that all of Laurent's memories and impulses are infantile. Daniel begins to rock him as if he were in a cradle, and Laurent's deepest wish emerges to the surface of his consciousness:

LAURENT: All this old blood came back up into my mouth when I saw you!
I'm afraid, Daniel! At night while I'm sleeping I sometimes start to cry and I wake up feeling awful. Then when I get to sleep again it's even worse and I begin screaming. Lena has to wake me up, she feels sorry for me. Yes! Now I know—I suddenly remember! It's just like this—the way it is now. You're following me down a hallway and the walls are all moldy, like these. I'm afraid. You hold out your hand—and then suddenly there's . . . nothing left.
Yes, that's it. . . . You catch me in the middle of the hanging sheets, and instead of killing me, you hold me in your arms and

---

* The Beacon Press edition, pp. 49–51, as quoted by Donald M. Kaplan in "Homosexuality and American Theatre: A Psychoanalytic Comment," *Tulane Drama Review*, vol. 9, no. 3 (Spring, 1965), pp. 33–34.

rock me gently back and forth. I discover a terrible joy, a horrible happiness, and I'm a little boy again. I'm a little boy and I'm back with Tony.

DANIEL: I give you this peace?

LAURENT: You erase everything. You wash everything clean. It's like the waves of the ocean washing the shore.

Laurent, in his guilt and fear of retribution wants the monster Daniel, whom he has completely identified with the monster of his dreams, to destroy him so he can be washed clean and start over again. Of course, Daniel cannot do this and wouldn't even if he could. His refusal prompts this dialogue which prefigures the events of the final scene:

LAURENT: If you don't want to save me, it's because you don't love me.

DANIEL: I don't love you.

LAURENT: Then I'm all alone.

With this, Laurent breaks down, begs Daniel for help, and passes out.

When the others enter the Laundry at this moment, they misinterpret the metamorphosis of Laurent and attribute to Daniel a supernatural power to transform people's lives. This idea of Daniel as a miracle-working God-figure is developed throughout the remainder of the play. Daniel at first resists it, but he is finally persuaded to accept the role and is about to face the huge crowd which has been gathered when Laurent reappears for their final and fateful confrontation.

All of his adult life, Laurent has been waiting for the miracle which Tony had promised him when he was a young boy: "The two of us would share our lives together in the delights of the world." This miracle has never come to pass and he resents the world because of it. This explains both his sadistic treatment of women and his destructive self-disgust. Laurent sees in Daniel the embodiment of his dream (for him Daniel is the incarnation of the ideal described by Marcuse in the passage quoted above): He lives above morality. He is free from all societal restraints to seek his own destiny. We know, in fact, that Daniel cannot do this, but Laurent resents the fact that Daniel's very existence reveals such freedom as a possibility, but cannot provide him with the means to achieve it for himself. This resentment is clear in the following speeches:

Daniel, you haven't the right to show yourself! You haven't the right to toss them into the boiling water of awakening, only to leave them later in their own mirror! Look at me—at what I've become: a worthless nobody! And I used to have such strength. . . . When you save people, you should save them completely—otherwise, it's better to leave them to their misery! . . . The Key! You have it, Daniel, and you must give it to me. Tell me why I've been tortured all these years by the vision of your face. You know and you're going to tell me!

As the action rushes to Daniel's murder, Laurent shouts, "You're my dream become reality—the reality must explain the dream." Of course, Daniel cannot do this and he turns to return to his attic prison rather than assume a role he could never play. Laurent chases after him and kills him, and when he returns to the rest of the group, he says: "There—it's finished! The dream is over. . . . When a dream becomes a reality it must be loved . . . or destroyed. Nothing else is possible."

The murder, then, is a perversion of a perversion. Homosexuality is an act of perverse disengagement. However, like all the other strategies of detachment, it can never be a totally successful life solution. Daniel represents the embodiment of the perfect solution, but he is a figure of fantasy who can only make Laurent more conscious than ever of the impossibility of his quest. Dr. Kaplan expands on this when he writes in the article I've already referred to as follows:

> An important ideological derivative of homosexuality protests a supramorality: In submitting to neither of your sexual choices, I exceed both. And in so doing, I fulfill my destiny, not on your terms but on my own. The protest here is against the Father who, on the most significant occasion in the homosexual's life—sexual conception —was heterosexual and procreative. "Psychoanalytic theory sees in the practices that exclude or prevent procreation"—I am again quoting Marcuse—"an opposition against continuing the chain of reproduction and thereby of paternal domination." The homosexual, then, is a rebel.
>
> But he is a rebel of a particular sort. "The freedom he demands," as Camus said of Sade, "is not one of principles, but of instincts." Thus, as an ideologist, when he sides with the victim against the oppression of God or society, the homosexual's ideologic style does not champion humanity, but merely himself. Ideology, whose sole program is instinct, that is, behaviour without responsibility—a pro-

gram ultimately without action—is merely nostalgic for justice and reformation but is actually seeking restoration of the spoilt child, a bit of which is lively in every victim, as well as oppressor. Intelligence, discrimination, and reason—the dawnings of the post-Oedipal child and the neutralizers of defiling domination—have little status in a homosexual ideologic style. . . .

Thus the homosexual gravitates toward the rebellious tradition of the anguished romantic and, like Sade, is susceptible to a confusion between individuality and egocentricity, liberty and libertinism, freedom and lawlessness. The homosexual engages in—to use Camus' cogent phrase—the "Dandies' Rebellion." *

*The Laundry* reveals the ultimate futility of disengagement as a life style. But it also indicates why it, like all romantic quests, haunts the human spirit—especially in times when other, more realizable possibilities seem so unsatisfying.

When one first discovers the theatre of Michel de Ghelderode, he gets the strange feeling that somehow this remarkable Belgian playwright doesn't belong to our times. (Lionel Abel has referred to him as "our man in the 16th century.") But this is misleading, for his apocalyptic visions so much like those of the Flemish painters Hieronymus Bosch and Pieter Brueghel whom he so greatly admired and by whom he was profoundly influenced, strike like lightning to the core of our twentieth-century nightmares. In fact, the theatre is just now beginning to catch up with him.

---

* Kaplan, *op. cit.*, pp. 36–37. Mention of Camus' phrase underscores the relevance of his definition of the Dandy to the central theme of this introduction: Particularly pertinent is the following:

The dandy is, by occupation, always in opposition. He can only exist by defiance. Up to now man derived his coherence from his Creator. But from the moment that he consecrates his rupture with Him, he finds himself delivered over to the fleeting moment, the passing days, and to wasted sensibility. Therefore he must take himself in hand. The dandy rallies his forces and creates a unity for himself by the very violence of his refusal. Profligate, like all people without a rule of life, he is coherent as an actor. But an actor implies a public; the dandy can only play a part by setting himself up in opposition. He can only be sure of his own existence by finding it in the expression of others' faces. Other people are his mirror. A mirror that quickly becomes clouded, it is true, since human capacity for attention is limited. It must be ceaselessly stimulated, spurred on by provocation. The dandy, therefore, is always compelled to astonish. Singularity is his vocation, excess his way to perfection. Perpetually incomplete, always on the fringe of things, he compels others to create him while denying their values. He plays at life because he is unable to live it. He plays at it until he dies, except for the moments when he is alone and without a mirror. For the dandy to be alone is not to exist.—*The Rebel*, Vintage Books, pp. 51–52.

Most of Ghelderode's plays derive from the dark yet coldly sensual world of Flanders. *Pantagleize* is a notable exception and that perhaps explains why it was the first of his plays to be given a major production in America. It's a play that transcends both history and nationality; it is of all times and places and hence will always strike audiences with its disturbing modernity.

Suzanne Langer has described the dramatic mode as the "mode of destiny." By this she means that the perpetual present moment which is the nature of theatrical performance is a very special kind of present: It is a present that is conscious of being derived from specific actions of the past, and it is also a present that is conscious of being oriented toward its own future. Thus, when we are conscious of ourselves as having a destiny we experience the present as embodying the past and the future simultaneously. It is this sense of destiny that T. S. Eliot was describing in the *Four Quartets* in the now famous lines:

> Time present and time past
> Are both perhaps present in time future
> And time future contained in time past.
> If all time is eternally present
> All time is unredeemable.

Now, in actual life most of us are not conscious of our impending future in this way, nor do we want to be. To be sure, we know that our actions will have consequences, but we do not usually have any sense of the future as a total experience which is coming because of our past and present acts. Such a sense of destiny only arises in those exceptional moments of psychic, emotional, or intellectual stress. And, hence as Eliot continues:

> . . . human kind
> Cannot bear very much reality.
> Time past and time future
> What might have been and what has been
> Point to one end, which is always present.

In short, most of us most of the time would prefer not to be conscious of ourselves as men of destiny. Like Eliot's women of Canterbury we want to be left "in our humble and tarnished frame of existence . . . small folk who live among small things." Like them, "we do not wish anything to happen . . . we have lived quietly, / succeeded in avoiding notice, / Living and partly living."

No playwright in the twentieth century was more conscious of what a heavy burden destiny can be than Michel de Ghelderode, and one of the continuing themes in his large body of work is man's abiding desire "to escape" from the bonds of the historical present into some kind of eternal mythic existence. Once in an interview when he was asked if he was "an escapist because you live in solitude and are distrustful of our world," he replied: "Perhaps you're right. In that way I'm like my Pantagleize or Christopher Columbus. Like them I sought freedom. Each of them is a synthesis of all travelers, all the wandering gypsies, all the 'seekers' of his time and of all time. Christopher Columbus was the man who escaped. *Escape!* What a magic word! But this problem of escaping seems to confront modern man as much as it did the Italian discoverer. Men have always tried to escape because destiny is hard."

*Pantagleize* is Ghelderode's drama of the destiny of Everyman. When the play opens, Pantagleize has no real identity in the society in which he lives. He is, as Ghelderode describes him in the program note to the first English production of the play, "unfit for anything except love, friendship, and ardor—a failure, therefore, in our utilitarian age, which pushes out onto the fringe everything that is unproductive, that does not pay dividends!" Pantagleize is vaguely uncomfortable that he does not have a sense of his own destiny, but he has accepted this fact and is really quite relieved that he is free of such a burden. He says to his servant Bamboola early in the play:

> I always believed I would have a destiny, a wonderful destiny, and in this childish belief I was just like you. And, alas, now I have reached the age when one slips into the category of failures. What have I done on this planet—except to wonder what I was going to do? What am I? . . . I am forty years old, and my destiny has never begun. Will it begin? Or is it my destiny to have no destiny? I am growing old. Mankind, milling all around me, I understand less and less. I have neither vanity, nor pride, nor love, nor self-respect. I have nothing but my queer name, my crucial age, and an insufficient intellectual ballast, all completely out of date.

But it soon turns out that even his name means nothing. Identity involves commitment. We are known by the choices we make, and life is constantly putting situations before us which demand that we identify ourselves. Everyman tried persistently to avoid making these choices; he much prefers to live quietly and peacefully, the friend of all men, the enemy of none. And yet life as it is lived denies the possibility of such neutrality. Flesh-and-blood men are always partisan; living is the taking of sides. And the great insight of Ghelderode's play is that neutrality is, in fact, the taking of sides by default. Pantagleize has no intention of getting involved with the revolution, or with anything else for that matter. But his innocent remark "What a lovely day!" starts a chain of events which enmeshes him inextricably in the revolution and leads to his death. In the process, however, this Chaplinesque character begins to live: He falls in love, he enjoys the power and prestige of being a leader of men, he is exhilarated as he participates unwittingly in desperate adventures, and he is confused as he faces the final judgment and death. Using the technique of a kind of modern baroque amplification to create a burlesque of man's condition, Ghelderode shows us that the contemporary Everyman does not choose his identity, rather it is thrust upon him. But strangely enough, when this occurs Pantagleize manifests a rich and warm humanity. His horoscope reads: "You, who are so far without a destiny, will find your destiny begin unexpectedly when you reach your fortieth year. So the stars foretell. Your destiny, suddenly aflame and as soon extinct—historic, perhaps—will begin with the dawn and end with the evening. On what will befall, the stars maintain a diplomatic silence." That historic day proves to be grotesquely absurd, but it is no laughing matter. As Pantagleize is being tried for his participation in the aborted revolution, he says: "What have I done? I wonder. Have we time to wonder what we do? Does anyone really know what he does here? . . . I am distressed. Distressed at having such a complicated destiny. Put a stupid phrase, an eclipse, a woman, and some treasure into a sack, shake them up, and out comes my destiny. I feel shrunk. I have left my philosophical heights. I used to fly very high, and here I am floundering on the common road. My noble philosopher's cloak is splashed with blood." And later, as he walks unknowingly to his death, Pantagleize remarks wearily: "It's overwhelming, having a destiny: it weighs heavy. . . . I shall never again say that the day is lovely. I shall never again bother myself with eclipses, or with my destiny. . . ."

*Pantagleize* is a lament. Like us all, he discovers he really doesn't want to have a destiny, for finally the destiny of each of us is to die. But this play, like all the dramas of disengagement and escape, presents an ambiguous picture of the human condition. We may indeed, and for good reason, seek to escape being identified in history by our own unique destiny. But in that one day in which Pantagleize's destiny was fulfilled, he revealed the richness, the joy, the pain, the sadness, and the ludicrousness of each man's destiny, and in so doing he affirms the humanity of us all.

# 23

# ANGER AND AFTER:
# A DECADE OF
# BRITISH THEATRE

WITH THE opening of John Osborne's *Look Back in Anger* in May of 1956, the British theatre entered what came to be known as its "anger" period, a decade that many commentators hailed as a renaissance. Playwrights popped up everywhere, and their plays were so different in tone, theme, and form that the change could only be described as revolutionary. Interestingly enough, it was Kenneth Tynan, who was to become the spokesman-critic of the new breed, who chronicled the mid-century death and rebirth of the London stage. Within the same month he reviewed the opening of Enid Bagnold's *The Chalk Garden* and John Osborne's *Look Back in Anger*. Of the former, he wrote:

> On Wednesday night a wonder happened: the West End theatre justified its existence. One had thought it an anachronism, wilfully preserving a formal, patrician acting style for which the modern drama had no use, a style as remote from reality as a troop of cavalry in an age of turbojets. One was shamefully wrong. On Wednesday night, superbly caparisoned, the cavalry went into action and gave a display of theatrical equitation which silenced all grumblers. This engagement completed, the brigade may have to be disbanded. But at least it went out with a flourish, its banners resplendent in the last rays of the sun.

Ten days later he was to write:

> Look Back in Anger is likely to remain a minority taste. What matters, however, is the size of the minority. I estimate it at roughly 6,733,000, which is the number of people in this country between the ages of twenty and thirty. And this figure will doubtless be swelled by refugees from other age-groups who are curious to know precisely what the contemporary young pup is thinking and feeling. I doubt if I could love anyone who did not wish to see Look Back in Anger. It is the best young play of its decade.

As Tynan predicted, this minority was important and for the next decade London was the most vital center of the theatre in the world. Osborne was soon followed by Behan (Irish, but first produced by Joan Littlewood at the Royal Court), Delaney, Pinter, Wesker, Kops, Arden, Bolt, a new John Whiting, Simpson, Ann Jellicoe, Edward Bond, and Tom Stoppard. Now, no one will ever try to argue that all of these playwrights are alike or are members of some "new school" of the theatre. But what links writers as different as N. F. Simpson and Robert Bolt is their willingness to try new things in the theatre. It is this willingness to try new things, and the insistence that the theatre must deal with different subjects if it is to be relevant to its audiences, that characterize the drama of "Anger and After."

To demonstrate the vitality and rich diversity of this decade of British theatre, I would like to discuss briefly four of the most significant plays produced during that time. They are Robert Bolt's A Man for All Seasons, Ann Jellicoe's The Knack, John Osborne's Inadmissible Evidence, and Harold Pinter's The Homecoming. (Certainly a play of John Arden's should also be included here; but I will be discussing his work at some length in the following chapter.)

Robert Bolt's A Man for All Seasons is one of the finest achievements of the modern theatre. It is a history play dealing with the life of the famous sixteenth-century statesman and churchman Sir Thomas More. But like all great history plays, it is more about the time in which it is written than the time about which it is written.

Bolt sees very clearly the effects that industrialization and collectivism have had upon the individual in the twentieth century. In his preface to the play he describes how in our time we have lost all conception of ourselves as individual men, and how, as a result, we have increasingly come to see ourselves in the third person. As this happens we are less and less able to deal with life's psychic, social, and spiritual collisions. Thomas More does not see himself in this way; he is "a man with an adamantine sense of his own self. He knew where he began and left off," and the action of the play is best described as a series of collisions between More and a group of powerful and able adversaries who would have him deny his selfhood to serve the wishes of his king. It is not my purpose here to describe the plot of the play, but briefly, King Henry VIII wanted his marriage to Catherine of Spain, who had not given him a son, annulled by the Pope so he could marry Anne Boleyn. Sir Thomas, although he could sympathize with the king, and even willingly stepped into the background so as not to be an obstruction in the king's divorce proceedings, refused to swear an oath that what the king was doing was right. Because of More's stature in society, the king would be content with nothing less. The play is the struggle of More, who had a tremendous love of life and a great capacity for it, to keep alive and still maintain his integrity, i.e., not make the oath. He is finally executed after a young man, whom he had helped earlier in the play, testified falsely that More was guilty of treason. But More could go to the gallows calmly, serenely, and able to say in all honesty: "I am the King's true subject, and pray for him and all the realm . . . I do none harm, I say none harm, I think none harm. And if this be not enough to keep a man alive, in good faith I long not to live."

The matter of the oath is the crucial issue of the play. In a collective society the individual tends to become an equivocal commodity, and when we think of ourselves in this way we lose all sense of our own identity. More's refusal to take the oath is Bolt's way of asserting that even under the greatest of pressures man can exist unequivocally; that it is possible to live in the modern world without "selling out." "A man takes an oath," Bolt says in the preface, "only when he wants to commit himself quite exceptionally to the statement, when he wants to make an identity between the truth of it and his own virtue; he offers himself as a guarantee." Such a commitment implies a self to guarantee. Because of his inviolable sense of himself, Sir Thomas More cannot take an oath that would in effect deny his whole being. For, as he says to his daughter, "When a man takes an oath, Meg, he's holding his own self in his own hands. Like water (*cups hands*) and if he opens his fingers then—he needn't hope to find himself again. Some men aren't capable of this, but I'd be loath to think your father one of them." He is capable of it, and as a result has a nobility of character that is rarely found in the modern theatre.

But such triumphs are not easily won. For Bolt, only those conflicts between real alternatives are meaningful; and, therefore, More's antagonists are not straw men. King Henry is a giant of man; he has a keen intellect, a sharp wit, a pleasing disposition (except when he is crossed), taste and sensitivity, and a gluttonous thirst for life. Only in the realm of ethics is this mercurial personality deficient. Cromwell is also a man of great power; historically, he was a successful administrator and was largely responsible for shaping much of present-day English law. His success was based on his shrewd understanding of what people wanted and his ability to manipulate persons and events to his own ends. More may have despised Cromwell as a pragmatist and an opportunist, but he never underestimated him. Norfolk, too, has significance as an antagonist. He lacked moral and intellectual courage, but he was a good friend. And the claims of friendship can sometimes be a more dangerous foe to integrity than open opposition. But if the claims of friendship are difficult to withstand, those of love are almost impossible. In this regard, More's faithful wife and family must also be considered powerful threats to his selfhood. His family life was the most meaningful part of More's existence, and his stand against the king meant not only poverty, pain, and disgrace, but more important his wife and children's lack of understanding and partial rejection of him. Only great spiritual courage, and the realization that his own self-respect was the foundation of these cherished relationships, made it possible for him to resist their claims. And, finally, there is More's strongest antagonist: the Common Man, that "plain simple man" who just wants "to keep out of trouble." Quite rightly, More cries out passionately, "Oh, Sweet Jesus! These plain simple men!" For it is the Common Man—sentimental, faithless, and concerned only for his own safety and welfare—who, out of his own sense of inadequacy, ultimately judges and executes the heroes of selfhood.

Sir Thomas More did not believe the natural end of man was martyrdom, and as the forces of opposition began closing in on him, this end was no temptation for him. In a moving speech to his daughter and son-in-law, he says:

> Now listen . . . God made the angels to show him splendor—as He made animals for innocence and plants for their simplicity. But Man

He made to serve wittily, in the tangle of his mind! If he suffers us to fall to such a case that there is no escaping, then we may stand to our tackle as best we can, and yes, Will, then we may clamor like champions . . . if we have the spittle for it. And no doubt it delights God to see Splendor where He looked for complexity. But it's God's part, not our own, to bring ourselves to that extremity! Our natural business lies in escaping—so let's get home and study this Bill.

The law, then, was More's defense, and although Bolt has no illusions about the sufficiency of human law, he does see it as the only defense man can create to fight against the forces of evil. ("The law is a causeway upon which so long as he keeps to it a citizen may walk safely.") Ultimately, because men and their laws are corruptible, More cannot escape that fatal web that has ensnared him; but he dies knowing that his soul is his own, and "a man's soul is his self." He died, as he lived, with full consciousness and pure respect for his own selfhood and the selfhood of all men.

In a time when social and economic forces tend to destroy individual integrity and the courage to accept the destiny of our own identity, many people have lost faith in the power and the possibility of heroism. Robert Bolt has not! His hero, Sir Thomas More, is able to look the modern world straight in the face and say:

> If we lived in a State where virtue was profitable, common sense would make us good, and greed would make us saintly. And we'd live like animals or angels in the happy land that needs no heroes. But since in fact we see that avarice, anger, envy, pride, sloth, lust, and stupidity commonly profit far beyond humility, chastity, fortitude, justice, and thought, and have to choose, to be human at all . . . why then perhaps we must stand fast a little—even at the risk of being heroes.

It would be difficult to pick a play so unlike *A Man for All Seasons* in tone, style, construction, and language as Ann Jellicoe's *The Knack*. One is a serious drama, the other slapstick farce; Bolt's play contains some of the most powerful dramatic language written in our century, while Miss Jellicoe achieves equally dramatic effects with dialogue that is monosyllabic and barren; *A Man for All Seasons* is heavy with significance, *The Knack* so light in spirit that it bobs about like a pretty red balloon on a breezy afternoon, but both plays have the power to jolt audiences.

In a way, there is nothing for the critic to say about *The Knack*. As a literary text the script is insignificant. What do you say about a text that saying "ping" for two pages to the tune of "The Blue Danube," or about a main character who shouts little more than "rape" throughout most of the last act? *The Knack* is not a literary experience (and is, therefore, immune to the techniques of literary criticism), but it is a theatrical experience of rare power. More so than most plays, it must be visualized rather than read. Miss Jellicoe has written a play for actors not readers, and in this regard the play is symptomatic of one of the major changes which has taken place in the theatre during the past twenty years.

We heard so much about the so-called Theatre of the Absurd during this period that one hesitates to mention it again now. Most of the discussions of this form of the avant-garde get tangled up in such things as Camus and Kierkegaard, despair and solitude, and black comedy and gray tragedy. The critics so caught up with these weighty concerns don't seem to realize that what the Absurdist playwrights were really revolting against was the tyranny of words in the modern theatre. In each of their plays there is an insistent demand that the gestures of pantomime are the theatre's most appropriate and valuable means of expression, the insistence that the mimetic gesture precedes the spoken word and that the gesture is the true expression of what we feel, while words only describe what we feel. The real aesthetic of this theatre is to be found in Artaud's *The Theatre and Its Double*. Artaud's basic premise is that it is a mistake in the theatre to assume that "in the beginning was the Word." The theatre is not a branch of literature, and a play is not a performed text! As Artaud put it: "The stage is a concrete physical place which must speak its own language—a language that goes deeper than spoken language, a language that speaks directly to our senses rather than primarily to the mind as is the case with the language of words."

This is the most significant thing about the so-called avant-garde theatre: it is a theatre of gesture. "In the beginning was the Gesture!" Gesture is not a decorative addition that accompanies words; rather it is the source, cause, and director of language, and insofar as language is dramatic it is gestural. The famous director Meyerhold was striving to achieve this in his attempts to restore vitality to the Russian theatre at the turn of the century. With the exception of Chekhov—and the affinity of Chekhov to the avant-garde is greater than is commonly supposed—most of the playwrights of that time were trying to transform literature for reading into literature for the theatre. Meyerhold correctly saw that these playwrights were in fact novelists who thought that by reducing the number of descriptive passages and, for the liveliness of the story, increasing the characters' dialogue, a play would result. Then this novelist-playwright would invite his reader to pass from the library into the auditorium. As Meyerhold put it in his essay "Farce":

> Does the novelist need the services of mime? Of course not. The readers themselves can come onto the stage, assume parts, and read aloud to the audience the dialogue of their favorite novelist. This is called "a harmoniously performed play." A name is quickly given to the reader-transformed-into-actor, and a new term, "an intelligent actor," is coined. The same dead silence reigns in the auditorium as in the library. The public is dozing. Such immobility and solemnity is appropriate only in a library.

There is a bit of intentional overstatement in this passage. Obviously, it is not a matter of suppressing speech in the theatre. It is not that language is unimportant in the theatre; it is rather a matter of changing its role. Since the theatre is really concerned only with the way feelings and passions conflict with each other, the language of the theatre must be considered as something more than a means of conducting human characters to external ends. It must capture the turbulence of experience. To change the role of speech in the theatre is to make use of it in a concrete and spatial sense, combining it with everything else on the stage. This is what these playwrights of revolt mean when they insist that the language of the theatre must always be gestural: it must grow out of the gesture, must always act and can never be only descriptive.

Ironically, no one has discussed the nature of gestural language more intelligently than a literary critic. R. P. Blackmur, in his now famous essay "Language as Gesture," defines what is meant when we say that language is gestural. He sees beyond the simple distinction that language is made of words and gesture is made of motion, to the reverse distinction: "Words are made of motion, made of action or response, at whatever remove; and gesture is made of language—made of the language beneath or beyond or alongside of the language of words." Working from this premise it is possible for Mr. Blackmur to consider that idea which is so important for anyone writing for the theatre: "When the language of words most succeeds it becomes gesture in its words." He sees that gesture is not only native to language but that it precedes it, and must be, as it were, carried into language whenever the context is imaginative or dramatic. Without a gestural quality in language there can be no drama. This is so since "the great part of our knowledge of life and nature—perhaps all our knowledge of their play and inter-play [their drama]—comes to us as gesture, and we are masters of the skill of that knowledge before we can ever make a rhyme or a pun, or even a simple sentence." Blackmur then goes on to define what he means by gesture in language:

> Gesture, in language, is the outward and dramatic play of inward and imaged meaning. It is that play of meaningfulness among words which cannot be defined in the formulas in the dictionary, but which is defined in their use together; gesture is that meaningfulness which is moving, in every sense of that word: what moves the words and what moves us.

This is the quality in words that many of the playwrights of England's "anger and after" period were trying to express when they wrote for actors. It is this quality, more than anything else, which makes Sophocles, Shakespeare, and Molière great dramatists. Now, I don't believe Ann Jellicoe is the next Molière, but *The Knack* is a significant play, significant because it indicates that the theatre is beginning the process of stripping away the nontheatrical verbiage. This is the necessary first step if we are ever to have a theatre in our time that can rival the great theatrical ages of the past. To the "literary" minded this may sound like sacrilege, but we should remember that while each week a new play of great literary merit opens, only to close shortly thereafter, a play like *The Knack* keeps running to full and delighted houses.

John Osborne started it all with *Look Back in Anger*, and this was soon followed by *The Entertainer* with Laurence Olivier in the Archie Rice role. Some people then believed that the quality of his work fell off and that he failed to live up to the promise of his early plays. This may be a fair assessment of his career as a play-wright to date, but in 1964 his *Inadmissible Evidence* opened and there can be no question that in the character of its protagonist, Bill Maitland, he has created one of the towering roles of the theatre in our times. The most remarkable thing about this character is the fact that while it is impossible to like him, he nonetheless always commands our attention. It is a strange sensation: to be mesmerized by mediocrity. Bill Maitland is an inelegant lecher, an addicted personality who alternates between too much whiskey and too many pills, an insensitive and unprincipled lawyer who just barely survives on the petty wretchedness of others, and finally is a failure in every human relationship in which he has participated. In an act of self-judgment in the play's courtroom prologue, he says about himself:

> I am almost forty years old, and I know I have never made a decision which I didn't either regret, or suspect was just plain commonplace or shifty or scamped and indulgent or mildly stupid or undistinguished. . . . I have depended almost entirely on other people's efforts. . . . And then, I have always been afraid of being found out.

Except to the most morbidly curious, such a character should be monstrously dull. But he isn't, and one of the chief reasons we find him so compelling is Osborne's incendiary brilliance of language. There is no one writing in the theatre today who has a surer mastery of stage rhetoric than he, and I believe the secret of his success lies in his ability to deal with disturbing themes without resorting to cheap or eccentric tricks of language. Jonathan Miller, the British writer-director, made a penetrating comment about this capacity when he said in an interview:

> There is an essay by George Orwell about Salvador Dali in which he says that the mediocre talent can often attract more attention than it is worth by dealing in evil. Dali is a man with a rather mediocre imagination who attracts much attention by dealing in extravagantly eccentric sick themes. . . . The thing about Osborne which is so attractive is that he doesn't have any need to resort to this sort of sickness in order to produce his effect. No one has his capacity for sustained pessimistic rhetoric, a scalding absolutely nihilistic pessimism. Theatre of Disgust, if you like.

Many people have seen *Inadmissible Evidence* as a play in which the young and angry Jimmy Porter of *Look Back in Anger,* having just reached middle age, discovers his own spiritual bankruptcy and turns his seemingly limitless capacity for bitter disgust away from the world and now directs it towards himself. Certainly, this is true. In *Inadmissible Evidence* Osborne has written a drama of middle-aged withering away in which Maitland not only reveals his emptiness ("We are the hollow men") but judges his mediocrity as well ("Not with a bang, but a whimper"). But such a reading of the play doesn't explain why Maitland judges himself as he does. It seems to me that only when we recognize that from the beginning Osborne has been writing dramas of disengagement will the full import of this play become clear.

Jimmy Porter is angry because he has come to believe that everything about society is mean and hypocritical. In his disgust for the world he has consciously chosen to step outside it, no matter how this decision may affect his wife and friends. But Jimmy's whole angry existence is totally dependent upon the continued existence of that society which he rails at so bitterly. The judgment which Osborne makes on the life of Jimmy-Bill now that he has reached forty is not directed at his anger but at his act of disengagement.

The play opens with a courtroom scene which is, in actuality, taking place within Maitland's own mind. Acting as his own defense attorney he attempts to present his case. In his analysis of the existing social system, he sounds quite reasonable and his charges read like a liberal middle class weekly journal of opinion. But the lawyer and the judge are the same person, and gradually the inadmissible evidence with which he ultimately indicts himself creeps into his defense-indictment. By the end of the prologue, he has acknowledged his failure and has judged himself guilty. The scene ends with him saying: "I should like to stand down if I may. I am not feeling very well . . . I am not equal to any of it. But I can't forget it. And I can't begin again."

The main body of the play consists of a number of scenes in which the inadmissible evidence of Bill's life is presented to us directly. We see what it means to be the disengaged man. As a lawyer he sees the law as something to use to his own ends rather than as a body of social value which he is committed to serve. ("I don't think the law is respectable at all. It's there to be exploited. Just as *it* exploits us.") In his relationships with his office fellows he is brutish, cruel, and insulting. In his dealings with his clients he is insensitive and inept. In a fascinating scene with his daughter—in which she says not a word—he reveals a blindness which is as staggering as it is pathetic. But it is finally in his relationship with women, particularly his wife and mistress, that we see the failure of disengagement as a strategy for living. Because he has no awareness of human otherness he has only succeeded, as he says in his self-indictment, in "inflicting more pain than pleasure." He has not found love; he cannot stand the presence of any woman who loves him; and he is no longer capable of being satisfied by those indiscriminate sexual conquests which seem to have filled a good share of his adult life.

Bill Maitland (né Jimmy Porter) chose to detach himself from every claim which society can make on the individual. At the end of *Inadmissible Evidence,* as we see him broken and alone on the stage, we know he has at last succeeded in making the final cut. It has been a meaningless achievement, and John Osborne who fathered the "angry" generation in the British theatre has demonstrated most convincingly that when anger over the failures of society becomes so extreme that it leads to disengagement from that society, the anger will eventually turn into a caustic self-disgust which can produce only isolation and impotence.

Probably no play written during the 1960s provided more discussion than Harold Pinter's *The Homecoming.* Newspapers on both sides of the Atlantic ran countless interviews and symposia with the most unlikely people about the play, and for months one of New York's favorite cocktail party games was "What does *The Homecoming* mean?" What does it mean? is always the wrong question to ask of a play. How does it mean? is a somewhat better one. But, finally, a work of art doesn't "mean" anything; rather, as Archibald MacLeish put it, "it is!" I think Pinter was implying this when he answered the question What does *The Homecoming* mean? by saying: "It doesn't mean anything." His answer was much like Chekhov's (with whom Pinter has so much in common) when he was asked by Stanislavsky, "Anton Pavlovich, as author of the play, explain what it means." Chekhov replied: "It doesn't mean anything. Listen, I wrote it down; it is all there." A play is not a theological treatise or a sociological essay, nor is it a psychological investigation. Therefore, to get at the "is-ness" of a play, we should not ask what it means; rather, we should examine it to see what happens.

What is happening in *The Homecoming?* To hear most people talk, Pinter's plays are supposed to be bizarre, surreal, and filled with what John Russell Brown has called "menace and muddle." Nothing could be further from the truth. When one examines the plays he discovers that their language is simple, direct, and exceedingly commonplace. Like Chekhov, Pinter's chief dramatic means are the trivial remark and the small gesture, which in their apparent inconsequence seem to hide deeper meanings, but which, in fact, ultimately reveal the truth about people in a given situation. It is as if Pinter were saying that the most ordinary people in the most ordinary situations are actually experiencing *King Lear, Oedipus the King*, or *Macbeth*—that the great dramas of history are occurring every day in the lives of each of us. But he achieves this by employing very simple and natural means.

To understand how it is done in *The Homecoming* I believe two quotations from Pinter can be helpful. In an interview given in 1962, he said:

> The speech we hear is an indication of what we don't hear. It is a necessary avoidance, a violent, sly, anguished, or mocking smokescreen which keeps the other in its place.

Later, he added:

> I'm not suggesting that no character in a play can ever say what he in fact means. Not at all. I have found that there invariably does come a moment when this happens, where he says something, perhaps which he has never said before. And when this happens, what he says is irrevocable, and can never be taken back.

These passages tend to describe Pinter's central technique in all of the plays written prior to *The Homecoming*. The action of each of them moved to reach that statement which was "irrevocable, and can never be taken back."

But in *The Homecoming* it is different. Here people say what they really mean almost from the beginning. It is the truth not of facts, but of an inner reality. In the first act, Pinter establishes the situation and reveals the condition of absence which "the homecoming" is to fulfill. Then Teddy and Ruth enter. But as soon as they arrive, Pinter designs the action to remove Teddy from the stage. Thus the first forward-moving scene is between Ruth and her brother-in-law, Lenny. It is a shocking scene precisely because the unspoken thought is verbalized. After a highly charged, sexually suggestive preamble, in which Ruth is clearly identified with Lenny's mother, the following dialogue concludes the scene between them:

> LENNY: . . . Just give me the glass.
> RUTH: No.
>    (*Pause.*)
> LENNY: I'll take it, then.
> RUTH: If you take the glass . . . I'll take you.
>    (*Pause.*)

LENNY: How about me taking the glass without you taking me?

RUTH: Why don't I just take you?

(*Pause.*)

LENNY: You're joking. (*Pause.*) You're in love, anyway, with another man. You've had a secret liaison with another man. His family didn't even know. Then you come here without a word of warning and start to make trouble.

(*She picks up the glass and lifts it towards him.*)

RUTH: Have a sip. Go on. Have a sip from my glass. (*He is still.*) Sit on my lap. Take a long cool sip. (*She pats her lap. Pause. She stands, moves to him with the glass.*) Put your head back and open your mouth.

LENNY: Take that glass away from me.

RUTH: Lie on the floor. Go on. I'll pour it down your throat.

LENNY: What are you doing, making me some kind of proposal?

(*She laughs shortly, drains the glass.*)

RUTH: Oh, I was thirsty. (*She smiles at him, puts the glass down, goes into the hall and up the stairs. He follows into the hall and shouts up the stairs.*)

LENNY: What was that supposed to be? Some kind of proposal?

(*Silence.*)

The word has become flesh. The masks of conversation have been shattered and the secret thoughts and desires behind the words are directly expressed. In *The Homecoming* the action moves beyond the "irrevocable" word to the irrevocable act.

If Pinter's basic technique is, as it were, to take the subtext of human experience and make it textual, it will require a new kind of naturalistic dialogue. It will also require that he conceive of his characters in a different fashion. In *The Homecoming* the Jungian archetype is made manifest. We can understand this when we ask the key question of the play—the question that is at the center of the play's is-ness: Whose homecoming is it? At first it would appear to be the son, Teddy, who is returning home to introduce his wife of six years to his father, his uncle, and his two brothers. Giving an ironic twist to the story of the Prodigal Son (for, ultimately, Teddy is lost, not found. At the end of the play Pinter uses a device he has often used before: Ruth forgets his name. He *is* a stranger even as she says her parting line to him, "Don't become a stranger."), it looks as though this is to be yet another Pinter play of menacing victimization. However, Teddy just is not in a central focus long enough for this interpretation to work. Once the family reunion is achieved he moves increasingly to the play's periphery, and his wife, Ruth, takes over the center. Indeed, from the point of view of emphasis, it would seem to be her homecoming. But it cannot be, since this is not, nor ever has been, her home. So whose is it?

I believe it is Jessie, Max's wife and the boys' mother, who has come home. The mother is the one person in the play each character is always talking about, and she returns, in a kind of Nietzschean recurrence, in the guise of the girl. From Ruth's opening scene, which I have already referred to, she assumes all the roles that Momma had played. She is the wife, the mother, the whore, and above all, she wants to belong.* Now, obviously, there isn't a one-for-one correspondence; there are ambiguities and differences. Jessie was made in the car and Ruth in a beach house. Lenny was not his mother's pimp, but in his relationship to Ruth he reveals what his real attitude to the mother was. These examples, and others like them, are the evocative ambiguities of all works of art.

Finally, the play is about wants—those basic wants which for most of us remain forever in the realm of forbidden fantasy. This is the significance of Sam's sudden and unexpected outburst at the end of the play. When he says "MacGregor had Jessie in the back of my cab as I drove them along," he is revealing what he had *wanted* to do all his life. For Ruth the homecoming is an act of self-discovery in which she begins to embody all of her possibilities as a woman. At the end of the play, in the form of a highly stylized tableau, Ruth has assumed all of Jessie's roles at once and the rest of the family has reassumed the relationships each of them had had with her. As Max says:

> Since poor Jessie died . . . we haven't had a woman in the house. Not one. Inside this house. And I'll tell you why. Because their mother's image was so dear any other woman would have . . . tarnished it. But you . . . Ruth . . . you're not only lovely and beautiful, but you're Kin. You're Kith. You belong here.

*The Homecoming* is a profoundly disturbing play. Even the vehemence with which some people rejected it indicates this. But why are we so disturbed? Perhaps it is because in our pluralistic society,

* The parallels to the biblical story of Ruth tend to underscore this.

where all of our roles tend to be separated from each other, our women want to come home to a oneness—a oneness of being mother, wife, and whore. And we men want her—our mother, wife and whore—home again.

# THE THEATRE
# OF JOHN ARDEN

THAT REMARKABLE decade (1956–1966) in the British Theatre which came to be known as the "Anger and After" period is usually considered one of the rich fruits of a new political dispensation and the great energy of that period is usually explained in political terms. Invariably such causes as the ascendency of the Post World-War II Labor government, the rise to power of the lower-middle class and the concomitant jumbling of all social classes, the widespread effect of national television (with the resultant infusion into the theatre of new dialects from all over the British Isles), the emergence of Joan Littlewood, with all her socialist tendencies, as a major figure in the theatre, and even the increase in the number of Jewish writers in the theatre are mentioned. However, while each of these explanations has some truth to it, I do not believe that this so-called renaissance was really so much a matter of politics as it was one of style. Even though the *movement* seemed to have anti-establishment origins, it certainly lacked that kind of political fervor which marked the American theatre of the 1930s. It is important for us to remember that practically every one of the playwrights who emerged into prominence in the last half of the 1950s was born in or after the year 1930. They did not know the poverty of the depression; they were not particularly pro-labor; they certainly didn't know the confusion and despair of the thirties; and that quality in their work which is attributed to political enthusiasm is more likely only a product of political irritation.

What they all shared was a straightforward commitment to deal more directly with reality—with life as it really is! And this commitment was most clearly evidenced in their use of language. The traditional language of the British stage had become, in their opinion, so unbelievably unreal; it was so formal, so apart from reality, so BBC-ish. Their real revolt was against these conventions, which is why I believe the social realism of the Anger playwrights was more a question of style than a political position.* And it is the very fact that this was primarily a revolution of style *alone* that, by and large, explains why this great watershed of talent seems to have dried up prematurely.

There were, however, some writers whose work did continue to grow, and one of the most exciting of them is John Arden. Born of middle-class parents in 1930 in Yorkshire, he graduated from Cambridge, studied architecture at Edinburgh, and was a practicing architect for two years before he began writing for the theatre. As a young playwright, Arden shared many of the attitudes and concerns of his contemporaries, and like them he was searching for new forms and new techniques to express these "radical" perceptions. But he differed from his colleagues in one most important way: in his exploration of the new he was also capable of embracing the best of previous traditions in the theatre. This combination has created one of the most interesting bodies of work in the contemporary repertoire. In fact, Arden's output is now sufficiently large (almost twenty plays) and has been sustained for a long enough period of time (better than fifteen years) that it is possible for us to discover certain continuing themes and attitudes in the richly diverse works of this man whom we must now consider a major playwright.

I have maintained that the British Theatre of the decade 1956–1966 was not political and that the revolution which John Osborne's *Look Back in Anger* started was more one of style than of political conviction. But this does not mean that this theatre was not profoundly social in its concerns, and no writer reveals this new social awareness more powerfully than John Arden. However, it is a differ-

---

* Nothing underscores this more clearly than the fact that with one exception (Olivier in *The Entertainer*) none of these writers attracted the great classical actors such as Ralph Richardson, Michael Redgrave, Alec Guinness, John Gielgud, or even Richard Burton and Paul Scofield to appear in one of his plays. Yet we have ample evidence that the political convictions of these performers—insofar as they have them—are quite similar to those of the actors—Albert Finney, Peter O'Toole, Nicol Williamson, and Ian Richardson—who came to fame by performing these new plays.

ent kind of social awareness than we are accustomed to think about when we use the term "social plays." * How is it different?

Arthur Miller, in his essay "The Writing of Social Plays," has said:

> It is necessary, if one is to reflect reality, not only to reflect why a man does what he does, or why he nearly didn't do it, but why he simply cannot walk away and say to hell with it.

Traditionally, great drama has always had the last judgment built into it. We may never know why a character cannot walk away and say to hell with it, but, in fact, all the characters in a play are beyond adjustment and beyond bargaining. A dramatic action is a judgment and each of the characters is a part of that judgment. Thus, the dramatic hero must always move from the question "To be or not to be?" to the assertion "Let be!" He is led, finally, to insist upon following things out to their inevitable end. The motive can be anything—will, moral purpose, fate, history, providence, the dignity of man, blind chance. The cost is usually self-destruction, but it can also be calamity, catastrophe, the fall of the sparrow, a plague on both your houses, the shadowy waters, the dark root of a scream, the mill race, or Oedipus' bleeding eyeballs. The effect may be catharsis, woe and wonder, or even "getting stoned." But, as I said, things are different now. This is not the kind of play our new playwrights are creating. How can there be that kind of commitment or monomaniacal singleness of purpose in a world where, as Duerrenmatt put it, "Creon's secretaries close Antigone's case," or in a world in which, to use J. Robert Oppenheimer's phrase, "We live too variously to live as one," or in a world where we can carry on wars of pacification. In short, how can we say "Let be!" in an age of ambiguity?

Brecht pondered that question. More recently it has been the central concern of writers such as Weiss, Kipphardt, and Hochhuth. And John Arden revealed both his involvement in the issue and his answer in his first published play, *The Waters of Babylon*, where in the final act his protagonist, Krank, says with the greatest passion:

KRANK: But I don't know what *you* are.
    Or you, Henry Ginger, or all of the rest of you,
    With your pistols and your orations,
    And your bombs in my private house,

---

* This is where I believe those critics who tend to compare the British drama of Anger and After to the American drama of the 1930s are all wrong.

And your fury, and your national pride and honour.
This is the lunacy,
This was the cause, the carrying through
Of all the insensate war
This is the rage and purposed madness of your lives,
That I, Krank, do not know. I *will* not know it,
Because, if I know it, from that tight day forward,
I am a man of time, place, society, and accident:
Which is what I must not be. Do you understand me?

PAUL: No

KRANK: The world is running mad in every direction.
It is quicksilver, shattered, here, here, here, here,
All over the floor. Go on, hurtle after it,
Chase it, dear Paul. But I choose to follow
Only such fragments as I can easily catch,
I catch them, I keep them such time as I choose,
Then roll them away down and follow another.
Is that philosophy? It is a reason, anyway,
Why I am content to hold such a disgusting lodging-house,
And why I'd be content to get you and your bombs out of it.

Krank emerges as the first of Arden's "characterless" characters. Characterless, in the sense that he does not have a destiny that leads to a judgment which is not cast in the shades of ambiguity. Serjeant Musgrave is also such a characterless character. History, not John Arden, condemns the protagonist of *Serjeant Musgrave's Dance*, and for that reason we are also extremely conscious of Black Jack's many positive qualities. The result is an ending to the play which is completely, and to many people confusingly, ambivalent. This ambivalence is the key to all of Arden's plays. This is even true of *Happy Haven*, although on the surface—because of its many farcical elements—it doesn't appear to be so. The very use of masks in this play not only solves specific acting problems, more importantly, it makes it possible for Arden to achieve an ambiguous reversal of mask and face within the structure of a morality play. Thus the resolution of *Happy Haven* is as ambiguous as any of Arden's other plays. There is no clearcut judgment on Dr. Copperthwaite and his patients, just as there was none between the Sawneys and the Jacksons in *Live Like Pigs*. In fact, *Happy Haven* is, in many respects, only a more stylized version of *Live Like Pigs* and might very well have been entitled *Live Like Guinea Pigs*. The ending of *Happy Haven*, with Mrs. Phineus holding Dr. Copperthwaite in her arms, is very similar to Annie's holding the skeleton in *Serjeant Musgrave's Dance.* It is a formal resolution, but its very formality makes manifest an unformulated version of the ambiguity of life's processes.

When we examine all of Arden's work we discover that his chief problem has been to find a dramatic form complex enough to encompass our contemporary reality in all of its concreteness and at the same time transcend both the dead end of social realism by the use of representative characters, and the limitations of naturalism, by the use of a kind of wild-eyed theatricality. All of his experiments have been attempts to find a dynamic form to express, as he put it,

> all modes of the spirit's life, all its directions, or focuses or motives, including those of childhood dreams, drunkenness or passion which are hardly rationalized at all.

But most important, he has sought to discover a form which would reflect the absence of any one solution to the problems of contemporary reality.

In this regard, Arden's work takes on one of the most significant characteristics of all recent modern art, namely, the disappearance of an individual point of view in a work of art. This is one of the central notions in all of Marshall McLuhan's theories of media and culture. It can be observed in much contemporary painting, and it is the animus of the Happening and various intermedia experiments. In the theatre, the first person to deal with the issue directly was Brecht. As early as his *A Man's a Man* (1927), he shows his new kind of hero, Galy Gay, triumph over Bloody Five precisely because he had no point of view. In the foreword to the play (which I quote at length in my essay on Brecht) he describes his protagonist as a *"new human type."* Brecht develops this kind of character more fully in some of his later plays where he uses the parabolic form (a form which Arden is to use also). The parabolic form of drama has an imagistic, mosaic-like quality which tends to break down causal determination, sequential connection, and final judgments.

The works of Peter Weiss provide other good examples of this tendency. In *Marat/Sade*, for instance, Weiss has categorically denied that de Sade's view is dominant. There is no single point of view in the play, rather there are multiple points of view and the play ends with no one of them having been affirmed. In his later play *The Investigation*, Weiss develops the idea that what happened to the Jews in the concentration camps can never be encompassed by a single point of view. The whole presentation is quite neutral; it is, in fact, a selection from the transcript of the Nazi war trials. Some may argue that this is not literature; and to them, Weiss replies: "I'm not trying to write literature." However, no matter what it is he has created, it has proven to be very powerful theatre; just as is *Marat/Sade*, which is to a large extent nothing but the presentation of already existing writings. Weiss, and many others like him, does not think of himself as a playwright but as a theatrician.

I can think of numerous other examples of this tendency in the arts, but perhaps none is more apt than Truman Capote's fictional document *In Cold Blood*. It is clear that Kenneth Tynan's anger over the book is largely the result of the fact that it lacks a point of view and that Capote has no positive attitude toward any of its characters. It is no longer "these two guys committed murder and these other guys will punish them." Rather, the murderer is the author, the reader, the whole society. Each one of us is involved in that murder; it is a tribal kind of experience in which we are all interrelated and participating. In short, the permanent source of true ambiguity is life itself. And for Arden—and so many other artists of our time—the chief responsibility of the artist is not to resolve these ambiguities by means of an artistic form, but rather to use form to reveal as clearly as possible life's ambiguities in all their complexity.

All of Arden's experiments with technique:

1. his use of use of the simplified techniques of characterization of the miracle and morality plays,

2. his attempts to achieve the robustness of Elizabethan drama coupled with an almost Jacobean tendency toward excess,

3. the borrowing from the poetic and fragmented form of Buechner's plays,

4. the use of the sung doggerel of the Victorian music hall,

5. the use of satirical ballad poetry and the parabolic epic structure of Brecht, are attempts to express this abiguity. But in spite of these efforts he continues to discover, as he once put it in an interview, that "life itself remains the most ambiguous and paradoxical phenomenon." (Just as *Mother Courage* and so many of Brecht's other plays reveal that life is more Brechtian than Brecht.) As a result, so long as Arden can suggest that life's inconclusiveness undercuts all viewpoints, including the viewpoint that there is no one solution to our contemporary dilemmas, then he is an ironist, at the same time

that he transcends his own irony. Sparky, in *Serjeant Musgrave's Dance,* sums it up best when he says:

> That's what I call life—it all turns up in the expected order, but not when you expect it.

For this reason the central duality in all of Arden's work resides in the basic conflict between the institutionalized society of men under the aegis of law and order and a community based on the relations of service, loyalties, and affection among individuals. This conflict might be described in a harsher and perhaps more Pirandellian way with the observation that the chaotic energy which keeps man alive, also threatens his social existence. All of our laws, social conventions, and other forms of public order are protections which we build to hedge in our instinctual drives. But these are frameworks against which we must continually rebel, lest we become sterile. This conflict explains why there can never be an answer to an Arden play, even though there seems to be an artistic resolution. How can man, with his idiosyncratic urge for anarchy, poetry, and sensual pleasure, ever be crammed into the tame yet violent structures of contemporary urban life which he knows are necessary?

This same duality finally explains the typical Arden protagonist. Each one is a rebel. But not a rebel who withdraws from society to oppose it; but rather one who remains involved in, and corrupted by, a society which he has come to loathe. In the end he is a person who has become the epitome of the corrosive society which made him. And when he learns this, usually through an act of self-discovery, he tries to destroy both society and himself. He is a kind of Everyman, with huge energy, who in his self-loathing and self-destructive willfulness refuses to control either.

However, all of the above may be a little bit misleading. For while it is true that Arden in embracing complexity and ambiguity, may be denying the validity of a theatre based upon rebellious and partisan political attitudes, or social reform, or even a theatre which has as its chief responsibility the coming to grips with significant contemporary issues, he is nonetheless a writer of social plays—a new kind of social play. Perhaps this will become clearer when we recognize that Arden is not concerned with the metaphysical implications of the human condition, nor is he concerned with psychological problems (although the psychology of some of his characters is fascinating). Arden's vision of life is communal. For him the community has value and it is always threatened by the corrupting forces of polity, which are as iniquitous as they are necessary and inevitable. And it is this belief in community that inspires the quality of festivity—the spirit celebration—which pervades each of his plays. As I said earlier, a celebration is a joyful response to a deed or an event, and its most important characteristic is that it implies and demands a public sanction. Arden's drama celebrates the spirit of community and its powers of survival in spite of man's strong inborn tendencies toward self-destruction.

Perhaps an example from one of the plays will be helpful here. Most audiences and critics have not understood the significance of the dance in *Serjeant Musgrave's Dance*. Actually, there are two dances in the play, and this is an important fact. Throughout the play the obsessed protagonist—who knows his duty, who believes that he has God and "The Word" on his side, but who does not know that the Word did and must always "become flesh"—was looking for a brother. He needed a public sanction for his mission. But, as Annie tells us, it turns out that his brother was Hurst, a man just like himself; and hence his ultimate failure in the pursuit of his mission is prefigured. His chief attempt to win the community's sanction for his cause was with a dance, a dance which he stops just at its climax. Because of his inability to accept the efficaciousness of the dance he must return to his words; these in turn lead him to the skeleton that marks his failure. Now, a dance is an act of celebration. It implies public sanction; it implies something which Musgrave does not have. Once it becomes clear to both the community and Musgrave that he does not have such a sanction, his doom becomes inevitable. And, *then*, upon his failure, the community begins to dance. It celebrates, and Arden celebrates its spirit, flawed though it may be. The spirit of celebration is at the center of his plays; it is, indeed, central to his vision of the theatre. In an interview in *Encore*, he said:

> I see myself as a practitioner of an art which is both public and exploratory: the exploring is done in public and is therefore full of danger—if you fail it is bound to be a pretty humiliating failure! But if you succeed, you will have done so by presenting, alive, on the stage, a tactile piece of human existence which will be recognized as true and meaningful and illuminating, and the recognition will be almost a ceremonious act between audience, actors and author—

it is the possibility of this happening with any play that keeps the business going.*

The English theatre in its most creative periods has always had as one of its chief concerns the probing of the existing forms of human organization. King Lear pulls his whole kingdom down upon his head in order to discover the very cornerstones of its superfluous existence. This is the challenge which the emergence of a new society constitutes for the old—a questioning of the foundations of its very existence. But in spite of all the probing, the community must continue to exist and must continue to celebrate itself, even if this is done only in the minds and imaginations of its playwrights. By relating himself to the most creative parts of his native tradition and at the same time maintaining his disturbing modernity, John Arden is, I believe, one of the most vital and significant playwrights of the contemporary British theatre.

* Encore (July–August, 1961), p. 41.

# THE ACHIEVEMENT
# OF ARTHUR MILLER

## I

We live in an instant age. Everything from the most complex information to giant buildings, from vast networks of electric circuitry to blenderized gourmet meals, can be produced or made available in a flash. It should be of little wonder then that we also tend to create instant major figures in the arts; and our theatre has been no exception. Of the five most important Americans writing for the theatre in the twentieth century—Eugene O'Neill, Thornton Wilder, Tennessee Williams, Arthur Miller, and Edward Albee—only O'Neill's reputation and stature were built cumulatively over a long period of time. And of the five, only O'Neill (and possibly Williams) approached the prodigious productivity of their Continental counterparts. Each of the other four achieved the status of "major" playwright with the professional production of his first or second full-length play. (Wilder: *Our Town*—first, 1938; Williams: *The Glass Menagerie*—second, 1945; Miller: *All My Sons*—second, 1947; Albee: *Who's Afraid of Virginia Woolf?*—first, 1962). Having such a large international reputation can be a heavy burden for an artist to bear at any time, but it is particularly difficult when it is thrust upon him early in his career.

This was definitely true for Arthur Miller. After *Death of a Salesman* was produced in 1949, he was considered by many as one of the world's most important living dramatists, and he was treated as a monument while he was still very much alive. Fortunately, Miller knew how to cope with such adulation and was not destroyed by it. But such conditions did create an atmosphere which has made it difficult to consider his artistic achievement with any objectivity. Now that a quarter of a century has elapsed since he first was catapulted to fame, it is possible for us to see the pattern of his work a little more clearly and to assess the plays of this man who many still believe to be America's most important dramatist.

Although one should be leery of critics who play the "periods game" and break down an artist's work into nice, tight little compartments, there do, nonetheless, seem to be two quite different patterns of concern in the plays that Arthur Miller has produced thus far. The first pattern emerges in the plays written up to and including the revised version of A View from the Bridge (1957). The second began to emerge in The Misfits (1960), Miller's only produced film, and has become increasingly manifest in his last three plays, After the Fall, Incident at Vichy, and The Price. I believe these patterns can be best discussed by treating them as separate yet related aspects of the playwright's own evolution as an artist.

In tracing this development, Erik Erikson's remarkable psychological biography, Young Man Luther, can be especially helpful. In this book, Dr. Erikson postulates the idea that in the lives of most people there are normally three periods of psychological crisis: the crisis of Identity, the crisis of Generativity, and the crisis of Integrity. These crises, he maintains, generally occur in youth, middle age, and old age, respectively, although there is always some overlapping and the pattern does vary slightly from individual to individual.

I believe that the first two stages in Erikson's pattern of psychological crisis are quite applicable to Miller's own development as a playwright, and also throw light on the major themes of everything he has thus far written. The central conflict in all of the plays in Miller's first period (The Man Who Had All the Luck, 1944; All My Sons, 1947; Death of a Salesman, 1949; An Enemy of the People, 1950; The Crucible, 1953; A Memory of Two Mondays, 1955; A View from the Bridge, 1955; A View from the Bridge, 1957) grows out of a crisis of identity. Each of the protagonists in these plays is suddenly confronted with a situation which he is incapable of meeting and which eventually puts his "name" in jeopardy. In the ensuing struggle it becomes clear that he does not know what his name really is, and, finally, his inability to answer the question "Who am

I?" produces calamity and his ultimate downfall. Strange as it may sound, Joe Keller, Willy Loman, John Proctor, and Eddie Carbonne are alike, caught up in a problem of identity that is normally characteristic of youth (one is almost tempted to say adolescence), and their deaths are caused by their lack of self-understanding. In every case this blindness is in large measure due to their failure to have resolved the question of identity at an earlier and more appropriate time in life. Miller presents this crisis as a conflict between the uncomprehending self and a solid social or economic structure—the family, the community, the system. The drama emerges either when the protagonist breaks his connection with society or when unexpected pressures reveal that such a connection has in fact never even existed. For Miller the need for such a connection is absolute, and the failure to achieve and/or maintain it is bound to result in catastrophe. He makes this very clear in his introduction to *The Collected Plays,* where he writes about *All My Sons* as follows:

> Joe Keller's trouble, in a word, is not that he cannot tell right from wrong, but that his cast of mind cannot admit that he, personally, has any viable connection with his world, his universe, or his society.*

Miller expands this idea even further in an article in *The New York Times* written on the occasion of the New York revival of *A View from the Bridge:*

> What kills Eddie Carbonne is nothing visible or heard, but the built-in conscience of the community whose existence he has menaced by betraying it. Whatever both plays (the other was *A Memory of Two Mondays*) are, they at bottom reassertions of the existence of community.†

Each of the plays written prior to *The Misfits* is a judgment of a man's failure to maintain a viable connection with his surrounding world because he does not know himself. The verdict is always guilty, and it is a verdict based upon Miller's belief that if each man faced up to the truth about himself he could be fulfilled as an individual and still live within the restrictions of society. But while Miller's judgments are absolute they are also exceedingly complex. There is no question but that finally he stands four-square on the side of the community, but until the moment when justice must be

* *The Collected Plays,* p. 19.
† *The New York Times,* Sunday, August 15, 1965.

served his sympathies are for the most part directed toward those ordinary little men who never discovered who they really were.

A Miller protagonist belongs to a strange breed. In every instance, he is unimaginative, inarticulate (as with Buechner's Woyzeck, the words that would save him seem always to be just beyond his grasp) and physically nondescript, if not downright unattractive.* His roles as husband and father (or father surrogate) are of paramount importance to him, and yet he fails miserably in both. He wants to love and be loved, yet he is incapable of either giving or receiving love. And he is haunted by aspirations toward a joy in life that his humdrum spirit is quite unable to realize. Yet in spite of all these negative characteristics Miller's protagonists do engage our imagination and win our sympathies. I think this ambiguity stems from the fact that his own attitude towards his creations is so contradictory.

On the one hand, there is no question but that he finds them guilty for their failure to maintain (or fulfill) their role within the established social structure; though there is something almost rabbinical in the loving sternness of his judgments.† On the other hand, while it is certainly true that the system is ultimately affirmed, it cannot be denied that the system is shown to be in some ways responsible for creating those very conditions which provoke the protagonists' downfall.

Despite these contradictions, each of the plays of Miller's first period is imbued with a sure sense of the world. The individual may struggle for his name, to be himself in difficult situations in what may seem to be an inimical world, but a sense of what Miller believes the world can and should be is always there. The issues facing each of the protagonists are clear-cut, and we cannot help but feel that if they had chosen otherwise—and such an alternative is open to them—the conflict would have dissolved. Unlike the most signifi-

* Henry Popkin underscores this fact when he points out that all the leading actors in the major productions of Miller's plays have been rough-hewn types: Lee J. Cobb, Thomas Mitchell, Ed Begley, Raf Vallone, Van Heflin, Arthur Kennedy, J. Carrol Naish, Jason Robards, and Pat Hingle.
† A number of critics have made the point that Miller's Jewish heritage is one of the dominant motivating forces in his theatrical mode. I do not quarrel with this view, particularly as it applies to the plays of his first period; they do seem to have several characteristics which we tend to associate with traditional Jewish family life. My own experience and background are such, however, that I do not feel competent to explore this dimension of Miller's work. Moreover, I do not believe the central conflicts of these plays and Miller's attitude toward his protagonists to be uniquely Jewish.

cant tragedies of the past—and Miller certainly had conscious aspirations to be a tragic writer during this period of his career—the catastrophes in these plays do not have a sense of inevitability, nor do they spring from the unalterable divisions of man's nature. The world of Arthur Miller's first plays is a hermetic one; one in which none of life's mysteries have been allowed to intrude. The reader or spectator may be caught up in the suspense of the plot, but he always knows where he is, just as Miller seems to know.*

It is this quality of certainty which characterizes *The Collected Plays*, published in 1957. This volume marks the completion of the first phase of his development, and one senses from the Introduction that Miller was capable of a kind of objective assessment of his own work which only an artist secure in his achievement could succeed in pulling off. Like his protagonists, however, Miller was in for a shock. The closed and tight world of the first plays was soon to be shattered. Unlike his protagonists, he was not destroyed. He emerged from a period of painful personal conflict to write plays with significantly new and wider dimensions.

## II

*The Collected Plays* was dedicated to Miller's second wife, Marilyn Monroe, who was to be the inspiration for his next work, *The Misfits* (1960). Much has been written about this relationship, and while I have no intention of adding to the pile of surmise and irrelevancy, I think it is undeniable that Miller's marriage to Miss Monroe had a profound effect on his attitudes, his sense of the world, his view of himself, and perhaps even on the nature of his dramatic form. These changes first became apparent in *The Misfits*, a screenplay which I consider the pivotal work in Miller's career as a playwright, although it has been strangely neglected in most appraisals of his work. One is aware that a transition is taking place because *The Misfits* is the first of Miller's dramas which is not concerned with identity. Each of the five characters is very much alone

---

* "I was trying in *Salesman*, in this respect, to set forth what happens when a man does not have a grip on the forces of life and has no sense of values which will lead him to that kind of a grip; but the implication was that there must be such a grasp of those forces, or else we're doomed. I was not, in other words, Willie Loman, I was the writer, and Willie Loman is there because I could see beyond him." From "Morality and Modern Drama; Arthur Miller, as interviewed by Phillip Gelb," *The Educational Theatre Journal*, October, 1958, pp. 198–199.

and none of them, like the wild mustangs who symbolize their condition, fit into the world as it exists; but identity is never one of the play's issues.* Gay, the chief protagonist, always knows who he is and the intrusion of Rosalyn into his life does not make him question his identity; rather, her presence comes to make him conscious of an absence, an emptiness, in his existence. Guido is certainly not a character with self-knowledge; in fact, he has numerous blind spots. But his blindness about himself is not central to the action and the situation never forces him to question his identity. Even the younger Perce, whose age, psychological condition, and family situation are rooted in an identity crisis, does not play this kind of role in the drama. If anything, his very presence points up the fact that this is *not* what the play is about. Rosalyn is a much more complex character. While she is "a woman whose life has forbidden her to forsake her loneliness," she also has the childlike innocence and trust of one who exists before the fall. She has no sense of herself at all, or perhaps it is more accurate to say that, like a child, she is an emerging self who has yet to have a consciousness of her own identity. Thus, in a way, all of these are new Miller characters, characters whose very natures preclude the crisis of identity from becoming a dramatic element.

A yet more noticeable change in *The Misfits* from the plays that preceded it is Miller's radically different attitude toward sex and the role of woman. In the plays of the first period, the woman is always in the background. She is never sexually interesting and is always a mother figure even when she is a wife. There is a marked streak of puritanism in Miller's view of women in these plays, a puritanism which is clearly underscored by such lines as "Our opposites are always clothed in sexual sin," or "It's a cold wife that prompts lechery." Quite unlike Tennessee Williams' plays written during the same period of time, desire is not a central part of Miller's universe and his plays are manifestly lacking in the sensual. Yet, if sexuality is submerged in the plays of the first period, it is not dormant, and in its repressed state sex plays an important role in the action. In fact, it is always the cause of catastrophe. Chris and Sue's relationship is the beginning of Joe Keller's undoing in *All My Sons;* Willy's affair in Boston is the cause of his separation

---

* Henceforth I shall usually refer to *The Misfits* as a play even though it is, in Miller's words, "neither novel, play nor screenplay." It is, he goes on, "a story conceived as a film, and every word is there for the purpose of telling the camera what to see and the actors what they are to say."

from Biff; Proctor's act of adultery with Abby is the source of his downfall; and Carbonne's incestuous and unacknowledged passion for Catherine is the cause of his demise. In every play the sexual sin brings on disaster. And the stability of the family—the value Miller always affirms—is inevitably shattered when sex rears its ugly and sinful head.

One can speculate—and many have—as to whether Miller's marriage to Miss Monroe (the puritan and the sex goddess) caused a shift in attitudes. There can be no question that a change did occur. It is first revealed in the actual evolution of *The Misfits*. Originally, this work was written as a short story for *Esquire* in 1957, when Miller was in Reno getting a divorce from his first wife. While in this city of sad, lonely, and oftentimes desperate people, his own solid family world having crumbled, Miller seems to have become aware of separateness and of a kind of people who have no place in a system. It is significant, however, that the short story reveals this misfit condition in terms of a totally masculine world. After his marriage to Miss Monroe, when he comes to redo the story for the film, a woman is added and that woman is his second wife. For the first time a woman shares the central focus in a Miller work. In fact, the role of Rosalyn is so dominant that at times she draws our attention away from Gay altogether.

It is interesting to note that there is no family in *The Misfits*—again, it is the first time—only the tortured comradeship of a group of people who belong nowhere. Like them, Miller seems to be cut off from the structures and strictures of the past, in a world that is lonely and adrift. "To life—whatever that is," Rosalyn says, in a toast after her divorce. No character in the earlier plays could have or would have made such a statement. Similarly, Gay's loose-end philosophy of "Just live," because "maybe all there really is is what happens next, just the next thing, and you're not supposed to remember anybody's promises," is a credo totally alien to the clearly defined and highly circumscribed attitudes of the previous plays.

But the aspect of *The Misfits* which I find most significant (and the element which clearly indicates that Miller is moving in a new direction) is the fact that it marks the beginning of what has become his growing involvement with the dramatic possibilities of otherness. The characters in *The Misfits* are not so much concerned with themselves as they are with finding a way to relate to each other. And in this Rosalyn is the catalyst. For the most part, the play focuses on separation, but by the end of the film Gay and Rosalyn have finally touched. For the first time they are fully aware of their need for each other, and yet in their need neither of them feels compelled to deprive the other of his or her selfhood. This ending is, at best, tentatively hopeful (not sentimental, as some critics have said). Like the quiet moment between Hannah and Shannon at the end of Williams' *The Night of the Iguana,* it is an intimation of the possible rather than an affirmation of it.

This moment has not been achieved without difficulty, however.* At the beginning of the film, both Gay and Rosalyn are very much alone. She has just gotten a divorce from a husband who wasn't there ("Why can't I just say he wasn't *there?* I mean, you could touch him but he wasn't there") and he has just put the latest of a long line of divorcées on a train back to St. Louis. But while the external situation is similar, their inner condition is totally different. Rosalyn is perpetually alone and she and the world have always been strangers. As a result she seems never to have been touched by life. Her open innocence is not assumed; rather it is the response of one who has never found a way to live. Gay, on the other hand, knows life all too well and wants no part of it. He is determined to stay free not just from the world of wages, but from anything that demands a commitment. He says, "I hunt these horses to keep myself free," and while this is true, Miller makes a more telling comment about him when he describes him as follows: "He needs no guile because he has never required himself to promise anything, so his betrayals are minor and do not cling."

To promise is the key to the whole work. Rosalyn has never really made any promises because she doesn't know how to, and Gay never has because he has refused to do so. (In renouncing his former wife and children, he broke the only real promise he ever seems to have made.) And yet promises are not only the basis of all enduring and meaningful human relationships, they are also the only things that can give stability to existence. In this regard the already quoted passage from Hannah Arendt's *The Human Condition* is once again pertinent:

* Though the whole story is under a kind of shadow of foreboding that the relationship between Gay and Rosalyn will explode, the tone of the work is never grim, morbid, or heavy. I believe Miller achieves this remarkable balance because the characters, with the possible exception of Guido, never feel sorry for themselves in their misfit and isolated condition.

The possible redemption from the predicament of irreversibility—of being unable to undo what one has done—is the faculty of forgiving. The remedy for unpredictability, for the chaotic uncertainty of the future, is contained in the faculty to make and keep promises. . . . Both faculties depend upon plurality, on the presence and acting of others, for no man can forgive himself and no man can be bound by a promise made only to himself.*

The central action of *The Misfits* is the steady movement of Gay and Rosalyn from two extremes of isolation until they can meet and make a promise to each other. And they make this promise with full respect for "the otherness" of the other.† The symbol of this promise is their decision to have a child. When Gay first proposes the idea, Rosalyn rejects it because the bond-promise still does not exist between them. It is only after the struggle with the mustangs that it can occur. Rosalyn must come to accept what the wild horses mean to Gay no matter how horrifying she finds the experience; and he, in turn, must come to see that true freedom can only be found in relationship, in the acceptance of otherness. His real act of freedom is the releasing of the stallion for Rosalyn's sake. Only then does he discover that he has "touched the whole world." Then they can make the deepest of human promises: to have a child.

### III

As I said earlier, the Arthur Miller of *The Misfits* is quite different from the author of the works included in *The Collected Plays*, and *The Misfits* marks a new departure not only in form but in tone and theme as well. The stern moralist has softened. For the first

* *The Human Condition* (Doubleday Anchor Book Edition), pp. 212–213.
† Although Miller never uses the word, this might be called love. Certainly, it is love in the way defined by Thomas Merton in *Disputed Questions*, which I have already referred to in the essay on Ugo Betti. Merton writes:

to love another as an object is to love him as "a thing," as a commodity which can be used, exploited, enjoyed and then cast off. But to love another as a person we must begin by granting him his own autonomy and identity as a person. We have to love him for his own good, not for the good we get out of him. And this is impossible unless we are capable of a love which "transforms" us, so to speak, into the other person, making us able to see things as he sees them, love what he loves, experience the deeper realities of his own life as if they were our own. Without sacrifice, such a transformation is utterly impossible. But unless we are capable of this kind of transformation "into the other" while remaining ourselves, we are not yet capable of a fully human existence.

time in his career Miller has not led his characters to the seat of judgment. He accepts, and even loves, these misfit souls; he does not judge them. From this point on, in each of the three plays which have followed *The Misfits*, he has been primarily concerned with the implications of otherness in both the private and the public levels of experience. Such a concern inevitably leads him to come to grips with those conflicts which are inherent in the crisis of generativity.

The identity crisis, which is at the heart of the plays of Miller's first period, is a crisis of consciousness. The generativity crisis is one of conscience. In such a condition, as Dr. Erikson describes it, the individual must face up to the fact that "I have done this and that; my acts have affected others in this or that way. Have I done well or ill? Can I justify the influence which, intentionally or unintentionally, I have had on others?" This is the essential drama of all Miller's plays beginning with *After the Fall*. It is the drama of someone who knows and accepts his identity and is conscious of his unique relationship to other people. The protagonists of Miller's first period struggled, for the most part unsuccessfully, to discover who they were. In his last three plays, Miller is concerned with the effect his protagonists have had on others and their capacity to accept full responsibility for what they have or have not done.

*After the Fall* is a dramatic revelation of a man who has come to realize that each one of us has, indeed, been born after the fall of man and that, if we are ever to know ourselves, we must recognize and accept the fact that we not only have a share in the fall, but perpetuate it.* All of Miller's heroes have a tremendous sense of guilt. In the earlier plays, however, they could never really acknowledge that the source of guilt was in themselves, and this was in large measure, as I have already pointed out, because they did not know themselves and, therefore, could not know their guilt, even though destroyed by it. Only when we become aware of other people as separate identities who exist in and for themselves, and not merely as extensions of our own needs and concerns, can we be capable of seeing how our deeds can and do affect them. With such awareness we come to recognize that we are responsible for what happens,

---

* In a special Foreword to the play written for its first publication in *The Saturday Evening Post,* Miller underscores this point when he writes: "The human being becomes 'himself' in the act of becoming aware of his sinfulness. He 'is' what he is ashamed of."

not only to ourselves, but, insofar as we relate to others, to them as well. This is the condition of Quentin at the opening of *After the Fall*. He is clearly caught up in a generativity crisis. He is painfully aware of the fact that he has acted on others; he is also aware of the people in his life *as* others.

In general, most people think of *After the Fall* as Miller's *mea culpa*. This is to miss the point of the play completely. In spite of all the flashbacks, this is not a memory play, any more than *Death of a Salesman* is one. The motive force of *After the Fall* is Quentin's desire and need to enter into a relationship with Holga. But desiring and needing Holga is no longer a simple thing because Quentin is also aware—and it is a new awareness for a Miller character—that to enter into a relationship with Holga is to be responsible for her and for what happens to her because of what he himself does and has done. (By extension, to relate to one individual is to accept a personal responsibility for what happens to all men. This is the significance of the many flashbacks to the concentration camp, and it is a theme which Miller develops further in *Incident at Vichy*.) *

Miller has called *After the Fall* a trial ("the trial of a man by his own conscience, his own values, his own deeds"). In a sense this is true, but it is also misleading. The play is certainly not a trial play in the same way that the earlier plays are, where the judgment is the final verdict and where the laws of life which have been violated are viewed as a taskmaster bringing us back to the paths of righteousness by making us more aware. The play is about commitment and choice. "Can I commit myself again?" is the agonizing question that Quentin asks himself. And to answer that question, he must face the evidence, must face up to the fact that everything that he has ever done *is* the evidence. ("A life, after all, is evidence, and

---

* Again, Miller makes this point clear in his Foreword: "Quentin . . . arrives on the scene weighed down with a sense of his own pointlessness and the world's. His success as an attorney has crumbled in his hands as he sees only his own egotism in it and no wider goal beyond himself. He has lived through two wrecked marriages. His desperation is too serious, too deadly to permit him to blame others for it. He is desperate for a clear view of his own responsibility for his life, and this because he has recently found a woman he feels he can love, and who loves him; he cannot take another life into his own hands hounded as he is by self-doubt. He is faced, in short, with . . . the terrifying fact of choice. And to choose, one must know oneself, but no man knows himself who cannot face the murder in him, the sly and everlasting complicity with the forces of destruction."

I have two divorces in my safe-deposit box.") But to search for a verdict is not the issue; in fact, it is a cop-out. How can there be a verdict when there is "no judge in sight?" And how purposeful are our own self-judgments? The real challenge facing Quentin is to accept the validity of the evidence without resorting to "the everlasting temptation of innocence." Not to accept is to live a life of "pointless litigation of existence before an empty bench."

The first stage of his acceptance is to become fully conscious of the otherness of all the people who have been a part of his life. (Significantly, as he recalls the past, Quentin is able to think of them as people rather than as extensions of himself. He is able to see his parents and his first wife as they were—at least in some respects—and also as they saw him, even when this was not a pleasant vision.) Such awareness leads him to acceptance of his responsibility for what has happened to them. He must accept his share of Lou's death, his inadequacy in his relationship with Louise, Maggie's lifeblood on his hands. But accepting the evidence involves much more than just acknowledging our role in the big events or the major relationships of our lives; it means facing up to the idea that everything we do affects other people. This is the significance of Felice, who weaves in and out of the play. Even the smallest gesture, which had no significance for Quentin, profoundly shapes her life.* That is part of the evidence too.

Quentin's presentation of the evidence (his past life) is not, however, the central point of the play. At the end of the first act, after glancing at Holga, he says: "It's that the evidence is bad for promises. But how do you touch the world without a promise?" Here we are back again with the main theme of The Misfits. Only with a promise can we touch the world, and a promise involves both an awareness of "what I had done, what had been done to me, and even what I ought to do" and a responsibility for the otherness of another human being.

After the Fall thus marks a real progression in Miller's attitudes. The question of identity is never an issue. The name theme of the earlier plays does, in fact, reemerge at the end of the play and it is important to see that when Maggie challenges him by trying to

* This prefigures the beginning of his relationship with Maggie. The opening episode with her is equally inconsequential/yet consequential. It has disastrous results because a relationship which could never be maintained grows from that encounter.

make him nameless ("You're on the end of a long, long line, Frank!"), Quentin is not only not destroyed, but able to accept his "own blood-covered name." The play also goes beyond *The Misfits*. Gay and Rosalyn had a glimpse of what relationship might be, but they still hadn't made the journey. At the end of the play they were still simply talking about it:

ROSALYN: How do you find your way back in the dark?
GAY: Just head for that big star straight on. The highway's under it; take us right home.

The trip "home" isn't easy. To get home you have to face up to your responsibility for others. This is something Gay has never done (having never made promises) nor has Rosalyn (who has never been able to transcend her isolation). Quentin, on the other hand, is in the process of the journey—all of the last plays are a part of the journey—and the first step is to accept the fact that we have affected and continually do affect other people's lives.

As Quentin goes to meet Holga, he goes with the knowledge that he is a murderer—that he bears the mark of Cain. He moves toward her with no sense of certainty, but with that kind of courage—probably the only kind there is—which is born of doubt. *After the Fall* significantly ends with a beginning ("Hello"), just as *The Misfits* did. However, now there is a knowing. The big question that we are left with at the end of the play is "Is the knowing all?" Miller, himself, does not seem to know the answer. But in *Incident at Vichy* and *The Price,* he carries the question further.

### IV

When compared to *After the Fall, Incident at Vichy* may seem to be a smaller play. In many ways it is, but it does reveal the next stage in Miller's development of his new theme: our personal responsibility for our murderous nature. *After the Fall* ends with Quentin acknowledging that we act as we do because "no man lives who would not rather be the sole survivor of this place than all its finest victims." He knows that he gave all of the people in his life "willingly to failure and to death that I might live." In *Incident at Vichy*, the psychiatrist Leduc knows the same thing and represents a similar attitude. But there are some important differences; Leduc has an anger which Quentin lacked. He directs this anger at himself (for thinking of using his own death as a way of taking vengeance on a wife he no longer loves), at all men for their failure ever to learn from man's history of slaughter and destruction, and especially at Prince Von Berg, whose special circumstances will save him from the Nazi horror. Moreover, though the anger turns to frustration when he must acknowledge that knowing isn't enough and that he has failed not only to "make part of myself what I know," but to "teach others the truth," he is in fact a better teacher than he realizes. In the climactic speech of the remarkable *agon* which closes the play, he says to Von Berg:

> . . . I have never analyzed a gentile who did not have, somewhere hidden in his mind, a dislike if not a hatred for the Jews. . . . Until you know it is true of you, you will destroy whatever truth can come of the atrocity. Part of knowing who we are is knowing we are not someone else. And Jew is only the name we give to that stranger, that agony we cannot feel, that death we look at like a cold abstraction. Each man has his Jew; it is the other. And the Jews have their Jews. And now, now above all, you must see that you have yours— the man whose death leaves you relieved that you are not him, despite your decency. And that is why there is nothing and will be nothing—until you face your own complicity with this . . . your own humanity.

He concludes the scene by saying: "It's not your guilt I want, it's your responsibility—that might have helped." In many ways this is only an amplification of the basic theme of *After the Fall*. What carries *Incident at Vichy* further is the fact that Von Berg, who strangely has much the same kind of innocence about life as Rosalyn and Maggie had, is shown to be capable of the pure act of courage. He gives up his freedom (and presumably his life) for another. To have such courage is to transcend the human. And yet it is precisely this kind of superhuman capacity that all of the most significant dramas in the theatre's history have celebrated as the source of man's greatness.

The major theme of *Incident at Vichy* is that responsibility is not just a question of personal relationships; it must also extend to the world. Here Miller broadens the focus of his theme. What was implied by the projection of the concentration camp in *After the Fall* becomes the subject of *Incident at Vichy*. The most interesting (and I think perhaps the most significant) realization of the theme emerges at the very last moment. When Von Berg comes out of the

Nazi office, having been cleared, he gives his pass (the means to freedom) to Leduc. The doctor not only does not want to take it, he is almost horrified at the thought of it. His final speech, together with Miller's stage direction, reads as follows:

> (*Leduc backs away, his hands springing to cover his eyes in the awareness of his own guilt.*)
> LEDUC (*a plea in his voice*): I wasn't asking you to do this! You don't owe me this!

The real mark of Cain—and the reason why there will always be a Melos, a Vichy, a Memphis—is that the murderer within us cannot stand the thought that someone else could and would give up his life for our sake. Such an act makes our guilt unbearable by destroying that balance of *quid pro quo* which we have created in an effort to justify our guilt. We suppose that the price life exacts for our existence should be fair, and the actions of a Von Berg or a Martin Luther King upset the balance of payments. We cannot permit ourselves to be in someone else's debt. There must always be a price. That is why there must also always be a Jew.

It is just this concern with life's balance of payments that Miller explores in his most recent play, *The Price*. At the end of *After the Fall*, as Quentin goes to join Holga, he asks himself, "Is the knowing all?" Is the hard-won awareness enough? Can such knowledge be the basis of a commitment to another human being? *Incident at Vichy* answers these questions, and the answer is "No! It is not enough." We must also, as Leduc puts it, "make part of myself what I know," and we must make others come to see this truth. The great insight of *Incident at Vichy* is that we fail in this because of our inability to accept the otherness of people, and, more important, because our guilt-ridden natures will not permit anyone to acknowledge our own otherness. Locked in the prison of self, our guilt demands that there be a price—no free giving like Von Berg's— because then solipsism becomes intolerable. It is this solipsism which makes us incapable of love, which makes us treat others and our relationships with them as commodities, as objects which, to use Merton's words again, "can be used, exploited, enjoyed and then cast off." This guilt is first revealed in our insistence that "vengeance be mine." Leduc sees this in his relationship with his wife and can acknowledge it to Von Berg because he still believes in his moral superiority over the Prince. But when Von Berg freely offers his own life to save the Jewish doctor, Leduc's essential guilt, of which his vengeance is symptomatic, is fully expressed. The ending of *Incident at Vichy* reveals that otherness is an ambiguous reality. Without it there can be no promises, and hence no love; but, at the same time, its very existence calls forth the murder which each of us carries within himself.

In *The Price*, Miller develops these themes further. This play, while longer than *Incident at Vichy*, is written with the same tight and simple form, and in it he returns to the family as the *locus* of the action.* The play consists essentially of the confrontation of two brothers who have been estranged for sixteen years. Each of them has reacted in different ways to the terror provoked by their father's failure in the Depression and has now returned to the old family brownstone to sell the parents' possessions before the building is demolished. Victor, a policeman with twenty-eight years on the force, has chosen the security of a humdrum but safe existence, justifying his (and his wife's) sense of failure on the grounds that he has sacrificed his own ambitions to take care of his broken father. Walter, on the other hand, while less talented than his brother, has become a famous and wealthy surgeon. He is a selfish and egocentric man who sacrificed everything and everyone to his drive for success. At the same time, he is also an extension of Quentin and Leduc. A few years earlier he has suffered a mental breakdown and has come to realize that because of his terror of failure he has, in effect, murdered life. He returns now, having seemingly and at long last conquered his guilt, to reestablish a relationship with his brother, who he believes has found a more meaningful existence through a life of self-sacrifice.†

As the two men confront each other—and their past, which is

---

* The family seems to provide the most hospitable context for Miller's theatre. He certainly is both more at ease and more direct when he writes out of and in terms of familial conflicts. If one can fault *Incident at Vichy* in any way, it would have to be because of its tendency to abstractness. Most of the characters represent attitudes and lack the sense of a felt life. Whatever passion they have tends, for the most part, to be rhetorical rather than an inherent quality of character. This is certainly not the case with Victor and Walter in *The Price*.

†† "The actor playing Walter must not regard his attempts to win back Victor's friendship as mere manipulation. From entrance to exit, Walter is attempting to put into action what he has learned about himself, and sympathy will be evoked for him in proportion to the openness, the depth of need, the intimation of suffering with which the role is played." From the author's Production Note, *The Price*, p. 117.

presented in all its accumulation through the furniture of the set—each of them comes to discover that he represents a different aspect of the same dilemma. Miller puts this very clearly in his Production Note to the play, where he writes:

> As the world now operates, the qualities of both brothers are necessary to it; surely their respective psychologies and moral values conflict at the heart of the social dilemma. The production must therefore withhold judgment in favor of presenting both men in all their humanity and from their own viewpoints. Actually, each has merely proved to the other what the other has known but dared not face. At the end, demanding of one another what was forfeited to time, each is left touching the structure of his life.*

The structure of life which both men are forced to accept as their own is a structure in which all of the positive aspects of otherness have been excluded. They have touched neither each other nor the world because they were not brought up to believe in one another but to succeed. In developing this idea, Miller is doing much more than challenging the whole American money ethos as he had in *Death of a Salesman*. This is a play about absence, and the absence at the core of the play is the absence of love. There is nothing at the center of these men's lives and never has been; there is nothing at the center of Victor and Esther's relationship; there was nothing at the center of Walter's broken marriage; there was nothing at the center of their parents' relationship or in the sons' relationships to their parents. The great revelation of the play is spoken by Walter, when he says to Victor:

> It's that there was no love in this house. There was no loyalty. There was nothing here but a straight financial arrangement. That's what was unbearable.†

The whole *agon* between the brothers hinges on the assumption that "there is such a thing as a moral debt." Both men have justified everything that they have or have not done, as well as everything that has or has not happened to them in terms of this imperative. This is particularly true of Victor. His wasted twenty-eight years are his moral capital, and until Walter finally forces him to acknowledge that in his heart he knows he has been living a lie, he has managed to believe that this capital was backed by the hard cur-

* *The Price*, p. 117.
† *The Price*, (New York, The Viking Press, 1968), p. 109.

rency of self-sacrifice. This explains both his insistent need to demand "a price" and also his need for vengeance even if it costs him
(symbolically) his life. Certainly Esther has supported him in this,
for their empty life together would have had absolutely no meaning
or justification if there were no valid moral indebtedness. Walter,
on the other hand, realized during his illness that he had paid the
price and why he had done so. Now, struggling with his guilt, he
comes—again with a reasoning similar to Leduc's—to act:

> I've learned some painful things, but it isn't enough to know; I
> wanted to act on what I know.

What Miller is challenging, however, is the whole idea of moral
debt based on "price." For whenever people try to relate to each
other in terms of the price to be paid, they will always get less than
they bargained for; the price is never enough. Both Walter and Victor have been wrong; in life there can be no question of success or
failure, or I gave more than you. And this is the significance of
Gregory Solomon, the used furniture dealer who has come to pur-
chase the junk heap of their past.

Solomon—the wise man—is one of Miller's greatest theatrical
achievements. Not because, as so many critics have noted, he is
Miller's first major comic figure, but rather because he represents
an expanded view of life that incorporates all of the most significant ideas and attitudes that the playwright has been working with
for almost almost a decade. Solomon's wisdom, simply stated, is
that it is silly for the brothers to worry about the price because it
will always be fair. Whether the final price offered for the furniture
is $1,100, $3,500, $12,000, $25,000, or $2.50 really doesn't matter
since, as he says, the price of the used furniture of our lives is only
a viewpoint and we can never deal with life's real issues in terms
of *quid pro quo*. The fairness of Solomon's price is underscored by
such lines as: "I'm not sixty-two years in the business by taking
advantage," "I used to be president" (of an appraisers' association),
"I made it all ethical," "Listen, before me was a jungle—you wouldn't
laugh so much. I put in all the rates, what we charge, you know—I
made it a profession, like doctors, lawyers—used to be it was a regular snake pit. But today, you got nothing to worry—all the members are hundred percent ethical." To a man who has spent most of
his ninety years picking up the pieces of other people's lives, usually
in times of misfortune, the price is a minor matter. "What happens

to people is always the main element to me." This is the source of Solomon's remarkable vitality. Even at his advanced age, he cannot help becoming involved again; just as he entered into his fourth marriage when he was in his seventies.

In addition to pointing up the fact that paying the price is finally irrelevant—both the brothers have paid a heavy price, but so what? Solomon's presence serves two other important functions. One of these is especially clear in the second half of the play. After dominating a good share of the first act, the old man is shunted to the bedroom shortly after Walter arrives on the scene, and the second act is primarily devoted to the conflict of the brothers. But Solomon does not disappear altogether, and each of his entrances is significant. In effect, he serves to keep the brothers honest; his interruptions deter them from arriving at false or illusory solutions. He first returns when they seem to have touched each other by recalling their parents as they were before the Crash. This is a purely sentimental response, and later revelations in the play make it clear that no renewed bond could ever be built upon such roseate memories. After Walter takes him back to the bedroom, this possibility is never raised again. Solomon's second appearance occurs just when Walter is offering Victor an administrative job at the hospital (page 86). This, too, is an illusory solution, because it reveals not only Walter's great sense of guilt, but his total inability to take in what has really been gnawing at Victor during all the years since their separation. For the same reasons that Victor cannot go along with Walter's idea to use the furniture as a tax deduction, he finds it intolerable to be offered this "gift" of a more meaningful job. He is unquestionably right that he is not suited for the job; but even if he were it would not lessen his resentment, only enhance it. Solomon's third entrance (page 93) comes just as the brothers think they are about to face the "dreadful" moment of truth. I believe that his remarks at this point to the effect that the government may catch up with them really apply as much to the revelations that are soon to follow as to the legality of Walter's proposition. Finally, he returns when the brothers have actually reached the bedrock of truth in the middle of Walter's last speech:

> WALTER (*humiliated by her. He is furious. He takes an unplanned step toward the door*): You quit; both of you. (*To Victor as well.*) You lay down and quit, and that's the long and short of all your ideology. It is all envy!

(*Solomon enters, apprehensive, looks from one to the other.*)
And to this moment you haven't the guts to face it! But your failure does not give you moral authority! Not with me! I worked for what I made and there are people walking around today who'd have been dead if I hadn't. Yes. (*Moving toward the door, he points at the center chair.*) He was smarter than all of us—he saw what you wanted and he gave it to you! (*He suddenly reaches out and grabs Solomon's face and laughs.*) Go ahead, you old mutt—rob them blind, they love it! (*Letting go, he turns to Victor.*) You will never, never again make me ashamed! (*He strides toward the doorway.*)

This is a painful moment, but it is the only one that is worth something. In a symbolic sense, Solomon has helped them to arrive at this point by preventing them from settling for anything less.

Solomon's other major function may be discerned in the numerous references to his daughter's suicide which are woven throughout the play. To my knowledge, no one has dealt with this theme, even though it is of the utmost significance. As a character, Solomon is much more than a Pirandellian *raisonneur* whose dramatic function is to lead the protagonists (and the audience) to a new kind of understanding of their situation. The reason Solomon is the "wise man" about the play's central issues is that he has experienced them himself. He does know. The first time his daughter is mentioned, her suicide is not mentioned, but simply that she had nothing significant to believe in. ("You're worse than my daughter! Nothing in the world you believe, nothing you respect—how can you live?") In equating Victor with his daughter, he is prefiguring the emptiness of the policeman's life, for Victor neither believes in nor respects the self-sacrifice he has used to justify his choice of what to to him is a failed life. (There *need* be nothing wrong with twenty-eight years of dedicated service to the police force!) And when Solomon continues, pointing out that if you cannot believe in the life you are living, then "my friend—you're a dead man!", the parallel to Victor is even more apparent.

Later, Solomon reveals that his daughter committed suicide fifty years ago, and openly admits that he has been haunted by it all his life. "And you can't help it, you ask yourself—what happened? What *happened*? Maybe I could have said something to her . . . maybe I *did* say something . . . it's all. . . ." As Solomon's voice fades into momentary silence, we cannot help being reminded of similar agonizing queries in the two previous plays.

The daughter is not mentioned again until the very end of the play. At this point Solomon is paying Victor "the price" for the furniture, and Esther has just lamented the brothers' failure to make a meaningful contact ("So many times I thought—the one thing he wanted most was to talk to his brother, and that if they could—But he's come and he's gone. And I still feel it—isn't that terrible? It always seems to me that one little step more and some crazy kind of forgiveness will come and lift up everyone. When do you stop being so . . . foolish?"). Solomon replies:

> I had a daughter, should rest in peace, she took her own life. That's nearly fifty years. And every night I lay down to sleep, she's sitting there. I see her clear like I see you. But if it was a miracle and she came to life, what would I say to her? (*He turns back to Victor, paying out.*) *

Solomon has lived life fully and he is also a wise man. The essential lesson he has learned is that the murder/suicide in each of us can never adequately explain or justify what we have done or have not done to others. We must accept our guilt knowing that it is just, but also with the full awareness that any attempt to seek revenge on others for the guilt for which we are responsible is to choose the road of nothingness.

As I said earlier, otherness is an ambiguous reality. Unless we can accept a person as another we can never really touch him, and without such contact we can never touch the world of all men. Yet since we can never really know another, he will always be the Jew, the stranger. ("Each man has his Jew; it is the other.") Here is the absurd contradiction that the intellect can never resolve. To live in relationship is to make the Kierkegaardian leap—knowing that none of us would ever know what to say to Solomon's daughter if she were to return, but knowing also that it is irrelevant to worry about "the price." This is the meaning of Solomon's laughter as the curtain falls. Life may be an absurd joke, but it is the only life we have. Arthur Miller may or may not have read Ugo Betti's *The Gambler*, but I think—at least at this point in time—that he would agree with the spirit expressed by Betti in the lines:

* *The Price,* p. 114.

To believe in God is to know that all the rules will be fair and that there will be wonderful surprises. (*The Gambler*, Act II)

## V

Earlier I observed that the dominant characteristic of the American theatre during the first half of the 1960s was its passionate commitment to the business of self-scrutiny. There is no new evidence that convinces me to alter that view. All of our serious playwrights have responded to the violent disturbances of our national life—Vietnam, racism, urban problems, assassination and murder, poverty in the midst of plenty—by seeking to give definition to the soulscape which forms our planetary and spiritual horizons. And no one has been more involved in this search than Arthur Miller.

In his adaptation of Ibsen's *An Enemy of the People*, Miller described Dr. Stockman as one who "might be called the eternal amateur—a lover of things, of people, of sheer living, a man for whom the days are too short, and the future fabulous with discoverable joys. And for all this most people will not like him—he will not compromise for less than God's own share of the world while they have settled for less than Man's." Although I am sure he has no such Promethean ambitions, Mr. Miller might well have been describing himself. Certainly no modern playwright writes with such moral earnestness and has a greater sense of social responsibility.

In a time when so many playwrights are dealing with modern man's isolation and loneliness, Miller—without denying either the loneliness or the isolation—is convinced that "the world is moving toward a unity, a unity won not alone by the necessities of the physical developments themselves, but by the painful and confused reassertion of man's inherited will to survive." His passionate concern that attention be paid to the aspirations, worries, and failures of all men—and more especially, the little man who is representative of the best and worst of an industrialized democratic society—has resulted in plays of great range and emotional impact. For the past quarter of a century a disturbingly large percentage of the plays written for the American theatre have tended to be case histories of all forms of social and psychological aberration. For Arthur Miller, who has been a major figure during the whole period, this has not been the case; he has insisted with a continually broadening range that courage, truth, trust, responsibility, and faith must be the central values of men who would—as they must—live together.

Though the dominant tone of the theatre in the mid-twentieth century is despair, Miller continually demands more; he seeks a "theatre in which an adult who wants to live can find plays that will heighten his awareness of what living in our times involves." Miller's own sense of involvement with modern man's struggle to be himself is revealed in his own growth as an artist and has made him one of the modern theatre's most compelling and important spokesmen.

# 26

# WHERE THE PEOPLE ARE

In this final chapter I should like to take a more personal tone. During the past five years I had been centrally involved in the creation of the California Institute of the Arts. This remarkable new institution is the first professional school in which all of the arts are both taught and practiced by one of the most talented and adventuresome groups of artists ever assembled in any one place. The opportunity to work with these several hundred men and women has made me acutely aware of the many new directions the arts have already taken in recent years and this awareness prompts an attitude of speculation as to what the nature of the arts, and particularly the art of the theatre, will be in the next few years to come.

We know that there has always been a continuing tension between rebellion and celebration in the arts. As the rebel, the artist is an adventurous explorer; he crosses the frontiers of our common life, and in his work by means of the right and redeeming word, shape, or tone he gives definition to those boundary situations of man's mind and spirit. In this role he is a maker of maps for the rest of the community, and these maps, in turn, celebrate the best and worst, the most beautiful and most painful experiences that men have thought and felt. In the past the artist's rebellion, and its attendant discoveries, was always rather easily measurable by a more or less stable tradition. To be sure there was change; indeed, oftentimes when we look back we can see that profound and radical changes were actually taking place. But at the time they were being experienced, these changes were imperceptible and almost glacierlike in nature. Tradition really meant the gradual assimilation and passing on of one's work on a person-to-person basis. But today it is different. Everything changes so fast that we all have trouble getting or keeping our bearings. However, this is not, as so many people seem to think, because our artists have tossed tradition and traditional disciplines out the window, but rather because they are being literally bombarded by *all* traditions at once and are forced to choose between them. In our times, because of the nature and the power of our media, each one of us is conscious of all past achievement—whether it be Western, Oriental, African, or what-have-you—*simultaneously*. And this confrontation has led in the arts, and everywhere else for that matter, to a widespread hybridization of forms, attitudes, and disciplines which many people find questionable and confusing, and which others dismiss as downright gibberish and junk. Some of it is all of those things, but I nonetheless sense a tremendous potential in this apparently confusing and manifestly chaotic condition.

I had my first important insight into the significance of this change when I attended the Venice Biennale in the summer of 1966. When I went to the American pavilion, certainly the grandest one in the park, I was amazed to discover that no one was there in spite of the fact that our country was represented that year by a number of very distinguished "color" painters. The Argentinian pavilion was quite crowded, but I attributed this, and I think correctly so, to the fact that Le Parc had won the painting prize (significantly, for works that were not composed with paint) and people were curious to see what the "winner's" work was like. However, the place that was really packing in the crowds was the Japanese pavilion. The major attraction of this show was a giant collage that covered two walls of the pavilion. This collage was made up of countless orifices, large and small, and to experience the work it was necessary to put your head, your hand, or a finger into these openings, and strange and wonderful things would happen to you when you did so. The significance of this work was that to experience it one had literally to participate in it, become one with it. The gulf between the seer and the thing seen had been bridged; the object and the viewer became one. People can say that this is not art, just as they dismiss Happenings and improvisations, conceptual or environmental art, random music, computer films, or antitheatre plays, but *that's where the people were*—hundreds of them at a time, from all over the world, each speaking a different language, and all of them having a marvelous time. What is more important, I know that these strange new forms of art are being created not by a bunch of faddish, undisciplined, irresponsible, campy, pretentious, self-indulgent, overaged hippies, but rather by highly trained and disciplined artists who have mastered the traditional forms and would be quite capable of working in them if they had chosen to do so.

We tend to forget that the real nature of the avant-garde in art, as its literature so clearly reveals, is at heart conservative and at times even reactionary. Ionesco puts this fact as well as anyone (although one could choose Shelley, Pater, or a host of others) when he writes:

> In the end I realized I did not want to write "anti-theatre" but "theatre." I hope I have rediscovered intuitively in my own mind the permanent basic outlines of drama. In the long run I am all for classicism: that is what the "avant garde" is. The discovery of forgotten archetypes, changeless but expressed in a new way. Any true creative artist is classical . . . the *petit bourgeois* is the person who has forgotten the archetype and is absorbed in the stereotype. The archetype is always young.

The artists of the avant-garde *are* "radical" only in the true sense of that word—they want to go back to the old roots. In using new techniques to return to these old truths they hope to be more real and direct, to be more truly communal and involving. Thus, more often than not, what appears in their work to be a shattering of tradition is actually, in fact, a reaffirmation of it.

One of the reasons we have failed to understand this is that there has been a tendency—and many artists have encouraged it—to regard the artist as an alien (highly respected, of course, but alien nonetheless) to society. But to think this way is to misunderstand what an artist does and what his role in society actually is. The artist has always been the seismograph of his age.* Like the rabbit in the submarine or the canary in the coal mine, his sensibilities perceive the currents of what is happening in the present moment long before the rest of society does. For this reason he is very much a part of our world. In this regard, we tend to forget that art is first of all an act of

---

* Obviously, he is more than a recorder of his age. To the extent that his capacities permit it, the artist also transcends his time and adumbrates the future. The artist who speaks only to his age, dies with his age. Thus, the artist is, ideally, a combination of seismograph and crystal ball.

discovery, an act which simultaneously reveals and reflects the reality of the present moment. I do not for a minute believe that Shakespeare wrote *Hamlet* to tell us about some prince who couldn't make up his mind, or was in love with his mother, or was ambitious for the throne; he wrote *Hamlet* to discover the Hamlet that was in himself and by giving form to that discovery he reveals the Hamlet that resides in each one of us. The same thing is true of Beckett in the writing of *Waiting for Godot*. And the reality that the arts of today are revealing is the interrelatedness of every aspect—the social, political, economic, and ideological—of our daily life.

I have observed in some of the earlier chapters that in the fifteen to twenty years after World War II there had been a tendency on the part of artists to shrink the world to a rebellious gesture. The predominant spirit during this time was one of protest and retreat and their work had become the violent graphs of the cornered man. From such movements as the Theatre of the Absurd or abstract expressionism in painting it is clear that man was defined by his estrangement and solitude and not by his participation in society. The dominant image of those times was one of man left face to face with himself. And Pirandello told us a long time ago what would happen when this condition prevailed:

> My friend, when someone lives, he lives and does not watch himself. Well, arrange things so he does watch himself in the act of living, a prey to his passions, by placing a mirror before him; either he will be astonished and dismayed by his own appearance and turn his eyes away so as not to see himself, or he will spit at his image in disgust, or will angrily thrust out his fist to smash it. If he was weeping he will no longer be able to do so, if he was laughing he will no longer be able to laugh. In short, there will be some manifestation of pain.

But then in the 1960s things began to change and I believe the most important of these changes was, as I indicated in the opening chapter of this section of the book, the shift in the artist's attitude toward technology. Technology came to be seen not as a dehumanizing enemy but as a great new resource that could be used in both material *and* spiritual ways so as to enhance the present and its possibilities. However, whenever we embrace anything—an attitude, an idea, even another person—we must remember that we are acted upon by the object of our embrace every bit as much as we affect it. There is no such thing as embrace without impunity. Thus when the artist came to embrace technology not only was his work affected; his whole sense of himself was changed.

I got one of my first insights into the nature of this change when I began interviewing some of the first applicants for admission to the California Institute of the Arts. I was astonished to discover the large number of team applicants. There were video groups, poetry groups, women's art communes, environmental designers, street theatre companies, and most of them had names—The Stonewall Jackson, the Videofreeks, the Write of Arting—like the then popular rock groups. As I talked to these groups (and invariably they insisted on having only one application form) I discovered that each of them thought of himself as interchangeable with the other members of the group; none of them felt the need to stress his or her own individual identity within the group, and hence insisted that their contribution to the work of the group be treated anonymously; but more important, they indicated that the most significant of man's recent achievements—the walks on the moon, organ transplants, the redesign of our cities—were *team* efforts and if art was to use the perceptions and the hardware that technology had made available to it the artist, too, had to work in teams. No longer does the artist see himself as Walt Whitman's "solitary singer."

However, the chief effect of the artist's embrace of technology is that it gives him a radically new sense of choice. This is the central theme of the reports of the Harvard Program on Technology and Society, and I have already alluded to this fact earlier in the book. We know that each one of us has opportunities for choice that were unthinkable a generation ago (and I believe the current tensions resulting from the gap between parents and children can in large measure be attributed to this fact), and more important, we know that we had better keep on making them. We don't need to be locked into anything because the number of choices available to us is greater than ever before and the possibilities for continuing new choices are rapidly increasing. Now I happen to think that the possibility for choice is at the very heart of the creative process; but when you also believe that one need not be bound permanently by his choices because new choices are made available to each of us every day, then your attitude toward what you create invariably changes. And this accounts for the growing dominance of the spirit of improvisation and impermanence in all of the arts.

Chartres Cathedral could only have been built because thousands of people over a very long period of time believed that not only would the building last forever, but more important, that its very existence celebrated religious meanings that were eternal. Well, today we don't build cathedrals anymore (the world's last great cathedral, the Cathedral of Saint John the Divine in New York City, is unfinished and will remain that way—the monies collected for its completion are being used to develop the church's mission in Harlem), rather we are building "collapsible churches," temporary structures which serve the needs of a given community and then will literally "fall down" as those needs change, which they will do with increasing rapidity. In the same way our artists are less and less concerned with creating lasting works of art. Because each day brings with it new choices, the artist comes to find joy in the creative process itself—indeed, involvement in the process of creating has tended to replace concern for the product or the object that is made. It is in this sense that we refer to our time as the "Age of the Happening," and that we have had trouble adjusting to it is underscored by the strange contradiction that there is a permanent collection of disposable art at the Museum of Modern Art.

Perhaps nothing has accelerated the growth of the spirit of impermanence in the arts more than television. (It is interesting to recall that the first international happening was Ruby's murder of Oswald on TV.) For television, more than anything else in modern society, emphasizes the temporary and expendable as opposed to the permanent. Everything created for this medium becomes something for rapid and largely uncritical consumption. And in a very real way so do the artists who work in and for it; they are something to be used and discarded. This kind of expendability is not always intentional. The artist himself does not necessarily think of his work, let alone himself, as being designed for instant consumption; but it does challenge artists to make things that really are expendable (Tinguely's self-destructing works are good examples of this phenomenon). Another factor which pushes in this same direction is the anonymous efficiency and professionalism of all the new media created by electronic technology. The industrial/electric revolutions have affected the arts in the same ways that they did everything else: All of the human mistakes can be cut out, but at the cost of individuality so that soon all evidence of ordinary human character or activity in the work is eliminated. This has produced two major reactions: a frantic search for the spontaneous and unpredictable or the pretense that the spontaneous humanity of the artist makes up for its absence in the work of art. In either case, the creator himself becomes his most meaningful creation.

As a concomitant to this is the inevitable breaking down of traditional forms that occurs with the advent of any new technology. We saw some time ago that the triumph of electrical technology over mechanical technology led to widespread hybridization in the established scientific disciplines: No longer do we think in terms of biology, chemistry, physics, etc.; instead the major new fields of scientific endeavor are called such hybrid names as geophysics, neurobiochemistry, and algebraic topology. The same thing is happening in the arts. The new technology not only tends to destroy the narrative style in all of the arts, and hence the decline of the linear and sequential, it has actually metamorphosed the very forms themselves. Painters have moved down off the walls into action; the new music is not only random, it is beginning to behave like an object in space; and as the new forms of the theatre move out of the theatre into the streets all the other arts are becoming more and more like theatrical performances. Forms are being transplanted everywhere, all the arts are reappraising the way in which forms shade over into each other in a world of multiplicity. Profound changes occur only when you break down boundaries, and we know that the artist has always been one of the first in any society who is capable of doing this. And as forms break down so do those hierarchies of value which governed them. The major impulse of contemporary music, for example, is nondifferentiation or the rejection of tonality. Tonality—the governance of a dominant note or tone—implies a hierarchy, while atonality insists upon the absence of such dominance. Thus in fulfilling this strong drive toward equalization there has been a flattening out, both technically and aesthetically, of those values which had given meaning and form to musical composition for centuries. Under such conditions the traditional forms of training hardly seem relevant. However, when the artist begins to doubt the necessity and relevancy of his discipline he soon comes to question one of the basic premises of all art: that albeit related, art and life are separate and distinct orders of human experience.

Increasingly, our artists do not think of art as something reserved for the high holy days of the spirit; in fact, in their desire to make art and life more interrelated and mutually involved, the very idea of "going" to a museum, a theatre, or a concert hall has become repugnant to them. I remember going to a performance of Robert Whitman's *Prune Flat* a number of years ago. It was given in the loft where he lived in SoHo (long before this came to be the "in" place for artists to work and live), and the work was a film but the actors in the film were acting live in front of the screen; it also had static visual images, strobe lights, and an electronic musical score. It all worked together, not in an additive but in a synthetic way, and I thought it was a very interesting and moving experience. Afterwards, I went up to Mr. Whitman and in an old-fashioned way, I asked: "Wouldn't this have been better if it had been performed in a theatre?" He replied, "That's just the point. We don't want it in theatres. We want it in the loft where we make it, where we do it, where we're all together, where you are a part of us, where you're totally involved with us, where we live, where we eat, where we make love, where we are related together. We want to break down the gulf that exists between the artist and the audience. We want, in effect, to destroy audiences." (And I know there are people who participatory theatre groups such as the Living Theatre, the Performance Group, or the Open Theatre resides in the fact that these believe, for quite different reasons, that they are succeeding in doing just that.)

This represents a radical shift in attitude. Certainly one of the most widely held traditional views of the artist's function is the one which asserts that the artist's main job is to take the chaos and complexity, the ambiguity and contradictions of actual life, and to impose on them a meaning and order by means of the unique powers of his temperament, the depth of his imagination, and his capacity to create form. Increasingly, the artists of today do not see this as their function. Rather, they believe that their obligation is to present the complexity and ambiguity of life as directly as possible. John Cage, who has been one of the major forces in moving the arts in this direction, states the position of many of these artists when he says: "For too long art obscured the difference between life and art. Now let life obscure the difference between art and life." In the theatre, for example, one of the major themes of the Absurdists is the bafflement men feel when facing a complex world. This bafflement reached the point of paralysis and for many of the most serious theatre artists writing at that time the theatre of the Renaissance Humanist tradition had reached the end of the road. The sense of vitality which many people find in Happenings or the do, for all of their limitations and transitoriness, celebrate the world's complexity and its total irrelatedness. The purpose of environmentalism is not to produce works of art for people to mull over, but to make the arts an immediately experienced social transaction. The Aristotelian aesthetic of improving the audience's moral well-being has been spurned in favor of professed involvement in social change. It is this shift of attitude which caught Herbert Marcuse's attention and which prompted him to point out in 1970 that the revolutions of the young were, in fact, aesthetic and not political. In their concern for life style and the quality of life they were demanding that art and life, politics and education, be totally interrelated and that art be not apart from life just as education should not be preparation for it. However, it should be pointed out that whenever anything becomes totally at one with the environment we cease to notice it. Thus, if these artists succeed in making art and life one, they will also have to accept the fact that they may no longer be thought of as artists.

The effects of these changes have led to two major movements in the theatre—the theatricalizing of everyday life and the politicizing of theatrical life. Unfortunately, history reveals that whenever this process has occurred in the theatre of the past the art of the theatre has become second-rate. And much too much of what's going on in our theatres today is second-rate. It is trying to be more political, but its politics are a whirligig of radical platitudes on monumental issues. What claims to be self-honesty is, in reality, terribly narcissistic. It has not only abandoned words for undulating gyrations, it has given up thought altogether and much of what is happening on our stages reflects that condition which Marcuse sees in our advanced technological society: "the elimination of mediated thought and the exploitation of desublimated sex." But probably the dreariest aspect of our current theatre is the high incidence of what Herbert Blau has described as "Christ figures putting on, pitying, or scourging those who are already profoundly guilty for not feeling guilty enough."

However, these conditions do not disturb me overly much. I believe the theatre of "The Post-McLuhan Age" is an embryo theatre, one in transition that is beginning a new cycle. When one looks back over the history of the theatre, he will observe that the periods of radical transition all share a number of common characteristics, the most important of which is that the clear line between the performance and the audience dissolves or at least becomes quite blurred. Just as with the Japanese collage I described earlier, the gap between the seer and the thing seen has been bridged so that the performance and those at the performance almost become one. This clearly happened as the Greek theatre emerged out of the tribal dance rituals; and it did again with the Atellan farces of republican Rome. The same thing is true of both the *commedia* and the medieval miracle and mystery plays. Even the physical nature of performance during these earlier periods resembles the "new" kinds of performance spaces which are currently in vogue.

Today's Happenings and improvisations, the street and guerrilla theatres, and the work of the Becks, Grotowski, Chaikin, Schechner, and even Peter Brook all indicate that the theatre is once again at a primitive starting point. These artists and their work do not as yet indicate what the future of the theatre will be, but I do believe it reveals a profound anxiety. We all know that we are living in an era of transition; a time in which almost all of the established modes of existence, all of the accepted and understood concepts and structures, have pretty well disintegrated and the new ones emerging are not yet clearly recognizable. In the midst of such chaos, in a world overcrowded with people, objects, and techniques, torn by conflicts and rotted by corruption, overshadowed by perils of unprecedented dimensions, confronted with an ever-increasing mass of unmastered life material—both within and without—it is no wonder we are anxious. And in our anxiety, we tend to turn to the surface levels of existence, to the sheer presence of the present, to the immediately palpable sensory appearance of objects and gestures. The despair of being unable to cast an anchor into the immense chaos of our world has been one of the chief reasons why so many of our artists have turned to the presentation of surfaces, to a pure, immediate materiality.* Hans Richter, the former Dadaist, wrote in 1964:

> It looks as if people today needed the instantly palpable material object to hold on to as a confirmation of their presence in the world; as if man could find himself substantiated only through his contact with his five senses, since in him all is broken up and uncertain. An inner void seems to force him outward, an urge to convince him of

* We see this tendency in so many forms: Jim Dine's self-portraits, the plaster figures of George Segal, the analytic novelistic techniques of Robbe-Grillet, *cinéma vérité,* and even concrete poetry.

his existence by way of the object, because the subject, man himself, got lost. . . . Our generation has become so greedy of presence that even a toilet seat is holy to us, we are not satisfied with seeing it pictured, we want to *have* it altogether, bodily. (*Dada, Art and Anti-Art*)

To many, this view of the present and its possibilities in the arts will seem grim indeed. But it should not be cause for despair. For while it is true that the artist of today faces insuperable challenges, he cannot respond to them as did Desdemona, when confronted with the horror of her situation, by saying, "Faith, Emelia, I'm half asleep." Rather, he must embrace the truth of Hofmannsthal's observation that "the necessary is always possible. History proceeds in just that way, that something hardly credible is treated by a few as if it could be immediately realized." But I am not really worried about the artist. Like Prospero, he will go back to Milan even if his dreams have been shattered and he is full of despair. The artist, if he is one, will always make the act of faith. He will always go on working. He is Yeats' "fiddler" and that is why no matter what happens "the fiddles are tuning all over the world." But it is absolutely necessary for the rest of us to listen (and hopefully hear) his tune because he is singing and playing *our* song. However, for those of us who cannot make such a commitment, these "fiddlers" urge us— and it is important that they do—to maintain as best we can that courtesy of the spirit which accepts the absence of spiritual consolations without complaint and is content to wait in stillness.

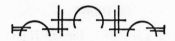

# INDEX